Digital E
Impacts, Influences and Challenges

Harbhajan S. Kehal
University of Western Sydney, Australia

Varinder P. Singh
University of Western Sydney, Australia

IDEA GROUP PUBLISHING

London • Melbourne • Singapore

Acquisitions Editor:	Mehdi Khosrow-Pour
Senior Managing Editor:	Jan Travers
Managing Editor:	Amanda Appicello
Development Editor:	Michele Rossi
Copy Editor:	Bernard J. Kieklak, Jr.
Typesetter:	Amanda Appicello
Cover Design:	Lisa Tosheff
Printed at:	Yurchak Printing Inc.

Published in the United States of America by
    Idea Group Publishing (an imprint of Idea Group Inc.)
    701 E. Chocolate Avenue, Suite 200
    Hershey PA 17033
    Tel: 717-533-8845
    Fax: 717-533-8661
    E-mail: cust@idea-group.com
    Web site: http://www.idea-group.com

and in the United Kingdom by
    Idea Group Publishing (an imprint of Idea Group Inc.)
    3 Henrietta Street
    Covent Garden
    London WC2E 8LU
    Tel: 44 20 7240 0856
    Fax: 44 20 7379 3313
    Web site: http://www.eurospan.co.uk

Library of Congress Cataloging-in-Publication Data

Digital economy : impacts, influences, and challenges / Harbhajan Kehal, editor, Varinder P. Singh, editor.
    p. cm.
  Includes bibliographical references and index.
  ISBN 1-59140-363-4 (hardcover) -- ISBN 1-59140-364-2 (pbk.) -- ISBN 1-59140-365-0 (ebook)
 1. Information technology--Economic aspects. 2. Information technology--Social aspects. 3. Electronic commerce. I. Kehal, Harbhajan, 1942- II. Singh, Varinder P., 1974-
  HC79.I55D5455 2004
  303.48'33--dc22
                          2004003777

British Cataloguing in Publication Data
A Cataloguing in Publication record for this book is available from the British Library.

All work contributed to this book is new, previously-unpublished material. The views expressed in this book are those of the authors, but not necessarily of the publisher.

Dedication

In Memory of My Parents,
Chaudhry Harkishan Singh Kehal and Sardarni Harnam Kaur Kehal

H.S. Kehal

To
My Parents,
Who have guided me with wisdom and always supported me in every
walk of life.

V.P. Singh

Digital Economy:
Impacts, Influences and Challenges

Table of Contents

Preface vii

Chapter I
Socio-Economic Impacts and Influences of E-Commerce in a Digital Economy 1
  Sushil K. Sharma, Ball State University, USA

Chapter II
Re-Intermediation and Deferment through E-Commerce: Neo-Austrian
Interpretation of Capital and Time 21
  Parthasarathi Banerjee, NISTADS, India

Chapter III
Risk and Investment in the Global Telecommunications Industry 39
  Irene Henriques, York University, Canada
  Perry Sadorsky, York University, Canada

Chapter IV
Reduction of Transaction Costs by Using Electronic Commerce in Financial
Services: An Institutional and Empirical Approach 62
  Thomas Pfahler, University of Bayreuth, Germany
  Kai M. Grebe, University of Bayreuth, Germany

Chapter V
The Spreading Use of Digital Cash and Its Problems 84
  Yutaka Kurihara, Aichi University, Japan

Chapter VI
Electronic Signature: The Core Legislation Category in Digital Economy 98
  Fjodor Ruzic, Institute for Informatics, Croatia

Chapter VII
**Impacts of the Digital Economy: The Shift to Consumer-Driven Competition and
Life-Span Products** 136
 Simon Mowatt, Auckland University of Technology, New Zealand

Chapter VIII
Digital Products on the Web: Pricing Issues and Revenue Models 154
 Gary P. Schneider, University of San Diego, USA

Chapter IX
On Software Piracy 175
 Sougata Poddar, National University of Singapore (NUS), Singapore

Chapter X
**An E-Classification of the World's Capital Cities: URL References to
Web Sites** 200
 Stanley D. Brunn, University of Kentucky, USA

Chapter XI
**Online Services and Regional Web Portals: Exploring the Social and
Economic Impacts** 217
 Helen Thompson, University of Ballarat, Australia

Chapter XII
**ICT Growth and Diffusion: Concepts, Impacts and Policy Issues in the Indian
Experience with Reference to the International Digital Divide** 236
 Saundarjya Borbora, Indian Institute of Technology Guwahati, India

Chapter XIII
Digital Technologies and the Cross-Border Expansion of South African Banks 252
 Joanne Roberts, University of Durham, UK
 Chipo Mukonoweshuro, University of Durham, UK

Chapter XIV
Technology and Culture: E-Commerce in China 273
 Alev M. Efendioglu, University of San Francisco, USA
 Vincent F. Yip, University of San Francisco, USA

Chapter XV
**Internet Economy of the Online Game Business in South Korea: The Case of
NCsoft's *Lineage*** 286
 Kyonghwan Park, University of Kentucky, USA

Chapter XVI
Opportunities and Challenges of the New Economy for East Asia 313
 Donghyun Park, Nanyang Technological University, Singapore

Chapter XVII
Digital Engineering Campus: Economics, Acceptance, and Impact 344
    Milind J. Mahajan, Mirash Infotech, India
    Sunil S. Umrani, Sunind Systems, India
    Narendra S. Chaudhari, Nanyang Technological University, Singapore

Chapter XVIII
Corporate Strategies in a Digital World: Supply Chain Management and
Customer Relationship Management – Development and Integration-Focus 359
    Purva Kansal, Panjab University, India
    Keshni Anand Arora, Indian Administrative Services, India

About the Editors 381

About the Authors 382

Index 389

Preface

Information and knowledge have emerged as major sources of wealth in the recent past. There is a digital revolution and it has impact and influences on the consumers, producers, investors, exporters, importers, public policy makers, academics, students, consultants, administrators, lawmakers and all others directly or indirectly involved in various processes of the new economy. It has also huge challenges for all of the above and the shape of things to come will be determined by their response to the fast moving changes, additions and modifications in the Information, Communication, Technologies (ICTs) and their applications.

The pace of the revolutionary changes in the ICTs and their applications and their impacts, influences and challenges are more pronounced in the developed countries. The rest of the world is also catching up with them fast in the digital stakes.

Public policy makers in both the developed countries and the rest of the world and administrators, who have even bigger challenges than policy makers, will have serious problems to tackle. Censorship and freedom will be in conflict with each other in relation to the use of and access to the ICTs.

ICTs have ushered in a new era of global communication, production, trade and investment. It has implications for all of the players in the economy and society irrespective of whether they reside and work in the developed countries or in the developing countries. The digital economy is transforming the lives of people beyond recognition. There is a revolution in the way that things are produced and traded before they reach the final consumer. Also there is a revolution of rising expectations as the world is getting transformed to a global village and the access to the good things in life will no more be in the domain of the rich and influential, whether in developed or developing countries.

The buzzword is e-commerce. The term e-commerce goes beyond doing business electronically. Doing business electronically means that the conventional processes are computerized and are done on the Internet, however now it seems that the Internet is not merely an alternative to make a channel for marketing or selling product online. Instead the electronic marketplace enables the seller to innovate the whole business process from the producer to consumer to service by integrating them in the seamless whole, where product choices and prices are updated according to the customer information in real-time on web stores.

About the Book

This book is not about how to use the web or how to set up your web page for a successful business. This book provides information from socio-economic angle. As a number of books are already available about e-commerce or digital commerce, most of them provide information mainly from a technical angle and the socio-economic aspect had been neglected. Contrary to that, we would like to present the picture of digital information economy from the socio-economic perspective. This book covers various aspects of global production, trade and investment and the effects of the Internet from a socio-economic angle.

While paying attention to the current status of intertwined issues of electronic commerce in technology, standards, policy and legal issues, the focus is on many economic issues and aspects of electronic commerce that other books do not cover. This book aims to provide relevant theoretical frameworks and the latest empirical research findings in this area.

The change in the flow of information, computing and communication in the recent past has greatly influenced the world economy. In the emerging "digital economy," the players as well as the rules of the game are changing fast. Along with it has come a lot of confusion and uncertainty. The digital economy may bring potential invasions of privacy, more sophisticated and far-reaching criminal activities and host of other unknown problems.

The audience of this book is diverse. In addition to the academics, students and other knowledge workers, this book is intended for the business people who are using the Internet to seek a new customer, suppliers and partners around the world.

If a business person is already directly involved in international trade and business and business trade, either as a manufacturer, distributor, exporter and importer, custom broker and freight forwarder, trade financer, diplomat, then this book is for him/her.

If he/she is involved in the international trade, perhaps as a lawyer, management consultant, trade show organizer, site developer, business school professor, executive educator or someone who advises international companies, then this book is also for him or her.

The assembling of the chapters and editing of this volume was a very onerous task but has proved to be highly worthwhile and rewarding in the end. The response to the call for chapters was overwhelming. We received proposals from top scholars, professionals and practitioners from various parts of the world. We have received chapters from the USA, Canada, Japan, Australia, New Zealand, Korea, Singapore, India and many other countries. Authors with background from various cultural groups and with firsthand knowledge of the socio-economic impacts, influences and challenges of the digital economy has contributed to this volume.

Choice of the chapters for this volume was a highly challenging task, as we received an overwhelming response. Which chapter to include and which to exclude was very difficult. Chapters included in this volume have gone through a very rigorous review process. The ultimate choice of the chapters for inclusion in this volume were guided by the quality, relevance and coverage of the vital issues and proper analysis and depiction of the impacts, influences and challenges of the digital economy. The brief summaries of the various chapters included in the book in the words of the contributors are provided below for the readers to make their own judgement:

The first chapter of this book is *Socio-Economic Impacts and Influences of E-Commerce in a Digital Economy* written by Sushil K. Sharma.

Electronic commerce or e-commerce is the exchange and processing of business transaction information using computers connected through a network. **E-commerce does have unique advantages for businesses.** It allows a shop, a show room or an office to open 24 hours a day, seven days a week. It also means that time zones are not a problem. A Web site can bring a prospect from the point of advertising and information directly to the point of sale, seamlessly, without involving any other medium. Adoption of new information technologies, particularly e-commerce, is expected to result in improvements in firm performance, such as reducing transaction costs and closer coordination of economic activity among business partners. E-commerce also is expected to facilitate entry into new markets or extension of existing markets and greater integration of systems with suppliers and customers. E-commerce is changing business economics and as a result many firms are re-engineering their core business processes. Suppliers and retailers are able to collaborate on product forecasts, product flow and inventory management decisions using the collaborative Internet-based networks between suppliers and retailers. In addition to reducing costs, e-commerce solutions permit customers to custom order products based on individual needs and preferences. Retailers are able to allow customers to mass customize orders based on virtually thousands of choices. The Internet's growth and e-commerce has begun to create fundamental change in government, societies, and economies with social, economic and political implications. These advances present many significant opportunities but also are having wide-ranging effects across numerous domains of society and policy makers.

As e-commerce continues to grow rapidly, it could have significant effects on the social and economic structures of economy. The impacts of these changes are diverse and may even widen the digital divide among nations, alter the composition of trade, disrupt labor markets and change taxation, may have ramifications for intellectual property rights, privacy protection, and data filtering, etc. Some of these effects of e-commerce are unintentional and create adverse business and personal conditions that could have societal consequences. Social and economic aspects of ICTs have been studied by a wide variety of researchers and practitioners for over 50 years. However, the influences of e-commerce are far bigger than imagined before. This chapter describes the various socio-economic impacts and influences that have been created by e-commerce in a digital economy.

The second chapter is *Re-Intermediation and Deferment through E-Commerce: Neo-Austrian Interpretation of Capital and Time* written by Parthasarathi Banerjee.

It is commonly believed that electronic commerce reduces intermediation and the time in a business circuit. This is an efficiency view. This borrows from the Chicago view. Alternatively, transactions cost economics (TCE) theorists argue that electronic commerce decreases transactions cost by way of reducing the distance between the producers and the customers. TCE too argues that dis-intermediation in electronic commerce reduces transactions cost and hence increases economic efficiency. In contrast to this efficiency theory of dis-intermediation and of quickened money, this chapter argues from Neo-Austrian perspective that efficiency can refer to technological changes alone. Efficiency, it is argued, fails to increase rate of profit or innovation. Electronic commerce is an innovation in trade. Electronic commerce brings in several layers of possible intermediaries. In this chapter authors argue that electronic commerce keeps transactions incomplete and extends the completion of transactions indefinitely and thereby; electronic commerce instead of shortening the business circuit would extend such a circuit indefinitely. Indefinite extension of business circuits—that is the lengthening of business transactions—increases effectively the period of production. Austrian theory argues that capital is time. This theory argues that a longer period of production implies a higher rate of profit and an increase in capital. Based on this theoretical stance, the authors argue that electronic commerce enhances capital and increases the rate of profit by lengthening the circuit of transaction through re-intermediation and through an increased period of production.

Velocity of money or goods in an economy, as the efficiency theorist suggests, refers to technical efficiency. This efficiency refers to particular states of affairs of technology. As a result this perspective fails to explain why such technological states change or why certain particular economic agents reap great profits. Moreover, efficiency theorists' "profit" is actually a rent earned. Interpreters of TCE have assumed that electronic commerce brings about a frictionless or transactions-cost-free market. They have wrongly committed TCE to such an explanation. Moreover, reduction of transactions cost would increase efficiency and would not increase rate of profit or the capital and even would not hasten innovation. It follows contrarily that electronic commerce would increase transactions cost.

Internet pricing has shown personalized effects based on quality differentiation and on personalized offerings. Electronic commerce has opened up the possibility of offering extremely variegated personalized pricing. This forum can also offer equivalents of typical market place bargains. Production organization of a vertically integrated corporation stood upon standardization. Production of apiece products with variegated quality, chosen often by the buyer himself, demands that the entire chain of logistics and the supply chains get linked to the electronic commerce platform and that the stages in production are increased immensely and at each step of production each apiece product contains unique information. Such a picture of an electronic-commerce-led economy shows that stages of production must increase, that different economic agents must undertake value addition at each stage, that variability must increase and that mass production of personalized wares must hasten. In short, electronic commerce demands that an economy increase both its division of labor and the long period of production.

A long period of production refers to the entire input-output table of an economy. A short period of production refers to a specific transaction chain of a business or a sector. Electronic commerce increases the length of both these periods. Shackle discussed profit and its rate from the perspective of lengthened periods of production and an increase in the division of labor amongst economic agents who are speculators. Electronic commerce has opened up this opportunity. In these commerce intermediations, in particular, cyber mediations have increased and will continue to increase. Neo-Austrian framework offers a cogent explanation as how electronic commerce increases the rate of profit and the capital in an economy based on electronic commerce.

The third chapter is *Risk and Investment in the Global Telecommunications Industry* written by Irene Henriques and Perry Sadorsky.

Access to affordable technology to improve the flow of information is essential to the development of an economy. Closing the Digital Divide could bring many benefits to developing countries. In many ways, developing countries have the most to gain from improvements in telecommunications and information technology. Bringing the benefits of IT to developing countries is possible, but the governments of these countries need to be aware that the process is going to cost money and require institutional changes.

International investors will frequently calculate the cost of equity for their existing investments and their proposed investments. Development planners must be able to make their own cost-of-equity calculations so that they can see first hand how their investment projects compare with other investment projects around the globe.

Consequently, it is necessary to have good measures of equity risk for managers, planners, policy makers and investors. The cost of equity is important in valuing new investment opportunities and in evaluating the ongoing performance of established business projects. This is especially true in the new economy IT industry where an understanding of equity risk aids in the examination of the relationship between the IT sector and economic development.

In this chapter, quantitative modeling and simulation techniques are used to estimate various risk measures and the associated cost of equity for the global telecommunications industry. The approach is to calculate several different cost-of-equity values and then use simulation techniques to build up a probability distribution for each company's cost of equity. In this way, a clearer picture of where a company's cost of equity lies is developed.

Estimates of the cost of equity for a particular company vary widely and depend upon the methodology used. For a particular company, cost-of-equity values based on systematic risk tend to be lower than cost-of-equity values calculated from downside risk measures. For some companies, downside cost-of-equity values are twice as large as cost-of-equity measures based on systematic risk. This is true, even though all of the cost-of-equity values use the same risk-free rate and same risk premium.

One of the insights that emerges from this study is the fact that the average cost of equity for telecommunications companies in developing countries is not always greater than the average cost of equity for telecommunications companies in developed countries. This is borne out by the high cost-of-equity calculations for companies like Cable & Wireless, France Telecom and Nextel. In general, it is difficult to find evidence of regional differences in the average cost of equity of telecommunications companies. This is useful to a development planner who can then use a portfolio approach in which high-risk investments are combined with low-risk investments to promote an investment in a developing country's telecommunications industry. Closing the Digital Divide could bring many benefits to developing countries but international investors and development planners must be able to make their own cost-of-equity calculations so that they can see first hand how their investment projects compare with other investment projects around the globe.

The fourth chapter is *Reduction of Transaction Costs by Using Electronic Commerce in Financial Services: An Institutional and Empirical Approach* by Thomas Pfahler and Kai M. Grebe.

The authors face the subject of analyzing the impact of the increasing utilization of information and communication technology (ICT) and electronic commerce on the co-ordination of specific transactions in financial services. Bank transfers and stock purchases, as two relevant business processes commonly occurring in the contractual relationship between a financial institution and its customers, will be considered in detail.

For that purpose, the conceptual framework for the target analysis has to be developed at first. This requires the definition of the most important terms and the explication of major ideas. The basic principals of the New Institutional Economics and the instruments developed in the context of the Transaction Cost Approach specifically serve as a theoretical background for the study and all further argumentation. Subsequently, the chapter develops and implements a proposal how to exemplify and to compare the above-mentioned processes under the varying influence of certain technologies. This new approach will be specified and the proceeding will be elucidated in detail. The authors refrain from attempting to quantify transaction costs in an absolute way and concentrate deliberately on comparative considerations. Transactions will be decomposed and classified into different phases according to their devolution over the period under observation. The intention is to reveal the basic phenomenon and to document the reasons of the current utilization of ICT in this sector by emphasizing relative reductions of transaction costs through the use of electronic commerce.

After the development of the approach to quantify reductions of transaction costs, the model will be applied exemplarily on the two selected transactions. In detail, the model takes into account seven different phases of a transaction and seven different modes of coordination.

The empirical section of the chapter concentrates on existing technological infrastructures, growth rates, and diffusions rates of certain information and communication technologies. Available data will be analyzed, particularly for Germany. Moreover, certain indicators are introduced to qualify in detail present developments and impacts of ICT.

In the final stage the attained results and consequences of the outlined developments are eventually systematized and summarized. The authors criticize and comment on crucial points concerning the elaborated approach, its significance and limitations as well as its explanatory power. Last, but not least, an attempt is be made to relate the diffusion rates of the investigated technologies in the empirical section to the insights on reductions of transaction costs derived from the theoretical cost model. This will lead to a four-quadrant scheme to illustrate and classify present and future impacts of electronic commerce on financial services. On the basis of this visualization the chapter concludes with deducing a couple of final predictions and with giving a future perspective.

The fifth chapter is *The Spreading Use of Digital Cash and Its Problems*, which is written by Yutaka Kurihara.

It has been several years since the words "digital cash" and other related terms were introduced into the modern lexicon. Needless to say, the progress made in communication and information technology (IT) has been rapid, and change in the area of digital cash is no exception. The volume of such transactions is rising, yet analysis of this revolution in payment is limited, particularly in the academic fields.

Although e-commerce has been growing rapidly and attracting much attention, digital cash has not been a focus of such attention. Digital cash has some problems associated with it that need to be solved before its use can continue to grow, and the rate of growth is slowing at present. The logic behind replacing cash, checks and magnetic credit cards with digital cash is bound to prevail in the end, but there are many barriers that need to be overcome.

The author proposes that material cost reduction and service price are cutting resultant factors of the demand for electronic wallet transactions and the means by which digital cash can spread, the technology of IC (integrated circuit) card reformation can be developed, and price cutting on the supply side can occur. The popularity of the personal computer and the Internet has also skyrocketed in recent years. A general price decline for computer and communication tools has been ongoing as well, helping to promote online-type transactions at the supply side.

Moreover, it seems that the spread of mobile telecommunications has contributed to the development of digital cash. In the near future, interactive television will be used to make transactions. IT (information technology) has undergone a global revolution in many fields. Ubiquitous instruments in IT fields have appeared recently allowing for digital cash to develop much further.

There are two points that will be emphasized in this chapter. The first point is that given the essential characteristics of electronic money, its advantages and disadvantages should be carefully examined. It is quite certain that digital cash will be promoted. It also seems that IT progress is unstoppable, and fortunately IT can make our world a more convenient and efficient place in which to live. Nevertheless, there are a number of concurrent challenges with this change. None of these challenges are apt to be resolved swiftly or painlessly.

The second point is this: since financial institutions cannot stop this trend, it would be prudent for them to view it as a business opportunity. If they do not find ways to adapt, they will become obsolete and completely fade away from the market. By promoting e-finance, a company can gain market share and negotiating power over suppliers, as well as earn a profit. Monetary authorities worldwide should pay careful heed to the trend as well, guiding the "sound" market to maturity, taking care not to confuse exercising leverage with excessive intervention.

The sixth chapter is *Electronic Signature: The Core Legislation Category in Digital Economy* authored by Fjodor Ruzic.

E-business, as well as all of the active participants in the digital economy environment, raises a host of new legal issues that must cope with the fact that the technical expectations imposed by participation in the digital economy will increase. Three basic segments of the digital economy are converging, and each of them consists of one core category:

- *Infrastructure:* telecommunications infrastructure (the members of the society must communicate)

- *Services:* the content (the goal of communications is to transfer the content)

- *Legislation:* electronic signature (the goal is to compile rules of intercommunication processes in which the electronic content is interchanged)

Businesses that offer services and have taken to the Internet seriously have a responsibility to their customers to offer services in a secure manner. Security is a fundamental requirement for e-business applications using signature-based forms. Lack of trust is a significant problem for any e-business — the parties evolved in the e-business processes must feel trust in the people and companies that are doing business. In many traditional business relationships, trust is based on a combination of judgement or opinion based on face-to-face meetings, or recommendations of colleagues, friends and business partners. However, the e-business environment generally does not involve human interaction and, therefore, this new context requires a new understanding of trust.

Several techniques help in establishing online e-trust:

- Electronic authentication

- Electronic signature

- Escrow payment services (online)

- Public Key Infrastructure (PKI)

With the advent of electronic signatures, e-business is changing the way we sign and store documents. Thus, any business that wants to succeed in the digital economy must deal with electronic signatures. It is considered an everyday activity whenever a law or other arrangement requires a signature of person. Signature is needed as a medium for authentication in order to identify the person (the signer), to indicate the person's approval of the information communicated and, to be legally applicable. Most of the national laws currently in force provide that a signature, contract, or other record relating to such transaction may not be denied legal effect, validity, or enforceability solely because it is in electronic form. Like a handwritten signature, an electronic signature can be used to identify and authenticate the originator of the information and, it can also be used to verify that information has not been altered after it is signed. Electronic signatures play a key role in enabling electronic business by helping ensure that electronic documents are unaltered and have not been forged.

Considering the functionality and applicability of such issues, this chapter finds one key category that links all of the separate e-business legal issues in one regulated scene — the answer is done by introducing electronic signature as equivalence with handwritten signature no matter what type of information technology is in use. There are more legal environments, solutions and applications of an electronic signature from which several examples are described accompanied with the e-business view on electronic signature utilization.

The seventh chapter is *Impacts of the Digital Economy: The Shift to Consumer-Driven Competition and Life-Span Products* authored by Simon Mowatt.

This chapter examines changes in innovation and competition made possible in two traditional industries by the adoption of integrated information and communication technologies. The two industry cases used are drawn from the consumer magazine segment of the printing industry and the grocery multiple (supermarket) segment of the retail industry. Both of these industries have benefited from changes in communication within the industry value system made possible by the adoption of digital information management and communication systems.

The primary research in these industries was undertaken by an empirical program of qualitative, interview-based research focused on innovation networks. The informants were involved in production, distribution and retail, and identified by prior secondary research. The research also employed a census questionnaire survey of consumer magazine publishing firms. The survey response was checked for representiveness against a random sample of the industry population and found to be robust.

The chapter highlights the importance of consumer-drive innovation in consumer-facing markets. The industries examined had previously been conditioned by the economics of manufacturing. The development of complex innovation networks to supply consumer needs is examined and the innovation process is explored in detail. For the process of consumer-driven innovation, the importance of linkages to end-consumer and market experts is acknowledged—something is enhanced by the use of digital technologies. The chapter acknowledges that the development of the innovation systems described was the result of firms reacting to consumer needs. But in addition to this, the chapter offers the concept of "life-span" goods as those developed from the outset as having a short life dependent on changing consumer tastes and fashions. Life-span goods are emerging as firms continue to explore the possibilities of proactively using innovation systems to forge links with consumers. Within this environment firms have been recently acting more as project orchestrators: using their skills in developing innovation teams based on the deep knowledge of consumer activities to identify and supply new market segments.

Production in the innovation systems identified is undertaken across firms and coordinated by shifting and temporary alliances. This presents a challenge to economic analysis and to the theories of the firm grounded in a transaction-cost framework. Network-based and sociologically grounded theories of the firm have previously attempted to resolve the inadequacies of contemporary economic theory by emphasizing the importance of social ties and long-term embedded relationships. However, the examples explored in this chapter highlight the role of new technology in short-term non-embedded relationships as well. The project-based firm is identified as having features that are problematic for economic analysis. Despite this the chapter suggests that changes in competitive pressures towards consumer-facing competition may increase the prevalence of project-based firms with industrial economies. Finally, the chapter concludes by exploring some avenues for future research that offer new pathways for future theoretical understanding of project-based and network organizations.

The eighth chapter is *Digital Products on the Web: Pricing Issues and Revenue Models* written by well read Gary P. Schneider.

Products that exist in digital form can be bought, sold, and in some cases delivered, online. Some products exist only in digital form, such as software and certain types of information databases. Many more types of products exist in physical form, but can be digitized. These products include many forms of intellectual property such as text, pictures, photographs, architectural drawings, choreography notes, sound recordings, and video recordings. In some cases, digital products arise from the transmission of other digital products, as in the case of telephone and fax transmissions. The pricing issues that arise in the sale of these products are different from those that sellers face when pricing physical goods. These pricing issues lead to interesting opportunities for devising revenue models. These pricing and distribution issues affect the nature, quantity, and quality of competition in markets for these products. Some digital products are made available at no charge. Thus, an alternative revenue stream that is somehow related to the product must be devised. Some digital products are bundled with other products (digital or physical) to avoid some of the problems inherent in the pricing of digital products alone. Another pricing strategy is to create an artificial distinction within a subset of digital products and use differential pricing to extract the highest revenue possible from each set of customers for the product. Perhaps the most common pricing method is to use a licensing approach of one kind or another. Many digital products are, in their essence, things that are experienced by customers. They often have no meaningful physical existence separate from their experience. Providers of digital products must maintain a current knowledge of underlying technologies that are used or could be used in the future for delivery of their products. The ability of customers to adapt and reformat digital products is also an essential characteristic of digital products, a characteristic that can be affected by changes in technologies as well. The success of revenue models for companies that sell digital products depend on the nature of the product, the characteristics of the buyers, and the traditional practices in the industry. For most digital products, the effect of pricing and distribution strategy does not derive so much from the introduction of the Internet into the marketing channel as from the products' very nature as digital products. This chapter examines the nature of digital products, their pricing issues, and the efficacy of various revenue models that have been implemented by companies that deal in digital products.

The ninth chapter is *On Software Piracy* by Sougata Poddar.

The pervasiveness of the illegal copying of software is indeed a worldwide phenomenon. Economists argue that when the piracy takes place at the end-users level, the original software developer finds it profitable to allow limited piracy when the effect of network externality is reasonably strong in the users' market. The author argues that when the piracy is of retail in nature, the same logic cannot be extended, and shows that it is always optimal for the original software developer to protect its software even when the effect of network externality is strong in the end-users' market. The author suggests that piracy depends on more fundamental issues like demand environment, market structure, the nature of piracy and the nature of competition. The other issue covered here is the economic impact of piracy on the welfare of a society. The author discusses various policy implications on regulating piracy in developing as well as developed markets.

The 10th chapter is by the well-known Professor Stanley D. Brunn, *An E-Classification of the World's Capital Cities: URL References to Web Sites.*

The world's capital cities perform various political functions for their populations, contain embassies, consulates, and missions of other governments, and serve as headquarters for major corporations, cultural and humanitarian organizations. While social scientists have classified major cities based on population size, number of corporation headquarters, banks, and airline connections, the emergence of ICTs suggests additional criteria. The author used the number of URL references to Web sites listed in the Google search engine for 199 world capitals. These cities had nearly 120 million hyperlinks in mid-2003. The capital cities in Western Europe had the most hyperlinks (15 million), followed by Southern and Northern Europe (13 and 10 million respectively), and Central America (10 million). The capitals with the most references to electronic information were: Singapore (6.6 million), Washington, D.C. (5.1 million), and Mexico City (4.2 million). The next largest cities are recognized as major European cities and world cities, including: Luxembourg, Paris, Tokyo, Monaco, Madrid, Berlin, Rome, and London. Several Central American capitals, Panama, San Salvador, and Guatemala City, were in the top 15. The top 15 capitals had 46 million hyperlinks or 31% of the total. The regions with the fewest hyperlinks were capitals in Southern Africa (only 603,000) and the Pacific Islands (only 410,000). These had less than 1% of the total. Five capitals had fewer than 6,000 URL references each. They were the capitals of Bhutan, Micronesia, Tonga, Mauritius, and Nauru. Small prosperous city-states and major capitals in Western Europe and North America had the most hyperlinks. The fewest links are found for capitals in poor and rural Sub Saharan Africa and Southeast Asia countries. Capitals with multiple government offices, strong ICT economies, and dominant tourist economies have the most hyperlinks per capita. These were mostly in wealthy Europe and North America. The lowest values were African and Asian capitals that were poor and/ or had repressive regimes. Regarding hyperlinks per capita, there were 48 capitals with more URL references than residents. The highest figures were for small city-states with dominant specialized functions, including administration, finance, tourism, telecommunications, and religion. These include: Vatican City, Vaduz, Singapore, Brussels, Luxembourg, Washington, D.C., Canberra, Ottawa, Monaco, Valetta, Yaren (Nauru), and Victoria (Seychelles). Those with the lowest per capita values were in South and Central Asia, West, East, and North Africa. Many have closed or repressive regimes or are poorly connected to the Internet. The major categories of information provided on the first "screen" of those capitals with the most hyperlinks were news stories, embassy (often US) information, and financial, tourism, and weather information. The first items of those capitals with the fewest hyperlinks were tourist sites, hotels, recreational activities, and local time. A number of subsequent topics are offered that merit additional research by scholars in various fields interested in e-commerce.

Online Services and Regional Web Portals: Exploring the Social and Economic Impacts is the 11th chapter written by Helen Thompson.

This chapter examines community empowerment, economic and business development, and equity of service as the issue of success and decline in regional and rural communities. This is explored with a particular focus on community informatics initiatives (CI) in Australia, there has been a vision for online services to be used to open up regional communities to the rest of the world. Government support has been seen as enhancing the competence levels of local communities so they become strong enough to deal equitably in an increasingly open marketplace. But how effective have regional portals and other online initiatives been? This chapter explores whether economic and social benefits are generated via establishing and sustaining regional CI initiatives. Theory relevant to online communities is introduced to provide a context for the presentation of two case studies. The first case outlines how a geographical portal has been established and progressively enhanced as a central component of a strategy to facilitate an increase in the uptake of ICT and e-commerce in the Ararat region. Benefits have included the efficient linking of Internet-based information and services, more effective promotion of local businesses, tourism and regional events and also significant skills development and learning opportunities for community members. Ararat Online has been recognized as an exemplar online community, effectively demonstrating how regional development and online technologies can be combined. The second case demonstrates how online services can be established to leverage the activities of a community of interest. The Young Australian Rural Network (YARN) is an interactive online community for young people working in rural industries to keep in touch, collaborate, share ideas and strengthen networks. "Ownership" is effectively shared between the Federal Government and young people with multiple opportunities provided for participation and involvement. For examples, the author discusses contributing to online discussions, building a community site, adding a link, publishing events or suggesting news items. In both cases the same comprehensive portal platform and toolset has been accessed in the delivery of each community's web-based services. This platform has been designed by the University of Ballarat to meet regional and rural needs and to reduce evident challenges in terms of infrastructure, cost and skill barriers, which often negatively impact on the success of CI initiatives. It has been found that communities, just like businesses, benefit from accessing assistance in identifying appropriate online services for their particular circumstances. Case studies, such as those presented in this chapter, are effective in illustrating the impacts, influences and challenges that can be experienced in operationalizing and sustaining regional CI initiatives. Dissemination of the critical learning from cases such as Ararat Online and YARN can inform others about diverse factors which impact on the effectiveness and long-term sustainability of regional CI initiatives.

Chapter 12 is *ICT Growth and Diffusion: Concepts, Impacts and Policy Issues in the Indian Experience with Reference to the International Digital Divide* authored by Saundarjya Borbora.

This chapter examines the role of technology in economic and social development in developing countries, with a particular emphasis on India as an example. The concepts of ICT Growth and ICT Diffusion are examined. ICT growth refers to the growth of IT-related industries and services and their effect on employment, export earnings and outsourcing of activities. ICT diffusion refers to IT-induced development, which increases productivity, competitiveness, economic growth and human welfare from the use of the technology by different sectors of the economy. The chapter focuses on the direct benefits of ICT growth, paying special attention to the service sector. But the role of IT in economic development has not received adequate attention in India. From this, the paper reviews Indian governments' successful policies encouraging ICT growth through the support of the export-oriented service industry. This industry has witnessed long-term growth primarily as the result of the increasing tradability and consequent internationalization made possible by changes in ICTs. However, the export focus policy has created enclaves within the Indian economy without significant forward and backward linkages. Whatever ICT diffusion is taking place is due to activities of industry and discrete public and private initiative at the absence of any specific central government policy for ICT diffusion in India. The chapter examines both international and domestic digital divides. Real disparities exist in access to and in the use of information and communication technology between countries, the International Digital Divide, and between groups within countries, the Domestic Digital Divide. Evidence suggests that International Digital Divide between may be increasing. Examining the present unequal access to ICT, it may be stated that new technologies reinforce the disparities between developed and developing societies. But late entrants such as India have the advantage of access to frontline technologies and cost-effective infrastructure development without the sunk costs in extent systems carries out by many developed countries. There exists real opportunities for promoting ICT diffusion through involvement of the society at large. This chapter suggests that in order to maintain its relative technological position and to increase its comparative advantage in the IT sector, government policy should focus on domestic ICT diffusion. The chapter reviews several local public, private and public-private initiatives to spread the use of ICT throughout Indian regions that has been successful and may serve to offer examples for future development. The author concludes that ICT-driven development may be achieved with supportive central government policies in order to maximize the wider economic and social benefits, lessening both the International Digital Divide and the Domestic Digital Divide.

The 13th chapter is *Digital Technologies and the Cross-Border Expansion of South African Banks*, which has been written by Joanne Roberts and Chipo Mukonoweshuro.

The increasing intensity of competition since the 1970s, together with the deregulation of financial markets and the internationalization of financial services, has driven the application of digital technologies in the financial services sector. However, the impact of digital technologies combined with the deregulation of financial markets has led to a growing concentration of financial service activity in the global cities of developed countries. Nevertheless, digital technologies do influence the financial services sectors in the developing countries, both in terms of the availability and cost of capital, consumer access to services and the organizational development of service providers. This chapter focuses on the impact and role of ICTs in the development of financial services organizations in the developing countries of Africa, and, in particular, on the international development of South African banking organizations.

Through a review of relevant literature and evidence, together with a number of case studies, this chapter explores the role of ICTs in the international development of South African banking organizations. The aim of this chapter is to explore the role of digital technologies in facilitating the cross-border expansion of South African banking organizations. Specific challenges do exist for financial sector organizations operating in Africa where the ICT infrastructure is poorly developed. Nevertheless, it is argued here that South African banking organizations derive important advantages from the use of

ICTs in their expansion into neighboring countries. Using Dunning's (1989, 1988) eclectic approach as a mechanism with which to assess the importance of digital technologies, ICT is explored both as an ownership-specific internal capacity, and as a locational-specific factor influencing the geographical pattern of international expansion, and as a facilitator of the internalization of cross-border banking networks. This chapter highlights the opportunities and challenges related to ICTs for South African banking organizations. In so doing, the chapter will make a contribution to the understanding of intra-African foreign direct investment in the banking sector and the emerging digital economy in developing countries.

A review of banking in Africa with particular attention focused on South Africa is provided, followed by an analysis of the internationalization of South African banking organization. The use of digital technologies in the delivery of services and the organization of banking networks is then explored before their role in the South African banking organization networks is investigated. Finally, conclusions are drawn regarding the role of digital technologies in the international development of South African banks.

Technology and Culture: E-Commerce in China is the 14th chapter of this book written by Alev M. Efendioglu and Vincent F. Yip.

The number of Internet users around the world has been steadily growing and this growth has provided the impetus and the opportunities for global and regional e-commerce. As part of this trend, over the recent years access to technology in China dramatically increased and it is projected that 10.3 million PCs were sold during 2002, making China the 3rd largest market after U.S. and Japan. Furthermore, China is now second only to the United States in the number of home Internet users with nearly 57 million people with web access at home. Internet subscriptions are growing by 5-6% every month, and in just three or four years 25% of the population could have Internet access, translating to over 250 million people. During 2002, 31.67% of Internet users in Shenzhen made online purchases. However, as with the Internet, different characteristics (infrastructure and socio-economic) of the local environments have created significant levels of variation in the acceptance and growth of e-commerce in different regions of the world and in China. The author's research focuses on the impact of these infrastructures (payment systems and access to technology), and socio-economic factors on e-commerce development in China. The findings provide insights into the role of culture in e-commerce, issues such as "socializing effect of commerce," "transactional and institutional trust," and "attitudes toward debt," that may impact a broader acceptance and development of e-commerce in China. To identify the current infrastructure and socio-economic influences on the development and growth of e-commerce in China, a 20-question questionnaire was administered to a total of 252 individuals that formed the study group. The study participants were located in Beijing, Shenzhen, Shanghai, Guangzhou, Wuhan, and Shandong during the time of the study, worked for different types of organizations (Joint Ventures, State-Owned Enterprises, Multi-National Corporations, etc.), resided and worked in different regions in China, and had different educational levels, professions, and gender. The participants identified some infrastructure and social issues that will impede and be obstacles to full development of e-commerce in China in the near future. Among the most identified and repeatedly mentioned issues were lack of credit cards (availability of them for the general public in China) and convenient payment means, poor distribution logistics, lack of specialized, trustworthy online merchants of reasonable size (too many small players facing many bottlenecks and without necessary resources to set up e-commerce systems), an imperfect legal system, and lack of large scale telecommunication transmission capability (broadband). Overall, the respondents were reasonably positive about the availability of hardware/software, government and industry support for IT in China and were overwhelmingly less positive when asked if the Chinese culture "supports" the propagation of IT and e-commerce. The group thought the Chinese consumer society was not quite ready (lack of confidence in technology and off-site transactions, online culture, and overall sophistication of the general public) and the conditions were not "ripe" for e-commerce. In this chapter, the authors present and discuss the findings in detail, and propose some strategies for success for e-commerce in China.

The 15th chapter is *Internet Economy of the Online Game Business in South Korea: The Case Of Ncsoft's Lineage* written by Kyonghwan Park.

This chapter attempts to lay the groundwork for in-depth discussions on the economic, social and cultural dimensions of the online game business as one of the most successful forms of the contemporary digital contents industry using the Internet. Theorizing the Internet as a "general purpose technology" is a useful framework to elucidate its "complementary" role in commerce and telecommunication sectors, and its "general-purpose" diffusion in socio-cultural spheres. However, the framework has an overall danger in downplaying the significant "discontinuity" of the emerging Internet economy, which takes the Internet "network" itself as a core, as an alternative economic resource and a social "space" of economic activities. Based on this problematic, this chapter explores the way in which the online game as a form of digital economy has evolved both through and within the "space" of the Internet.

For an empirical analysis, this chapter investigates the case of the South Korean online game company NCsoft's Lineage: the blood-pledge. The rapid success of NCsoft's Lineage is mainly indebted to two factors. The first is the formation of South Korean national innovation systems (NISs) in the recent development of the Internet broadband infrastructure. Since the 1997 financial crisis, the South Korean government has implemented massive projects to construct nationwide, high-speed Internet networks in order to boost a knowledge-based and techno-intensive national economy. About 24,000 broadband-based Internet-cafés on every street corner in built-up areas played a crucial role in the success of the online game business, not only because Internet-cafés provided high-quality Internet service along with low price, but also because they were pivotal "off-line" places of the online game users' communities. The second is the company's technology-intensive, elaborate efforts at constructing the cyberspace of Lineage as a social space in-between the real and the imaginary. Lineage is a spatial simulacrum consisting of not only hyper-real images of basic realities, but also its own spatio-temporal scale. It is a distinct social space in which game users share common time-space compressed experiences and socialize with other game users in order to survive the cyber-society of Lineage. In short, the broadband Internet infrastructure and the construction of the game users' community constitute two necessary conditions for the economic success of the online game business.

Although a digital economy could not be completely separate from conventional economic principles, the online game business contains emerging forms of new economic space not only in-between the real space and the virtual space, but also between the production and the consumption. The author conceptualizes such a socio-cultural economy of the Internet business as the economy of a "third" space. The case of NCsoft Lineage implies the third space is not just social, but also economic space with the game users' real consumption of simulacra and its spread effects on other off-line economic sectors. The emergence of the digital economy containing certain forms of new economic space would give rise to a neo-economic environment in which many businesses such as e-business could explore new economic opportunities.

The 16th chapter is *Opportunities and Challenges of the New Economy for East Asia* which is written by Donghyun Park.

The first part of the chapter discusses the economic impact of the New Economy on East Asia. First, the author discusses the potential economic benefits of the New Economy for the region. The author argues that East Asian countries should focus on applying existing IT technology to improving the efficiency of the manufacturing sector, the main engine of the region's economies. Second, the author points out that while the IT revolution may enable East Asian countries to leapfrog some technological barriers, it does not enable them to leapfrog sound economic policies. Furthermore, the potential of IT will remain largely unfulfilled in the absence of complementary investments such as a sound infrastructure for transportation and logistics. Third, East Asian countries must fulfill certain pre-conditions to make sure that the New Economy takes hold. Above all, they must liberalize their telecommunication sectors so as to improve the quantity and quality of telecom services. They should also make the necessary investments in human resource development. In short, although the New Economy holds out tremendous economic potential for East Asia, realizing that promise will require a lot of determination and hard work. That promise is already being realized in the more developed countries of the region, namely Japan and the NIEs, and the author looks at some examples of their success in the New Economy.

The second part of chapter deals with the implications of the IT revolution for regional development. The second part is essentially an application of the first part, which addressed the broader issue of economic development, to the narrower issue of regional development. East Asian countries suffer from significant inter-regional economic inequalities. Such inequalities inevitably interfere with well-balanced economic development and impose costs on both the magnet cities and the rest of the country. A more balanced pattern of development is therefore desirable, and IT can make significant contributions toward this objective. In particular, by reducing the concentration of information and knowledge in the main city and disseminating those valuable resources to the rest of the country, IT reduces the inequality of opportunity that lies at the root of the inter-regional economic inequality. However, IT by itself will not enable poorer regions and cities to catch up with the main cities, and will facilitate regional development only if the other fundamental ingredients of regional development are in place.

In the last section, this chapter summarizes the main points and provides some concluding thoughts. In addition, policy implications of the analysis for FDI in Asia, along with implications for potential foreign investors, especially in the telecommunications industry are given. FDI into IT sectors can not only be profitable for the investors, but also can promote the host country's economic growth.

Digital Engineering Campus: Economics, Acceptance, and Impact is the 17th chapter of this book written by Milind J. Mahajan, Sunil S. Umrani, and Narendra S. Chaudhari.

Widespread uses of many web-based, e-learning approaches have established the usefulness of these technologies. The cost of development of contents is a major component for appropriate "soft" infrastructure for such web-based, e-learning approaches. To have a wider impact of these technologies on the society, we need to have the models to keep the development cost self-sustainable within the society. In advanced countries, in the educational sector, the costs are mostly borne by government / public supported educational institutions. In developing countries like India, there is not sufficient financial support. However, there is a huge market. Tapping such a market at an early stage is important.

To highlight these issues, in this chapter, the authors introduce two existing web-based, e-learning approaches, and examine economic and social aspects of their usage in the society. Specifically, the authors first briefly introduce an e-learning initiative in Singapore. Secondly, the authors introduce a scenario in developing countries like India. The demand for an engineering degree within India has led to widespread engineering education within the country. While there are a few "elite" institutes like IITs, that have been funded heavily by government, offering engineering degrees, the wider societal impact is increasingly being driven by a large number of private educational institutions. However, such an expansion has resulted in concerns for maintaining necessary educational standards. The cost-effectiveness and success of low-cost, web-based, e-leaning initiatives is the main focus in the discussions within this chapter.

In this respect, the authors briefly introduce the role of universities and other government agencies for monitoring educational standards. Next, the authors give a scenario of an engineering education at a wider level with a focus on a typical state. The authors have chosen to focus on Maharashtra state for this purpose. A brief sketch of the socio-economic perspective for the adoption of web-based, e-learning in the context of engineering education in India is examined. The impact of non-governmental organizations (NGOs) is illustrated through the detailed description of a case study regarding the experiment called "Digital Engineering Campus" (DEC). DEC is an NGO initiative to provide supplementary educational facilities for engineering colleges in India. Considering the economic as well as social benefits, using the detailed case study of DEC, authors argue that developing countries like India have tremendous growth potential in web-based education. Further, the experiences of developed countries with web-based education will prove to be highly beneficial for developing countries like India.

The last chapter of this book is *Corporate Strategies in a Digital World: Supply Chain Management and Customer Relationship Management – Development and Integration-Focus* written by Purva Kansal and Keshni Anand Arora.

These days, the majority of management literature stresses the concept of "learning organizations," i.e., an organization's capacity to change. However, it is not easy for people to accept this fundamental especially when it comes to the Internet and technology's growing importance in business operations. They claim it as a temporary trend that will leave little visible change in the way business is conducted. For these businessmen the philosophy seems to be "keep making better products and offering new services, and the customers will keep buying." They ignore changes occurring in the buying habits of customers and ignore the impact of technology.

There are some businesses that are happy to follow the leader and adopt tools like supply chain management. Supply chain management is a recognized discipline to shorten cycle times, reduce inventories, decrease logistics' costs and streamline communication process across the business network.

On the other hand are the businessmen who understand the learning organization concept and develop a forward orientation. They are prepared to ride the technology wave to new heights and accomplishments by using technology as a defining element in business operations. This chapter suggests a new approach for this new breed of Entrepreneurs. In this chapter, the authors are trying to give supply chain management a customer orientation and study its results. The authors highlight the synergistic advantage of linking supply chain management with customer relationship management into a tightly knit network using technology. The main focus is on finding solutions to deal with Internet-empowered customers and to learn how to apply technologies demanded in the new digital economy.

All the chapters included in this book are original and have been published for the first time. This book covers various aspects of global production, trade and investment and the effects of the Internet from a socio-economic angle.

While paying attention to the current status of the intertwined issues of electronic commerce in technology, standards, policy and legal issues, the focus is on many socio-economic issues and aspects of the electronic commerce that other books do not cover. This book aims to provide relevant theoretical frameworks and latest empirical research findings in this area.

Acknowledgments

A collaborative project like this doesn't exist in vacuum. Such projects cannot be kept running without enormous support and help. Producing a book is just like entering a long-term relationship with many partners like contributors, reviewers, editors, and a publisher. It is appropriate to acknowledge all of those people we know who have directly or indirectly shaped our work by contributing to the successful production of this book.

We would like to express an especially warm note of thanks to Professor Mehdi Khosrow-Pour, Chief Editor, Idea Group Publishing, which made the start of this project possible by planting the seed of inspiration by suggesting this project to us.

We wish to thank all the contributors for their excellent contributions to this book. Many of the contributors also served as reviewers for the chapters written by other contributors and assisted the editors in producing a wonderful product. Thanks go to all those who provided constructive reviews to enhance the quality of the book. Irrespective of having congested schedules, these people responded promptly and enthusiastically to all our requests. However, some of the individuals need a special mention as their help set the benchmark. These include: Professor Alev M. Efendioglu, Professor Vincent F. Yip, Mr. Kwonghwan Park, Dr. Saugata Poddar, Professor Yutaka Kurihara, and Dr. Fjodar Ruzic, among others. A special vote of thanks is due to Professor Stanley D. Brunn for providing us access to his listserv, introducing us to potential authors and contributors and encouraging us to persist with the project until successful completion. A special vote of thanks is also due to Professor Gary P. Schnieder for kindly accepting our invitation and making a highly valuable contribution within the tight delivery schedules.

A special environment at the University of Western Sydney in Australia facilitated our work on this project. The cooperative attitude of all the colleagues had a direct impact on the successful completion of this task.

Special thanks go to the publishing team at Idea Group Inc. particularly to Jan Travers, who via her timely emails prompted us to always meet the deadlines and keeping the project on schedule. We also acknowledge the help of Michele Rossi, Jennifer Sundstrom and Amanda Phillips for their unstinting support to this project.

We would like to express our sincere thanks and gratitude to our families, who have been supportive and patient throughout this venture, without which this project could not have been completed successfully. We are highly grateful to Mrs. Harbans Kehal for her great moral support and encouragement that bolstered us in tough situations.

A special mention must be made of Harinder Samatani for his technical help in the editing process and also for his contribution with his computing and linguistic skills.

In closing, we wish to acknowledge the unselfish help and technical support provided by Dr. Kiranjit Sohi during the end days of the project.

H.S. Kehal
V.P. Singh
January 2004

Chapter I

Socio-Economic Impacts and Influences of E-Commerce in a Digital Economy

Sushil K. Sharma
Ball State University, USA

Abstract

Innovations in information and communications technologies have created a digital revolution that is changing the way the world works, learns, communicates and transacts business. E-commerce continues to show strong growth and has been influencing the social and economic growth of nations. On one hand e-commerce technologies have helped nations to accelerate their economic growth and to provide more opportunities for businesses to grow, but it has also created many challenges and effects across numerous domains of society, and for policy makers. These issues involve economic productivity, intellectual property rights, privacy protection, and affordability of and access to information, among other concerns. This chapter describes the various socio-economic impacts and influences that have been created by e-commerce in a digital economy.

Introduction

The revolution in computing and communications of the past few decades, indicate that technological progress and use of information technology will continue at a rapid pace. The Internet's growth and e-commerce has begun to create fundamental change in government, societies, and economies with social, economic and political implications (Boulton et al., 2000; McGarvey, 2001). These advances present many significant opportunities but also are having wide-ranging effects across numerous domains of society, and for policy makers. Issues involve economic productivity, intellectual property rights, privacy protection, and affordability of and access to information, among other concerns (Sharma and Gupta, 2001; 2003b). Electronic commerce promises to be the momentum behind a new wave of economic growth (Mariotti and Sgobbi, 2001). E-commerce has already improved business value by fundamentally changing the ways products are conceived, marketed, delivered, and supported. The relationship and interaction of various stakeholders such as customers, suppliers, strategic partners, agents, and distributors is entirely changed. On the positive side, e-commerce has been creating opportunities for individuals and businesses in the new economy. E-commerce is helping organizations to reduce transaction, sales, marketing, and advertising costs. E-commerce is also helping businesses to reach global markets efficiently 24 hours per day, seven days per week, 365 days per year. Many of the benefits come from improved consumer convenience, expanded choices, lower prices, and the opportunity for better interactions with partners, suppliers and targeted customers for service and relationships. E-commerce has also improved product promotion through mass-customization and one-to-one marketing.

Adoption of new information technologies, particularly e-commerce, is expected to result in improvements in firm performance, such as reducing transaction costs and closer coordination of economic activity among business partners (e.g., Malone et al., 1987; Mukhopadhyay et al., 1995). E-commerce specifically (especially B2B) is predicted to result in lower coordination or transaction costs due to automation of transactions online, as well as productivity and efficiency gains (Amit and Zott, 2001; Lucking-Reiley and Spulbur, 2001; Wigand and Benjamin, 1995). E-commerce also is expected to facilitate entry into new markets and the extension of existing markets (Garicano and Kaplan, 2001), and greater integration of systems with suppliers and customers (OECD, 1999; Timmers, 1999; Wigand and Benjamin, 1995). As e-commerce continues to grow rapidly, it could have significant effects on the social and economic structures of economy. The impacts of these changes are diverse and may even widen the digital divide among nations, alter the composition of trade, disrupt labor markets, and change taxation (Anonymous, 2000). Widespread use of the Internet for e-commerce may have ramifications for intellectual property rights, privacy protection, and data filtering, etc. Therefore, in the digital economy, it is becoming imperative to know how e-commerce affects organizations and society and raises social concerns. Some of these effects of e-commerce are unintentional and create adverse business and personal conditions that could have societal consequences. Social and economic aspects of ICTs have been studied by a wide variety of researchers and practitioners for over 50 years (Dutton, 1999a; 1999b). However, the influences of e-commerce are far bigger than imagined before (Sharma and Gupta, 2003b).

This chapter describes the various socio-economic impacts and influences that have been created by e-commerce in a digital economy. The chapter is divided into four sections. The first section provides the definition and components of the digital economy. The second section discusses the positive influences of e-commerce for businesses. The third section discusses the details of sociological influences of e-commerce. The fourth and concluding section discusses the economic impact of e-commerce in the digital economy.

Digital Economy

The essential in the new economy is a structural shift from the industrial economy toward an economy characterized by information, intangibles and services and a parallel change toward new work organizations and institutional forms. Many new terms have been coined for this new economy such as "knowledge-based economy," "borderless economy," "weightless economy," "networked economy," "digital economy," "the information-based economy," and "the networked economy" to name a few (Woodall, 2000; Sharma et al., 2004). A digital economy is a convergence of communications, computing, and information. The new economy is basically about coordination, innovation, selection and learning (Gärdin, 2002). The combination of networked computing technologies and new business models is creating entirely new markets, industries, businesses, and work practices today to form a digital economy. The new economy or digital economy is based more in the form of intangibles, information, innovation, and creativity, in expanding economic potential (Persaud, 2001) and is based on the exploitation of ideas rather than material things. The focus of the new economy moves from processing material input into material output toward creation, trading and distribution of knowledge, intellectual property and intangibles. The symbiosis between changing production and business processes and information and communication technologies (ICT) is the driving force toward the new, digital economy. The key to understanding the new economy is services and the measurement of services. The modern industrial enterprise is largely a producer of services integrated or embedded in the product. A large part of this service production concerns the use of information in some form (Gärdin, 2002). The essential elements of the digital economy are:

- digitalization and intensive use of information and communication technologies (ICT);

- codification of knowledge;

- transformation of information into commodities; and

- new ways of organizing work and production.

This implies that much of information and many services are available online. A widely distributed access to the networks, the intra- and Internet, and of skills to live and work in the Information Society is the basis for the digital economy. The new economy is a combination of services and ICT. Malone, Yates and Benjamin elaborate on the growing concern that the benefits of the digital economy are not evenly distributed within society (Bouwman, 1999). The two major concerns are the role of technologically-sophisticated workers in the digital economy and the equity of the benefits-sharing as digitization of information changes the structure of businesses and industries. For example, the dramatic expansion of inequality and educational differentials, and disparities in access among different groups seem to follow the perfect labor market scenario. In this scenario, the most qualified workers receive much of the benefits, but both firms and poorly qualified workers tend to lose out (Kauffman and Walden, 2001). Many of these socio-economic influences are discussed in the next section.

Positive Influences of E-Commerce for Businesses

Electronic Commerce or e-commerce is the exchange and processing of business transaction information using computers connected through a network. **E-commerce does have unique advantages for businesses**. It allows a shop, a showroom or an office to open 24 hours a day, seven days a week. It also means that time zones are not a problem. A Web site can bring a prospect from the point of advertising and information directly to the point of sale, seamlessly, without involving any other medium. E-commerce has reinvented the way businesses operate. E-commerce has also allowed the establishment of completely new types of businesses such as online shopping and Internet banking. These new ways of thinking, and processes involved in commerce, provide many benefits and advantages. E-commerce brings substantial net benefits to the economy. The real impact of e-commerce is its ability to reduce costs and prices and make doing business more efficient. The increased productivity will result from lower production costs, lower inventory holding costs and lower overall input costs to a business. These savings permeate through the entire value chain and impact significantly in business interactions with other businesses (Sharma and Gupta, 2003a).

The Internet is providing considerable opportunities for firms to streamline their business operations as well as offering greater choice and lower prices to customers shopping online or alternatively obtaining product information before making a store or catalogue purchase. A large number of enterprises have migrated to Internet-based systems for increased efficiencies, lower costs and the ability to operate in real time across different platforms. E-commerce is changing business economics and as a result many firms are re-engineering their core business processes. Suppliers and retailers are able to collaborate on product forecasts and product flow and inventory management decisions using the collaborative Internet-based networks between suppliers and retailers. In addition to reducing costs, e-commerce solutions permit customers to custom order products based on individual needs and preferences. Retailers are able to allow customers to mass customize orders based on virtually thousands of choices. Internet-based systems are more efficient in communicating customized product information to suppliers. The entire value chain makes better decisions collaboratively with the end result being vastly improved performance throughout the entire chain. The Net economy or digital economy will result in lower prices for consumers, better information access and increased competitiveness of small and mid-size businesses. It will also pave the way for a true global trading community.

Social Impacts and Influences of E-Commerce

As e-commerce continues to grow rapidly, it could have significant effects on the structure and functioning of a society at an individual and aggregate level (Granovetter, 1985). The social impacts of these changes are discussed in this section.

E-Commerce and the Digital Divide

The term Digital Divide means a lack of equal access to computer technologies and the Internet in particular, creating a gap between those who have and those who *have not*. The Internet, information and communication technologies (ICTs) and growth of e-commerce has created enormous influence on services, market structure, competition and restructuring of industry and markets. These changes are transforming all areas of society, work, business, and government. The use of information and communication technologies (ICTs) for e-commerce deepens and intensifies the socio-economic divisions among people, businesses and nations. New leadership, better policies, improved infrastructure, greater trust and determined efforts to raise ICT-related skills and competencies across the economy and society in general to move toward greater and more equal digital opportunity. On one hand, e-commerce has provided new opportunities for economic growth. On the other hand, it has created a social problem of digital divide. Digital divide refers to the disparity between those who have use of and access to information and communications technologies (ICT) and those who do not. More than two-thirds of the world population still is deprived of access to information and communication technologies (ICTs). There is a complicated patchwork of varying levels of ICT access, basic ICT usage, and ICT applications among socio-economic groups. Many disparities are getting even larger (Lambert, 2000). Disparities in the location and quality of Internet infrastructure, even the quality of phone lines, have created gaps in access (Quay, 2001). There are gaps in the adoption of digital technologies among different social groups and firms, depending on income levels, education, gender, and ethnic groups and, for firms, depending on industry structure, business size (large firms versus SMEs) and location. Millions of technologically disenfranchised have-nots, who cannot afford the cost of that technology and training, are walled off from potentially life-changing tools and knowledge. Therefore, they feel isolated in the virtual world. For example, although growth has been very strong in Europe, particularly in Sweden and Finland, the United States still accounts for more than three-quarters of all e-commerce transactions. Despite the promise of "borderless" trade, most e-commerce is still national or within the continents (Bassols and Vickery, 2001). Hindered by poverty and a poor telecommunications infrastructure, the gap between developing nations and developed nations is widening further and, therefore, those nations that are not able to jump on the e-commerce bandwagon and have poor access to the Internet suffer from a great disparity in wealth. Many countries are trying to formulate multi-faceted social policy approaches to improve access conditions, education, skill development and training to reduce digital divide gaps (Rombel, 2000; Morrisett, 1998).

E-Commerce and Marginalization

In many countries, the formal sectors in the economy are becoming less labor-intensive and are able to provide employment opportunities to only specialized workers. With the use of the Internet to conduct business, fewer people are required as jobs are automated or made obsolete (World Employment Report, 2001, 2002). This also means that those who are employed in the formal sectors require greater skills and knowledge. This implies that the other half is either unemployed or is in the informal sector of the economy. According to Tores, Bhorat, Leibbrandt and Cassim (2000), those in the informal sectors may be employed — as they are involved in "survivalist" activities, yet they remain in poverty. They are therefore marginalized as they are pushed to the periphery due to their inappropriate education or skills. They are further marginalized as the gap in the knowledge attained between themselves and those in the formal sectors (using the Internet to conduct business) grows (Abrahams et al., 2001).

The use of ICT (such as e-commerce) has brought greater than the existing marginalization (Machipisa, 1999). These sentiments are echoed by the World Employment Report (2001), which says that the use of technologies such as e-commerce is positively correlated with economic growth — both on a national and organizational level. It also states that in countries where ICTs are relatively expensive, many people (particularly previously marginalized, e.g., rural people) are further marginalized. These persons are marginalized to a greater degree than before, i.e., they are being excluded from the electronic market place and are simply ignored by "electronic players." The Internet is becoming a prerequisite for economic development and companies that can quickly access information about conditions in export markets can respond rapidly to changes. On the other hand, those organizations or business people who do not have access to such facilities are unable to respond. Again, they are left out of the mainstream of activities (Abrahams et al., 2001; Licker, 2000).

Social Disparities and Change of Life Styles

Changes in households' roles, division of labor, responsibilities and relationships take place, at least partially influenced by the adoption and use of modern information and communication technologies. Home-based e-work and other combinations of time and place flexibility have created a variety of important effects on partnerships, families and family life. Important research questions are boundaries and overlap between work and leisure or family activities, the availability of space and other resources for home-based e-work and its impact on social contacts and career prospects (Gershuny, 2000). Four groups have been identified that could have problems in coping with new information and communication technologies: inhabitants of remote and less-developed regions, older workers, women and the disabled. The relationship between the adoption of new information and communication technologies and the development of income distribution is very complex. Several important causal chains, effects and mechanisms must be investigated and at least some of them seem to be contradictory in the sense, that the adoption of ICT can cause both growth and reduction of income disparities.

Domestic use of information and communication technologies has both beneficial and harmful impacts. Evidence is mixed with regard to various competing theories about the impact of computing on individual well-being. Some data suggest that increasing Internet use is associated with social isolation, withdrawal, and stress. Although the data also suggest that Internet "addiction" may be limited to about ten percent of Internet users and it is not necessarily associated with how much time an individual actually spends online. Conversely, some studies suggest that Internet use enhances family bonds and friendship formation since e-mail and multi-user domains may foster communication between family members and friends. E-commerce has also created another kind of problem which is known as an X problem. A few magazine reports indicate that as many as 600,000 people are hooked on Internet pornography. The report says online sex addicts go to porn sites, X-rated chat rooms and other sexually-oriented content. The Internet survey indicates that one percent of all Internet users are addicted to online porn.

Social Isolation

E-commerce has been an important facilitator of new flexible work forms. Types of flexible work refer to:

- the location of work, with a flexible location including, e.g., working on the move, working from home and working from tele-centers or satellite offices;

- the working time with non-standard arrangements like flexible hours or "flexitime" schemes, part-time work, job-sharing, compressed working weeks, annualized working hours and zero hours (contracts under which the employer does not guarantee to provide work and pays only for work actually done);

- contractual arrangements like outsourcing, use of agency workers, temporary/ fixed term contracts, casual.

The ranks of telecommuters have grown rapidly throughout the late '90s, as employees have wired homes with high-speed Internet connections and multiple phone and fax lines. Fueling the trend is an office-space crunch in most major cities. Instead of leasing new office space or expanding the existing headquarters, it's vastly less expensive to provide workers with laptops and phone lines and tell them to stay home. Given the historically tight job market, the fierce competition for talent, and the record high turnover among workers, many executives see telecommuting as a perk to woo new recruits—no different than offering them company cars, subsidized Internet access or stock options. Telework has a considerable variety of forms. It includes, among others, work of employees of a company away from the workplace (part-time or full-time, at home or in another places, such as tele-centers), home-based work freelancers, home-based part-time or temporary work as a secondary activity and, in recent times, mobile working, made neither in the workplace nor at home (or tele-center). Early research indicates that so-called telework centers may boost productivity. To cope with the high price of commercial real estate and the shortage of information technology workers, many companies are opening outpost offices in different countries. Each office has a conference room equipped with three large video screens so programmers and engineers can collaborate from remote locations. However, there are various serious social effects of telework. E-commerce has far reaching implications in a social context. On one hand, it provides all the comfort of shopping from home, on the other side, it removes old-fashioned human interactions for social needs (Gershuny, 2000).

The chief problem appears to be the fear of losing touch. Telecommuting could be seen as a different social class with a different set of rules. The fact that traditional workers could be seen as failures in such a society further increases rifts between social classes. As Internet use grows, it is observed that workers spend less time with friends and family, shopping in stores or watching television, and more time working for their employers at home — without cutting back their hours in the office. The more hours people use the Internet, the less time they spend with real human beings (Kraut et al., 1998). More people are working at home on the Internet for their employers and are working more hours at home since they gained Internet access without cutting back at the office, actually reporting increases in time spent working both at home and at the office (Gershuny, 2000; Heikillä et al., 1998).

E-commerce makes it possible for an older consumer to purchase almost all needs from home and have those items delivered. But this can lead to social isolation. The only time there is any personal contact in this situation is when the consumer signs for the packages and when they call up customer service. Due to such phenomenon, there are fewer people active in their neighborhoods than in the 1960s. Many researchers are trying to find answers by working on various issues, such as: How might online communities help reverse this trend? How can local neighborhoods, street corners, apartment buildings, school playgrounds, etc., be turned into bustling, chattering communities where people feel connected and care about others? Random encounters in chat rooms are not enough. Continuing collaborations are needed that encourage trust and collaboration in local health groups, community groups, parent-teacher associations, local conservation groups, community activists or political action groups. Hopefully online communities of the future will help reduce social isolation, enrich local neighborhood communities and encourage development of social capital. Corporate cultures that are traditionally strengthened and reinforced through informal discussions of stories, ritual and specialized language can no longer be maintained. Therefore, geographic dispersion is the primary factor contributing to a weakened culture.

Another issue is ensuring the safety standards of tele-workers. Some feel that an employer should be responsible for preventing or correcting hazards in a home office, passing an unprecedented burden of liability onto the employer. Employers must take steps to reduce or eliminate any work-related safety or health problems they become aware of through on-site visits or other means. But determining how much responsibility an employer has for a tele-worker's home office is unclear. Should an employer be responsible for making sure a tele-worker's office is ergonomically sound or for snowplowing services on the porch and driveway of a traveling salesperson's home?

Loss of Individuality

Maintaining a customer base has become a very important asset in today's economy for the organizations to gain competitive advantage. Therefore, organizations use sophisticated tools to reach customers and get their personal data recorded into their databases. Many believe that e-commerce technology is eroding personal privacy because consumers have no control over their personal data that merchants have collected during their shopping experiences. Also, personal record keeping systems of merchants are not regulated or restricted. People fear that if the trend of collecting information continues, they may lose their individuality since they would have no control over the information about them (Kling and Linowes, 1996; Hatch, 1996).

The Internet expands our experience of community. This expansion challenges traditional notions of the community and the individual. The Web provides so many manifestations of individuality that it causes an inflation of individuality. Individuality is no longer a definition of who we are, which was won the hard way, through explorations of the social and economical boundaries of survival. Individuality is more and more a definition of who we are, which was acquired through countless hours of mediated experiences through television and the Web. An important component of the sociological implications of the information age is that the breaking down of distances that is at the heart of the process should not be allowed to impinge on the essence of individuality. There is clearly the need to ensure that an electronic counterpart of physical individuality is evolved so that there is a true breaking down of distances without a loss of identity. There is already wide recognition of such a need across the world and various efforts are in place to create such e-identities (Miyazaki and Fernandez, 2000).

Privacy

The transition from the Paper Age to the Digital Age has brought with it new issues surrounding the usage of personal information. Privacy has now become a major issue internationally. The rise of intrusive technologies and the Internet has resulted in a surge in awareness about the importance of privacy. Pressure is being put on companies to develop privacy policies to protect consumers who are liberally sharing their personal information in this new environment (Miyazaki and Fernandez, 2000). The rush by large corporations to engage in electronic commerce has meant more personal information is being gathered, shared, sold, and disseminated than ever before. However, the privacy issue moves far beyond protecting personal information on the Internet. In a larger sense, our privacy is being violated daily as new and all encompassing surveillance technologies come on the market. It is also clear that the emergence of ever pervasive and intrusive technologies is representing a threat not only to privacy, but also to fundamental freedoms as citizens. We are building mechanisms and accepting them by allowing their implementation and use, in which we are, virtually, potentially building an electronic prison for ourselves. The potential mechanisms to diminish our basic freedoms are now being put in place (Ambrose and Gelb, 2001).

Technology has meant a wide-scale loss of privacy in comparison to what we enjoyed just 20 years ago. It is not just our personal information that is being abused. We are subject to almost daily scrutiny of our lives. In most countries, video surveillance cameras are accepted as a way of life to combat crime. Computers can now talk to other computers and, if properly programmed, can exchange information between machines automatically. Computers can monitor every aspect of our online activities. In the work place, electronic monitoring of employees is not unusual. In many corporations, it is becoming a standard practice in the name of administrative efficiency. Geo-positioning satellite (GPS) technology can now send email, faxes and messages to our pagers and, now, even to our cars. But that same technology can also pinpoint exactly where we are at any given time of the day. Whether we are in our car and just a short walk away from where we parked, someone somewhere will be able to know our location. This is just another bit of information that will end up somewhere in a database for possible current or future use by someone. Employers can monitor every aspect of employees' movements through these technologies. All of this will be in the name of administrative efficiency, monitoring productivity and being cost-effective. In time, governments will find persuasive reasons to also monitor our activities. It appears that society is whistling cheerfully as we descend willingly into the fast approaching dark tunnel of encroaching technological tyranny. The threats to our freedoms are even wider than ever imagined (Gupta and Sharma, 2001; Zaret and Sawyer, 2000).

The Impact of E-Commerce on Local, Social, and Political Values

E-commerce may have a significant, impact on local political and social life and on local values such as privacy, freedom of information and the right of free speech. Commerce, particularly local commerce, is a social activity that promotes community connections, reinforces community values, establishes community identity, and supports community development. Telecommuting or virtual mobility of labor permitted by global networks can have significant effects on policies, institutions, and social patterns—regional social infrastructure (e.g., housing, health care, and transportation), immigration law, dress standards, eating habits, and others. In the United States, with its many local tax authorities and its heavy dependence on sales tax to run local government, a significant shift from local to Internet commerce would have serious ramifications. On the face of it, this would put local businesses (which are taxed) at a competitive disadvantage, and it would certainly reduce the funds available for local social services. One interesting possibility is that the United States may respond to these pressures by moving toward a European-style, value-added tax.

Economic Impacts and Influences on E-Commerce

The promise of significant economic growth places electronic commerce high on many public and private sector agendas. Starting from basically zero in 1995, it is predicted to reach $1 trillion in 2003-05 (IDC, 1999). On the other hand, it could have significant effects on the structure and functioning of economies at the firm, sector and aggregate level. The impacts of these changes are diverse and likely to impinge on prices, the composition of trade, labor markets and taxation revenues. Adapting policy frameworks and institutions to these changes and ensuring that the full potential benefits of e-commerce are reaped will pose a number of challenges for structural policy. This section provides an overview of these issues.

Organizational Changes of Enterprises

E-commerce can influence the process of governance in various ways and in varying degrees, from improving the current mechanisms of delivery of services to transforming the entire mechanism and the nature of services themselves. The role played could be:

1. Purely technical in terms of automation of tedious tasks earlier done by humans,

2. To a facilitating/supportive role leading to more participatory and all-encompassing decision-making and implementation processes,

3. To a completely innovative role that involves new services and new mechanisms to deliver these services.

E-commerce can lead to increased participation, inclusion and integration on one hand and increased marginalization, loneliness and exclusion from information and communication on the other.

All enterprises face internal as well as external changes due to the emerging e-commerce technologies. They influence the way in which enterprises position themselves in the market and the way they collaborate with others. These new technologies have consequences for intra-organizational changes of production and working issues. The implementation of modern ICTs creates impacts on business relationships with partners and concurrently, the internal and external enterprise organizations with regard to its competitiveness. For any organization, the adoption of an e-commerce strategy generally entails redefining its value chain and re-engineering internal functions and processes to adapt to and benefit from the new information systems implemented. The dramatic changes in the way information flows throughout the organization deeply affect its entire value chain. A shift of importance of single functions of an enterprise is to observe. Value is shifting from production to product development, procurement, sales and marketing, and the provision of after-sales services. These are also the areas where e-commerce solutions are going to play a vital role in increasing companies' collaborative capabilities with partners along value chains. Co-operation motives can be cost and risk reduction, knowledge transfer or just the reduction of time to market. Unfortunately, costs are still the main incentive for business activities or even the reason to shut down business activities. Reduced expenditures due to lower charges can be directly used in marketing, research and development, etc. In cooperation, enterprises can exploit the better cost position of the partner or use economies of scale.

Through the new possibilities of electronic collaboration and IT-supported production, it is expected that productivity will comparatively grow with the introduction of new ICT technologies. ICT technologies are becoming an important part of business processes and have become indispensable to stay competitive in new market constellations. They are necessary to reduce time to market, to find the best offer with the best price and most suitable partners for one's business. Productivity is the relationship between output and input. It should be viewed as value adding in addition to optimizing. It is a total concept that addresses the key elements of competition, i.e., innovation, cost, quality and delivery. Therefore, an increase in productivity can be achieved by enhancing the value-added content of products/services, or by decreasing the unit cost of production, or a combination of both (Uzzi, 1997).

E-Commerce and Local Businesses

Whitten and Steinfield show that as electronic commerce grows, it will create an important socio-economic side effect which will be increased competition with the traditional businesses in any given local community (Steinfield, Mahler and Bauer, 1999a; 1999b). Their study indicates that although local businesses may gain from the efficiencies afforded by electronic commerce, both in better serving their local constituencies and by reaching out to distant markets. In general local merchants are ill-prepared to take full advantage of electronic commerce due to various reasons, and thus are unlikely to see gains from it (Steinfield, Mahler and Bauer, 1999a; 1999b).

Distant Web-based businesses have several advantages over their local physical businesses. Based on Steinfield et al. (1999a; 1999b), such advantages include, but are not limited to: access to a wider potential market; lower sunk costs because a building or rented space in each market is not required, and they may operate with less or no inventory; better economies of scale arising from a larger customer base, and consequent volume discounts on inputs; lower costs due to the ability to bypass many of the intermediaries in the retail distribution value chain (Wigand and Benjamin, 1995; Wigand, 1997); a higher degree of transaction automation, leading to improved service and lower labor costs and the ability to rapidly respond to changes in the market through price adjustments which can be almost in real-time (Bailey, 1998), as well as changes in product mix and marketing approach. These economies can potentially enable Web-based retailers to easily undercut the prices of local retailers who formerly faced little or no competition. Using transaction cost theory, one can conclude that electronic commerce implies new competition for local retailers, particularly those offering products that are readily obtainable from other sources, and that are easily transported (Steinfield and Whitten, 1999; Steinfield et al, 1999a; 1999b).

Community-Level Impacts of Electronic Commerce

E-commerce has many positive influences at the individual level whereby local buyers gain more value and greater access to suppliers. However, the results at the aggregate community level may be undesirable for local residents. Some of the community-level social costs of electronic commerce are: job losses, particularly in relatively unskilled areas already quickly disappearing in the digital economy; loss of local shopping options that, even with higher prices, afforded some conveniences; decreased attractiveness of the local community due to the loss of boutiques or other businesses that enhanced the quality of community appearance and life and reduced tax income from business, resulting in a reduction in the ability to fund government services that enhance community life (Whitten, 1999; Steinfield et al., 1999a; 1999b).

Clearly not all communities will be affected equally. Some may even find that electronic commerce leads to significant growth in jobs, tax revenues and service levels. Larger communities may be less vulnerable for a number of reasons. They may have more competitive local business, and their larger population may make the effects of any loss in business less noticeable. Community culture may play a role, such as university towns having more Web-savvy consumers. The nature of the local economy — for example, a prevalence of firms in high-tech vs. heavy industry vs. services, such as tourism — may also influence the relative attractiveness of Web commerce and the vulnerability of local businesses. Even the extent to which a community is geographically isolated, influencing the availability of nearby businesses within driving distance, and the resulting competitiveness of local firms once they are exposed to Web competition, can be a factor (Steinfield and Whitten, 1999; Steinfield et al., 1999a; 1999b; Choi et al., 1997).

Bundling or Tying Arrangements

E-commerce offers opportunity for building or bundling several products and services together. Many companies now offer a complete package of trading, information, logistics and supply chain management services. The bundling of such products and/ or services may provide a convenient solution for buyers, and a way in which competing service providers can differentiate their offerings to attract more customers. In some cases it may also be a more efficient and economical way to provide both products and/ or services, resulting in lower prices and promoting the development of a new competitive product or service. On the other hand, this may arise between competing outlets – particularly when some outlets are independently owned and operated but others have vertical links with manufacturers. Some wholesale operations could be squeezed out or replaced by Internet intermediaries. Potential issues may include:

- Suppliers refusing to deal with independent offline or online distributors because they have developed their own online retail Web sites;
- Suppliers refusing to deal with independent online distributors; and suppliers discriminating between price and quality or quantity of goods distributed via online and offline distribution channels.

E-commerce may have an impact on existing franchising arrangements, particularly where contractual terms provide for territorial limits. Many businesses may have entered into franchising arrangements on the understanding that they would have exclusive territorial rights, whereas for certain types of goods, e-commerce transcends global boundaries and thus would create a problem for franchising arrangements if these are territory-based. Also, in the new environment of e-commerce, franchise products will face competition both locally and globally.

Impact on Tax, Trade and Regulatory Policies

E-commerce has a strong impact on taxation and tax policy. Concerns have been expressed that e-commerce could result in the erosion of tax bases. Consumption taxes are levied on the principle of taxation at the place of consumption and according to rates set in individual countries, or in individual states in the case of federal nations. E-commerce, however, has the potential to undermine the application of domestic and national tax rules. Tax planning for an e-business differs from tax planning for a traditional bricks-and-mortar company. Historically, the generation of income depended on the physical presence of assets and activities. This physical presence, or permanent establishment, generally determined which jurisdiction had the primary right to tax the income generated. Because of the growth of electronic commerce, new e-business models (including digital marketplaces, online catalogs, virtual communities, subscription-based information services, online auctions, and portals) have emerged. Each allows taxpayers to conduct business and generate income in a country with little or no physical presence in that country. The separation of assets and activities from the source of the income represents a significant departure from historic business models. This change creates new tax planning challenges and opportunities (Penbera, 1999; Olin, 2001; Anonymous, 2000; Sharma and Gupta, 2003b).

Impact on Employment and Labor Policy

The growth of e-commerce is likely to have both direct and indirect impacts on labor markets as well as the composition of employment. Since e-commerce may create more knowledge-based products, it is likely to drive widespread changes in the labor market, shifting the composition of workers required to produce and deliver a product or service (Anonymous, 2000). There will be shifts in the kind of skills needed. Faster rates of innovation and diffusion may also be associated with a higher turnover of jobs. This may create more turbulence as workers will need to enhance their skills from time to time. This may result in reallocation of labor to the changing needs of the economy (Sharma and Gupta, 2003b; Anonymous, 2000).

One important change due to ICT is occurring in employment within economic sectors. Changes occur regarding the polarization of wages around skills, demand for specific qualified work (e.g., replacement of traditional craft and production engineering skills towards computer design skills), a need for ongoing training, other forms of work contracts, and a shift to a smaller core workforce. Businesses will incur ICT costs including cost of new applications, developer time, software licenses, any hardware or software, support and maintenance costs, and business costs associated with making the transition to the new system, etc. The challenge remains to predict support and maintenance costs for the new technology, business costs associated with making the transition to the new system and other hidden costs. Considering the fast development of technological changes it is therefore getting much harder to ascertain the long-term impact of any technology choice (Penbera, 1999).

Competitive Environment – Influence on Monopolistic Trends

Internet-driven e-commerce will have a significant impact on the competitive environment of commerce. Because in e-commerce the entry cost is low, and transaction costs are lower, it allows small entrepreneurs to enter the marketplace easily. On the other hand, e-commerce especially facilitates enterprises whose success depends on network effects—"winner-takes-all" situations for companies with significant market share—which further facilitate their growth and market dominance. This effect may create problems for competition and antitrust policy. Certain players may become monopoly holders, which will have greater (and dire) consequences for competition. The recent evidence from Microsoft case has shown that there is considerable potential for weakening the competitive process. The monopolists will have strong interests in locking customers into network relationships. The concepts like trust, reputation, loyalty, pricing and commitment take on new meaning for online business (Uzzi, 1997).

Since e-commerce would transcend geographical boundaries, many big firms of known brands may not only expand their markets, but also may enter into new business activities across the broad spectrum of business activities. This may help to reduce the costs and prices, but it will create the danger of creating an e-commerce monopoly by a few corporations or networks of corporations. Many firms may use a low-price strategy to grab the market and eliminate the competition. Several mergers and alliances, in which two or more firms combine to achieve a large market share and have large economies of scale, can result in eliminating meaningful competition (Sharma and Gupta, 2003b).

Impact on Prices

Electronic commerce is widely expected to improve efficiency due to reduced transaction and search costs, increased competition and more streamlined business processes. Lower search costs may also lead to Internet consumers being more sensitive to price changes. By reducing search costs and increasing the flow of information, e-commerce might effectively shift power from producers to consumers and make it harder for firms to maintain higher prices (Bakos, 1997). However, empirical evidence does not support this claim in all cases. Brynjolfsson and Smith (1999) found that average prices on certain items in a particular industry sold through the Internet were lower than their equivalent purchased through traditional retailers. However, in certain cases prices of goods sold through the Internet were higher than those charged by traditional retailers. Brynjolfsson and Smith (1999) justified this phenomenon by arguing that certain reductions in cost are offset by higher overhead costs elsewhere. They also indicate that increases or decreases in price depend on the size of the market (Sharma and Gupta, 2003b).

The Threat to SMEs

The adoption of e-commerce technologies is important for the ongoing survival of SMEs. The Internet can remove many of the competitive advantages of larger companies and provide opportunities for smaller enterprises. It can also include a cost-effective way for SMEs to market their business, launch new products, improve communications and information and identify potential partners (Sharma et al., 2003). However, SMEs also have to be aware that the Internet and e-commerce will create more sophisticated and demanding customers with higher expectations in terms of 24-hour access to company and product information and quicker responses to information requests.

From a theoretical perspective, small business and rural enterprises can benefit greatly with e-commerce as they gain access to more customers (even globally) and can even compete with large businesses since e-commerce is a "level playing field." Since SMEs are known for greater internal efficiencies, they may have an advantage over large businesses. However, recent studies indicate that the adoption of e-commerce by small business (as either a buyer or supplier in B2B and/or B2C environments) has not been as rapid as would be anticipated. Reasons cited for this include the cost, technology hurdles, and lack of expertise. E-commerce demands fundamental shifts in business strategies, operations and technologies. Many participating SMEs indicated that they have limited access to information about the business models and technologies that are the basis of e-commerce success. Lack of knowledgeable staff in SMEs is also responsible for non-adoption of e-commerce. This will result in SMEs being non-competitive in an e-commerce environment (Auger and Gallaugher, 1997).

Conclusions

As electronic commerce grows, there will be important socio-economic side effects. Although IT has the potential to reduce disparities between nations, asymmetric access to its benefits by different sections of society can have far reaching social and economic implications. Our research suggests that e-commerce technologies are helping organizations, societies and nations to accelerate their socio-economic growth and to provide more opportunities for businesses to grow, but it has also created many challenges and effects across numerous domains of society, and poses many challenges for policy makers. In this chapter we have identified a comprehensive set of socio-economic variables that are influenced by e-commerce. Further empirical validation could be done for these variables in different countries.

References

Abrahams, S., Parenzee, V., Chong, L.A.P. and Licker, P. (2001). The Role of E-commerce in the Economic and Social Marginalization and Demarginalization of Selected Populations in South Africa – An Empirical Research Report presented to the Department of Information Systems University of Cape Town in partial fulfillment of the requirements for Information Systems.

Ambrose, Jr., S.F. and Gelb, J.W. (2001). Consumer privacy regulation and litigation: The Business Lawyer. *Chicago*, 56(3), 1157-1178.

Amit, R. and Zott, C. (2001). Value Creation in E-Business. *Strategic Management Journal*, 22, 493-520.

Anonymous. (2000). E-commerce: Impacts and policy challenges. *Organization for Economic Cooperation and Development. OECD Economic Outlook*, 67, 193-213.

Auger, P. and Gallaugher, J. (1997). Factors affecting the adoption of an Internet-based sales presence for small businesses. *The Information Society, 13*, 55-74.

Bailey, J. (1998). Internet price discrimination: Self-regulation, public policy, and global electronic commerce. Paper presented to the *Telecommunications Policy Research Conference*, Washington, D.C.

Bailey, J. and Brynjolfsson, E. (1997). In search of 'friction-free markets': An exploratory analysis of prices for books, CDs, and software sold on the Internet. Presented to the *Twenty-Fifth Annual Telecommunications Policy Research Conference*, Washington, D.C.

Bakos, J.Y. (1997). Reducing buyer search costs: Implications for electronic marketplaces. *Management Science, 43*(12), 1676-1692.

Bernardes, E. S. (2000). The Socio-Economic Impacts of E-Commerce: A Review. In E. Brynjolfsson and B. Kahin (Eds.), *Understanding the Digital Economy: Data, Tools, and Research*. Cambridge, MA: MIT Press 2000. Retrieved from the World Wide Web: http://misrc.umn.edu/workingpapers/workingpapers.htm.

Boulton, R.E.S., Libert, B.D. and Samek, S.M. (2000). A business model for the new economy. *The Journal of Business Strategy, 21*(4), 29-35.

Bouwman, H. (1999, April). E-commerce: cyber and physical environments. *Electronic Markets, 9*(1).

Choi, S. Y., Stahl, D. and Whinston, A. (1997). *The economics of electronic commerce*. Indianapolis, IN: Macmillan Technical Publishing.

Dutton, W. H. (Ed.). (1996). *Information and Communication Technologies - Visions and Realities In The Media Economics & Media Culture Programme, and the Virtual Society?* Oxford: Oxford University Press.

Dutton, W. H. (1999a). *Society on the Line*. Oxford: Oxford University Press.

Dutton, W. H. (1999b). The Web of Technology and People. *Prometheus, 17*(1), 5-20.

E-commerce Development Report. (2002).

Garicano, L. and Kaplan, S.N. (2001). The Effects of Business-to-Business E-Commerce on Transaction Costs. *The Journal of Industrial Economics*, *49*(4), 463-485.

Gärdin, O. (2002). The New Economy New challenges for the statistical system. *The International Association for Official Statisticians Conference*, London 2002.

Gershuny, J. (2000). *Changing times. Work and Leisure in Post-industrial Society.* Oxford: Oxford University Press.

Granovetter, M. (1985). Economic action and social structure: The problem of embeddedness. *American Journal of Sociology, 91*(3), 481-510.

Gupta, J.N.D and Sharma, S.K. (2001). Cyber Shopping and Privacy. In A. Gangopadhyay (Ed.), *Managing Business with Electronic Commerce: Issues and Trends.* Hershey, PA: Idea Group Publishing.

Hatch, D. (1996). Privacy: How Much Data Do Direct Marketers Really Need. In R. Kling (Ed.), *Computerization and Controversy*, (2nd ed.). San Diego: Academic Press.

Heikillä, J., Kallio, J., Saarinen, T. and Tuunainen, V. K. (1998). Grocery Shopping for the Elderly and Disabled: Finnish EC Experiments. *Electronic Markets,8*(2), 17-19.

INTERNATIONAL DATA CORPORATION (IDC). (1999, March). Internet insights, 1999. *The Grey Sheet*, 33(21-22).

Kauffman, R.J. and Walden, E.A. (2001, Summer). Economics and e-commerce: survey and research directions. *International Journal of Electronic Commerce*, *5*(4), 4-115.

Kling, R. and Linowes, D. F. (1996). Information Technologies and the Shifting Balance between Privacy: Your Personal Information Has Gone Public. In R. Kling (Ed.), *Computerization and Controversy* (2nd ed.). San Diego: Academic Press.

Kraut, R., Steinfield, C., Chan, A., Butler, B. and Hoag, A. (1998). Coordination and Virtualization: The Role of Electronic Networks and Personal Relationships. *Journal of Computer Mediated Communication, 3*(4). Retrieved from the World Wide Web: http://www.ascusc.org/jcmc/vol3/issue4/kraut.html.

Lambert, C. (2000). Grappling with the digital divide. The Earth Times. Retrieved from the World Wide Web: http://www.earthtimes.org/j an/featuregrapplingwithjan 25_01.htm.

Licker, P. (2000). Countering e-commerce marginalization through demand-centred measures. Bitworld 2001 Conference Paper, University of Cape Town.

Lucking-Reiley, D. and Spulber, D.F. (2001). Business-to-Business Electronic Commerce. *Journal of Economic Perspectives*, *15*(1), 55-68.

Machipisa, L. (1999). Africa lags behind in the information race. *Daily Mail & Guardian*. Retrieved from the World Wide Web: http://www.mg.co.za/mg/za/archive/1999oct/features/28oct-africa_tech.html.

Malone, T., Yates, J. and Benjamin, R. (1987). Electronic markets and electronic hierarchies: Effects of information technology on market structure and corporate strategies. *Communications of the ACM, 30*(6), 484-497.

Mariotti, S. and Sgobbi, F. (2001). Alternative paths for the growth of e-commerce. *Futures, 33*(2), 109-125.

McGarvey, R. (2001). New corporate ethics for the new economy. *World Trade, 14*(3), 43.

Miyazaki, A.D. and Fernandez, A. (2000). Internet privacy and security: An examination of online retailer disclosures. *Journal of Public Policy & Marketing, 19*(1), 54-61.

Morrisett, L. (1998). Bridging the digital divide: The impact of race on computer access and the Internet use. Retrieved from the World Wide Web: http://www2000.ogsm. vanderbilt.edu/papers/race/science.html.

Mukhopadhyay, T., Kekre, S. and Kalathur, S. (1995). Business Value of Information Technology: A Study of Electronic Data Interchange. *MIS Quarterly, 19*(2), 137-156.

OECD. (1999). *The economic and social impacts of electronic commerce*, chapter 1. Paris.

Olin, J. (2001). Reducing international e-commerce taxes. *World Trade, 14*(3), 64-67.

Penbera, J.J. (1999). E-commerce: Economics and Regulation. *S.A.M. Advanced Management Journal, 64*(4), 39-47.

Persaud, A. (2001). The knowledge gap. *Foreign Affairs, 80*(2), 107-117.

Quay, R. (2001). Bridging the digital divide. *Planning, 67*(7), 12-17.

Rombel, A. (2000, December). The global digital divide. *Global Finance, 14*(12), 47.

Schroeder, R. (1994). Cyberculture, Cyborg Post-Modernism and the Sociology of Virtual Reality Technologies: Surfing the Soul in the Information Age. *Futures, 263*(51), 519-528.

Sethuraman, S.V. (1997). Urban Poverty and the Informal Sector. ILO. Retrieved from the World Wide Web: http://www.ilo.org/public/english/employment/recon/eiip/publ/ 1998/urbpover.htm.

Sharma, S.K. and Gupta, J.N.D. (2001). E-Commerce Opportunities and Challenges. In M. Singh & T. Thompson (Eds.), *E-Commerce Diffusion: Strategies and Challenges*. Australia: Heidelberg Press.

Sharma, S. K. and Gupta, J.N.D. (2003a). Creating business value through E-commerce. In N. Shin (Ed.), *Creating Business Value with Information Technology: Challenges and solutions*. Hershey, PA: Idea Group Publishing.

Sharma, S. K. and Gupta, J.N.D. (2003b). Adverse effects of E-Commerce. In L. van Heerden and J. M. van Heerden (Eds.), *The Economic and Social Impact of E-Commerce*. Hershey, PA: Idea Group Publishing.

Sharma, S. K., Wickramansinghe, N. and Gupta, J.N.D. (2004). What Should SMEs Do To Succeed in Today's Knowledge-Based Economy? In N. Al-Qirim (Ed.), *(forthcoming)*. Hershey, PA: Idea Group Publishing.

Steinfield, C. and Klein, S. (1999, April). Local versus global issues in electronic commerce. *Electronic Markets, 9*(1).

Steinfield, C. and Whitten, P. (1999). Community Level Socio-Economic Impacts of Electronic Commerce. *Journal of Computer Mediated Communication, 5*(2). Retrieved from the World Wide Web: http://www.ascusc.org/jcmc/vol5/issue2/ steinfield.html.

Steinfield, C., Kraut, R. and Plummer, A. (1995). The impact of interorganizational networks on buyer-seller relationships. *Journal of Computer Mediated Communication* [Online], *1*(3). Retrieved from the World Wide Web: http://www.ascusc.org/jcmc/vol1/issue3/steinfld.html.

Steinfield, C., Mahler, A. and Bauer, J. (1999a, April). Electronic commerce and the local merchant: Opportunities for synergy between physical and Web presence. *Electronic Markets, 9*(1).

Steinfield, C., Mahler, A. and Bauer, J. (1999b). Local Versus Global Markets in Electronic Commerce: Towards A Conceptualization of Local Electronic Commerce Strategies. In E. Bohlin, K. Brodin, A. Lundgren, A. and B. Thorngren (Eds.), *Convergence in Communications and Beyond*. Amsterdam: Elsevier Science Publishers.

Timmers, P. (1999). *Electronic Commerce: Strategies and Models for Business-to-Business Trading*. New York: John Wiley & Sons.

Tores, L., Bhorat, H., Leibbrandt, M. and Cassim, F. (2000). Poverty and the labor market. In J. May (Ed.), *Poverty and inequality in South Africa – meeting the challenge*. Claremont, South Africa: David Philip Publishers (Pty) Ltd.

Uzzi, B. (1997, March). Social structure and competition in interfirm networks: The paradox of embeddedness. *Administrative Science Quarterly, 42*, 35-67.

Wigand, R. and Benjamin, R. (1995). Electronic commerce: Effects on electronic markets. *Journal of Computer Mediated Communication, 1*(3). Retrieved from the World Wide Web: http://www.ascusc.org/jcmc/vol1/issue3/vol1no3.html.

Woodall, P. (2000). Survey: The new economy: Knowledge is power. *The Economist, 356*(8189), 27-32.

World employment report 2001. (2001). Life at work in the information economy ILO. Retrieved from the World Wide Web: http://www.ilo.org/public/english/support/publ/wer/overview.htm.

World employment report 2002. (2002). Life at work in the information economy ILO.

Zaret, E. and Sawyer, S. (2000). Protect yourself online. *Macworld, 17*(7), 64-69.

Chapter II

Re-Intermediation and Deferment through E-Commerce:

Neo-Austrian Interpretation of Capital and Time

Parthasarathi Banerjee
NISTADS, India

Abstract

Contrary to the common belief that e-commerce disintermediates—or even while reintermediation takes place the economic circuit fails to get lengthened—this chapter argues following the Austrian perspective, that through e-commerce consumption gets deferred and the economic circuit lengthens. Inappropriate use of transaction cost theory, in particular, has often weakened the received theory. This implies that e-commerce increases capital because capital is time according to the Austrian theory. Consequently the efficiency-focus of received theory is replaced by a capital-enhancing theory of this new commerce. Several novel functions of intermediaries including coordination have been utilized to support the departure from the efficiency perspective. Citing several well-known examples from the literature has adumbrated this argument.

Introduction

It is commonly believed that electronic commerce (Ecom) reduces intermediation and the time in a business circuit. Several authors have argued that dis-intermediation resulting from the use of Ecom increases economic efficiency and reallocates resources better. Alternatively, transactions cost economics (TCE) theorists argue that electronic commerce decreases transactions cost by way of reducing the distance between the producers and the customers. Proponents of increasing economic efficiency through dis-intermediation in electronic commerce have employed TCE as well. We argue from a Neo-Austrian perspective contrary to this efficiency theory of dis-intermediation and of quickened money that this efficiency perspective is limited to technological changes alone (Baumol, Panzar & Willig, 1986). In so far as Ecom is purely technological there would be gains in economic efficiency arising out of changes in technological relations. However, mediation in the market is only limitedly technological. Mediation refers more to the market microstructure. Moreover, Ecom can affect efficiency through means other than dis-intermediation.

In contrast, we argue that efficiency fails to increase rate of profit or the pace and spread of innovations. For us, intermediation refers to not just a certain value chain, such as a typical SIC industrial segment. Contrarily, intermediation goes beyond a market segment to the depth of market microstructure (O'Hara, 1997) to provide for coordination (Richardson, 1960, 1972, 1998) in two modes; first, amongst the competitors (including potential competitors and complementors), and second, between the producer and its consumers. Efficiency perspective refers to the continuation of the same basic structure of intermediation but accentuated and hastened through elimination of several mediatory links. We argue contrarily from the Austrian perspective that Ecom transforms the intermediation structure in order to afford higher coordination, higher capital and increased rate of profit—and all this by virtue of a new market microstructure of intermediation. Ecom is an innovation in trade and linkages in an economy and we would argue that it substitutes the previous intermediary-based value chain by a new coordination across several value chains and specifically along the scope dimension (North, 1989). It appears that this commerce ushers the economy to a new institutional mooring. This innovative coordination is afforded by generation of new and novel cybermediaries (Sarkar, Butler & Steinfeld, 1995). Further, Ecom brings in several layers of possible intermediaries such as the virtuals and the aggregators, and as a result tends to keep transactions incomplete. This significant departure from transactional completeness to incompleteness forces deferment of consumption and consequently increases capital and the period of production. It extends the completion of transaction indefinitely and thereby Ecom, instead of shortening the business circuit, the proverbial value chain, would extend such a circuit indefinitely along both vertical and horizontal dimensions.

Indefinite extension of business circuits, that is, the lengthening of business transactions, increases effectively the period of production. We argue that the lengthened circuit or the period of production necessarily demands more intense cooperation than what could be provided by the simple value chain intermediation. Noticing that Austrian theory recognizes capital as time that is as the period of production, we can recognize that Ecom enhances capital twice, first by lengthening the period and second by deepening coordination. This theory argues that a longer period of production implies a potentially higher rate of profit and an increase in capital. Based on this theoretical stance we argue that Ecom enhances capital and increases the rate of profit by lengthening the circuit of transaction through a mechanism of deferment of consumption, known otherwise also as the period of production. Lengthening of period comes through re-intermediation and through increased deferment of consumption.

Background

Ecom and the diffusion of information technology, in general, have been believed to contribute to transformation of value chains internal to a firm and to an industry (Porter, 1985). Such a value chain recognizes the vertical dimension and refers to an industry segment. It was argued (Malone, Yates & Benjamin, 1987) that consequent to transformation of inter-linkages there would be dis-intermediation or the shortening of the circuit in the market. A comparison between the two modes of reaching customers seemed inevitable (Brynjolffson & Smith, 1999). It was believed that the end result of dis-intermediation would be added value to customers and to the producers. This belief was strengthened by an additional belief in the disutility of a trader. A trader was looked down upon as an irritant causing disruptions and adding significant costs (Benjamin & Wigand, 1995). The trader did not seem to have any contribution to make to the market microstructure. This argument concludes that intermediation could be terminated altogether thus offering to both producers and the consumers additional value through effects such as direct sales, in particular by a dominant producer commanding price or quality (Bailey & Bakos, 1996). This hypothesis of threatened intermediaries, as Sarkar et al. (1995) coined it, is based upon a certain reading of the theory of transactions costs economics (TCE) (Williamson, 1975, 1985; Coase, 1990). Another approach though not far off from the TCE is agency theory, used by Picot, Bortenlanger and Hohrl (1997) to argue that principals henceforth armed with additional information would either dispense away with most of the services hired till date from the agents or, would design stronger and more effective system of incentives and monitoring. This would enable the principal to minimize upon the costs of monitoring and hence agents, such as all the intermediaries, would become obsolete.

Possibly Sarkar et al. (1995) were the first to indicate that intermediations would possibly increase. They renamed such mediations as the cybermediaries. They argued that the proponents of dis-intermediation employed a flawed TCE logic, the latter properly employed would show that mediation must increase in Ecom. In subsequent years empirical studies on the extent of cybermediation by a large number of contributors have pointed out the increasing incidences of mediations (Giaglis, Klein & O'Keefe, 2000; Burton & Mooney, 1998; Meck, 2001; Domowitz, 2001; Chircu & Kauffman, 2000; Story, Straub, Stewart & Welke, 2000). The key paper by Sarkar et al. employed TCE to argue that intermediation would possibly increase consequent upon introduction of Ecom. Most contributors agreed to this formulation by Sarkar et al., and these contributions have enriched the argument based upon TCE. The transactional logic employed has identified mediation as one component in the value chain necessary to reduce the otherwise high costs of transactions.

Issues have been conflated here, however. Accounting costs have wrongly been assumed to represent the costs of transaction. TCE argues (Williamson, 1975) that transaction costs arise because parties in an exchange behave opportunistically. The cost necessary to overcome opportunism or in other words, costs borne to protect property rights when an opportunistic exchange partner is faced (Barzel, 1989) is known as the transaction cost. It follows that in Ecom where parties may not transact repeatedly or do not have trust such transactions costs will rise instead of disappear. Coase's (1990) theorem shows that formation of a firm alone can force costs of transactions to remain limited. In other words TCE would demand either the birth of a firm or the birth of trusted intermediaries. The former implies that Ecom will cease to operate because vertical integration or appearance of firms would take place. The latter, close to most of the TCE proponents of cybermediation, shows that mediation possibly now through new partners will necessarily remain following introduction of Ecom.

Schmitz (2000) takes up agency theory to defend the thesis that mediation will remain or else increase following introduction of Ecom. Fallacy in Sarkar et al.'s (1995) approach is that mediation has been considered as a singular service. Schmitz, in contrast, argues based on agency theory and the theory of market microstructure that mediation has multiple aspects. Three aspects have been considered and these are: first, to hold inventory in order to service immediacy and insurance; second, to reduce asymmetric information by building reputation; and finally, to gather, collate and disseminate information on the market. Schmitz argues further that intermediation in Ecom does not increase marginal cost to the principal (the producer) and the intermediaries must produce the three types of services jointly, that is the market in lieu of having three different types of intermediaries would have only one type.

Sarkar et al. (1995) indicated that Ecom necessarily engenders mediation in the following areas of search and evaluation, needs assessment and product matching, customer risk management, product distribution, product information dissemination, purchase influence, provision of customer information, producer risk management, and transaction economies of scale and for integration of customer and producer needs. This detailed listing appears to cover the three modes described by Schmitz (2000). Meck (2001), for example, indicates three groupings of cybermediation, which are aggregation of buyer demand and seller products, searching and matching, and pricing and facilitation. Domowitz (2001) similarly applying the TCE logic vindicates reintermediation in Ecom. Most authors applying the TCE agree to the emergence of certain broad types of mediation. What, however, seems to be missing in this discussion is the relevance of increasing returns and the consequential restructuring in industrial segments that are adopting Ecom.

Restructuring through the cycle of intermediation followed by dis-intermediation and finally through cybermediation has been underscored as exogenous. The basic teaching from studies on increasing returns suggests, however, that a pull in demand on the structural elements in a market has a cascading effect. This cascade pulls through the economic inter-linkages across not only segments along a vertical direction but more often and more vigorously across the direction of scope (Richardson, 1996, 1997, 1998).

As a result, novel divisions of labor and novel microstructures of the market appear especially along the scope linkages (Katz & Shapiro, 1985; Silver, 1984). Such structures in turn demand further employment of information technology for linkages and for transactions. This cycle of increasing and synergistic spawning of divisions in market and in the diffusion of Ecom thus displays increasing return. Ecom consequentially restructures the previous market arrangement along directions of scope, and therefore the cascading effect of restructuring can be felt through a large number of interrelated industrial segments subsequent to introduction of Ecom in a lone segment. Contributions by previous scholars sadly missed this point of both lengthened intermediation and the cascading effect of restructuring following Ecom along markets other than where it was initially introduced. This re-intermediation in other markets is of great consequence since they alter very significantly structures and interrelationships amongst markets.

Evidences and Departure to a New Theory

Evidences of re-intermediation are in plenty. There are, however, other related changes in the market, such as in the emergence of a novel framework of liability (Valimaki & Martikainen, 2001), or the emergence of new relationships between the wholesaler and the retailer (Nettesine & Rudi, 2000), or in offerings of greatly dispersed prices (Pan, Ratchford & Shankar, 2001). Several databased searches and research on price offerings on the electronic commerce have shown that prices offered on Internet are often not lower than other modes of retail sales. Internet pricing has shown personalized effects based on quality differentiation and on personalized offerings. Ecom offerings have been compared to mass customization (Wind & Rangaswamy, 2000), necessitating the spawning of very large number of novel intermediaries. Technology has allowed firms to identify and track customers, on the online stores as also on Web sites. Firms now can create individual consumer profiles matched by all other relevant information on choices, demographics, cultures, and preferences. Internet retailers can deploy complex pricebots and can effectively discriminate price offers based on such profiles of preferences, etc. Ecom has thus opened up the possibility of offering extremely variegated personalized pricing. This forum can also offer equivalents of typical marketplace bargains. It follows logically that retail offers on Ecom cannot disintermediate and eliminate stages of intermediation necessary to gather market and competitive intelligence. Market clearing in Ecom therefore necessarily requires a very large increase in information transacted and processed (Aoki, 1990). These in turn demand services from new entrepreneurs offering specialized facilities for search and offer. Ecom market thus increases the market along the dimension of scope.

Along with personalization of pricing, the electronic retailer can now design its product offers on personalization of the qualities of the products. This results in offers of extremely variegated products, which in turn calls for revolutionary changes in the entire system of production that once through Tayloristic mode had developed along the line of corporatization and mass production of mass-standard goods. Mass customization and co-production of a new product offered especially through cooperation along the direction of scope have increased enormously the number of products on offer. Co-development of products by a group of competitors' complementors or collaborators in association with current or potential customers and the strategy of producing products' versions have catapulted previous industrial vertical segments into a jumbled up flux of cross-connected firms. Expansion along scope direction has deferred consumption of a good. Consequently the period of production has increased. This expansion has created numerous linkages or mediations along the scope axis before a product can be consumed. Expansion along vertical organization consumes a product necessarily earlier than through expansion along scope-axis.

Production organization of a vertically integrated corporation stood upon standardization. Production of apiece products with variegated quality, chosen often by the buyer herself, demands that the entire chain of logistics and the supply chains get linked to the electronic commerce platform and that the stages in production are increased immensely and at each step of production each apiece product contains unique information. This has resulted in enrichment of information and subsequent differentiation of previously firm-internal business activities. This is a classic example of increasing return-based expansion in divisions of labor. Such a picture of electronic-commerce-led economy shows that stages of production must increase, that different economic agents must undertake each stage especially to take care of the need for insurance and for generation of asymmetric information appearing often as specialization, that variability must increase and that mass production of personalized wares must hasten. In short, electronic commerce demands that an economy increase both its division of labor and the long period of production.

Velocity of money or goods in an economy refers to technical efficiency. This efficiency refers to particular states of affairs of technology. Enhanced efficiency and finally efficiency-equalization in the equilibrium must refer to a static picture of unchanged structure. Increasing return in association with continuous innovation in production and trade stands upon a dynamic equilibrium (Richardson, 1996). Such a dynamic equilibrium necessarily implicates structural transformation of the market and its microstructures. As a result, the efficiency perspective by remaining structurally contained and constrained fails to explain why such technological states do change or why certain particular economic agent reap in profit. Moreover, efficiency theorist's "profit" is actually a rent earned. Profit, however, is speculatively earned. Surprise must be a cornerstone in profit making. Efficiency theorists fail to underscore how electronic commerce brings about novelty and surprises in the trade and commerce.

Interpreters of TCE have assumed that Ecom brings about a frictionless (Brynjolffson & Smith, 1999) or transactions-cost-free market. They have wrongly committed TCE to such an explanation and this is my first objection. Second, reduction of transactions cost would increase efficiency and would not increase the rate of profit or capital and would not hasten innovation. About my first objection I must point out that TCE refers not to an accounting cost in an economy, instead it refers to cost due to opportunism or due to increased difficulties in protecting one's property rights. Cost of information is an additional element. Therefore TCE proponents of electronic commerce wrongly refer to accounting cost. Moreover, we would argue that Ecom couldn't reduce opportunism either inside a firm or in an economy. It follows then Ecom would in all likelihood increase transactions cost. Regarding the second objection, TCE refers to the efficiency that an organization or firm achieves in transaction costs when this firm replaces the erstwhile market-based opportunistic and costly transactions. Ecom is by definition inter-firm or inter-agent and cyber mediation of transactions cannot reduce the cost owing to opportunism. In fact in all likelihood such costs would increase because trust is recognizably the most intractable problem in this commerce. Increase in efficiency following reduction in transaction cost, according to TCE framework, happens through vertical integration. For example, electronic commerce has opened up a direction that disintegrates the verticality of a large corporation. Bringing closer the buyers and sellers has been putatively the transaction-cost-reducing factor; whereas we observe that costs even while reduced on this count is an accounting cost. Accounting cost reduction is fictional and this reduction cannot ensure achievement of profit or even of long-term efficiency.

There, however, is another aspect of TCE and externality. We know following the formulation (in the Pigovian tradition) on externalities by Coase (1960) that the extent a property owner can affect others without paying for these effects there arises a social cost, which is greater than their private costs. Coase argued that owing to imperfections in property rights this externality that is the divergence between private costs and social costs appear and the institution of price fails to clear such externalities. This phenomenon gives rise to transactions costs. Our empirical observations suggest that Ecom pulls through economic agents across several segments of industries along the scope direction or else Ecom pulls through agents who are in the complimentary sectors. Ecom is therefore a potential source of externality. However, social costs arise because according to Coase transactions fail to operate through price interfaces. Coase argued that there were not enough decompositions or partitions between specializations. In other words, if only enough specializations or separations between economic agents fail to appear consequent to introduction of Ecom, the social costs will rise. A solution to the rise in such costs could be dis-intermediation resulting into the formation of M-form firms. Contrarily separations in economic agencies or in specializations will engender transactions through price interfaces. Ecom achieves this feat. In Ecom price interface is regained. Transactions previously entrapped in non-price modes are released through increased division of specializations, in other words through increased intermediations. Ecom therefore engenders mediations in the market.

A long period of production refers to the entire input-output table of an economy. A short period of production refers to a specific transaction chain of a business or a sector. Electronic commerce increases the length of both these periods. Vertical integration linked up several such industrial sectors. Ecom and associated expansion along the direction of scope have crossed boundaries of specific transaction chains or of industry sectors. Increases in these periods take place because of several other factors as well. With an increase in the division of labor there would be increases in asymmetric information, insurance and valuation risks, joint productions of services and other goods, increased asset specificities, information impactedness and reduction in internal production. Innovations increase in Ecom because each economic agent has incentives to speculate and each agent looks for rewards from surprises that it might bring about in offerings, timings, and linkages. Electronic commerce reminds us about the traders of the earlier times when apiece goods were traded based on highly asymmetric information. Cantillon referred to this and Shackle defined the Neo-Austrian version of profit based on that understanding of Cantillon. Austrian theory argues that capital is time. This time is the period of production in an economy. An increase in the period of production is a reflection on the increase in rate of profit and of capital in an economy. So we could summarize that Ecom increases speculative profit by furthering the period of production that results from novel and increased cyber-mediations.

Shackle argued about surprise. He discussed profit and its rate from the perspective of lengthened periods of production and the increase in division of labor amongst economic agents who are speculators. Electronic commerce has opened up this opportunity. In these commerce intermediations in particular, cyber mediations have increased and will continue to increase. Transactions cost must increase because a principal cannot check opportunism and lack of trust between agents any longer. We have argued how the TCE framework fails in explaining the emergent phenomenon of electronic commerce. Neo-Austrian framework offers a cogent explanation as to how electronic commerce increases rate of profit and the capital in an economy based on electronic commerce. Moreover, to counter the looming increase in costs of transactions, Ecom offers furthered mediations (that is specializations) in price-based transactions. An increase in such price-based transactions alone can contain social costs and Ecom through increased mediations offers this as a distinct possibility.

Intermediation and Coordination

Received theory presents intermediation as the structure of a market. Microstructure of a market (O'Hara, 1997; Goodhart, 1989) refers to dynamics of transactions, relations, expectations and the time. Intermediaries served the most essential function of the microstructures of a market. Economic agents who interpolate them in between the producer of a good or services and its consumer are intermediaries according to the structural theorist. As a result of this structural emphasis the presence and the relevance of an intermediary can be analyzed in terms of costs of transactions. A dispersed microstructure of intermediation can remain operative only so long as transactions costs (Coase, 1990) do not favor formation of vertically integrated (Williamson, 1985) or multidivisional firms (Chandler, 1990). This appears to be a static view of the market. This approach is static because it can indicate substitution of one structure by an alternate structure alone and it fails to indicate other functions of structures.

We would argue that the microstructure of intermediation serves a major function. This function is coordination, which elongates the period between production and consumption. Elongation of this period is absolutely necessary to the formation of capital because capital is nothing but deferment of consumption. Static coordination achieves this elongation in a limited sense while coordination of dynamic situations enhances this period substantially. The static structural account on the microstructure of intermediation fails to capture this key aspect of coordination, which is a central theme in economic thinking because in its absence competition and innovation fail. Coordination between agents in a market is the key to the puzzle that the market survives through transformation, and that agents undergo changes in order to live through. Ecom refers to structural changes in market mediations and hence in the microstructure. Such changes lest reduced to anarchy or disruption must adhere to coordination, or more properly to coordination of expectations. Equilibrium or more particularly a dynamic equilibrium cannot be attained or maintained without the intervention of coordination. Coordination without mediation is impossible. We will take up two modes of coordination. Intermediaries are there in order to coordinate between two groups: first between several producers—current, potential and complementing, and second between producers and customers—current and potential. The former refers to aspects of competition relating to interoperability and inter-dependent innovations. The latter refers to aspects of creating and managing demand in the context of uncertainties. We discuss these two aspects in the present section very briefly on coordination with customers and in the following section on coordination amongst producers.

Ecom mediates between price quantity and most importantly the product (innovation) decisions of the producer, and the utility expectations of the customers. Under the circumstances of no-innovation, or of one single homogeneous product enjoying monopoly a la Chamberlin (1933), there is no need for coordination between the producer and the customer. However, following Richardson's (1996) argument, a market experiences a sequential competition between succeeding monopolists (contrary to Chamberlin's picture of co-existing monopolists) when there are continuous innovations in product. This sequential competition is between a current product and a future product (and not as suggested by Chamberlin between two near-identical current products). In Chamberlin's analysis a product can be substituted but completely only following the completion of the life cycle of the product. In sequential competition, as suggested by Richardson, all of the products get substituted having fulfilled only partially their life cycles, and as a result firms follow a strategy of offering versions of products. Our understanding of market making refers to such versions or sequences of products. A particular product brought out through innovation can be produced necessarily in shorter quantities. Prices that can be fetched support only normal and not a monopolist's profit.

A product version or a sequence necessarily must make a market through arousing customer expectations on future utility. A sequence of utilities implies therefore that changes in customer's perceptions or expectations of utilities take place in harmony with producers' perceptions or expectations. In other words, producer and customer must have mediated relations, which make it possible for the two parties to adhere to a common frontier of utility ensemble. In static non-sequential competition the role of mediation remains very restricted. In sequential competition innovations in products would fail in the absence of mediations. In other words, mediation being based upon sequential competition must increase in such innovation-led increasing-return-experiencing markets. Ecom based mediation serves precisely this function of increasing mediation.

Moreover previous markets with near-zero innovations in products could afford to make calculations on prices and quantities, such as the average cost, marginal cost and marginal return. In sequential competition no product can complete its life cycle and hence calculations of quantities and prices remain no longer exogenous. Price-quantity variables now come under the scanner of negotiated endogenous settlements. Uncertainties about the potential product and information asymmetries between the current product market and that of the market of the product next in sequence necessarily implicates microstructures in the market who can bear the risk, who can provide insurance, or hold the stock-in-progress, and who above all can calculate on durability of the current product. This switch to sequential competition therefore relegates monopolistic price-quantity variables to non-importance and substitutes those by new endogenous and negotiated variables, which are sequentially differentiated prices. Microstructure of mediation becomes the absolute necessity. Ecom therefore in lieu of dis-intermediation demands vigorous intermediation through novel market microstructures.

Finally, a future product and its arrival as well as its power to fulfill the expectations of the customer must defer the consumption of that potential product. Consumption of the current product is given up in expectation of the arrival of the future product. Deferment thus takes place twice at the levels of both consumption and production. Ecom and its intermediary-based coordination therefore shift the consumption through elongating the chains of price-based intermediation. This often happens through several kinds of limit orders or limit pricing, or through other modes of negotiated and insured shifts. Dispersion of prices can happen only when intermediation advances to raise buffers for absorbing the shocks. Price dispersion in Ecom can be afforded because enough mediated buffers have been put in place. This brief account above on customer-producer coordination shows us how intermediation and deferment increases in Ecom. To recall, this deferment is of the first kind arising from customer-producer coordination of expectations. We now look at the deferment of the second kind.

Deferment and Normative Coordination

In this section we elaborate upon coordination that appears necessarily between producers. The context of production is a sequential competition that is production of future products through innovations and based upon increasing returns and along dynamic equilibrium. Successions of short-lived products from several producers must entangle them in a web of expectations on successions. Another aspect of a product is that a product in the future must remain interoperable with a set of other products emergent from complementors lying in the scope direction. Richardson (1997, 1998) did not elaborate upon inter-operability. There are two possible courses, in the first inter-operability can be considered as non-sequential that is when inter-operable elements are pre-reconciled and they reflect a situation of timeless equilibrium. In the second aspect, it may refer to an input-output system—an interdependent succession of events through which intermediate products get apportioned to the final consumable products. Input-output systems allow for technological changes because consequent to technological changes or changes in tastes, etc., the successions or the relative apportionments might change. This second mode, even if not immediately and directly as in a Leontieff system, conceals the element of time and therefore does not depend on pre-reconciliation and on equilibrium conditions. Richardson seems to have preferred the first mode. We argue instead that the second mode alone can explain time-based, technological and unforeseen changes that remain operative over any inter-operable system.

This second mode is close to the Austrian understanding of time-dependence of capital and yet it is different in significant manners from it, based as this proposal is on Shackle's (1972) argument. In fact, we begin from Shackle's argument and develop this idea a bit more. Normative coordination is this additional element that Shackle did not explain. Normative coordination we wish to argue is an outcome of the "capital as time" thesis of Shackle. We do so more because strategy apprehends and orients this dimension of time. Criticality of time in orienting one's product-lines or technology constitutes a strategic move, and such a move must be able to influence and orient the moves of other firms. This capability to be able to orient the orientations of other firms, dependent on the expectation of expectations, can be achieved by strategic knowledge. Two corollaries follow. First, we have now a new definition of capability that is the capability to leverage strategic knowledge about others. Second, a strategic knowledge is about the processes in other firms and is about the possibilities of their orientations towards their own strategic advantages. This dimension of orientation is captured by the second mode of inter-operability. Time enters here because orientations appear in possible cascades. A particular ex-post orientation tells us about the choices committed and acts executed. Success in orienting processes of other firms by leveraging strategic knowledge toward one's own advantage becomes strategic only when this resultant orientation accrues a Cantillon profit or only when this ex-post inter-operation appears as "capital as time." An orientation through normative coordination of several intermediate products is an act of deferment of the consumption. A deferment of consumption achieved through elongation of the period of production or through elongation of the divisions of labor constitutes capital. It follows then that strategic acts are undertaken to increase capital. Such strategic acts become possible through normative coordination.

Shackle (1972) argued, "... capital is time ... capital is the manifestation of the role of time lapse in the productive process ... capital is delay. But delay is an inconvenience, a disutility, a discomfort, something which will not be borne except for a reward. ... capital seems to ... offer a prize for the endurance of delay ... (as) a marginal balance." A pure Austrian approach assumes that deferments are pre-reconciled amongst parties. Pre-reconciliation takes place through coordination or inter-operability of the first mode, as described above. However, there are opportunism and cheating, there are technological changes never foreseen, and there are changes in utilities. Such changes moreover happen along temporal successions. Richardson (1960) does not recognize such changes. In contrast, Richardson's schema fits in with the Austrian schema of plan-coordination. Departures that Richardson, and following him Leijonhufvud (1993) and Krafft and Ravix (2000), made consisted in recognizing that pre-reconciled plans would still take time— a duration that information needs to flow across firms and a time called "gestation lags" that would remain invariable across investment commitments of firms. The problem of aligning pre-reconciliation with plans (which in equilibrium surely would be equivalent to strategy) is then a problem of quickening of computation (this alignment is computationally feasible). Krafft and Ravix (2000) find out the computational algorithm with two forms, namely "maintain competitive investments under a maximum threshold level" and "maintain complementary investments over a minimum threshold level"— and they argue that "viability of the industrial system is ensured only if the two conditions are proved simultaneously." This leads them to argue that firms must act for coordination of both competitive and complementary investments.

Time lag in this model does not take into consideration delays or deferments owing to possibilities. A possibility to link up with or be complemented by a set of alternatives at any point of time is afforded by a technological innovation. This is the first objection. The second objection is that deferment is capital and it happens not because of a "market failure." In the Richardson-type of argument delay is undesirable. Krafft and Ravix argue for institutions that could alleviate problems of delay. These institutions can take up several forms, such as sequential contract from the property rights approaches of Hart (1988), Grossman and Hart (1990), et al., where there is information delay say due to uncertainty but there is no investment delay; or, if there is irreversible investment while there is no information delay a firm needs to make right decisions regarding profitability of a competitive investment (Dixit & Nalebuff, 1991). Other forms of coordination that might be taken up include informal market relation, licensing, strategic alliances, and formal agreements of various sorts, vertical integration or simply integration. The nature of the institution, it is argued (Langlois and Robertson, 1995; Teece, 1980, 1986, 1988) would depend on the type and length of delay. Teece (1986) argues that if the delay is caused by an autonomous innovation (which is relatively independent of other stages of production) then several types of institutions might emerge depending on the internal capabilities of the relevant firms. In case the innovation is systemic (in which simultaneous changes in several stages of production is required) Langlois and Robertson (1995) argue that there is the likelihood of vertical integration. Similarly when there are delays in both types and the delays are long, vertical integration resolves the simultaneously present coordination problems, because the incumbent will have to generate information on strategies that other firms can implement as well as the incumbent will have to muster coordination of the entire chain of systemic innovation. In case the innovation is autonomous and the delays necessarily shorter a large number of cooperation tools would suffice. And when there is only one type of delay in market-based transactions or when both the delays are of near zero duration simple market-based relations would be able to resolve the coordination problem. Institutional arrangements of the type of vertical integration according to this argument appear necessary only under specific circumstances.

According to this thinking, longer delay caused by systemic innovation can be managed as per a pre-reconciled plan. There is little uncertainty involved. Autonomous innovations according to this argument would experience shorter delay. Both these appear to us as unsustainable. Systemic innovations we understand as ex-post. Systemic innovations appear through an uncertain mechanism called by Shackle as "orientation." The delays and their lengths are attributable to this orientation. Delay as deferment refers to the postponement of the consumption with the expectation that there would be a profit at the margin. The longer the delay or the "average period of production," the higher is the capital. "It is this orientation of the presently co-existing objects which solely contains what we are measuring when we examine the 'period of production'. Orientation is thought, design, intention, and expectation. Thought is mutable and elusive, thoughts in different minds about 'the same' objects need have little in common" (Shackle, 1972). An ex-post systemic technology offers solution to the plans "now" made but there is little to ensure that such plans would indeed be executed. The binding to a plan is ordinarily verified through committed or irreversible investments. The average period of production is computed from such plans "accepted for the time being as a basis of immediate action, but by no means guaranteed" (Shackle, 1972). Technology dictates the current configurations that would give the plans stability in some "short period." Invariably advances in technology would tend to shorten this period "but the pace of innovation would itself be limited by economic considerations, by commercial organization and habits and by contracts" (Shackle, 1972). We might understand an average period as per the plans made by all participants to be the production net in an epoch, and the short period as per the plans made by participants to a systemic technology (as in a chain of Ecom usage) while a period even shorter as per plans made by those few who participate in an autonomous technological innovation, involving as it were a few firms through Ecom. However, we must emphasize that lengths of periods are determined more by economic states of affairs than by technological innovations. Increase in the average period, for example, Shackle argues, is never realized to the full because the production net is too lengthy and circuitous and negotiation with the net too protracted owing to the presence of durable equipment or the inertia caused by irreversible investment.

Epochal increase in the average delay reflects the general rise in capital and in divisions of labor. Systemic increase in delay reflects an increase in divisions of labor. The velocity with which an intermediate product might move through Ecom intermediaries reflects technological pace and the productivity but that hastened velocity cannot compensate for the lengthened divisions of labor. Prior to its appearance, technology is uncertain. However, following its appearance, it determines the circuit of production and hence the plans for production. Human ingenuity reflected in the strategic moves, however, bypasses such determinations by inventing and innovating further on economic organization of production. This is a step that a firm takes with the hope of reaping a profit, which is beyond technological rent (the Schumpeterian profit) and which belongs to the Cantillon profit. The firm resorts to strategic surprise and evocation of expectation. Modes through which expectations can be raised include of course lengthening of the production net, bringing about novelties and surprises in combining resources or in design of contracts and finally in innovating upon new technologies and in engendering divisions of labor. To underscore, Ecom affords best such requirements of mediation.

Coordination under such circumstances must look forward to the future. The coordination discussed above referred to the plans made previously. Concurrent coordination refers to the adjustment process. However, plans for deferment of consumption and on surprisingly new forms of intermediate products and combinations thereof are unique to a firm. This plan refers to the present and the future. Incumbent firms expect that novel routes of production net will emerge from its strategic choices. Firms belonging to the strategic milieu expect that expectations of the incumbent follow a path that is advantageous to them. Coordination of expectations can be achieved through intermediations, acting as a surrogate for dialogues amongst the parties. A dialogue often continues for rather long, however, often taking off to a rounding up through the evolution of norms. A norm is not a rule. It is not a routine either. A norm is always robust when it speaks only of what parties are not expected to do and when it allows freedom to parties to write whatever their expectation guides them to. A norm sets down injunctions then. Injunctions allow a very large space to the parties in a dialogue to expect the expectations of others.

Strategic expectations of economic agents, several producers complementors and intermediaries experience deterrence caused by durability of investment. Durability reduces uncertainty, shows commitment and exacts reciprocal durability of investment from other parties. Ex-post plan and existing technological paths are durable too. Novelty in technology or innovation and reduced durability of investment allow economic agents to engender differentiation of labor and increase in lengths and numbers of nested circuits of a production net. An agent defers the consumption with the expectation of profit. Profit would be allowed to this agent only if there are other agents who participate in the deferment and each of whom holds expectations on profits. The deferment must complete itself at a future time on approaching the average period of production. Similar to the normative dialogue these expectations need to follow norms in order to bring about completion of a particular production net. Norm guides the expectations of agents by disallowing them certain paths and the agents with the freedom to expect expectations of others keep generating short-period nests and an average period dialogue by remaining within the norm. Short periods remain nested within the overall structure of the average period.

To put in another way, it follows from our analogy that divisions of labor do not possess uniqueness or some unique rationale. Divisions of labor across firms or across several groups, such as the intermediaries, would then, we argue, be contingent to a situation of expectations. Such divisions retain fluidity. Designing an end consumable product through severalties of coordination might take several paths with several alternative and possible divisions amongst the participants who all join in the deferment-based expectations of expectation. The only binding that these groups or firms would consider necessary is what we have called normative binding. A great deal of ambiguity can be allowed in such engagements. Participants who could only guess based on partial and always evanescent evidences offered by the partners, use as it were a mix of axiomatic and subjective probabilities, or better still would be to think about potential. This potential gelled in time is the capital.

The argument of Krafft and Ravix or Leijonhufvud regarding the failure of the market to offer solutions to a coordination problem when there are two types of delays, namely that on information delay and investment gestation lags, has led to organizational and inter-organizational solutions. They include Teece or Langlois and Robertson, who have found vertical integration of several firms as solutions to longer delays or varieties of contracts as solutions to shorter delays. We observed that delays when caused by strategic intentions or by changes in market tastes or through increased divisions of labor, all of which appear consequent to Ecom, bring about uncertainties of expectations about future. The received argument refers to the alignment between plans made in the past and the current states of affairs. The proposed alignment in received theories offers technological solutions (that tend to reduce delays) that raise efficiency and organizational solutions in the form of dis-intermediation. However, institutional solutions are different from such organizational solutions. Coordination in Ecom is an institutional problem and therefore it requires an institutional solution. Normative coordination is an institutional solution. Normative coordination limits the failures in coordination. An institution might not offer a particular organizational solution as the preferred mode. Several organizational or quasi-organizational, including contractual, solutions might be considered as specific solutions. Vertical solution, we would argue, need not be considered as the only preferred solution to coordination with long deferment. Vertical solution can be considered only when information being exchanged across firms refers to a pre-reconciled plan. Information that cannot unambiguously describe a situation or that can remain incomplete evidence and is required to adjust to envelopes of expectations on the future cannot even while exchanged help formation of vertical integration. Ecom offers such intricacies and hence eludes organizational solution such as achieved through dis-intermediation. Moreover, deferment in the received theories is undesirable and technological solutions that raise efficiency have been proposed for reduction of its length. We argue technology fails to reduce the duration of average period of production. Contrarily technology increases this period of deferment, which represents capital. Technologies from firms who are not vertically integrated and who make non-durable investments need not reduce the deferment period, and in circumstances might even hasten deferment.

Conclusions

At the end of the day following the introduction of Ecom there could be fewer intermediaries in a vertical value chain. However, vertical value chains have lost their attractiveness in a time of increasing returns based on scope-wise innovations in product. Products in this setting of Ecom offer sequential competition. Firms and their customers coordinate their expectations based on the next versions of products. Similarly, firms that are competing in sequence or at the same time must coordinate their expectations on each other because products from their stables must fulfill obligations of interoperability, as well as satisfy mutually agreed upon restrictions on quantity and prices. Coordination amongst producers too affords a cascaded deferment of both consumption and completion of a systemic product. These two types of coordination involve incompleteness of contracts, uncertainties and liquidity of investment. The length between production and consumption thus must create enough number of economic agents who can trade in risks, insurances, information and liquidity. The intermediaries, who in this Ecom environment are the cybermediaries, offer this service as the microstructure of market. Cybermediaries therefore emerge to fulfill this novel task. The economic-value-adding activities by these cybermediaries lengthen the circuit of production that terminates in consumption. A lengthened circuit indicates deferred consumption and a consequent rise in capital and in profit. Ecom therefore requires possibly more quantity of intermediation and surely novel modes of mediation. Necessarily little of this novel mediation takes place along the previous value chain. Most of the novel cybermediations appear in the scope direction and away from the vertical industrial segment. The economy under Ecom increases in the scope but not through Chandlerian large multidivisional firms. The economy increases through highly differentiated and variegated cybermediaries who lengthen the circuit of capital and as a consequence of increasing the riskiness of a business increase the profit. This profit does not arise in technological innovations particularly of the kind that increase efficiency. Contrarily this profit is strategic because the cybermediaries arrange and then rearrange the configurations of a market and thus through bringing about surprise the cybermediaries reap enhanced profit.

References

Aoki, M. (1990). The participatory generation of information rents and the theory of the firm. In M. Aoki, B. Gustaffson and O.E. Williamson (Eds.), *The Firm as a Nexus of Treaties*. Los Angeles: Sage Publications.

Bailey, J. and Bakos, Y. (1996). An exploratory study of the emerging role of electronic intermediaries. *International Journal of Electronic Commerce, 1*(3), 7-20.

Barzel, Y. (1989). *Economic Analysis of Property Rights*. New York: Cambridge University Press.

Baumol, W., Panzar, J. and Willig, R. (1986). On the Theory of Perfectly Contestable Markets. In J. Stiglitz & F. Mathewson (Eds.), *New Developments in the Analysis of Market Structure*. Cambridge, MA: Macmillan.

Benjamin, R. and Wigand, R. (1995, Winter). Electronic markets and virtual value chains on the information superhighway. *Sloan Management Review, 36*(2), 62-72.

Brynjolfsson, E. and Smith, M.D. (1999). Frictionless commerce? A comparison of internet and conventional retailers. Working Paper, MIT Sloan School of Management. Retrieved from the World Wide Web: http://ecommerce.mit.edu/papers/friction.

Burton, A.F. and Mooney, J.G. (1998, November). The evolution of electronic marketplaces: An exploratory study of Internet-based electronic commerce within the American Independent Insurance Agency system. *Australian Journal of Information Systems*, 20-44.

Chamberlin, E.H. (1933). *Theory of monopolistic competition: A reorientation of the theory of value*. Cambridge, MA: Harvard University Press.

Chandler, A.D., Jr. (1990). *Scale and Scope: The Dynamics of Industrial Capitalism*. Cambridge, MA: The Belknap Press of Harvard University Press.

Chircu, A.M., and Kauffman, R.J. (2000). Reintermediation strategies in business-to-business electronic commerce. *International Journal of Electronic Commerce, 4*, 17-42.

Coase, R. (1960, November). The problem of social cost. *Economica, N.S, 4*, 386-405.

Coase, R. (1990). The nature of the firm. In O.E. Williamson (Ed.), *Industrial Organisation*. Aldershot: Elgar.

Dixit, A. and Nalebuff, B. (1991). *Thinking Strategically*. New York: Norton.

Domowitz, I. (2001). Liquidity, transaction costs, and reintermediation in electronic markets. eBusiness Research Center, Pennsylvania State University, WP 4-2001.

Giaglis, G.M., Klein, S. and O'Keefe, R.M. (2000). *Disintermediation, reintermediation, or cybermediation? The future of intermediaries in electronic marketplaces.* (Mimeo.)

Goodhart, C.A.E. (1989). *Money, information and uncertainty.* London: Macmillan.

Grossman, S. and Hart, O. (1990). The costs and benefits of ownership: A theory of vertical and lateral integration. In O.E. Williamson (Ed.), *Industrial Organization.* Aldershot: Elgar.

Hart, O. (1988). Incomplete contracts and the theory of the firm. *Journal of Law, Economics and Organization, 4*(1), 119-140.

Krafft, J. (2000). (Ed.). *The Process of Competition.* Cheltenham: Edward Elgar.

Krafft, J. and Ravix, J.L. (2000). Competition and Industrial Coordination. In Krafft (Ed.), *Competition and Industrial Coordination.*

Langlois, R.N. and Robertson, P.L. (1995). *Firms, markets and economic change.* London: Routledge.

Leijonhufvud, A. (1993). Towards a Not-too Rational Macroeconomics. *Southern Economic Journal, 60*(1), 1-13.

Malone, T., Yates, J. and Benjamin, R. (1987). Electronic markets and electronic hierarchies. *Communications of the ACM, 30*(6), 484-497.

Meck, A. (2001). Shopbots, powershopping, powersales: New forms of intermediation in E-Commerce – An overview. Beitrag 203, Volkswirtshaftliche Diskussionsreithe, Universat Augsburg.

North, D.C. (1989). A transaction cost approach to the historical development of polities and economies. *Journal of Institutional and Theoretical Economics, 145*, 661-668.

O'Hara, M. (1997). *Market microstructure theory.* Oxford: Blackwell Publishers.

Pan, X., Ratchford, B.T. and Shankar, V. (2001). Why aren't the prices of the same item the same at Me.com and You.com? Drivers of price dispersion among e-tailers. EBRC Working Paper 11-2001. Pennsylvania.

Picot, A., Bortenlanger, C. and Hohrl, H. (1997). Organization of electronic markets: contributions from the new institutional economics. *The Information Society, 13*, 107-123.

Porter, M. (1985). *Competitive Advantage: Creating and Sustaining Superior Performance.* New York: The Free Press.

Richardson, G. B. (1960). *Information and Investment.* Oxford: Oxford University Press.

Richardson, G.B. (1972). The organization of industry. *Economic Journal, 82*: 883-896.

Richardson, G.B. (1996). Competition, innovation and the increasing returns. DRUID Working Paper no. 96-10, Aaolborg: DRUID.

Richardson, G.B. (1997). Economic analysis, public policy and the software industry. DRUID Working Paper no. 97-4, Aalborg: DRUID.

Richardson, G.B. (1998). Production, planning and prices. DRUID Working Paper no. 98-27, Aaolborg: DRUID.

Romer, P. M. (1987). Growth based on increasing returns due to specialization. *American Economic Review, 77*(2), 56-62.

Sarkar, M.B., Butler B. and Steinfeld, C. (1995). Intermediaries and cybermediaries: A continuing role for mediating players in the electronic marketplace. *Journal of Computer Mediated Communication, 1*(3), Special Issue on Electronic Commerce. Retrieved from the World Wide Web: http://www.ascusc.org/jcmc/vol1/issue3/vol1no3.html.

Schmitz, S.W. (2000, March). The effects of Electronic commerce on the structure of intermediation. *Journal of Computer Mediated Communication, 5*(3). Retrieved from the World Wide Web: http://www.ascusc.org/jcmc/vol5/issue3.

Shackle, G. L. S. (1972). *Epistemics & Economics: A Critique of Economic Doctrine.* Cambridge: Cambridge University Press.

Storey, V., Straub, D., Stewart, K. and Welke, R. (2000, July). A conceptual investigation of the Electronic Commerce industry. *Communications of the ACM, 43*(7), 117-123.

Teece, D. (1980). Economics of scope and the scope of the enterprise. *Journal of Economic Behavior and Organization, 1*(3), 223-247.

Teece, D. (1986). Profiting from technological innovation: implications for integration, collaboration, licensing and public policy. *Research Policy, 15*, 285-305.

Teece, D. (1988). Technological change and the nature of the firm. In G. Dosi, C. Freeman, R. Nelson, G. Silverberg and L. Soete (Eds.), *Technical Change and Economic Theory.* London: Pinter.

Valimaki, M. and Martikainen, P. (2001). *Online intermediary liability framework.* Helsinki, Finland: HIIT.

Williamson, O.E. (1975). *Markets and Hierarchies.* New York: The Free Press.

Williamson, O.E. (1985). *The Economic Institutions of Capitalism.* New York: Free Press.

Wind, J. and Rangaswamy, A. (2000). Customerization: The second revolution in mass customization. eBusiness Research Center, Pennsylvania State University, WP 06-1999.

Chapter III

Risk and Investment in the Global Telecommunications Industry

Irene Henriques
York University, Canada

Perry Sadorsky
York University, Canada

Abstract

In this chapter, quantitative modeling and simulation techniques are used to estimate various risk measures and the associated cost of equity for the global telecommunications industry. Our approach is to calculate several different cost-of-equity values and then use simulation techniques to build up a probability distribution for each company's cost of equity. In this way, a clearer picture of where a company's cost of equity lies is developed. Closing the Digital Divide could bring many benefits to developing countries but international investors and development planners must be able to make their own cost-of-equity calculations so that they can see first hand how their investment projects compare with other investment projects around the globe.

Introduction

The new economy can be characterized in a number of different ways but one way to look at the new economy is to identify industries that are undergoing the greatest amount of structural change and have the greatest opportunity for growth. Three industries stand out as having particularly promising futures: biotechnology, energy and information technology (IT). Collectively these three industries may be called the BET economy. Of these three industries, the IT industry (broadly comprised of the technology, media and telecommunications (TMT) sub- industries) is the one industry that can contribute the most to productivity improvements in countries. Technological progress can lead to process innovation (lower cost ways of producing existing products) or product innovation. Furthermore, from neoclassical growth theory, technological improvements are the only way to increase the living standards in countries that have reached the golden rule. An increase in technology raises the production function and increases the steady state amounts of capital stock and output. In terms of economic performance, maximizing productivity growth is the single most important objective for a country to have since increases in productivity growth lead to higher living standards.

Productivity growth can be influenced by a number of different factors or drivers. Broadly speaking, these factors include macroeconomic policy, regulatory environment, innovation, industrial structure, human capital, management strategies and policies, trade, and investment. For large industrialized countries like those in the G7 or G10, economic performance depends in large part on coordinating the actions between these various drivers to enhance productivity. The shortage of the necessary resources to accomplish this objective is not that large of a problem. For developing countries, the situation is often much more difficult because, in addition to successfully coordinating the actions of the various drivers, developing countries also face a shortage of financial capital. As a result, foreign investment is becoming an increasingly important driver behind productivity growth in developing countries.

Business growth and the overall wealth generation process are hindered in developing economies by the lack of affordable credit. This is particularly true in the IT industry. New firms starting out in IT are often very small and face high start-up costs. These firms usually have no source of financial capital to draw from, which means that they need to seek external funding. In developing economies, the selection of financial instruments available to start up companies is very limited (Chong and Micco, 2003). The source of financial capital -where it exists- tends to be scarce and commands a very high price. This problem is particularly acute in South America and Africa where domestic savings rates are much lower than in other developing parts of the world. As a result, foreign investment into developing countries can provide a much-needed source of financial capital.

Financial capital is probably the scarcest commodity in the world. More people demand financial capital at any one time than are able to supply it. Financial capital is scarce, mobile and very sensitive to economic and political conditions. Consequently, those who have financial capital to invest are very selective about where they invest. Domestic and global investors typically prefer investments with high returns and low risks. Risk management is, therefore, an important component of global investing. Savings is the only source of financial capital and the relationship between savings, investment and economic growth has been well documented (Miles and Scott, 2002). The role that foreign direct investment plays in aiding a country's economic development has also been extensively studied.

Foreign investment can be categorized as either foreign direct investment (FDI) or foreign indirect investment (portfolio investment). FDI adds to the receiving country's GDP because it involves investment in physical capital (roads, buildings, plants, machinery and equipment, etc.). Portfolio investment has a less direct impact on economic growth when it involves the buying and selling of existing equities and bonds. Of course, portfolio investment used to finance initial public offerings adds directly to GDP.

There are a number of interesting trends regarding foreign investment (Miles and Scott, 2002). First, richer countries tend to invest more overseas. Second, FDI assets (liabilities) as a percentage of industrialized countries GDP are 16% (17%). Thus, a lot of FDI is conducted between the rich industrialized countries. Third, total outward investment by the industrialized countries is currently around $1500 billion (US) of which one-third is FDI and two-thirds is portfolio investment. By comparison, FDI in 1990 was $300 billion (US) and this was approximately equal to portfolio investment. Portfolio investment is currently the fastest growing part of foreign investment. Fourth, FDI tends to be less volatile than portfolio investment.

Developing or emerging economies seeking foreign investment must be aware of these trends and realize that, while FDI might be the preferred choice of foreign investment, portfolio investment is a much larger pool of money to tap. Portfolio investment, however, requires risk management on the part of both the seller and the buyer. Provided a developing or emerging economy can offer attractive risk and return characteristics to investors of financial capital, portfolio investment should not be overlooked as a source of investment capital.

Consequently, it is necessary to have good measures of equity risk for managers, planners and investors. The cost of equity is important in valuing new investment opportunities and in evaluating the ongoing performance of established business projects. This is especially true in the new economy IT industry where an understanding of equity risk aids in the examination of the relationship between the IT sector and economic development.

The purpose of this chapter is to calculate the cost of equity for the global telecommunications industry using a sample of 26 firms in 19 countries. The companies in the sample are chosen primarily based on their inclusion in the www.adr.com telecommunications database and having a reasonable length of market data (five years). Quantitative modeling and simulation techniques are used to estimate various risk measures and the associated cost-of-equity values for the telecommunications industry in each country in the sample. The methodology is similar to that used by Sadorsky (2003) and Sadorsky and Henriques (2003). The risk measures include systematic risk (Brealey and Myers, 2003; Campbell, Lo and Mackinlay, 1997), total risk (Shapiro, 2003), downside risk (Estrada, 2000, 2002; Harvey, 2000; Alexander, 2001), regret (Dembo and Freeman, 2001), and value at risk (JP Morgan/Reuters, 1996). A brief discussion of each of these risk measures is provided. The risk measures are then used to calculate the cost of equity (which is equal to a risk-free rate plus the product of a risk measure and a market risk premium) in the global telecommunications industry for each company in the sample. For each company, the different cost-of-equity values are compared and contrasted. Moreover, a comparison between different cost-of-equity values is made with companies in similar regions of the world.

Background

The term Digital Divide usually refers to the overall gap in information technology and communication usage between developed and developing countries (Lu, 2002). Currently there are huge differences in the ability of people around the world to communicate both locally and globally. The International Telecommunications Union (ITU) provides free statistics, available on their Web site, on IT usage rates in five broad regions of the world. These regions are: Africa, Americas (including North, Central and South), Asia, Europe, and Oceania. Total telephone subscribers per 100 inhabitants in 2002 ranged from a low of 6.60 in Africa to a high of 89.83 in Europe (Table 1). The number for the Americas (64.92), represents the average of high wire-line usage in North America and low wire-line usage in South America. For example, Canada and the United States have 101.26 and 114.70 total telephone subscribers per 100 inhabitants while Peru and Venezuela have 13.67 and 36.78 total telephone subscribers per 100 inhabitants. Statistics on cellular

Table 1. IT usage statistics (2002)

	Africa	Americas	Asia	Europe	Oceania	World
Wireline						
subscribers per 100 inhabitants	6.6	64.92	23.89	89.83	88.93	36.35
Cellular subscribers						
as % of total telephone subscribers	61	45.8	50.3	55.1	54.6	51
% digital	86.3	53.5	80.2	55.4	80	65.8
subscribers per 100 inhabitants	4.19	29.74	12.19	50.21	48.53	18.77
Internet usage						
users per 10,000 inhabitants	99.62	2421.02	557.56	2079	3330.47	972.16

Source: http://www.itu.int/ITU-D/ict/statistics/

subscribers in 2002 show a great deal of variation. Africa had the lowest number (4.19) of cellular subscribers per 100 inhabitants while Europe had the highest (50.21) number of cellular subscribers per 100 inhabitants. Similarly, 2002 statistics on Internet usage also reveals vast differences between regions of the world. Africa only had 99.62 users per 10,000 inhabitants while Oceania had 3,330.47 users per 10,000 inhabitants. The high number of Internet users for Oceania is heavily influenced by the widespread usage of the Internet in Australia and New Zealand. The Americas also have a high number of Internet users and this number is heavily influenced by the large number of Internet users in Bermuda, Canada and the United States. Collectively, the statistics reported in Table 1 indicate that IT communication tends to be the highest in the prosperous regions of the world.

Access to affordable technology to improve the flow of information is crucial to the development of an economy. Currently four-fifths of the world's cellular subscribers live in developed economies. The prospects for growth in cellular phone subscribers is largest in the developing countries. For many large developing countries, like Russia, it can take up to ten years to get a fixed line telephone (Economist, 1999). The problem, of course, is that it doesn't make economic sense to install wire-line services in regions of the world where there are very few people. Cellular phone services provide an affordable alternative to expensive wire-line telephone because cellular phone companies only need to install transmission towers to send and receive signals and do not have to dig holes in the ground. It is much cheaper and easier to install transmission towers. With lower costs, cellular phone companies can break even with a small number of subscribers and also more easily tailor cellular phone packages to regional tastes. Cellular phone companies also bring much needed competition and foreign investment to the telecommunications industry in many parts of the world.

Internet usage is an important determinant in closing the Digital Divide (Jain, 2002). Internet access brings many benefits to a country and its citizens. These benefits include information on health and education, finding lower prices for goods and services, increased business efficiency, the creation of new jobs, and increased trade. Here, however, the problems (costs) associated with installing wire-lines re-surface. In North America and Europe, two regions of the world with high Internet usage rates, the vast majority of Internet traffic travels across wire-line. Wireless Internet is available but at a higher cost. In developed countries, wireless products are seen as a luxury. In developing countries, because of the high cost of laying fixed wire-line, wireless technology is seen as more of a necessity. As a result, the demand for wireless products in developing countries may just possibly drive technological innovations in wireless products.

E-commerce is one area where the Digital Divide is extreme. The statistics are startling. Currently, three-quarters of all e-commerce is done in the United States and 90% of all commercial Web sites are located in the United States. There are vast opportunities awaiting companies and countries that participate in the globalization of e-commerce (Iyer, Taube and Raquet, 2002). Macroeconomic advantages include innovation (through bigger rewards in a global market place and knowledge diffusion through the use of the Internet), efficiency (by transparency through intermediaries and global availability of information) and trade (via global reach to export goods and the opportunity to export services). Microeconomic advantages of international e-commerce growth include service (with customized and integrated services worldwide and global knowledge about consumer's preferences), distribution (lower costs by bypassing retailers and global reach through electronic channels) and costs (create new distribution channels through electronic supply chain integration and global selection of suppliers). Clearly, consumers and businesses in both developed and developing economies stand to gain from the globalization of e-commerce.

Closing the Digital Divide could bring many benefits to developing countries. Bringing the benefits of IT to developing counties is possible but the governments of these countries need to be aware that the process is going to cost money and require institutional changes. Bortolotti, D'Souza, Fantini and Megginson (2002) have completed a study in which they examined the financial and operating performance of 31 national telecommunications companies in 25 countries that were fully or partially privatized through public share offerings. Firm profitability was measured in several different ways including return on assets, returns on sales and return on equity. Their results indicate that the financial and operating performance of telecommunication companies significantly improved after privatization, but that regulatory changes also played a major role.

Methodology

This section, which follows the methodology in Sadorsky and Henriques (2003) and Sadorsky (2003), describes the empirical approach used to calculate the various risk measures and associated required returns. The cost of equity for a firm is the minimum rate of return required to induce investors to buy or hold the company's stock. This required rate of return consists of a risk-free rate (representing the time value of money) and a premium for risk. Alternatively, the cost of equity is the rate used to capitalize corporate cash flows. It can be used to measure the required rate of return of future equity investments as long as the future investments are very similar to the current projects being undertaken by the firm.

Any required rate of return on an equity investment consists of a risk-free rate and a risk premium.

$$RR_i = R_f + (RP_M)(RM_i) \tag{1}$$

In equation (1), RR_i is the required return on equity i (or alternatively, the cost of equity), R_f is the risk-free rate, RP_M is the market risk premium and RM_i is a risk measure for equity i. Several risk measures are considered and studied. Systematic risk (SR) is measured by the capital asset pricing model (CAPM) beta (Brealey and Myers, 2003). Systematic risk has a long history and is one of the most widely used measures of risk (Brealey and Myers, 2003; Campbell, Low and Mackinlay, 1997). Systematic risk calculated from the CAPM also has its critics and Fama and French (1997) is one well-known example of this. Total risk (TR) is measured by the standard deviation of stock returns. Total risk is also widely used and is particularly appropriate in segmented markets (which describes the stock markets in developing countries). Total risk, the combination of systematic and unsystematic risk, is important to the value of the firm. Total risk may have a negative impact on the firm's expected cash flow because financial distress is most likely to occur for firms with high total risk (Shapiro, 2003). Companies experiencing financial distress face business uncertainty and this uncertainty imposes costs on consumers, suppliers and employees. When a company is in financial distress, suppliers often charge higher prices than normal. In addition, some customers become concerned about the long-term commitment of the company and cancel orders. Consequently, high total risk is likely to adversely affect a firm's value via lower sales and higher costs.

Value at risk (VAR) is a well-known measure of the expected losses in extreme downturns (Alexander, 2001; JP Morgan, 1996). VAR is the expected loss to be exceeded during a particular time period with a specific probability. The greater the value of VAR, the greater the potential loss within the defined time period for a particular confidence interval. It is usual to assume a 95% confidence interval and a time period of one month. In this case, VAR is the expected loss to be exceeded with a 5% probability during the next month. For example, assume that the United States stock market (measured by the S&P 500) has a VAR of $9. This means that for every $100 invested in the United States stock market, there is a 5% chance of losing $9 or more in any given month. Equation (2) specifies the VAR calculation.

$$VAR = (1 - \exp(-1.645\sigma)) * 100 \tag{2}$$

In equation (2), 1.645 is the critical value for a 95% confidence interval, assuming a normal distribution for stock returns, and σ is the monthly standard deviation of the monthly continuously compounded total returns.

Another perhaps lesser known measure of risk is downside risk. Downside risk (DR) is measured using semi-standard deviation of returns.

$$\Sigma_B = \sqrt{(1/T)\sum_{t=1}^{T}(R_t - B)^2} \quad \text{for all } R_t < B \tag{3}$$

In equation (3), R_t are monthly returns and B is the benchmark. There are a number of different benchmark returns and consequently several different measures of downside risk. A popular choice for B is the arithmetic mean (μ) of the continuously compounded monthly returns. In this case, equation (3) reads Σ_μ. Other measures for the benchmark include the risk free rate (f) and zero (0) (Estrada, 2000; Harvey, 2000). Downside risk was discussed by Markowitz (1959) who recognized that investors have asymmetric preferences towards risk. Most investors like upside risk, but dislike downside risk. Investors are interested in minimizing risk for two reasons. First, only downside risk or safety first is relevant to an investor. The idea of safety of principal can be traced to Roy (1952) who proposed that investors prefer safety of principal first and will set some minimum acceptable return that will protect this principal. Second, asset returns may be non-normally distributed. A downside risk measure is an appropriate risk measure to use when asset returns are non-normal. Nawrocki (1999) and Sortino and Satchell (2001) provide a good review of downside risk and Bernstein (1998) provides a good historical perspective of risk.

Recently, Dembo and Freeman (2001) have introduced regret as a measure of downside risk

$$\text{Regret} = -E(\min(0, R-B)) \tag{4}$$

where E is the mathematical expectations operator, R is return and B is the benchmark. As in equation (3), the benchmark, B, can be time varying or fixed. Notice that regret has the same form as the pay-off function to a put option with a strike price equal to the benchmark return. In this chapter, regret is measured using a risk-free benchmark (f) and the zero benchmark (0).

Data

The data used in this study consist of monthly data on 26 telecommunications companies' total returns (price returns plus dividends) over the period from January of 1997 to December of 2002. The total return series are expressed in American dollars. The data were collected from the Center for Research in Security Prices (CRSP) database. Total returns on the value weighted U.S. market portfolios of NYSE, AMEX and NASDAQ stocks are also included in the data set. The companies were selected on the basis of their inclusion in the www.adr.com telecommunications database and a continuous set of stock price data over the period from January of 1997 to December of 2002.

American depository receipts (ADR) is a name for foreign company shares that trade on a local stock exchange and have receipts that trade on a U.S. exchange like the New York Stock Exchange (NYSE). ADRs are an easy way for U.S. investors, or international investors with a U.S. trading account, to buy the shares of foreign companies. ADRs were first introduced in 1927 by Morgan Guaranty. Currently approximately 70% of the ADRs (330 companies) trade on the NYSE. To round out the sample and for comparison purposes, three U.S. companies and one Canadian company were included in the data set. All companies in our sample trade on NYSE.

Risk Measures

Monthly summary statistics for the 26 global telecommunications companies are reported in Table 2. Mean monthly continuously compounded returns are very small and

Table 2. Summary statistics

Company	Country	mean	stdev	Sharpe ratio	rho	beta	skewness	kurtosis
APT Satellite Holdings Ltd.	Hong Kong	0.00	0.26	-0.06	0.39	1.76	2.14	7.78
Asia Satellite Telecom	Hong Kong	0.01	0.15	0.11	0.62	1.63	0.19	-0.40
BCE Inc.	Canada	0.02	0.10	0.70	0.53	0.94	0.39	0.72
BT Group PLC	U.K.	0.00	0.11	-0.20	0.59	1.18	-0.21	-0.59
Cable & Wireless	U.K.	-0.03	0.16	-0.63	0.56	1.55	-0.35	0.38
China Mobile Ltd	China	0.02	0.17	0.34	0.61	1.78	1.06	1.44
Deutsche Telekom AG	Germany	0.01	0.15	0.09	0.54	1.40	0.34	0.00
France Telecom	France	0.01	0.21	0.09	0.47	1.71	0.59	2.00
Indonesian Satellite Corp	Indonesia	0.02	0.21	0.22	0.35	1.28	1.87	6.60
Nippon Telegraph & Telephone	Japan	-0.01	0.11	-0.40	0.47	0.90	0.65	0.11
Nokia OYJ	Finland	0.04	0.17	0.64	0.65	1.94	0.07	-0.29
Philippine Long Distance	Philippines	-0.02	0.13	-0.54	0.51	1.16	0.55	0.33
Portugal Telecom	Portugal	0.00	0.11	-0.03	0.48	0.95	0.10	0.57
SK Telecom	Korea	0.04	0.21	0.54	0.47	1.67	1.64	3.58
TDC A/S	Denmark	0.01	0.13	0.05	0.49	1.11	0.26	1.99
Telecom Argentina	Argentina	-0.02	0.22	-0.31	0.44	1.65	0.46	1.02
Telecom Italia	Italy	0.01	0.10	0.18	0.46	0.79	0.51	0.52
Telefonica de Argentina	Argentina	-0.02	0.20	-0.39	0.43	1.47	0.83	2.80
Telefonica del Peru	Peru	-0.03	0.15	-0.89	0.54	1.38	0.47	1.21
Telefonica SA	Spain	0.01	0.12	0.07	0.61	1.24	0.49	0.61
Telefonos de Mexico	Mexico	0.02	0.11	0.63	0.66	1.21	-0.04	0.47
Telekomunidasi Indonesia	Indonesia	0.02	0.20	0.29	0.46	1.59	0.92	2.05
Vodafone	U.K.	0.01	0.11	0.24	0.47	0.91	0.01	-0.65
Nextel	U.S.	0.03	0.24	0.32	0.54	2.19	0.50	0.64
AT&T	U.S.	-0.01	0.12	-0.25	0.45	0.96	0.62	0.85
Verizon	U.S.	0.01	0.10	0.13	0.31	0.55	1.10	2.39
Average		0.01	0.16	0.03	0.50	1.34	0.58	1.39
US Market		0.00	0.06	-0.15	1.00	1.00	-0.46	-0.46

Notes: Means (rates not percentages), standard deviations, rho, skewness, and kurtosis reported for monthly stock return values. Sharpe ratios calculated for annual values.

range from a low of -3.00% to a high of 4.00%. The sample average for the mean monthly return was 1.00% and the mean monthly return on the U.S. market index was 0.00%. The five-year period from January of 1997 to December of 2002 was one characterized by no capital appreciation in the broad-based stock market. Most of the stock returns had some evidence of either skewness or kurtosis. Most of the companies in the sample had high standard deviations and, as a result, the values for the Sharpe ratios are low. Risk-averse individuals prefer high values of the Sharpe ratio. BCE had the highest value of the Sharpe ratio in the sample (0.70) and this value was 23 times larger than the Sharpe ratio for the sample company average. On a risk-adjusted basis, BCE was a better investment than the value-weighted U.S. market. In comparison, Telefonica del Peru, with a Sharpe ratio of -0.89, was a particularly risky investment. The variable rho measures the correlation between monthly company total returns and monthly U.S. market total returns. All of the rho values are positive indicating that each company's stock returns are positively correlated with the broad based U.S. market. U.S. companies do not necessarily have the highest correlation with the U.S. market. For example, Telefonos de Mexico had the highest correlation with the U.S market while Verizon had the lowest correlation. This result is useful to investors interested in building a portfolio of global telecommunications stocks.

The second column in Table 3 reports company beta values. Company beta values are calculated from a single factor market model. More specifically,

$$R_{it} = \alpha_i + \beta_i R_{mt} + u_{it} \tag{5}$$

where R_{it} is the company return, R_{mt} is the return on the U.S. stock market index, and u_{it} is the error term. Systematic risk (SR) is measured by the beta, β_i, and idiosyncratic risk (IR) is measured by the standard deviation of the residuals $\hat{u}_{it}$.

Many of the company betas are larger than unity (Table 3). Company beta values show considerable variation and range from a low of 0.55 for Verizon to a high of 2.19 for Nextel. Notice that in this sample, two U.S. companies have the lowest and highest values for systematic risk. Based on these risk measures, Verizon stock is much less risky than the U.S. market while Nextel stock is much more risky than the U.S. stock market. The systematic risk values indicate that there is a wide variation in the risk of these telecommunications companies. The company average systematic risk measure is 34% larger than the systematic risk value for the U.S. stock market.

As discussed in Harvey (2000) and Estrada (2002), the single factor model in equation (5) can also be used to calculate two downside beta measures. The first measure, downside beta 1 (DB1), is calculated as the coefficient on the market return using observations when company returns and U.S. market returns are both negative. The second measure, downside beta 2 (DB2), is calculated as the coefficient on the market returns when U.S. market returns are negative.

For each company, ten risk variables are calculated (Table 3). The risk variables are systematic risk (SR) measured by beta, total risk (TR) measured by the standard deviation of returns, value at risk (VAR), downside risk (DR) measured by the semi-standard

Table 3. Risk measures

Company	SR	TR	VAR	Σ_μ	Σ_f	Σ_0	DB1	DB2	REGf	REG0
APT Satellite Holdings Ltd.	1.76	0.26	-35.00	0.13	0.16	0.13	2.33	2.74	0.12	0.08
Asia Satellite Telecom	1.63	0.15	-22.20	0.10	0.12	0.10	2.02	2.35	0.08	0.06
BCE Inc.	0.94	0.10	-15.33	0.07	0.08	0.05	1.04	1.38	0.05	0.03
BT Group PLC	1.18	0.11	-17.19	0.08	0.11	0.08	1.57	1.94	0.07	0.05
Cable & Wireless	1.55	0.16	-22.99	0.12	0.16	0.13	2.14	2.28	0.10	0.07
China Mobile Ltd	1.78	0.17	-24.19	0.10	0.11	0.09	1.59	2.49	0.08	0.05
Deutsche Telekom AG	1.40	0.15	-21.63	0.10	0.12	0.09	1.63	2.03	0.08	0.06
France Telecom	1.71	0.21	-29.24	0.14	0.16	0.13	2.64	2.12	0.09	0.07
Indonesian Satellite Corp	1.28	0.21	-29.41	0.12	0.13	0.11	2.27	1.82	0.09	0.06
Nippon Telegraph & Telephone	0.90	0.11	-16.74	0.07	0.10	0.08	1.05	1.25	0.08	0.05
Nokia OYJ	1.94	0.17	-24.51	0.12	0.12	0.10	1.70	2.51	0.07	0.05
Philippine Long Distance	1.16	0.13	-19.42	0.08	0.12	0.10	1.52	1.60	0.09	0.06
Portugal Telecom	0.95	0.11	-17.17	0.08	0.10	0.08	1.45	1.55	0.07	0.04
SK Telecom	1.67	0.21	-28.64	0.11	0.11	0.09	1.44	2.35	0.08	0.05
TDC A/S	1.11	0.13	-19.19	0.09	0.11	0.08	1.96	1.62	0.07	0.04
Telecom Argentina	1.65	0.22	-30.12	0.15	0.18	0.15	2.12	2.28	0.11	0.09
Telecom Italia	0.79	0.10	-15.06	0.06	0.08	0.06	0.97	1.22	0.06	0.03
Telefonica de Argentina	1.47	0.20	-27.75	0.13	0.16	0.14	1.96	2.07	0.11	0.08
Telefonica del Peru	1.38	0.15	-21.34	0.10	0.14	0.12	2.21	2.41	0.10	0.07
Telefonica SA	1.24	0.12	-17.55	0.08	0.10	0.07	1.41	1.83	0.06	0.04
Telefonos de Mexico	1.21	0.11	-15.99	0.07	0.08	0.06	1.16	1.80	0.05	0.03
Telekomunidasi Indonesia	1.59	0.20	-27.95	0.12	0.13	0.11	1.89	2.37	0.09	0.06
Vodafone	0.91	0.11	-16.76	0.08	0.10	0.07	1.25	1.32	0.06	0.04
Nextel	2.19	0.24	-32.13	0.16	0.17	0.14	2.55	3.07	0.10	0.08
AT&T	0.96	0.12	-18.29	0.08	0.11	0.08	1.09	1.38	0.08	0.05
Verizon	0.55	0.10	-15.68	0.06	0.08	0.06	0.69	0.65	0.06	0.03
Average	1.34	0.16	-22.36	0.10	0.12	0.10	1.68	1.94	0.08	0.06
US Market	1.00	0.06	-9.04	0.04	0.07	0.04	0.98	1.47	0.05	0.02

deviation of returns, using three different benchmarks, two downside beta measures, and two measures of regret.

The TR values range from a low of 0.10 to a high of 0.26. The sample average for TR is almost three times larger than the TR for the U.S. market.

The -35.00 VAR value for APT Satellite Holdings means that for every $100 invested in this company there is a 5% probability of losing $35.00 or more in any given month. Based on the VAR measure, this company is very risky to invest in. Telecommunications companies are, as a group, very risky and this is clearly demonstrated by the average VAR value of -22.36. By comparison, the U.S. stock market has a VAR value at -9.04 and this value is well above the telecommunications industry average. The average downside risk measures are each larger than twice the corresponding values for the U.S. market (Table 3). The average values for downside beta 1 (DB1) and downside beta 2 (DB2) are each larger than the average value for systematic risk. The results in Tables 3 show that the global telecommunications industry is a very risky industry to invest in.

A correlation matrix between mean stock returns and the ten risk variables indicate that company stock returns are most highly correlated with the two measures of regret (Table 4). Market returns are the least correlated with systematic Σ_μ. Total risk and downside risk are very highly correlated with each other and downside risk, and VAR are very highly correlated with each other. Total risk is perfectly correlated with VAR. The risk measures, downside beta 1 and downside beta 2, are each less highly correlated with market returns than is systematic risk.

A cross section regression analysis is used to investigate the relationship between mean returns and various risk variables (Table 5). The adjusted R^2 values for these regression models range from -0.03% to 20%. The probability value associated with the estimated coefficient on the risk variable indicates that each of the risk variables (Σ_f, Σ_0, REGf, and REG0) is statistically significant. None of the regression models exhibit evidence of mis-specification as evident from the RESET test. These results provide evidence of a linear relationship between market returns and these four risk variables.

Table 4. Correlations

	MEAN	SR	TR	VAR	Σ_μ	Σ_f	Σ_0	DB1	DB2	REGf	REG0
MEAN	1.00	0.21	0.10	-0.09	0.01	-0.37	-0.36	-0.17	0.11	-0.48	-0.42
SR	0.21	1.00	0.82	-0.82	0.86	0.73	0.74	0.77	0.96	0.60	0.70
TR	0.10	0.82	1.00	-1.00	0.93	0.83	0.84	0.80	0.79	0.80	0.81
VAR	-0.09	-0.82	-1.00	1.00	-0.93	-0.83	-0.85	-0.80	-0.78	-0.81	-0.82
Σ_μ	0.01	0.86	0.93	-0.93	1.00	0.92	0.92	0.87	0.81	0.78	0.87
Σ_f	-0.37	0.73	0.83	-0.83	0.92	1.00	0.99	0.88	0.72	0.91	0.97
Σ_0	-0.36	0.74	0.84	-0.85	0.92	0.99	1.00	0.87	0.73	0.93	0.97
DB1	-0.17	0.77	0.80	-0.80	0.87	0.88	0.87	1.00	0.78	0.75	0.82
DB2	0.11	0.96	0.79	-0.78	0.81	0.72	0.73	0.78	1.00	0.63	0.71
REGF	-0.48	0.60	0.80	-0.81	0.78	0.91	0.93	0.75	0.63	1.00	0.95
REG0	-0.42	0.70	0.81	-0.82	0.87	0.97	0.97	0.82	0.71	0.95	1.00

Several risk measures (REGf, REG0) exhibit a high degree of explanatory power as indicated by the high R^2 values. These R^2 values range from 18% to 23% and there is no evidence of mis-specified functional form. Notice how little of the variability in market returns can be explained by systematic risk.

Table 5. Cross section regression analysis

	c_1	c_2	R squared	R squared adj	RESET
SR	-0.01	0.01	0.05	0.01	0.21
	0.41	0.21			
TR	0.00	0.04	0.01	-0.03	0.26
	0.96	0.59			
VAR	0.00	0.00	0.01	-0.03	0.15
	0.93	0.61			
Σ_μ	0.00	0.00	0.00	-0.04	0.95
	0.69	0.97			
Σ_f	0.03	-0.22	0.13	0.10	0.99
	0.02	0.05			
Σ_0	0.03	-0.23	0.13	0.09	0.77
	0.01	0.05			
DB1	0.01	-0.01	0.03	-0.01	0.77
	0.16	0.38			
DB2	0.00	0.00	0.01	-0.03	0.57
	0.87	0.56			
REGf	0.04	-0.46	0.23	0.20	0.93
	0.00	0.00			
REG0	0.03	-0.44	0.18	0.14	0.93
	0.00	0.02			

Regression equation is: $MR_i = c_1 + c_2 RV_i + u_i$

Notes: MR is the mean stock return and RV is the risk variable. White's (1980) heteroskedasticity corrected probability values are reported below coefficient estimates. RESET shows the probability values for a Ramsey (1969) regression specification F test with 2 and 22 degrees of freedom.

The Cost of Equity

The cost of equity is important in valuing new investment opportunities and evaluating the ongoing performance of existing business projects. From equation (1) any required return consists of a risk-free rate and a risk premium.

$$RR_i = R_f + (RP_M)(RM_i) \tag{6}$$

In equation (6), RR_i is the required return on equity i, R_f is the risk-free rate, RP_M is the U.S. market risk premium, and RM_i is a risk measure for equity i. This section focuses on ten risk measures based on systematic risk (RM_{SR}), total risk (RM_{TR}), value at risk (RM_{VAR}), three measures of downside risk (RM_{DR}), two measures of downside beta, and two measures of regret. The appendix contains the equations for the cost of equity calculations.

In order to calculate the cost of equity for each company, numerical values for a risk-free rate and market-risk premium are required. In the calculations of the cost of equity, a risk free rate of 1.19% was used as this was the value of the three-month U.S. Treasury bill rate at the end of December 2002. A market risk premium of 4.0% was employed. With globalization and capital market convergence, the U.S. market-risk premium may by the best proxy for the global market risk premium (Pettit, Gulic and Park, 2001). Estimates of the U.S. market-risk premium range from 3% to 8%. In this chapter, we choose a market-risk premium of 4%. This value is slightly higher than the 3% market-risk premium now being advocated (Tully, 2003), but 3% is also lower than the 5.5% global market-risk premium previously used by other authors (Estrada, 2000, 2002).

For almost all companies, the cost of equity based on systematic risk is the lowest of the cost-of-equity measures (Table 6). The cost of equity based on systematic risk varies from a low of 3.41% (Verizon) to a high of 9.95% (Nextel). Telecom Italia has the lowest cost of equity using total risk or value at risk. APT Satellite Holdings has the highest cost of equity using total risk or value at risk. For most companies, the cost of equity ranking is $CE_{TR} > CE_{DRj} > CE_{SR}$ (j = μ, 0, f). In some cases $CE_{DRj} > CE_{VAR}$ and, in other cases, the ranking is reversed. The differences between these risk measures can be very large. For example, Telefonica de Argentina has a CE_{SR} of 7.08% per year while CE_{TR} and CE_{DR0} are 14.92% and 14.25% per year respectively. This suggests that an investor in Telefonica de Argentina stock would be expecting to earn 7.08% per year if the cost of equity was calculated using systematic risk. By comparison, this investor would expect to earn 14.92% per year if the cost of equity was calculated using a total risk measure. In other words, there is a substantial difference in risk-adjusted expected returns. The cost of equity sample averages for the telecommunications companies are 6.56% for systematic risk, 12.00% for total risk, 10.49% for downside risk ($CE_{DRμ}$) and 11.09% for value at risk. These cost of equity measures are much higher than the corresponding values for the U.S. stock market as a whole. The cost of equity calculated using downside beta measures are almost always greater than the cost of equity calculated using systematic risk. On average, the cost of equity calculated using downside beta 1 (beta 2) is 21% (36%) larger than the average cost of equity calculated using systematic risk.

Table 6. Cost of equity

Company	CE_{SR}	CE_{TR}	CE_{VAR}	$CE_{DR\mu}$	CE_{DRI}	CE_{DRO}	CE_{DB1}	CE_{DB2}	CE_{REGI}	CE_{REGO}	AVERAGE
APT Satellite Holdings Ltd.	8.23	19.38	16.68	13.55	10.65	13.77	10.50	12.15	11.03	15.23	13.12
Asia Satellite Telecom	7.72	11.79	11.02	10.84	8.46	10.48	9.27	10.59	8.03	10.92	9.91
BCE Inc.	4.95	8.22	7.97	7.52	5.76	6.38	5.34	6.71	5.28	5.73	6.39
BT Group PLC	5.93	9.15	8.80	8.97	7.63	9.23	7.47	8.94	7.23	9.08	8.24
Cable & Wireless	7.38	12.23	11.37	12.13	10.34	13.59	9.74	10.32	9.54	13.59	11.02
China Mobile Ltd	8.32	12.89	11.90	10.51	7.84	9.45	7.56	11.16	7.63	9.77	9.70
Deutsche Telekom AG	6.79	11.48	10.76	10.47	8.25	10.18	7.71	9.29	7.80	10.39	9.31
France Telecom	8.02	15.80	14.14	14.03	10.34	13.73	11.75	9.67	9.18	12.87	11.95
Indonesian Satellite Corp	6.32	15.90	14.21	12.03	8.90	11.21	10.25	8.45	8.49	11.36	10.71
Nippon Telegraph & Telephone	4.79	8.93	8.60	7.72	7.31	8.37	5.39	6.17	7.70	9.36	7.43
Nokia OYJ	8.94	13.07	12.04	12.25	8.33	10.55	7.99	11.21	7.24	9.65	10.13
Philippine Long Distance	5.84	10.31	9.79	9.13	8.39	10.22	7.28	7.61	8.52	11.11	8.82
Portugal Telecom	4.97	9.14	8.79	8.59	7.20	8.55	6.99	7.40	6.86	8.19	7.67
SK Telecom	7.87	15.44	13.87	11.59	7.94	9.58	6.96	10.58	7.82	9.99	10.16
TDC A/S	5.61	10.19	9.69	9.31	7.52	9.15	9.05	7.69	7.05	8.44	8.37
Telecom Argentina	7.80	16.33	14.52	14.78	11.73	15.80	9.67	10.29	10.92	15.91	12.77
Telecom Italia	4.36	8.08	7.86	7.20	6.18	6.82	5.08	6.08	6.18	6.66	6.45
Telefonica de Argentina	7.08	14.92	13.48	13.07	10.82	14.25	9.02	9.46	10.43	14.87	11.74
Telefonica del Peru	6.70	11.33	10.64	10.27	9.70	12.30	10.05	10.84	9.89	13.44	10.52
Telefonica SA	6.17	9.34	8.96	8.35	6.94	8.14	6.83	8.52	6.63	7.80	7.77
Telefonos de Mexico	6.01	8.55	8.27	8.06	6.12	7.06	5.84	8.39	5.45	6.01	6.98
Telekomunidasi Indonesia	7.57	15.03	13.56	12.46	9.04	11.45	8.75	10.68	8.56	11.64	10.88
Vodafone	4.83	8.94	8.61	8.49	6.85	7.97	6.18	6.46	6.44	7.84	7.26
Nextel	9.95	17.56	15.41	15.88	10.96	14.67	11.38	13.47	9.67	14.51	13.35
AT&T	5.04	9.72	9.28	8.55	7.59	8.95	5.55	6.71	7.66	9.53	7.86
Verizon	3.41	8.39	8.13	6.92	6.14	6.56	3.95	3.78	6.44	6.79	6.05
Average	6.56	12.00	11.09	10.49	8.34	10.32	7.91	8.95	7.99	10.41	9.41
US Market	5.19	5.19	5.19	5.19	5.19	5.19	5.12	7.09	5.19	5.19	5.37

While systematic risk is a very well known and widely used measure of market risk, the results in this chapter suggest that a prudent investor in global telecommunications companies might also wish to calculate risk measures based on total risk, value at risk, downside risk, and regret. Unfortunately there is no simple answer to the question, "which is the appropriate risk measure to use?" nor is the use of downside risk without its' critics (Nawrocki, 1999). Different individuals have different attitudes and preferences towards risk (Bernstein, 1998). One possible approach would be to use the simple average value of the ten cost-of-equity calculations. The average value for each company is presented in the last column of Table 6. These cost-of-equity average values range from a low of 6.05 for Verizon to a high of 13.35 for Nextel. The South American and Indonesian companies have fairly large values for the average cost of equity. Contrary to what one might expect, the average cost of equity for telecommunications companies in developing countries is not always greater than the average cost of equity for telecommunications companies in developed countries. This is borne out by the high average cost-of-equity values for Cable & Wireless, France Telecom and Nextel. In general, it is difficult to find evidence of regional differences in the average cost of equity of telecommunications companies.

In order to more fully develop the usage of the cost-of-equity values (Table 6) and risk measures (Table 3), we perform two simulation experiments to build distributions for each company's cost of equity. In the first simulation, we assume that for each company in our sample, the cost of equity can be approximated by a normal distribution with a mean and standard deviation calculated from that company's ten cost-of-equity values. A number of different distribution functions (exponential, extreme value, normal, logistic, triangular, Weibull, uniform and Pareto) was fit to each company's cost-of-equity values.

For each company, the normal distribution ranked high (usually in the top four) for chosen fit. For each company, 5,000 simulations were performed and the minimum, mean, maximum, 5% value, and 95% values recorded. The results are reported in Table 7.

These results show not only the average cost-of-equity value for each company, but also show the 90% confidence interval. For example, the average cost-of-equity value for Telecomm Argentina is 12.78%. There is one chance in 20 that the cost of equity will be below 8.01%. There is one chance in 20 that the cost of equity will be above 17.53%. Thus we are 90% certain that the true cost of equity will be in the 8.01% to 17.53% range.

Simulation two is more elaborate in that the uncertainty is modeled directly into the components of equation (6). A triangular distribution function with parameters 0.5, 1.19 and 2.25 was assumed for the risk-free rate. A normal distribution with mean 4 and standard deviation 1 was assumed for the market-risk premium. A normal distribution was assumed for each company's risk measures using company sample values for the mean and standard deviation. For each company, 5,000 simulations were performed and the minimum, mean, maximum, 5% value, and 95% values recorded. The results are shown in Table 8.

The mean values recorded in Tables 7 and 8 are for each company, fairly similar. The 5% and 95% values for each company vary between the two tables and in some cases the 90% confidence interval is larger in Table 8 than it is in Table 7. The results in Table 8 are more precise because the randomness was modeled directly into the components of equation (6). Our suggestion is therefore to not rely on just one cost-of-equity value but to calculate several different cost-of-equity values and then use simulation techniques to build up a probability distribution for each company's cost of equity. In this way, a clearer picture of where a company's cost of equity lies is developed. After all, two different distributions can have the same mean values but have very different shapes. For project evaluation and investing, for example, distributions that are skewed to the right are much preferred to distributions that are skewed to the left.

Table 7. Cost of equity (simulation 1)

Company	Minimum	Mean	Maximum	5%	95%
APT Satellite Holdings Ltd.	-0.59	13.12	24.42	7.94	18.29
Asia Satellite Telecom	4.35	9.91	14.73	7.69	12.14
BCE Inc.	1.95	6.39	10.77	4.55	8.22
BT Group PLC	4.17	8.24	12.34	6.50	9.98
Cable & Wireless	4.22	11.02	17.99	7.98	14.05
China Mobile Ltd	2.80	9.70	16.21	6.76	12.65
Deutsche Telekom AG	3.98	9.31	14.77	6.85	11.77
France Telecom	2.99	11.95	21.89	7.96	15.94
Indonesian Satellite Corp	-0.49	10.71	21.40	6.22	15.19
Nippon Telegraph & Telephone	1.81	7.43	12.67	5.04	9.82
Nokia OYJ	2.91	10.13	16.92	7.01	13.25
Philippine Long Distance	3.24	8.82	14.85	6.30	11.33
Portugal Telecom	3.43	7.67	12.07	5.72	9.61
SK Telecom	0.77	10.16	19.75	5.81	14.52
TDC A/S	3.06	8.37	13.43	6.19	10.55
Telecom Argentina	2.13	12.78	24.19	8.01	17.53
Telecom Italia	2.57	6.45	10.46	4.65	8.25
Telefonica de Argentina	-0.78	11.74	22.80	7.45	16.03
Telefonica del Peru	3.50	10.52	17.08	7.74	13.28
Telefonica SA	3.96	7.77	11.93	6.09	9.44
Telefonos de Mexico	2.73	6.98	11.22	5.06	8.89
Telekomunidasi Indonesia	2.18	10.88	19.12	7.12	14.63
Vodafone	2.58	7.26	12.08	5.21	9.31
Nextel	3.94	13.35	24.45	9.12	17.58
AT&T	1.66	7.86	13.54	5.27	10.44
Verizon	-0.68	6.05	12.46	3.29	8.80

Notes: For each company 5,000 simulations were calculated from a normal distribution using that company's cost of equity mean and standard deviation.

Table 8. Cost of equity (simulation 2)

Company	Minimum	Mean	Maximum	5%	95%
APT Satellite Holdings Ltd.	-0.14	12.88	30.40	6.27	20.66
Asia Satellite Telecom	2.50	9.74	19.35	6.00	13.86
BCE Inc.	1.53	6.34	12.75	3.83	9.24
BT Group PLC	1.14	8.13	15.08	5.18	11.22
Cable & Wireless	1.18	10.86	22.50	6.52	15.69
China Mobile Ltd	1.93	9.52	21.90	5.36	14.32
Deutsche Telekom AG	2.20	9.19	19.68	5.51	13.43
France Telecom	1.96	11.82	25.80	6.74	17.91
Indonesian Satellite Corp	0.55	10.61	29.02	5.12	17.04
Nippon Telegraph & Telephone	1.67	7.40	15.67	4.50	10.70
Nokia OYJ	1.82	9.94	22.00	5.79	14.67
Philippine Long Distance	0.92	8.74	18.37	5.23	12.68
Portugal Telecom	1.73	7.60	14.68	4.72	10.75
SK Telecom	-1.01	10.00	33.01	4.62	16.39
TDC A/S	2.09	8.30	17.27	5.09	11.87
Telecom Argentina	2.37	12.62	27.30	7.38	18.68
Telecom Italia	2.01	6.42	14.23	3.99	9.20
Telefonica de Argentina	1.83	11.61	25.74	6.79	17.15
Telefonica del Peru	1.80	10.34	22.43	6.01	15.29
Telefonica SA	1.40	7.66	14.76	4.72	10.95
Telefonos de Mexico	1.50	6.88	13.63	4.21	9.88
Telekomunidasi Indonesia	1.38	10.71	27.16	5.83	16.77
Vodafone	0.49	7.23	16.25	4.40	10.41
Nextel	1.91	13.10	30.72	7.36	19.85
AT&T	1.42	7.82	15.75	4.78	11.21
Verizon	1.37	6.10	14.42	3.46	9.12

Notes: 5,000 simulations were performed for each company in the table. A triangular distribution function with parameters 0.5, 1.19 and 2.25 was assumed for the risk free rate. A normal distribution with mean 4 and standard deviation 1 was assumed for the market risk premium. A normal distribution was assumed for each company's risk measure using company sample values for the mean and standard deviation.

Future Trends

Countries around the world are experiencing an increase in the convergence of global-ization, financial markets and technology. Economic growth is tied closely with this convergence and it is expected that this convergence will continue into the foreseeable future. This convergence comes at a time when equity market volatility is high, thereby emphasizing the need for the practice of good risk management techniques. Policy makers in both developed and developing counties realize that economic growth is driven by enhancements in productivity and productivity growth, in turn, is driven by increases in technology. Affordable and reliable telecommunications are essential to the wealth and creation process of any country (Landes, 1998). Privatization and favourable regulatory changes in the global telecommunications industry can lead to greater productivity and profits. Privatization also requires well functioning capital markets, as new sources of debt and equity are required for those companies in industries being privatized.

The telecommunications industry is characterized by high fixed costs, increased compe-tition due to privatization and huge opportunities for growth in developing countries. As in all industries, companies can compete on price or product differentiation (including quality). In some regions of the world, it is just too costly to install wire-line services. In these instances, wireless services present a viable alternative. The build-out of new telecommunications services requires financial capital. Globalization (broadly character-ized as in increase in the trade of goods and services and an increase in foreign investment) can help by increasingly matching owners of scarce financial capital with those who need it. But foreign investment comes at a price. Namely, that investors compare various investment projects in a particular risk class and choose the one with the highest return. Telecommunications companies in developing countries can attract foreign capital if they offer a competitive risk-adjusted expected return.

Equity investors, in particular, because they rank after debt holders for claims on company assets, must have good measures of risk-adjusted, expected returns. In the future, investors and policy makers alike should make the cost-of-equity calculations made in this chapter to help gain a better understanding of the tradeoffs between risk and return in the global telecommunications industry.

Conclusions

Access to affordable technology to improve the flow of information is essential to the development of an economy. Closing the Digital Divide could bring many benefits to developing countries. In many ways, developing countries have the most to gain from improvements in telecommunications and information technology. Bringing the benefits of IT to developing countries is possible, but the governments of these countries need to be aware that the process is going to cost money and require institutional changes.

The basic economic production function mixes capital with labour, energy and materials to produce output. Capital consists of physical capital (buildings, plants, machinery), human capital (knowledge) and social capital (customs and institutions) (Landes, 1998; Helliwell, 2002). Smooth, well functioning feedback between these three types of capital is essential to promoting a fertile economic environment for entrepreneurs and business and provides the most direct path to productivity improvements and high living standards.

International investors will frequently calculate the cost of equity for their existing investments and their proposed investments. Development planners must be able to make their own cost-of-equity calculations so that they can see first hand how their investment projects compare with other investment projects around the globe.

Consequently, it is necessary to have good measures of equity risk for managers, planners, policy makers and investors. The cost of equity is important in valuing new investment opportunities and in evaluating the ongoing performance of established business projects. This is especially true in the new economy IT industry where an understanding of equity risk aids in the examination of the relationship between the IT sector and economic development.

Estimates of the cost of equity for a particular company vary widely and depend upon the methodology used. For a particular company, cost-of-equity values based on systematic risk tend to be lower than cost-of-equity values calculated from downside risk measures. For some companies, downside cost-of-equity values are twice as large as cost-of-equity measures based on systematic risk. This is true, even though all of the cost-of-equity values use the same risk-free rate and same risk premium.

The cost of equity is an essential ingredient for investors seeking estimates of risk-adjusted returns from an equity investment. The cost of equity is also crucial to project evaluation and project evaluation is crucial to the success of any firm. Small changes in the cost of equity can have large impacts on the net present-value calculation of a project valuation. Large cost-of-equity values lower present-value calculations while small cost-of-equity values raise present-value calculations. The results in this chapter suggest that, while systematic risk is a well known measure of equity risk, a prudent investor in global telecommunications companies might also wish to calculate risk measures based on total risk, value at risk, downside risk, and regret. Our approach is not to rely on just one cost-of-equity value but to calculate several different cost-of-equity values and then use simulation techniques to build up a probability distribution for each company's cost of equity. In this way, a clearer picture of where a company's true cost of equity lies is developed. Simulation results are insightful because different distributions can have the same mean values but have very different shapes. For project evaluation and investing, for example, distributions that are skewed to the right are much preferred to distributions that are skewed to the left.

One of the insights that emerges from our study is the fact that the average cost of equity for telecommunications companies in developing countries is not always greater than the average cost of equity for telecommunications companies in developed countries. This is borne out by the high cost-of-equity calculations for Cable & Wireless, France Telecom and Nextel. In general, it is difficult to find evidence of regional differences in the average cost of equity of telecommunications companies. This is useful to a development planner who can then use a portfolio approach in which high-risk investments are combined with low-risk investments to promote an investment in a developing country's telecommunications industry. Provided a developing or emerging economy can offer attractive risk and return characteristics to investors of financial capital, funds from portfolio investment should not be overlooked as a source of financial investment capital.

Acknowledgments

We thank an anonymous reviewer and the editor for helpful comments.

References

Alexander, C. (2001). *Market Models: A Guide to Financial Data Analysis*. New York: John Wiley & Sons.

Bernstein, P. (1998). *Against the Gods: The Remarkable Story of Risk*. New York: John Wiley & Sons.

Bortolotti, B., D'Souza, J., Fantini, M. and Megginson W. (2002). Privatization and the sources of performance improvement in the global telecommunications industry. *Telecommunications Policy, 26*, 243-268.

Brealey, R. and Myers, S. (2003). *Principles of Corporate Finance* (7th ed.). New York: McGraw Hill.

Campbell, J.Y., Low, A.W. and Mackinlay, A.C. (1997). *The Econometrics of Financial Markets*. Princeton: Princeton University Press.

Chong, A. and Micco, A. (2003). The internet and the ability to innovate in Latin America. *Emerging Markets Review, 4*, 53-72.

Dembo, R.C. and Freeman, A. (2001). *The rules of risk*. New York: Wiley.

The Economist. (1999). Survey: Telecommunications, the world in your pocket. October 19, 1999.

The Economist. (2001). Survey: Global equity markets. May 5, 2001.

Estrada, J. (2000). The cost of equity in emerging markets: A downside risk approach. *Emerging Markets Quarterly, 4*(3), 19-30.

Estrada, J. (2002). Systematic risk in emerging markets: the D-CAPM. *Emerging Markets Review, 3*, 365-379.

Fama, E.F. and French, K.R. (1997). Industry costs of equity. *Journal of Financial Economics, 43*, 153-193.

Harvey, C. R. (2000). Drivers of expected returns in international markets. *Emerging Markets Quarterly, 4*(3), 32-48.

Helliwell, F.F. (2002). *Globalization and Well Being*. Vancouver: University of British Columbia Press.

Iyer, L., Tarube, L. and Raquet, J. (2002). Global e-commerce: Rationale, digital divide, and strategies to bridge the divide. *Journal of Global Information Technology Management*, 5(1), 43-68.

Jain, R. (2002). The internet in developing countries. *Journal of Global Information Technology Management*, 5(1), 1-3.

JP Morgan/Reuters. (1996). RiskMetrics Technical Document. Retrieved from the World Wide Web: www.jpmorgan.com.

Landes, D.S. (1998). *The Wealth and Poverty of Nations: Why some are so rich and some so poor*. New York: Norton.

Lu, M. (2001). Digital divide in developing countries. *Journal of Global Information Technology Management*, 4(3), 1-4.

Markowitz, H. (1959). *Portfolio Selection: Efficient Diversification of Investments*. New York: John Wiley & Sons.

Miles, D. and Scott, A. (2002). *Macroeconomics: Understanding the Wealth of Nations*. New York: John Wiley & Sons.

Nawrocki, D. (1999, Fall). A brief history of downside risk measures. *The Journal of Investing*, 9-25.

Pettit, J., Gulic, I. and Park, A. (2001). The equity risk measurement handbook. *EVAluation*, 3(3). Retrieved from the World Wide Web: www.eva.com.

Ramsey, J. (1969). Tests for specification errors in classical linear least squares regression analysis. *Journal of the Royal Statistical Society B*, *31*, 350-371.

Roy, A.D. (1952). Safety first and the holding of assets. *Econometrica*, *20*(3), 431-449.

Sadorsky, P. (2003). Equity risk in the global information technology industry. International Research Foundation for Development, *World Forum on the Information Society, Virtual Conference 1*, Feb. 17 - 28 2003. Retrieved from the World Wide Web: www.irfd.org\events\wf2003/vc.html.

Sadorsky, P. and Henriques, I. (2003). Risk measures and the cost of equity in the new economy biotechnology industry. *Global Business and Economics Review*, 5(1), 37-55.

Shapiro, A.C. (2003). *Multinational Financial Management* (7th ed.). New York: John Wiley & Sons.

Sortino, F. and Satchell, S. (2001). *Managing downside risk in financial markets*. New York: Butterworth-Heinemann Finance.

Tully, S. (2003, June). Can stocks defy gravity? *Fortune*, *147*(12), 44-50.

White, H. (1980). A heteroskedasticity-consistent covariance matrix estimator and a direct test for heteroskedasticity. *Econometrica*, *48*, 817-838.

Appendix

The risk measures (RM) and associated cost of equity (CE) are calculated as follows:

$$RM_{SR} = \beta_i / \beta_M = \beta_i$$

$$CE_{SR,i} = R_f + (RP_M)\, \beta_i \qquad\qquad (A1)$$

$$RM_{TR} = \sigma_i / \sigma_M$$

$$CE_{TR,i} = R_f + (RP_w)\, \sigma_i / \sigma_M \qquad\qquad (A2)$$

$$RM_{DRj} = \Sigma_{ji} / \Sigma_{jM}\ , j = \mu, 0, f$$

$$CE_{DRj,i} = R_f + (RP_M)\, \Sigma_{ji} / \Sigma_{jM} \qquad\qquad (A3)$$

$$RM_{VAR} = VAR_i / VAR_M$$

$$CE_{VAR,i} = R_f + (RP_M)\, VAR_i / VAR_M \qquad\qquad (A4)$$

$$RM_{DBj} = \beta_{ji} / \beta_{jM} = \beta_{ji}\ \ j = f, 0$$

$$CE_{DB,ji} = R_f + (RP_M)\, \beta_{ji} \qquad\qquad (A5)$$

$$RM_{REGj} = REG_{ji} / REG_{jM}\ \ j = f, 0$$

$$CE_{REG,ji} = R_f + (RP_M)\, REG_{ij} / REG_{Mj} \qquad\qquad (A6)$$

Chapter IV

Reduction of Transaction Costs by Using Electronic Commerce in Financial Services:
An Institutional and Empirical Approach

Thomas Pfahler
University of Bayreuth, Germany

Kai M. Grebe
University of Bayreuth, Germany

Abstract

This chapter introduces the Transaction Cost Approach as a means of analyzing specific transactions in financial services by using the theoretical framework of New Institutional Economics. It argues that transaction costs can be assessed and used to compare different business processes. Furthermore, these costs allow a detailed explanation why certain underlying technologies which form the basis for transactions become widely accepted whereas others do not prevail. The authors emphasize the relevance of this approach and its application to the field of electronic commerce both on a theoretical and practical level to document and to interpret current trends in this sector on the one hand, and to predict future developments on the other hand.

Introduction

The authors analyse the impact of the increasing utilization of information and communication technology (ICT) and electronic commerce on the coordination of specific transactions in financial services. In particular, two business processes commonly occurring in the contractual relationship between a financial institution and its customers will be considered: bank transfers and stock purchases. The chapter focuses explicitly on the relationship between a bank and its customers which, in contrast to internal and inter-bank processes that have already been subject of intensive research, has been neglected so far.

The basic principles of New Institutional Economics and the instruments developed in the context of the Transaction Cost Approach serve as theoretical background for the study and further discussion. The chapter develops and implements a proposal how to exemplify and to compare these processes under the varying influence of certain technologies. Therefore, a cost model is developed that will be used in the following to assess two basic transactions in this specific area. The intention is to reveal the basic phenomenon and to document the reasons for the current utilization of ICT in this sector by emphasizing relative reductions of transaction costs by means of electronic commerce. The basic statements and conclusions are underlined and illustrated for Germany in an empirical section. At the end of the chapter, future perspectives and impacts on the chosen topic will be given and derived.

Electronic Commerce

The need to explain the most important terms and definitions in this context arises directly from the topic chosen. Choi/Stahl/Winston (1997) define electronic commerce as "a new market offering a new type of commodity, such as digital products through digital processes." This specification already indicates the potential scope and the enormous consequences which result from the use of electronic commerce.

More fundamentally, electronic commerce can be seen as any economic activity on the basis of electronic connections (Picot/Reichwald/Wigand, 2001). Hence, it follows that the underlying technology is crucial to promote the acceptance and the use of electronic commerce. The use of digital lines and early devices to generate and to exchange information between participants in the economic cycle was a first step. The introduction of telephone and telefax services can be seen as the advent of a massive development which turns out to be the "digital revolution." Phone lines can be used to connect computers to the Internet, and digital data highways have been implemented to overcome limitations and to assure rapid processing. Mobile phones or Personal Digital Assistants (PDA) enable users to interact and to participate in new as well as in established markets from almost anywhere at any time.

Electronic commerce can generally take place between two businesses, between a business and an administration, or between a business and a consumer. In the following, only the relationship between a business and its customers will be investigated. The object of the analysis is the financial sector.

Financial institutions hold special positions in the business cycle and differ in many ways from other corporations or firms. Economically, they perform the functions of liquidity equalization, of processing information and of conducting several transformations. Special laws and directives are applied and the services offered are abstract and immaterial (Büschgen, 1998). Moreover, these services need explanations and need to integrate an external factor: the bank customer.

In view of these facts it seems evident that the financial sector is likely to be more affected by the emergence of new technologies than other sectors might be. Consequently, banks have internally been using information and communication technologies for a long time to process a large number of highly standardized operations. In the last few years, especially the core business of banks has been at the center of attention—and it has changed in several ways. The interface between the institution and its customers has become increasingly important. New ways of contacting and transacting have been implemented for mutual benefit and changed their relationship. Customers are now much more integrated in the transaction process and may easily arrange their affairs through the use of electronic commerce without having to be on site. Banks will be able to reengineer business processes, offer new products and reduce personnel costs.

New Institutional Economics

There are many possible approaches to investigate different aspects of information and communication technology and electronic commerce. This chapter chooses the perspective of New Institutional Economics, more precisely the Transaction Cost Approach, which has been developed since the 1950s because of certain deficits in the Neoclassical Theory. The criticism leveled is that the use of a market or of the legal system is neither free nor without frictions (Williamson, 1990). On the contrary, institutions have to be taken into account and transaction costs arise.

Ostrom (1990, p.51) states as follows:

> *"Institutions" can be defined as the sets of working rules that are used to determine who is eligible to make decisions in some area, what actions are allowed or constrained, what aggregation rules will be used, what procedures must be followed, what information must or must not be provided, and what payoffs will be assigned to individuals dependent on their actions.*

Transactions

The basis of the Transaction Cost Approach was established by Coase in 1937, who questioned the reason for the existence of firms. He concludes that, "there is a cost of using the price mechanism" during the transactional process between individuals. The term "transaction" was introduced into the economic context by Commons (1990, p.58), who reasoned:

> Transactions [...] are not the "exchange of commodities," in the physical sense of "delivery," they are the alienation and acquisition, between individuals, of the rights of future ownership of physical things, as determined by collective working rules of society.

Other authors do not limit the relevance to property rights. Williamson (1985, p.1) claims that a transaction "occurs when a good or a service is transferred across a technologically separable interface." This definition will be the basis for all further discussion in this context. Many differing points of view can be found, but there is at least agreement that transactions are not free.

Transaction Costs

Arrow (1969, p.48) defines these specific costs in a very general way and found that transaction costs are "costs of running the economic system," whereas Williamson (1989, p.142) considers them as the costs of "planning, adapting, and monitoring task completion under alternative governance structures." This latter explanation is the basis for the development of the cost model and will be referred to later on when two transactions are compared which are accomplished in various ways.

Transaction costs may occur in markets, within firms and corporations or in the political framework (Richter/Furubotn, 1996). They may be fixed costs or variable costs. During the transactional process, transaction costs are generated before, during and after the actual transaction takes place (Coase, 1937). For example, costs of gathering information, costs of preparing the transaction, costs of monitoring or contracting costs can be distinguished in the different phases of a transaction. The specific amount of the transaction costs accruing varies, and depends for example on the specificity of a necessary investment in this transaction, on the frequency of occurrence or the uncertainty in respect to environmental factors or the contractual partner. In the context of all further investigations, uncertainty and opportunism can be excluded because the analysis considers the contractual relationship between a financial institution and its customers.

Quantification of Transaction Costs

After transaction costs have been identified and introduced as a new cost category, the question is how to measure these costs and how to use them for economic analysis. Different approaches can be found, for example from a macroeconomic or microeconomic perspective. In addition, many case studies focus on certain markets or specific aspects in or between corporations.

One of the most famous studies is the analysis of the development and importance of transaction costs for the United States over a period of 100 years by North and Wallis (1986, p.97). For them, transaction costs "are the costs associated with making exchanges, the costs of performing the transaction function." All economic activities are divided into activities which mainly transform input into output and those which are basically involved in coordination and transaction processes. North and Wallis (1986) demonstrate an increase of transaction costs of the whole transaction sector from 26.1% to 54.7% of GDP between 1870 and 1970 and conclude that transaction costs are as important as production costs in highly industrialised nations.

Demsetz (1968, p.35) focuses on the New York Stock Exchange (NYSE) and defines transaction costs as "the cost of exchanging ownership titles." He points out that these costs decrease with an increasing trade volume and thus explains the concentration processes at the NYSE.

Criticism

The most serious problem of the Transaction Cost Approach is the lack of a consistent terminology. Even for a basic term like transaction costs there is disagreement about its components, determinants and applicability for certain issues. Moreover, Niehans (1987) points out that transaction costs "become difficult, perhaps impossible, to quantify."

This lack of transparency is evident and basically the criticism is justified. But as the Theory of New Institutional Economics and the Transaction Cost Approach are comparatively young disciplines in economic science, a fairly standardised terminology will probably be developed in the future. Undoubtedly, transaction costs are relevant in industrial nations and make up an increasing part of all costs caused by economic activity. Last but not least, it is important to note that there is no imperative to measure transaction costs absolutely or in a direct way. The approach developed in the next section will link the Transaction Cost Theory to a specific subarea of Electronic Commerce in Financial Services.

The Cost Model

The preceding sections have developed the conceptual framework for the target analysis by defining the most important terms and by explaining the basic ideas. Now our own proposal to measure transaction costs will be introduced. We refrain from attempting to quantify these costs in absolute terms but concentrate deliberately on relative considerations. As the focus in this context is on the relevant interface between a bank and its customers, internal and inter-bank transactions will be left out of consideration. Our approach describes and illustrates a new way to combine the business perspective of a financial institution and the personal perspective of a customer. As business modularity can hardly be used to extend internal processes and to bridge the contrast between both perspectives, the given theoretical framework used in Banking and Finance is insufficient for the very specific investigation in this chapter: Only monetary factors have been considered so far. This new approach includes monetary as well as non-monetary factors, which are both covered by the underlying notion of transaction costs. The latter can actually be more important and they may represent the major proportion of all the costs that arise. Therefore, a relatively new framework to measure transaction costs has to be developed.

Phases of a Transaction

In a first step, the transaction will be subdivided and classified into different phases according to their evolution over the period under observation (Picot, 1982). Seven steps can be well-defined:

> Before a transaction can take place, certain preparations have to be made. To initiate a bank transfer or a stock purchase, all necessary information has to be collected. This phase is called "information seeking." Afterwards, the form has to be completed ("preparation") by the customer. All details have to be checked ("review") before the instructions are forwarded ("transmission") from the customer to the financial institution. The latter has to verify the given data ("inspection") and starts processing the task. Subsequently, an order confirmation is generated and transmitted back to the customer ("confirmation"). The transaction is terminated when the customer has received this piece of information and checked all of the particulars ("final checkup") (p.270).

Modes of Coordination

The model differentiates between seven modes of coordination. Each transaction can be arranged in a traditional way by visiting a bank. Another possibility offered by most European commercial banks is to send in a request by mail. Using a telephone to transmit the required information, utilizing facsimile communication or interactive video-text services are additional options. As a result of extensive technological progress, online processing and mobile processing of transactions via the Internet is commonly used nowadays.

Traditionally, a customer visits his bank during its office hours from time to time. He has to leave his home to get there, and typing errors may occur while completing the form manually. If he has to queue at the counter before it is his turn, the transaction may be very time-consuming. The confirmation of the order completion will be received at the next visit to the bank. A second alternative would be to post the order form by mail. Even though there is still no device to protect a customer from typos, informal language and errors, there is no need for him to go to his bank (which may be located far away) at a certain time: The next postbox will do. A confirmation of the order completion will also be received by mail several days later. By accomplishing a transaction via telephone it is not necessary for a bank customer to leave his home anymore. Although it may be more difficult to collect all information and to prepare the order, the transmission itself and the generation of the order confirmation is partially automated and comparatively fast. Telephone circuits can be used to transmit facsimiles and to receive information via faxback, too. Most European banks offer or have offered this option for certain groups of customers. No matter whether the order form is drawn up manually or by using a computer, the bank has to review all instructions and enter them into the system.

BTX is the German version of interactive video-text. With regard to the stock market, it is possible to receive and realize up-to-date market prices and to interact spontaneously. Other information can be acquired easily and fast in comparison to the media mentioned above, and error messages will occur in the case of typos in the electronic order form. By using a computer with a connection to the Internet, a customer can initiate transactions at home and is not restricted to office hours any longer. Typos and other errors will usually be reported before the order form is transmitted electronically. The exchange of information takes place instantly, the confirmation of the order completion will be generated and received directly after the acknowledgement on the part of the bank. Most services mentioned in the context of an online transaction are available for mobile devices, too. The crucial advantage is the stand-alone aspect: No other equipment is needed to seek information and to interact rapidly with markets from almost any location at any time.

The verbal description of these reflections can be transformed into a qualitative ranking on an ordinal scale. The matrix (Table 1) summarizes the potential relative reduction of transaction costs and illustrates which technology has the largest impact on the process described.

Table 1. Simple matrix for the phases in the transaction process and the mode of accomplishment

No.	Phase	Manual	Mail	Phone	Fax	BTX	Online	Mobile
1.	Information Seeking	0	0	0	0	+ + +	+ + + +	+ + + + +
2.	Preparation	0	0	-	-	0	+ + + + +	+ + + +
3.	Review	0	0	+	0	+ + +	+ + + +	+ + + + +
4.	Transmission	0	+	+ + +	+ +	+ + + +	+ + + +	+ + + + +
5.	Inspection	0	0	+	0	+ + + + +	+ + + + +	+ + + + +
6.	Confirmation	0	+	+ + +	+ +	+ + + +	+ + + +	+ + + + +
7.	Final Checkup	0	0	0	0	0	0	0

Enhancements of the Model

Although this table already reveals potential benefits and disadvantages of certain technologies, its explanatory power is limited to ordinal statements. Assuming that the chosen type of transaction costs can be measured on a relational scale, the values above can be transformed into numerical values. Thus it is possible to introduce a simple scoring model and to deduce more tangible conclusions than those derived from these first ordinal assessments.

The aggregated value (AV) of a mode will be defined as the sum of all allocated part values (PV) multiplied by their weightings (w). Each part value ranges from 0 to 1 and all part values together sum up to 1. Below the formal description of the basic model is given:

$$\textbf{(II)} \ AV_j = \sum_{i=1}^{m} PV_{ij} \times w_i$$

$$\textbf{(II)} \ 0 \le w_i \le 1$$

$$\textbf{(II)} \ \sum_{i=1}^{m} p_i = 1$$

The assumption is made that there are equal occurrences of transaction costs for bank transfers and stock exchanges. No matter which of the two transactions is investigated in the model, the same amount of costs (or reduction of transaction costs) is measured for each combination of mode of coordination and phase of the transaction. In more precise terms, the difference between a bank transfer and a stock purchase is the importance of the specific phase in the evolution of the transaction as a whole. This is taken into account by weighting the different steps according to their relevance in the transactional process. Thus it is crucial for an order to be transmitted to the stock market immediately, whereas a bank transfer may even take one more day without serious consequences. Table 2 gives an overview of all assigned weightings.

Table 2. Phases in the transaction process and weightings for bank transfers and stock purchases

No.	Phase	Weighting (Bank Transfer)	Weighting (Stock Purchase)
1.	Information Seeking	10%	20%
2.	Preparation	15%	5%
3.	Review	15%	5%
4.	Transmission	20%	30%
5.	Inspection	10%	5%
6.	Confirmation	20%	30%
7.	Final Checkup	10%	5%

Table 3. Enhanced matrix concerning stock purchases for the phases in the transaction process and the mode of accomplishment

No.	Phase	Manual	Mail	Phone	Fax	BTX	Online	Mobile	Weighting
1.	Information Seeking	0	0	0	0	3	4	5	10%
2.	Preparation	0	0	-1	-1	0	5	4	15%
3.	Review	0	0	1	0	3	4	5	15%
4.	Transmission	0	1	3	2	4	4	5	20%
5.	Inspection	0	0	1	0	5	5	5	10%
6.	Confirmation	0	1	3	2	4	4	5	20%
7.	Final Checkup	0	0	0	0	0	0	0	10%
I.	Sum (AV)	0.00	0.40	1.30	0.65	2.85	3.85	4.35	
II.	Potential Relative Reduction of TAC	0%	9%	30%	15%	66%	89%	100%	

Table 4. Enhanced matrix concerning stock purchases for the phases in the transaction process and the mode of accomplishment

No.	Phase	Manual	Mail	Phone	Fax	BTX	Online	Mobile	Weighting
1.	Information Seeking	0	0	0	0	3	4	5	20%
2.	Preparation	0	0	-1	-1	0	5	4	5%
3.	Review	0	0	1	0	3	4	5	5%
4.	Transmission	0	1	3	2	4	4	5	30%
5.	Inspection	0	0	1	0	5	5	5	5%
6.	Confirmation	0	1	3	2	4	4	5	30%
7.	Final Checkup	0	0	0	0	0	0	0	5%
I.	Sum (AV)	0.00	0.60	1.85	1.15	3.40	3.90	4.70	
II.	Potential Relative Reduction of TAC	0%	13%	39%	24%	72%	83%	100%	

For instance, information seeking and a rapid transmission to the financial institution involved as well as a quick confirmation of a completed transaction is much more important for stock purchases than for bank transfers. The latter may even take several days before the final completion without serious consequences for any party.

Now that all necessary steps have been taken, the scoring model can be applied using all assigned values and weightings. Advantages, restrictions and required technological devices are summarized in one new enhanced matrix for each transaction (Tables 3 and 4), and each combination of a transactional phase and a mode of coordination has been assessed and evaluated.

The total number of points acquired in the scoring model will finally be the basis for additional conclusions on the relative percentages of potential reductions of transaction costs.

Session costs and insurance costs will always be limiting factors in mobile banking deployment. Similar restrictions could be found for any other mode of coordination mentioned in the chapter. Therefore, all reasoning is done on a relative basis. At this point, the assumption is made that there is no relative reduction of transaction costs if a transaction is accomplished in the traditional way without the use of technology (i.e., a manual transaction). Using the most sophisticated medium at a given point of time (i.e., mobile devices), a potential relative reduction of 100% can be achieved in comparison to the remaining media. Specific potential relative reductions of transaction costs can now be derived for all other modes in between.

Premises and Hypotheses

As models are created to simplify and to explain real coherences or circumstances, premises may not be neglected. In this case, several simplifications have to be made:

- There are only the seven ways mentioned above to accomplish the transaction
- There is an absence of progress or new trends at the chosen point of time
- The same medium is used during the whole transaction process
- There are only two parties engaged, the bank and its customer
- The technical infrastructure has already been acquired and established
- The final result of each process is the same

In addition, several hypotheses are introduced, some of which will be referred to and tested later on:

- There has been an enormous increase in the use of information and communication technology in the last decade
- For this reason business processes have changed to a great extent
- For a national economy, the requirement for electronic commerce is the diffusion of information and communication technology
- Customers act in a rational way and prefer those modes of coordination which help to decrease the amount of accruing transaction costs
- Financial institutions are aware of these changes and the potential reduction of transaction costs, and they offer new modes of interaction for their customers
- Relative reductions of transaction costs are decisive for the development and the use of a new mode of transaction as well as the diffusion rates of the underlying technologies

Criticism

The cost model developed in this section is limited to investigating and determining transaction costs for a chosen area and for specific transactions only. Conclusions about the amount of a reduction cannot be automatically transferred to other situations, and there are several premises constraining its explanatory power. Furthermore, the utilized scope of "transaction costs" involves monetarily measurable parts as well as non-monetary components. As the deduction of reductions of transaction costs has been conducted by the verbal description of processes, these steps may not be easy to comprehend, nor unambiguous. As a matter of fact, two major weaknesses of any scoring model are the assigned weights which can hardly be objectified and the compensatory effects which may result from adding up all part values. Nevertheless, these aspects apply for all different modes of transaction that have been investigated in this context. Consequently, the scoring model enables comparative analysis to be carried out for different modes of coordination. Changing the assigned values in a reasonable way neither affects the general assessment of a single transaction in a significant way nor does it have an impact on the general conclusions derived.

Empirical Considerations

Transaction costs have been surveyed indirectly in the cost model by comparing different institutional designs. A similar approach will be taken in this section. Due to the lack of data concerning the number and the volume of transactions actually accomplished, further investigations will focus on the analysis of potential transactions in most areas. Therefore, infrastructure facilities and institutional as well as technical requirements will be reviewed for Germany.

The diffusion rates of certain underlying technologies which are necessary for electronic transactions will give an idea of the resulting potential relative reductions of transaction costs. Several regression models will be introduced and used to describe actual trends and developments. The coefficient of determination (r^2) serves as a measure to test the quality of the applied model.

With regard to the banking sector, it is important to note that there has been a permanent decrease in the number of commercial banks and branch offices in Germany over the last twenty years (Figures 1 and 2).

From 1990 (4,711 institutions) to 2001 (2,696 institutions) there has been a decrease in the number of commercial banks of about 42%. The regression model for this period predicts 2,087 institutions in 2010:

$$f(x) = -107,736x + 218635,905 \text{ and } r^2 = 0.9344$$

Figure 1. Number of commercial banks in Germany, 1980-2001

Figure 2. Regression models for the number of commercial banks in Germany, 1980-2001

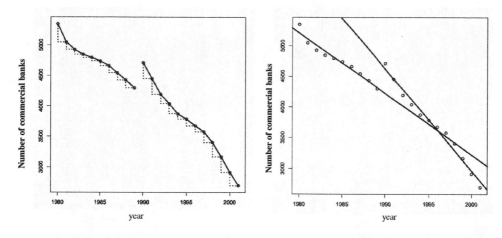

As shown in Figure 3 and 4, for this reason the number of inhabitants per commercial bank has steadily increased (from 1,375 inhabitants in 1981 to 1,880 inhabitants in 2001).

Using the regression model for the period from 1993 to 2001, this number will have reached 2,199 by 2010:

$$f(x)=41.517x-81249.894 \text{ and } r^2=0.9252$$

Figure 3. Development of inhabitants per commercial bank in Germany, 1980-2001

Figure 4. Regression model for the development of inhabitants per commercial bank in Germany, 1980-2001

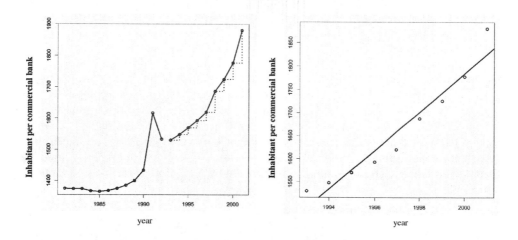

Figure 5. Development of telephone
mainlines in Germany, 1980-2001

Figure 6. Personal computers per
Internet User in Germany, 1991-2001

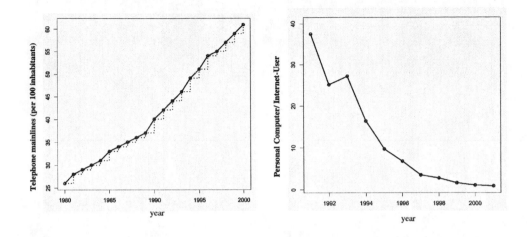

Another indicator for the emergence of new technologies and the use of electronic commerce is the number of telephone mainlines per inhabitant. These are required for transactions via phone or fax and can be used to access the Internet. The number has increased from 26 in 1980 to 61 in 2000 (Figure 5).

$$f(x)= 1.779x -3499 \text{ and } r^2=0.9812$$

The number of Internet users in Germany has grown from 0.3% in 1991 to more than 36% in 2000. Today, more than one third of the population browses the net regularly or at least from time to time. This fact and the enormous growth rate create a considerable potential of customers which may accomplish bank transfers and stock purchases in the future.

The development of the number of personal computers per 100 inhabitants in Germany since 1990 can be approximated by another linear regression model:

$$f(x)= 0.1398x -276,1 \text{ and } r^2=0.9877$$

A comparison between these data and the number of people browsing the Net may be even more interesting. Figure 6 relates the number of available personal computers to the number of Internet users. The latter increases much faster because not every single Internet user owns a personal computer, several individuals can use one device to get access to the Internet, and it is now possible to be connected via PDA (personal digital assistant) or mobile phone, which are commonly used. The increase of mobile phones per 100 inhabitants in Germany can be approximated by the following regression model:

$$f(x)=0.45405x-904.25649 \text{ and } r^2=0.9863$$

Figure 7. Number of online accounts in Germany, 1995-2001

Figure 8. Regression model for the number of online accounts in Germany, 1995-2001

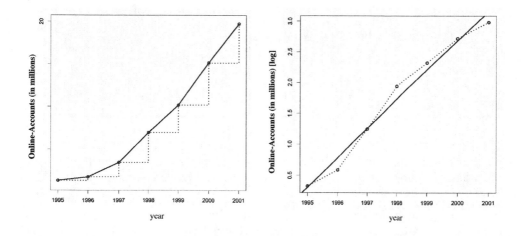

The number of online accounts has been increasing considerably over the past years as the cost model has predicted (Figures 7 and 8). As bank transfers are highly standardized and common transactions, they are processed via new media more and more often:

$$f(x)=0.47462x-946.55059 \text{ and } r^2=0.9766$$

Figure 9 displays the development of German security accounts. Figures on how these accounts are administered have not been available. Since 1995, the number has increased from about 16 million to 34 million. As the value of r^2 indicates, the regression model does

Figure 9. Number of security accounts in Germany, 1995-2000

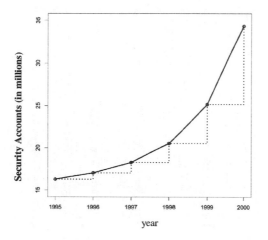

not describe current developments very well in this case, but the figures definitely reveal an increasing interest in stocks and in the capital market. Most of the newly established accounts are probably governed online or by using mobile devices:

$$f(x)=0.14315x-282.88639 \text{ and } r^2=0.8686$$

Future Trends

The increasing use of information and communication technology as the most important requirement for electronic commerce has been documented in the last section. Most of the predictions and hypotheses which could be derived from the cost model have been tested, at least for Germany.

It has been pointed out that the banking sector is facing dramatic changes and that the required infrastructure is constantly being improved. More and more individuals are utilizing information and communication technology to change their way of executing transactions—in financial services as well as in other economic areas. At present it is possible to realize relative reductions of transaction costs of 89% by using online banking instead of accomplishing a bank transfer in a traditional way, and to realize a reduction of 83% by switching to online brokerage for stock purchases. Transaction costs which commonly arise from the interface between a financial institution and its customers are crucial. But the success of a new mode of transaction does not solely depend on reductions of transaction costs: The diffusion rate of the underlying

Figure 10. Four quadrant scheme for the classification of present and future impacts of electronic commerce on financial services

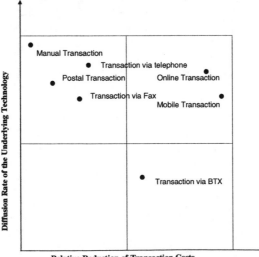

technology is another key aspect. To enable further predictions of sectoral trends and tendencies, all modes of coordination referred to are finally classified in a four-quadrant scheme to illustrate present and future impacts of electronic commerce on financial services (Figure 10).

Postal transactions and transactions via fax are inferior to other modes and will soon be negligible. In Germany, BTX has already merged with online and Internet services. Manual transactions will decrease, but they will still remain very commonly executed. Until new modes of transacting are developed and accepted, online and mobile transactions will continue to dominate other forms in this sector and gain even more importance.

Referring again to the famous study by North and Wallis (1986), it should be underlined that transaction costs are of extreme importance nowadays and that they have been increasing significantly over the last decades. This applies to a national economy as a whole as well as to specific economic areas. The increase originates from the growing complexity of business processes and transactions, the high level of the division of labour and the growing number of possibilities to act and to interact in general. By using Electronic Commerce instead of the so-called "traditional ways" of interaction, these costs can be reduced and limited to a great extent, depending on the specific mode of coordination. In the future, reductions of transactions costs will be made possible by the spread and the use of new technologies and modern communication and information facilities, i.e., by the development and the extension of an adequate technological infrastructure. However, it will have to be an issue of further investigation to what extent these costs can be reduced and in which areas new transaction costs will arise. Differences in the development of certain countries and of specific sectors will then help to illustrate and to understand the complex impacts of ICT.

Conclusions

The model developed in this chapter intends to explain how transaction costs can be reduced by the use of electronic commerce and its underlying technologies. Its academic background is the Theory of New Institutional Economics. Quantifying these costs and the potential reductions of transaction costs in an absolute way has not been possible in this context. Nevertheless, by comparing alternative institutional methods (Williamson, 1985) of accomplishing the same transaction, the model is able to illustrate specific trends and general tendencies in the banking sector under certain premises. At present, transactions which are accomplished by using mobile devices lead to a maximal relative reduction of transaction costs, and newer modes of transacting dominate traditional methods from this particular point of view. Some of these older forms have already been discontinued whereas others may not disappear completely from business life. But provided that all individual participants act in a rational way, they should lose more and more of their former importance.

Hopefully, new quantitative as well as qualitative indicators will be developed in the future to assess the emergence and the amount of transaction costs in a national economy as well as for specific enquiries. For this purpose, information and communication technology itself should contribute to a significant extent by making it possible to acquire, process and analyse relevant data.

References

Arrow, K. J. (1969). The Organization of Economic Activity: Issues Pertinent to the Choice of Market Versus Nonmarket Allocation. In The Analysis and Evolution of Public Expenditure: The PPB system. Vol. 1 U.S. Joint Economic Committee, 91st Congress, 1st Session. Washington D.C.: U.S. Government Printing Office, 59-73.

Bössmann, E. (1983). Unternehmen, Märkte, Transaktionskosten - Die Koordination ökonomischer Aktivitäten. *Wirtschaftswissenschaftliches Studium, 12*, 105-111.

Burgelmann, R. A. (1984). Designs for Corporate Entrepreneurship in Established Firms. *California Management Review, 26*, 154-166.

Büschgen, H. E. (1998). *Bankbetriebslehre: Bankgeschäfte und Bankmanagement.* Wiesbaden: Gabler.

Chandler, A. D. (1977). *The Visible Hand - The managerial Revolution in American Business.* Cambridge: Belknap Press.

Choi, S. Y, Stahl, D. O. and Whinston, A. B. (1997). *The Economics of Electronic Commerce–The Essential Economics of doing Business in the Electronic Marketplace.* Indianapolis, IN: Macmillan Technical Publishing.

Clark, C. (1957). *The Conditions of Economic Progress 2.* London: Macmillan.

Clement, M., Geißler, J. and Schneider, I. (2000). Mobile Commerce. In S. Albers (Ed.), *Marketing mit interaktiven Medien.* Frankfurt: FAZ.

Coase, R. H. (1937). The Nature of the Firm. *Economica, 4*, 386-405.

Coase, R. H. (1960). The Problem of Social Cost. *Journal of Law and Economics, 3*, 1-44.

Commons, J. R. (1932). The Problem of correlating Law, Economics, and Ethics. *Wisconsin Law Review, 8*, 3-26.

Commons, J. R. (1950). *The Economics of Collective Action.* Madison, WI: University of Wisconsin Press.

Commons, J. R. (1990). *Institutional Economics - Its place in Political Economy I.* New Brunswick, CT: Transaction Publishers.

Demsetz, H. (1968). The Cost of Transacting. *Quarterly Journal of Economics, 82*, 33-53.

Eissrich, D. and Frambach, H. (1998). *Zum Verständnis des Transaktionskostenbegriffs in der Ökonomischen Theorie.* Wuppertal: Arbeitspapiere des Fachbereichs Wirtschaftswissenschaft.

EITO/EEIG. (2001). *European Information Technology Observatory - Yearbook for the Information and Communication Industry.* Mainz: Eggebrecht.

EITO/EEIG. (2002). *European Information Technology Observatory - Yearbook for the Information and Communication Industry*. Mainz: Eggebrecht.

Furubotn, E. G. and Pejovich, S. (1972). Property Rights and Economic Theory - A Survey of Recent Literature. *Journal of Economic Literature, 10*, 1137-1162.

Goldberg, V. P. (1976). Toward an Expanded Economic Theory of Contract. *Journal of Economic Issues, 10*, 1025-1028.

Kaas, K. P. and Fischer, M. (1993). Der Transaktionskostenansatz. *Wirtschaftswissen schaftliches Studium, 22*, 686-693.

Kiwit, D. (1994). Zur Leistungsfähigkeit neoklassisch orientierter Transaktions kostenansätze. *ORDO, 45*, 105-134.

Klein, B., Crawford, R. G. and Alchian, A. A. (1978). Vertical Integration, Appropriable Rents, and the Competitive Contraction Process. *Journal of Law and Economics, 21*, 297-326.

Michaelis, E. (1985). *Organisation unternehmerischer Aufgaben - Transaktionskosten als Beurteilungskriterium*. Frankfurt: Lang.

Niehans, J. (1987). Transaction Costs. In J. Eatwell, M. Milgate & P. Newman (Eds.), *The New Palgrave - A Dictionary of Economics*. London: Macmillan.

North, D. C. (1986). The New Institutional Economics. *Journal of Institutional and Theoretical Economics, 142*, 676-679.

North, D. C. and Wallis, J. J. (1986). Measuring the Transaction Sector in the American Economy. In S. L. Engerman & R. E. Gallmann (Eds.), *Long-Term Factors in American Economic Growth*. Chicago: University of Chicago Press.

North, D. C. and Wallis, J. J. (1994). Integrating Institutional Change and Technical Change In Economic History - A Transaction Cost Approach. *Journal of Institutional and Theoretical Economics, 150*, 609-624.

Osterheld, I. (2001). *Transaktionskostenrechnung und Unternehmensstrategie*, Wiesbaden: Gabler.

Ostrom, E. (1990). *Governing the Commons*. Cambridge: Cambridge University Press.

Ouchi, W. G. (1980). Markets, Bureaucracies, and Clans. *Administrative Science Quarterly, 25*, 129-141.

Picot, A. (1982). Transaktionskostenansatz in der Organisationslehre. *Die Betriebswirtschaft, 42*, 267-284.

Picot, A., Reichwald, R. and Wigand, R. T. (2001). *Die grenzenlose Unternehmung - Information, Organisation und Management*. Wiesbaden: Gabler.

Raab, U. H. (1995). *Öffentliche Transaktionskosten und Effizienz des staatlichen Einnahmesystems*, Berlin: Duncker & Humblot.

Richter, R. and Furubotn, E. G. (1996). *Neue Institutionenökonomik*. Tübingen: Mohr.

Schumpeter, J. A. (1987). *Theorie der wirtschaftlichen Entwicklung*, Berlin: Duncker & Humblot.

Thiele, M. (1994). Neue Institutionenökonomik. *Das Wirtschaftsstudium, 23*, 993-997.

Wegehenkel, L. (1980). *Transaktionskosten, Wirtschaftssystem und Unternehmertum*, Tübingen: Mohr.

Williamson, O. E. (1979). Transaction Cost Economics: The Governance of Contractual Relations. *Journal of Law and Economics, 19*, 1537-1568.

Williamson, O. E. (1985). *The Economic Institutions of Capitalism*. New York: Free Press.

Williamson, O. E. (1989). Transaction Cost Economics. In R. Schmalensee and R. Willig (Eds.), *Handbook of Industrial Organization, I*, Amsterdam: North Holland.

Williamson, O. E. (1990). A Comparison of Alternative Approaches to Economic Organization. *Journal of Institutional and Theoretical Economics (JITE), 146*, 61-71.

Williamson, O. E. (1998). The Institutions of Governance. *American Economic Review, 88*, 75-79.

Windsperger, J. (1983). Transaktionskosten in der Theorie der Firma. *Zeitschrift für Betriebswirtschaftslehre, 53*, 889-903.

Appendix

Table 5. Number of commercial banks and inhabitants per commercial Bank in Germany (From Deutsche Bundesbank, 2002, Monthly Statistics and Reports on Banking, 1980-2001)

Year	Number of Commercial Banks in Germany	Inhabitants per Commercial Bank in Germany
2001	2,696	1,880
2000	2,912	1,777
1999	3,168	1,725
1998	3,404	1,687
1997	3,578	1,620
1996	3,675	1,593
1995	3,785	1,570
1994	3,872	1,548
1993	4,038	1,530
1992	4,191	1,533
1991	4,451	1,617
1990	4,711	1,433
1989	4,297	1,400
1988	4,429	1,385
1987	4,543	1,375
1986	4,662	1,368
1985	4,739	1,365
1984	4,798	1,367
1983	4,848	1,374
1982	4,930	1,374
1981	5,052	1,375
1980	5,355	n.a.

Table 6. Number of telephone mainlines in Germany (From Eurostat, 2002, Database NEW CRONOS, Table TEL4)

Year	Number of Telephone Mainlines in Germany	Number of Telephone Mainlines per 100 Inhabitants in Germany
2000	50,220,000	61
1999	48,300,000	59
1998	46,530,000	57
1997	45,200,000	55
1996	44,200,000	54
1995	42,000,000	51
1994	39,900,000	49
1993	37,500,000	46
1992	35,800,000	44
1991	33,700,000	42
1990	32,000,000	40
1989	28,847,800	37
1988	27,823,200	36
1987	27,007,100	35
1986	26,189,300	34
1985	25,391,800	33
1984	24,420,600	31
1983	23,385,600	30
1982	22,571,600	29
1981	21,645,900	28
1980	20,535,000	26

Table 7. Number of personal computers in Germany (From Eurostat, 2002, Database NEW CRONOS, Table PC1)

Year	Number of Personal Computers in Germany	Number of Personal Computers per 100 Inhabitants in Germany
2001	29,000,000	35.3
2000	27,640,000	33.6
1999	24,400,000	29.7
1998	22,900,000	27.9
1997	19,600,000	23.9
1996	17,100,000	20.9
1995	14,600,000	17.9
1994	12,300,000	15.1
1993	10,200,000	12.6
1992	8,800,000	11
1991	7,500,000	9.4
1990	6,500,000	8.2

Table 8. Number of internet users in Germany (From Eurostat, 2002, Database NEW CRONOS, Table INTERN2)

Year	Number of Internet Users in Germany	Number of Internet Users per 100 Inhabitants in Germany
2001	30,000,000	36.5
2000	24,000,000	29.2
1999	14,400,000	17.6
1998	8,100,000	9.9
1997	5,500,000	6.7
1996	2,500,000	3.1
1995	1,500,000	1.8
1994	750,000	0.9
1993	375,000	0.5
1992	350,000	0.4
1991	200,000	0.3

Table 9. Mobile Phones per 100 Inhabitants in Germany (From Eurostat, 2002, Database NEW CRONOS, Table TEL4)

Year	Mobile Phones per 100 Inhabitants in Germany
2000	59
1999	29
1998	17
1997	10
1996	7
1995	5
1994	3
1993	2
1992	1
1991	1

Table 10. Number of online accounts in Germany (From Homepage of the BDB, 2002, http://www.bdb.de/pic/artikelpic/062002/19-06-2002-Entwicklung-Onlinekonten 2001.pdf)

Year	Number of Online Accounts in Germany
2001	19,740,000
2000	15,130,000
1999	10,160,000
1998	6,960,000
1997	3,480,000
1996	1,800,000
1995	1,390,000

Table 11. Number of security accounts in Germany (From Homepage of the BDB, 2002, http://www.bdb.de/pic/artikelpic/122001/TzZ_Depots.pdf)

Year	Number of Security Accounts in Germany
2000	34,332,000
1999	25,194,000
1998	20,586,000
1997	18,304,000
1996	17,063,000
1995	16,303,000

Chapter V

The Spreading Use of Digital Cash and Its Problems

Yutaka Kurihara
Aichi University, Japan

Abstract

It has been several years since the words "digital cash" and other related terms were introduced. Although e-commerce has been growing, digital cash has not been a focus of much attention. Digital cash has some problems associated with it that need to be solved before its use can continue to grow. There are two points the author emphasizes in this chapter. The first is that the essential characteristics of digital cash, its advantages and disadvantages, should be carefully examined. The second point is since financial institutions cannot stop this trend, it would be prudent for them to view it as a business opportunity. Monetary authorities should pay careful heed to the trend as well, guiding the "sound" market to maturity, taking care not to exercise excessive intervention.

Introduction

It has been several years since the words "digital cash," "e-money," "e-cash," and other related terms were introduced to the modern lexicon. Needless to say, the progress made in communication and information technology has been very rapid, and the area of digital cash is no exception. The volume of such transactions is rising, yet there has been little analysis of this revolution in payment, particularly in academic fields. Investigating the influence and problems of this trend is an inevitable and important task, not only from a practical standpoint but from a theoretical one as well.

Although e-commerce has been growing rapidly and attracting much attention, digital cash has not been a focus of such attention. Digital cash has some problems associated with it that need to be solved before its use can continue to grow, and the rate of growth is slowing at present. We can say that digital cash is not used in practice. The logic behind replacing cash, checks and magnetic credit cards with digital cash is bound to prevail in the end but there are many barriers that need to be overcome.

In the past, I have classified digital cash into an electronic wallet type and an online type.[1] I then proposed that material cost reduction and service price cutting[2] were the resultant factors of the demand for electronic wallet transactions and the means by which digital cash could spread, the technology of IC card reformation could develop, and price cutting on the supply side could occur. The popularization of the personal computer and the Internet has also prevailed, as well as the stabilization in demand of Internet-based commercial dealings as a key factor of development for online transactions on the demand side. General price decline for media equipment, typically computers, has been ongoing as well, helping to promote the online-type transaction at the supply side.

It is said that electronic commerce in the United States more than tripled from 1997 to 1999. Moreover, it seems that the spread of mobile telecommunications such as cellular phones contributed to the development of digital cash. In the near future, television, etc., will be used to make transactions. IT (information technology) has undergone a global revolution in many fields. Ubiquitous instruments in IT fields appeared recently, allowing for digital cash to develop much further.

The purpose of this chapter is to analyze the inter-relational characteristics of digital cash, financial institutions, and financial authorities. Section 2 specifies the definition of digital cash, including a new payment instrument, the debit card. Section 3 investigates the advantages and the disadvantages of digital cash. Here I will address the problematic aspects of digital cash that have been clarified through our ongoing experiments and that are observable in society at large. Section 4 considers the connection between digital cash and the financial institution. In section 5, I analyze the relationship of digital cash to monetary policy and the decision making of the policy authorities. Finally, section 6 is a brief conclusion.

What is Digital Cash?

It is difficult to actually define what "digital cash" is. The classification has traditionally been either "IC card type (wallet use)" or "Network type (online use)." The IC card type digital cash has the value in itself, while the network type digital cash is data maintained on a personal computer or host computer (Figure 1). Recently, however, digital cash as a combination of both types has appeared. The distinction between the two is murkier than before.

Pertinent here are two forms of transaction: the "closed loop" and the "open loop." In a closed loop transaction, the transfer of the monetary amount is in the form of digital cash. For instance, a purchaser applies for an issue of funds from a financial institution (typically a bank), the digital cash is electronically transferred as payment for the commodity or service purchased, and the seller (vendor, etc.) settles the transaction at the value paid. This transaction is not transferable to any other users. The tools of the closed-loop transaction are the IC card and network digital cash.

On the other hand, digital cash issued once is susceptible to being reused for subsequent settlements in an open loop where revolving-liquidity exists. This is a pitfall of the IC card

Figure 1. IC card type and network type

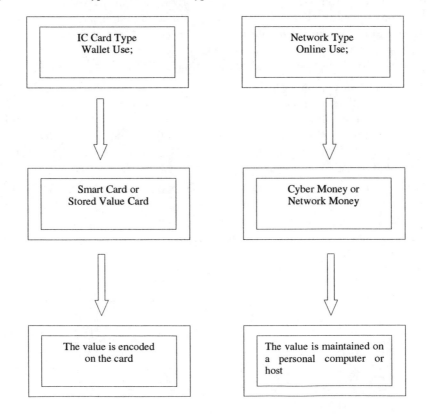

IC Card Type Wallet Use;	Network Type Online Use;
Smart Card or Stored Value Card	Cyber Money or Network Money
The value is encoded on the card	The value is maintained on a personal computer or host

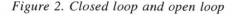

Figure 2. Closed loop and open loop

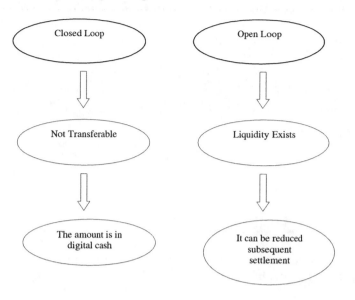

type closed loop transaction that is in the mainstream now (Figure 2). Cash can be reused and divisible much more immediately while collection of non-cash instruments can be delayed when drawn on non-local payer institutions (Hancock and Humphrey, 1998).

It would be worth pausing to consider whether digital cash is truly money. Though credit cards, checks, debit cards, etc., have become remarkably widespread for making payments in electronic form, the differences between these and digital cash are important ones (BIS, 1996). A lot of people are using a new batch of credit cards that can be acquired online (Tringham, 2000). Such financial tools should not be classified as digital cash, and from the standpoint of monetary policy the distinction is particularly important.

What I am focusing on here is a form of digital cash that builds information on "pseudo-cash," in other words the digital cash itself, into the card and the network, and transacts with it. The entity of digital cash has these facets: a) a concluded settlement; b) non-specificity (no defined purpose); c) the transfer; d) circulation (freely usable); and e) anonymity. It is necessary to assign a concrete classification to digital cash as a legal financial instrument unique and separate from deposit currency, time deposit, certificate of deposit (CD), trust funds, etc., which must not be classified as digital cash. It follows that the debit card, the pre-paid card, the credit card, and the check as listed above do not fall under the digital cash definition in spite of being traded in electronic form.

The non-specificity of digital cash far exceeds that of other electronic monetary instruments such as pre-paid phone cards. It is inferior to traditional cash and does not exist in closed-loop transactions. The circulation of digital cash also is low now, and it is doubtful whether anonymity exists in the form of currency deposits. Also, digital cash is not under the constraints of the laws governing traditional currency. However, our stated examples fit within the realm of the above-mentioned definition and thus should be classified as digital cash.

Advantages and Disadvantages of Digital Cash

In this section, I analyze the advantages and the disadvantages of digital cash.

Advantages of Digital Cash

It is common knowledge that both types of digital cash have the advantage of reducing the cost, the time, and the human-error risk of transactions for both the payer and the payee.

Santomero and Seater (1996) argued that the amount of pre-paid values stored on (including digital cash) products by households will be functions of the types of consumer goods that can be purchased using them, the availability of terminals that accept them, and the compatibility of competing digital cash products with each other. Furthermore, Kane (1996) reasoned that time-of-day flexibility and the protection from violent crime provided by electronic banking and TV shopping may be desirable services that paper cash transactions simply cannot offer. Kwast and Kennickle (1997) have illustrated that income, financial assets, age, and education all play important roles in determining household use of digital cash products.

Due to the availability of the IC card, we do not need to carry much cash on our person or deal with the annoyance of loose change. The IC-type transaction has the additional merit of transaction privacy.

As for the network type transaction, not having to go to the scene of the purchase is one key advantage. And there is high security against theft or loss. Furthermore, it allows sellers to save on handling costs and increase business opportunities even if they traditionally have a small-scale clientele. Low-cost transactions are highly likely as cross-border business dealings increase. The cost of handling transactions electronically is approaching the level that makes even relatively small purchases with electronic payment means feasible. Such non-paper exchanges can now have a cost advantage over traditional payments.

Also stemming from this would be the proliferation of related commodities such as computers and software, and the creation of a specific demand for such network transaction services.

Banks (2002) defines digital cash as "an electronic currency, created through special software, that can only be used on the Internet." He also says that most online B2C payments are handled through credit cards. Throughout the rest of the world payment methods vary and include electronic payments, direct debits, and credit cards. While this is cost-effective for most transactions, it is not efficient for smaller "micro" transactions.

Disadvantages of Digital Cash

Despite the bright prospects that digital cash can offer, the flip side of the digital coin reveals some serious dilemmas. Here is a list of some important problems.

1) Who pays the cost of a digital cash system?

   The cost of creating digital cash is high (Rosenblum, 1996). Because it is expensive to invest in the advanced technology of the IC cards and equipment and to set up the required minimum infrastructure, the commitment to this mode of transaction must be authentic, official, and for the long term.

2) How are the users protected?

   This is a legal question as well as an "economic and technological" one. A standard has been emerging around the world that in online-type transactions, a debt incurred from the fraudulent use by another person of one's registered identity or account is the sole responsibility of the registered owner[3]. Still, the U.S. Commerce and Trade Code (Title 15, Chapter 41, Subchapter 6, Section 1693g) states that a consumer's liability for an unauthorized transfer shall not exceed a) $50, or b) the monetary amount or value obtained in the unauthorized electronic funds transfer, whichever is less. Japan's commerce code has no equivalent safeguard at present.

3) Problems facing the issuing entity

   What happens when the issuing entity experiences an emergency, along the lines of bankruptcy for instance? In the case of the European Central Bank (ECB), it assumes that the issuance of digital cash is the same as the acceptance of the deposit for those who issue it. Thus the issuing organization should be limited specifically to the financial institution in order to a) defend the settlement system, b) protect the consumer, c) properly execute monetary policy, and d) promote competition. It should be noted that there is some debate within Japan's Ministry of Finance about whether the issue of digital cash should be allowed via other entities as well as traditional financial institutions.

4) Customer selection criteria

   Aspects of customer eligibility could become more technology based. For instance, being unable to use a personal computer could mean being denied certain services. Users need to perform difficult and different procedures in order to participate in it in some cases.

5) How and where would taxes be levied and what would be an appropriate global standard?

   It is feasible that taxation of digital cash could be circumvented. And neither the World Trade Organization nor the U.S. has much will to tax network trading. Elsewhere in the world, the stance on the issue varies.

6)   What could be done to combat high crime?

High crime such as counterfeiting will be significantly more difficult to pursue in the digital financial realm than it has been traditionally (Winer, 2002). At the consumer level as well there are a number of serious security concerns associated with IC-type financial transactions, including the ease with which an IC card can be lost or stolen, not to mention the possibility of its use in cash laundering, which has been noted before. Despite the privacy advantage of using digital cash, IC-type transactions are not all that widespread (Berger et al., 1996). But there is a serious crime risk among network-type transactions because of the sheer volume of them[4].

7)   The issue of user privacy

Privacy is a difficult issue as it is inseparable from security. Hackers have also aimed at collecting information and using it fraudulently. The principal drawback of e-transactions is the lack of privacy features associated with traditional cash transactions. The anonymity that can be achieved by dealing in cash is missing. But blinding causes another problem. How does the bank identify double-spenders if the coin-holder can't be identified? Essentially, the balance between individual financial privacy rights and legitimate law enforcement interests is a problem.

The battle that emerges is between the privacy afforded to a consumer by means of anonymous digital cash verses the desire of law enforcement to ferret out crime. The fact of complete anonymity guarantees that some money laundering will be easier to pull off.

Digital Cash and Financial Institution Management

Many banks in developed countries have adopted several kinds of Internet banking services, and some financial institutions that specialize solely in Internet banking have been established. The possibility of cost reductions in customer services, severe competition, and a rapid increase in consumer use of the Internet have all contributed to the boom in Internet banking[5].

The spread of digital cash is understood to have brought about an evolution in financial settlement. For one thing, no longer do we need to be physically present at a shop or a bank or even an ATM. We are free from having key activities of our daily lives dictated by the hours, the location, and the protocols of the business establishment. In this respect, the advantage of digital cash is substantial, as described in the previous section. Moreover, even with the extra costs of incorporating the system into our financial institutions, economies of scale are such that a broad customer base is assured (Davidson, 1997; Redman, 1997).

Several major companies have announced an interface standard to be used for bank services that is expected to further reduce the construction cost of the digital system. Moreover, a movement to recognize such a global standard is growing in the United

States. I can imagine, then, the possibility that some new types of financial settlements not dealt with by the banks will emerge with the spread of digital cash. In Japan such new transactions are being realized today. With regard to this, non-banking institutions pose a threat to banks and other traditional financial institutions. It is certain at least that the trend will push down cash handling costs (Timewell, 1996), and the following may also develop as symptomatic of financial industry digitization:

1)   Overall decrease in the number of bank branches and staff.

2)   Banks with fewer of their own branches (commercial mega-banks and some trust banks, etc.) have an advantage (Orr, 1997; Cline, 1998).

3)   A reduction in service fees in the case of net settlements or immediate settlements (The Banker, 1997), as well as through use of one's personal computer for banking transactions.

4)   By the acquisition of business information concerning commercial distribution, a bank has the means to create a monopoly.

5)   When institutions other than banks join the settlement network, it increases the possibilities of systemic risk.

6)   Likely to occur are tie-ups with credit-card companies and similar institutions having their own set infrastructures (Business Week, 1995).

7)   Shifts in these types of risks are forecast. Rather than the traditional concerns such as interest rates, liquidity, and market fluctuations being at the center of attention (Basle Commitment on Banking Supervision, 1998), operation risks may become the focus. Having to lower the cost of information acquisition while globalization continues to influence worldwide business trends makes it difficult for banks to establish a central standard of technology and risk-management operations[6].

8)   If competition turns severe, confidence and reputation become more important than before.

Each is trying to provide a better way of streamlining digital payments or replacing cash. Of course, some new trend in the financial realm will have a ripple effect. There is the view that any move to ensure that banks are not deprived of their vested right to profit from certain transactions, for instance, would disturb the development of electronic banking. Paper-based transactions are still the mainstay, according to Humphrey and Pulley (1998), BIS (2000), and Weiner (2000), not only in the United States but in the other countries as well.

Banks have a vested interest in keeping payment systems as slow as possible — the longer money takes to get from one bank account to another, the more use can be made of it. This is why banks are not pioneers when it comes to more efficient ways of making payment. Yet if they do not establish a relationship with the new payment schemes, they risk losing their franchise (Shirreff, 2001).

New banks entered the market for merchant acquisition and a price war broke out, reducing profit margins. All sorts of banks now complete fiercely to act as acquirers for individual traders (Revell, 2001).

Recently, digital cash helps to buoy the current bank merger wave (Solomon, 1999). Mergers may pool risks and make it easier to launch successful credit card or electronic cash operations just by capturing the infancy of less risk.

Digital Cash and Policy Authorities

Digital cash or the Internet payment has excited economists to speculate whether any of the possible forms of money will make the present methods of operating monetary policy impossible or much difficult. It is easy to predict that digital cash will influence policy authorities. However, digital cash is seen as a bank-issued debt, or in other words, a deposit. It circulates under the assumption, the trust, or the guarantee that 100% of it can be converted to cash (a central bank note). The digital cash itself does not possess the finality of the settlement. I doubt that the policy authorities will be greatly influenced by it anytime soon. The mechanism of digital cash essentially is no different than a bank note[7].

How the policy authorities might be influenced by the appearance of digital cash is laid out in the following:

a) **Problem concerning management of the cash supply**

I will discuss this problem in some detail. The debate continues about difficulties managing the cash supply because settlements with deposit currency will decrease as settlements by digital cash increase (BIS, 1996). So there are fears that the function of deposit creation will decrease. However, there would be no change in the cash supply if the issued digital cash were to be converted immediately to traditional currency. Or if non-depository digital cash issuers hold their digital cash in their own checking account, the cash supply will not be altered (Congressional Budget Office, 1996; Hancock and Humphrey, 2000). The problem might instead reside in what the monetary amount is and the length of time it is kept as digital cash. For instance, there would be no change in the multiplier if the digital cash is issued against a bank deposit, but the multiplier increases if digital cash is issued against a treasury bond, for example. Moreover, it's feasible for the multiplier to become unstable at the diffusion interval of digital cash. However, in the case where digital cash is increasingly substituted for paper cash, authorities would better be able to manage high-powered cash. And regarding the national debt as well, it would not be particularly difficult for monetary authorities to gain better control of finances.

Then what would happen relating to deposit payment preparation? The effect of the multiplier exists as long as demand continues for the cash that the central bank issues or prepares for deposit payment. However, as digital cash prevails, the comparative ratio of deposit payment preparations shrinks. Though the spread of digital cash naturally decreases the preparation requirements for payment, the multiplier rises and so does the possibility of the trend having an effect on monetary policy.

There is a possibility that a rise in the inter-bank market interest rate would rise because of a lack of deposit payment preparations. It can also be assumed that the confidence multiplier could expand to infinity, because a legal preparation framework does not currently exist. However, since a) the issuing body handles payment preparation, b) part of it is converted into cash and a deposit, and c) the lending demand is limited, the independent acceleration of such a movement may not occur.

The interest rate elasticity of cash-card substitution is a function of the level of digital cash adoption in the economy and this elasticity is high at low interest rates. This may result in perverse effects from attempts to contract (expand) bank credit and liquidity by raising (lowering) interest rates.

Finally, when the digital currency of one country is converted into the digital currency of another, cash-supply management becomes difficult.

b)   **Problem of cash demand**

The function of cash is as a) a value standard, b) a payment instrument, and c) a stored value. Digital cash is viewed as chiefly functioning as a payment instrument. Tobin's "stock theory" is useful when thinking about this. The cost of going to a bank, changing a deposit into cash, and the cash demand are positively correlated. If I apply this theory, then it follows that digital cash decreases the cash demand. However, it is true that liquidity will rise, so digital cash has the possibility of making the overall cash demand unstable.

The influence of digital cash was considered from the cash-supply side and from the demand side in a) and b) of this section. Then, the shift of the multiplier and the cash demand that may result cannot be predicted accurately. At this time, what should policy authorities do? According to standard economic theory, if the shock of the economic fluctuation is real, stabilizing the amount of the cash supply rather than the interest rate reduces the breadth of the shift in real GDP. Conversely if the shock to the cash demand is large, stabilizing the interest rate rather than the cash supply reduces the change in real GDP (Poole, 1970). Therefore, when an unanticipated cash shock occurs in the market in the guise of digital cash, financial authorities should stabilize the interest rate.

There has been much discussion about whether monetary authorities should give precedence to controlling the cash supply (or the exchange rate) as an intermediate goal over attaining price stability or economic growth. A typical example in which the cash supply has been targeted as the intermediate goal is Germany (Gerlach, 1999). However, if authorities adopted such an approach, their control over the cash supply would disrupt the stable relationship between the cash supply and inflation, and thus economic growth as well. So it appears preferable for monetary authorities to control interest rates instead of the cash supply in the digital cash environment. Woodford (2000) says macro-economic stabilization depends only upon the ability of central banks to control a short-term nominal interest rate.

c)   **Problem of the expansion of foreign currency use**

If part of domestic economic activity is based on foreign currency, its influence, which is conveyed by the domestic currency's short-term interest rate, can pull down the "real economy." Moreover, the influence of monetary policy can become insignificant, being limited to bank lending in domestic currency. Price changes for goods and services provided by foreign countries may influence the domestic economy as well.

The impact on domestic short-term interest rates would not be weak, but would be relatively strong as long as the policy authorities control the "high-powered" money. However, it's possible that the effect of fluctuations in the domestic short-term interest rate on the long-term rate is weakened through arbitrage trading. The mechanism of arbitrage trading buffers itself against much influence from the movements in short-term interest rates. However, this is not limited to the digital cash environment alone.

d)   **Problem of taxation**

Tax evasion and trends toward tax cutting would lead to a decrease in revenue.

e)   **Restrictions and supervisory problems**

Via the Internet, money is easily transferred to and deposited in financial institutions overseas, especially into those countries having few or no regulatory controls. This risks creating the domino effect of currency contagion and transferring some of the corruptive influences of the recipient country to the originating country. Restriction and supervision of such transactions is virtually impossible without the countries' mutual cooperation. Moreover, the individual scope of the financial institutions poses their own problems, since financial systems differ among countries. The problem of the scope of deposit insurance is present as well.

f)   **Problem of cash laundering, etc.**

Government intervention regarding code keys and other transaction aspects may arise. Wanting to adopt such measures is natural for the authorities, but in conflict with the issue of personal privacy (Mester, 2000).

Finally, the authorities lose profit, because cash (not digital cash) is a debt with no interest and the authorities acquire interest from assets. Or the substitution of privately issued digital cash for government-issued currency reduces seignorage[8]. But the pursuit of profit is not their objective, nor is it the goal of the central bank, as the ECB says.

Conclusions

Here I have laid out the advantages and disadvantages of digital cash. It's easy to believe that there are many advantages to promoting digital cash. It also seems that the progress of IT is unstoppable, but fortunately this will make our world a more convenient and efficient place to live.

Nevertheless, there are a number of concurrent problems. None of these challenges are apt to be resolved swiftly and painlessly. I have analyzed these issues not only from the customer standpoint but also regarding financial institutions and authorities.

For financial institutions, this trend cannot be stopped, and so it would be prudent for them to view it as a business opportunity. If they do not find ways to adapt, they will become obsolete and fade away completely from the market. By promoting e-finance, a company can give market share and negotiating power over suppliers, as well as earn a profit. The authorities should pay careful heed as well, guiding the "sound" market to maturity and taking care not to confuse it with excessive intervention. At the same time, they must maintain a sound financial system.

As online marketplaces are created, the choices that are made in their construction will shape the experiences of consumers. To make online shopping more familiar it may be useful to simulate the physical world, to bring into the virtual world analogs of physical objects and spaces. It is also incumbent on those who stand to benefit from e-commerce to make positive efforts to educate both the media and the public regarding e-commerce and its security (Jarupunphol and Mitchell, 2002). Now, many potential participants are reluctant to participate in e-commerce because of payment confidentiality, payment integrity, and payment authorization concerns. Software agents have the potential to take on characteristics of people in the new marketplace.

We cannot turn back now. What we need to do is analyze this trend not just from a practical perspective but also from a theoretical one. Much research ahead is also anticipated within the academic fields.

Endnotes

[1]   In detail, see Kurihara (2000).

[2]   See, for example, U.S. Department of Commerce (1998).

[3]   The settlement service for which insurance is included.

[4]   Counterfeiting has broadened to include digital cash as well as paper cash. And the liquidity, speed and anonymity of digital cash tends to be higher than that of paper cash.

[5]   See, for example, Lubove (1996), U.S. Department of Commerce (1998), and Mackintosh (1999). In Japan it is becoming preferable to avoid low interest rates.

[6]   Salomon (1996) also suggests the possibility that some computer software companies may be competing against financial institutions.

[7]   However, a current system is subject to radical change if it is first established outside of an existing system; for example, a second central bank.

[8]   Lacker (1996) has applied this result in a general equilibrium model.

References

The Banker. (1997, October). Getting smart.

Banks, E. (2002). *E-finance*. Chichester: John Wiley & Sons.

BIS. (1996). Implications for central banks for the development of electronic cash.

BIS. (2000, March). Statistics on payment systems in the Group of Ten countries.

Basle Commitment on Banking Supervison. (1998, March). Risk management for electronic banking and electronic cash activity.

Berger, A. N., Hancock D. and Marquardt, J. C. (1995). A framework for analyzing efficiency, risks costs, and innovations in payment system. *Journal of Cash, Credit and Banking, 6*, 815-830.

Business Week (1995). The future of cash. June 12.

Cline, K. (1998, March/April). The smart card disconnection. *Banking Strategies*.

Congressional Budget Office. (1996). Emerging electronic methods for making payments. Washington, D.C.: U.S. Government Printing Office.

Davidson, S. (1997, April). Survey forecasts retail trends; Banking industry. *American Community Banker, 6(4)*.

Gerlach, S. (1999). Who targets inflation explicitly? *European Economic Review, 43*, 801-813.

Hancock D. and Humphrey, D.B. (1998). Payment transactions, instruments, and systems: a survey. *Journal of Banking and Finance, 21*, 1573-1624.

Humphrey, D. and Pulley, L. (1998, November/December). Unleashing electronic payments. *Banking Strategies*.

Jarupunphol, P. and Mitchell, C.J. (2002). E-commerce and the media – influences on security risk perceptions. In W. Cellary & A. Iyengar, *Internet technologies, applications and social impact*. Boston: Kluwer Academic Publishers.

Kane, E. J. (1996). Comment on alternative monies and the demand for media of exchange. *Journal of Money, Credit and Banking, Part2, 28*, 961-964.

Kurihara, Y. (2000). *Currency integration in the EU* (in Japanese). Japan: The Chunichi Newspaper.

Kwast, M. and Kennickle, A. (1997). Who uses electronic banking? Results from the 1995 survey of consumer finances. Washington D.C.: Division of Research and Statistics, Board of Governors of the Federal Reserve System.

Lacker, J. (1996). Stored value cards: costly private substitutes for government currency. *Federal Reserve Bank of Richmond Economic Quarterly, 82*, 1-25.

Lubove, S. (1996, October). Cyberbanking. *Forbes*.

Mackintosh, J. (1999). Mondex reaches Japanese smart card deal. *The Financial Times*, February 15, 4.

Mester, L. J. (2000, March/April). The changing nature of the payment system: should new players mean new rules? *Business Review (Federal Reserve Bank of Philadelphia)*.

Orr, B. (1997, August). Smaller banks into Internet banking. *ABA Banking Journal*.

Poole, W. (1970). Optimal choice of monetary policy instruments in a simple stochastic macro model. *Quarterly Journal of Economics LXXXIV*, 197-235.

Redman, R. (1997, September). Making a virtual connection. *Bank Systems & Technology*.

Revell, J. (2001). Emerging methods of payment. In P.M. Gardner & P.C. Versluijs, *Banks Strategies and Challenges in the New Europe*. New York: Palgrave.

Rosenblum, H. (1996, *November/October*). Electronic cash: hype and reality. *Banking Strategies*.

Salomon, F. (1996). Opening windows with the internet. *Eurocash*, June 6.

Santomero, A. M. and Seater, J. J. (1996). Alternative monies and the demand for media of exchange. *Journal of Money, Credit and Banking, Part2, 28,* 942-960.

Shirreff, D. (2001). Small change to virtual cash, *The Financial Times*, Jan. 11, 17.

Solomon, E. H. (1999). What should regulators do about consolidation electronic cash? *Journal of Banking and Finance, 23,* 645-653.

Timewell, S. (1996, August). Shopping for cash, *The Banker*.

Tringham, M. (2000). Digital cash catches on. *The Times*, July 28, 30.

U.S. Department of Commerce (1998). The emerging digital economy.

Weiner, S. T. (2000). Electronic payments in the U.S. economy: an overview. *Economic Review (Federal Reserve Bank of Kansas City) 4th Quarter*.

Winer, J. (2002). How to clean up dirty money. *The Financial Times*, March 28, 1.

Woodford, M. (2000). Monetary policy in a world without cash. *NBER Working Paper No.W7853*.

Chapter VI

Electronic Signature:
The Core Legislation Category in Digital Economy

Fjodor Ruzic
Institute for Informatics, Croatia

Abstract

E-Business, as well as all of the active participants in the digital economy environment, raises a host of new legal issues that must cope with the fact that the technical expectations imposed by participation in digital economy will increase. Besides technology implementation, it is evident that the biggest barriers to E-Business today come from the notion that people don't trust the security and authenticity of the E-Business environment. Since the companies doing E-Business activities are not operating in an unregulated world, the old rules still apply in the new digital environment. Considering the functionality and applicability of such issues, this chapter is finding one, generic shaped, key category that links all of the separate E-Business legal issues in one regulated scene – the answer is done by introducing the electronic signature as the equivalent of a hand-written signature no matter what type of information technology is in use. There are more legal environments, solutions and applications of electronic signature from which several examples are described accompanied with the E-Business view on electronic signature utilization.

Background and Introduction to the Digital Economy

Digital economy is the infrastructure development of modern society towards full coverage of information society attributes. Information society is coming through three-revolution convergences:

- digital revolution, that opens the ways for

- economic revolution, that in turn, strengthens

- social revolution.

In the scope of the information society development, the core categories should be recognized, introduced and activated (Castells, 2000). The information society under-lined with information-communications systems' full utilization and knowledge-based economy and social activities, functions just like any society. There is the community of the people that communicate to exchange opinions, knowledge, etc., and act under social rules agreed to by most of its members. Thus, we can acclaim three basic segments of the information society, each of them consisting of one core category:

- infrastructure - telecommunications infrastructure (the members of the society must communicate)

- services - the content (the goal of communications is to transfer the content)

- legislation - *electronic signature* (the goal is to compile rules of intercommunication processes in which the electronic content is interchanged).

E-Business, as well as all of the active participants in the digital economy environment, raises a host of new legal issues which is being driven by four key factors:

- *electronic medium* – doing activities, business in digital form, in real-time over open digital networks without paper or traditional legal and security methods raises new legal issues;

- *geographical constraints* – although a digital economy is not constrained by geographical borders, countries have different laws, languages, cultures;

- *business models* – new ways of doing business electronically in a digital economy environment may present unfamiliar and unknown legal constraints;

- *legislation models* – legislators and courts alike are transforming laws as they struggle to address the features and implications of the digital revolution and digital economy, as well.

All of these facts are considering E-Business systems, too. What makes the positive future scenario of the E-Business systems in the age of the information-communications systems development on which the digital economy is based? It is almost undoubtedly the Web development process, which is on the road in recent days. This development is correlating with the integration of the telecommunications development, content integrity and legislation definition improvements. Most of the new services are Web-based or Web-oriented that makes the clear future for E-Business development in order to fulfill information needs in the modern society.

Information technology is reshaping today's economy and transforming businesses and consumers. This is about more than e-commerce, or e-mail, or e-trades, or e-content. It is about the "e" in economic opportunity that makes the arena for new digital economy. Technology and electronic commerce are changing the way that all industries and companies are doing business. From the automotive industry to the healthcare industry, from banking to retailing, virtually every company is moving quickly to take advantage of the tremendous opportunities offered by doing business electronically.

The e-marketplaces are changing the way business is done, and as they do so the technical demands are increasing. The marketplace would assume the role previously exclusively held by the personal relationship, assessing the reliability and worthiness of potential manufacturers. Products could be triple or quadruple sourced, as desired, provided market liquidity is evident. The time from design to production and shipping could be significantly reduced, thus providing greater agility to respond to changing market conditions or fashion sense, and in an integrated environment could reach right down to the fabric cutting room floor. Thus, ideally, communication is improved, transaction costs reduced, time-to-market is significantly reduced, and the entire process made more fluid and responsive.

Electronic commerce has changed the way business is conducted significantly. Businesses are focusing on conducting as much as possible through the Internet - be it payments of bills or ordering an appliance. For all of these things to happen through the Internet, there is a need for massive infrastructure comprising servers, operating systems, applications, software and the information-communications systems (embedded into Internet terminology). E-Business needs the support services of service providers and communications providers who make things happen through the Internet. Telecommunications technologies like WAP (Wireless Application Protocol), VoIP (Voice over Internet Protocol), have emerged, and many more new technologies are in the E-Business environment. All are occurring before the impact of the existing or previous technology slowly sets in our minds.

Related technology issues for any E-Business environment are faced with:

- *Convergence:* all information appliances will be connected to some version of the Internet. At the same time, the cost of moving people and goods around is going to go up, and the cost of moving information around is going down. The result: a massive restructuring not only of the economy but also of the human landscape.

- *Standardization:* E-Business will operate in a much more open standards world than it has in the last decade. The tremendous private and public investments in Internet technology over the past year also mean that it will be very difficult for any single company to invest sufficiently in research, development and marketing to promote large-scale proprietary standards.

- *Globalization:* E-Business goes to the future of the Internet worldwide, and it's clear that some of greatest impact of information-communications systems will be in developing global E-Business, marketplaces and alliances.

Currently and in nearly future, the critical technologies for E-Business environment are:

- Embedded computing,

- Wireless technology,

- Intelligent agents,

- Open and transparent communications infrastructure,

- Simulation and data visualization.

These constraints reshaped management challenges for most of the subjects acting within the digital economy. New technologies of data visualization, simulation techniques and broadband telecommunications platforms will become important E-Business tools (Volti, 2001). E-mail, networked groupwork and intelligent agents will rise in use among all organizations, improving communication and logistical coordination through an e-logistic environment.

Under these terms exists a new generation of employees and customers who will use information technology and the Internet as part of growing up. Their expectations about media, about service, about communications, and about transactions will be vastly different from a decade ago, and their behavior patterns will turn out to be the biggest surprise that information technology delivers to business in the next century.

And, what are the defining characteristics of E-Business? This is partly defined by the nature of the business activity. Typical features would include:

- A broad range of suppliers and products, with a strong representation of buyers, thus providing a critical mass of participants to establish the market, and the liquidity to buy or sell as needed;

- Well-established technical specifications and requirements for participation in the market;

- Quality assurance for the market, with feedback loops regarding product quality, fulfillment history, and financial transactions;

- Paperless transactions with enforceable legal agreements;

- Online contracts with digital signatures to associate authorized agents with specific documents;

- Security of the market, with strong user authentication, high standards for document integrity, transaction security, and preservation of the privacy of data of the participants.

It is evident that the technical expectations imposed by participation in the digital economy will increase. Businesses with high levels of e-competence will have a competitive advantage over those who do not. What are the requirements for successful participation? The answer will change, from industry to industry, but the minimal requirements would include a strong telecommunications infrastructure, with open Internet connectivity, and routine telecommunications services, along with a commitment to modern technical standards, system security, and *transparent legislation and regulation environment.*

Businesses that offer services and have taken to the Internet seriously have a responsibility to their customers to offer services in a secure manner (Ang, Dubelaar & Lee, 2001). With increasing networks across the globe for mission critical electronic commerce, securing the networks would be the primary focus. Various technologies and concepts is in place such as Virtual Private Networks (VPN), Secure Sockets Layer (SSL), Secure Electronic Transactions (SET) and many more to overcome and mitigate risks of transacting over the Internet. While security of operating systems, applications, physical, logical security are addressed by the respective organizations, the areas that are exposed are the networks and communication lines which leave the organization's gates. *Security* is a fundamental requirement for E-Business applications such as e-mail, purchase orders, the transmission of credit card information and workflow automation using signature-based forms

Secure and Trustworthy E-Business

The unprecedented global growth of the Internet, the promise of E-Business, and the emergence of mobile business have a profound effect upon the way organizations operate. The digital economy, that leverages the benefits of technological convergence and new business models, offers unparalleled advantages for an immense variety of service providers and their customers in the cyber marketplace. Providers see significant economies in operating in an E-Business environment that has global reach, with the prospects of cost reductions being passed on to the customer. Similarly, for online consumers, the Internet offers infinitely expanded buyer information and a range of choices that are daunting to comprehend. However, in spite of these apparent benefits the transition to the digital economy has not been without problems. For many organizations there is continuing uncertainty over which operating model to adopt, and the rather intimidating lessons of some high profile failures. The global E-Business environment will continue to pose difficult and far-reaching management challenges to leaders of online businesses. Some of these challenges are already evident and have a profound effect upon the ways of doing business. Among them, and of paramount importance, is the issue of how E-Business can maximize its value to consumers and simultaneously retain their trust and confidence.

It is evident that the biggest barriers to E-Business today come from the notion that people don't trust the security and authenticity of E-Business environment. Building consumer trust and confidence requires thoughtful analysis of the nature of the relationship between buyers and sellers. This notion is also about privacy in the E-Business environment (E-Privacy). In the context of E-Business, E-Privacy has to be established as a core value that connects organizational culture with the best interests of the consumer. The value of E-Privacy can be viewed as an important indicator of business success. Worldwide, many high profile business failures are attributable to the lack of recognition accorded E-Privacy, and the lack of commitment to it as a consumer issue. The consequences of this oversight can lead to an erosion of consumer loyalty, negative publicity, and the loss of potential business.

When examining barriers to the implementation of E-Business, numerous studies have singled out consumers' lack of trust as a major factor. Some people reduce the trust problem to one of security, arguing that if security issues are resolved, people will be happy to transact online. However, when the trust problem is broken down into its constituents, privacy, ease-of-use or the credibility of information on the Web is revealed to be as important to consumers as security.

As far as the introduction of a new e-payment system is concerned, one should not underestimate the power of the media and reputable institutions in approaching consumers and assuring them of the system's security. Since the average consumer is unlikely to be able to assess the objective security of, say, an encryption algorithm, this issue remains, to a large extent, one of trust – namely trust in familiar information sources. Thus, a well-orchestrated marketing effort would help give consumers enough pre-interactional trust to understand, accept and use the new E-Business system. Thus, security and trust mechanisms inhibit the free flow of business information required to achieve the full potential of business benefits promised by E-Business investments.

Lack of trust is a significant problem for any E-Business – the parties evolved in the E-Business processes must feel trust in the people and companies doing business on the Internet. In many traditional business relationships, trust is based on a combination of judgement or opinion based on face-to-face meetings, or recommendations of colleagues, friends and business partners. However, the E-Business environment generally does not involve human interaction and, therefore, this new context requires a new understanding of trust. Trust must be established and managed continuously in a wide range of E-Business activities.

The basis of trust is in ethics, and the topic is frequently discussed in the context of social and democratic processes (Conte & Castelfranchi, 1995). It is also a fundamental requirement of economic activity where the behavior of people and organizations takes place in conditions of uncertainty (Jones & Wilikens, 2000). When one party is dependent on the behavior of another party, the uncertainties give rise to risks. The notion of trust within an E-Business environment involves having confidence in the other parties, and hence having an expectation that the risks will not result in financial or any other loss.

The specific application of trust in the E-Business environment involves several key factors:

- *Identity:* the ability to identify party, good, service and to locate them in physical space, including identification and location services such as digital certificates;

- *Reputation*, and recommendations from parties who are themselves trusted or experienced; and proxies for reputation, such as brand names and seals of approval;

- *Security* of the E-Business environment including transaction data, integrity, authentication and non-repudiability, secrecy and privacy with alternatives that reduce the risk of data disclosure.

E-Business is generally considered to evidence many of the characteristics that render trust very important. The parties commonly have little or no knowledge of one another. They are also usually in different locations. They therefore cannot depend on physical proximity, handshakes, body-signals, a common legal jurisdiction, or even necessarily a definable jurisdiction.

The context of use and domain of application of the E-Business system being designed should be taken into account. Context of use can be viewed as an important requirement for the design. Different applications require diverse levels of security. Buying food can be done with a credit card with basic cryptographic protection, while electronic banking needs more sophisticated authentication and security mechanisms. Several techniques help in establishing online e-trust:

- Electronic authentication,

- Electronic signature,

- Escrow payment services (online),

- Public Key Infrastructure (PKI).

Trust in E-Business systems is influenced by factors such as anonymity, security, reliability, and the amount of control that parties have, as well as the reputation of the entity that introduces the system. There are a number of guidelines that address the different facets of security required for E-Business systems in the digital economy. Issues of trust and security are connected to exchange, storage and management of business and personal information. These techniques includes basic tasks to be done in order to achieve a secure and trustworthy environment:

- Providing a clear and prominent policy on security with clear visibility of the security techniques employed;

- Explaining security measures in management and storage of the data;

- Establishing a customer support line on security-related issues;

- Supplying regular information updates on changes and upgrades in security;

- Taking into consideration security issues specific to the type of E-Business system;

- Giving users access to their data, allowing them to change it, and timely delete outdated information (it can assist in building trust relations with customers);

- Minimizing the security costs (both financial and temporal) imposed on users;

- Creating a security management culture (by educating employees and implementing strict information handling policies within the company);

- Building a trust policy and trust recovery plan in the event of a security breach likely to undermine trusted relationships with customers.

From the wealth of information that proliferates on the topics of the Internet, or e-commerce specifically, there is a consensus on basic risks. Any transaction or message, financial or otherwise, would be subject to the risks. In an ordinary commerce environment, plenty of avenues are available to address these risks through formal signatures and other mechanisms that would ensure secure transactions. The major risks facing E-Business environment are considering key issues:

- *Identity or authenticity of the person:* Who sent the message? Does the sender have the authority to bind the organization he or she represents?

- *Data Integrity:* Is the message complete or has it been altered? Is it true that the copy of the message has not been altered?

- *Denial of Service:* Launch of an attack which would bring down the service.

- *Non Repudiation:* Proving up the message in court, ensuring that the sender cannot falsely deny sending the message, ensuring that the sender cannot falsely deny the contents of the message.

- *Confidentiality:* Ensuring that information is not disclosed to unauthorized parties.

While E-Business flourishes through the Internet, in the digital world, laws and statutes must be drafted and enacted to resolve disputes amongst parties. Issues will arise in the courts of law whether documents with electronic signatures are valid or otherwise and the extent of reliance that can be placed on the third parties. Any secure transaction is sure to have its share of disputes and losses. These may be due to negligence by one of the third parties or the parties to the transaction, or technological failures or any other reason.

If the information-communications systems are used for day-to-day business and private interests – to buy consumer goods, submit tax forms or to send confidential messages – there will ultimately be the need for a digital identity. Other existing solutions – identification using credit card numbers, etc. – are simply makeshift solutions that are being used temporarily in certain areas. Normally speaking, identity is something very complex. It does not merely refer to name, date of birth, color of eyes and all those other features contained in personal identification documents, but also means a person's entire personality, background and integrity.

Digital identity means considerably less than all these everyday meanings: first of all, that a person owns and uses a digital ID – in other words, an ID expressed in zeros and ones that can be transmitted via the Internet (or any other data network). This ID is digital or is also termed an electronic certificate. It confirms not just name and e-mail address of a person, but may also confirm other information - the name of company where a person is working, etc. – and the validity of the digital signature.

When a machine or a person issues someone with a certificate, this is confirmation of the existence of this person, including the name and one or two other details. This identity is invaluable for the entire digital economy - it forms a foundation for trust. But whether this person is honest, creditworthy or reliable, or whether the machine is operated by a reputable company – i.e., what in fact belongs to identity in a broader sense of the word – remains unknown.

Nevertheless, this manner of ensuring reliability is also indispensable for the digital economy. This is carried out using other means, beyond the scope of electronic signature technologies. In the case of companies with a good Web presence – with a shop system, SSL, credentials, supplier brand, general terms and conditions, quality labels, etc. – this is a good indication of their reliability, and the legislator has provided for legal provisions (remote sales law, EU e-commerce guideline, etc.).

Basic E-Business Legislation and Regulation

Companies doing E-Business activities are not operating in an unregulated world. The old rules still apply in new digital environment. And new statutes and regulations aimed at digital violations are quickly emerging. When it comes to regulations, however, ignorance is not bliss. Advertising, sweepstakes, unsolicited commercial e-mail (Spam), trade regulation compliance, securities laws, tax regulatory compliance, and other regulatory issues all can pose significant challenges for E-Business. Doing E-Business activities in a borderless medium raises special challenges, given that many jurisdictions have inconsistent laws regulating E-Business, e-commerce, e-signatures, etc.

At the core of all of E-Business activities is the fundamental question: "Is it legal?" And the answer to that question will depend on what law applies and how online activities are structured. Yet determining what law applies is easier said than done when transactions are being conducted in what is essentially a borderless medium. At the same time, the Internet is profoundly changing the law that applies to these business activities.

The law that governed our transactions six months ago may not be the law that governs our transactions today or, even if the prior law is still relevant, it may apply in ways we never contemplated because of legal developments in the interim (Zoellick, 2001). Many countries have already enacted numerous statutes and regulations related to some aspect of E-Business activities. In some cases, these laws represent an experiment designed to anticipate and resolve issues that have not yet arisen, and in other cases these laws represent significantly conflicting approaches to a common set of issues.

Some of the outmost areas of regulation and legislation in the digital economy cover several key issues:

- *Electronic Transactions and Contracts (e-commerce):* The electronic communication of documents, as well as electronic advertising, contracting, and payment, are clearly the future of e-commerce. Companies have embraced e-commerce in order to decrease costs, streamline transactions, and increase sales. To really do high-value deals online, however, companies must feel confident that the transactions they enter into today will be legally enforceable and binding tomorrow. In the paper-based world, putting a contract on company letterhead and using ink signatures help to provide that reassurance. Concern over what that means in the digital world has produced an explosion of legislation at national, and international levels.

- *Electronic Finance (services, Tax and Customs):* The proper characterization of a transaction for tax purposes is probably the most difficult issue in the taxation of e-commerce. Nevertheless, characterization is critical to determining how an e-commerce transaction will be treated for income tax and consumption tax (VAT) purposes. Local, national, and international tax authorities and organizations are struggling with these concepts and trying to decide whether new legislation will be needed or whether existing rules can be applied to the new concepts.

- *Intellectual Property Laws (trademarks, copyrights, and patents):* Companies face unprecedented challenges both in protecting their intellectual property worldwide and in minimizing the likelihood that they might be infringing someone else's intellectual property rights (Sang, 2002).

- *Privacy and Personal Data Protection:* Thanks to information-communications systems, it has never been so easy to collect, reproduce, disseminate, and compile personally identifiable information. Organizations have never faced such daunting privacy issues regarding the increasingly indispensable information and, E-Businesses should address the attendant privacy issues in order to avoid legal liability. Given the current media and legal climate, and the fact that electronic communications and technology tracking abilities will only increase in the future, concerns about the privacy of electronic communications are recognized in many countries, and many privacy-related bills are now pending at both the national and international scene.

- *Information Security (Cybersecurity, Cybercrime):* New information and communications technologies give rise to new opportunities for their abuse, which in turn give rise to legal restrictions. This notion arises the need to legislate against a variety of new abuses and frauds – or old frauds committed in new ways. Cyber-crime may cause serious financial damage, and computer-related offences frequently involve more than economic loss. Damage can be a waste of time, or the loss of privacy and security. The most significant harm and danger caused by cyber-crime is the threat of lost reliability and lost trust in cyber-space. There is another aspect of harmful and dangerous activity within E-Business environment – the digital content broadcasting. There is no consensus yet, neither on what kind of content should be prohibited, nor how it can be handled.

- *Consumer Protection:* Considering the functionality and applicability of such issues, it is worthy to find one, generic-shaped, key category that links all of these separate issues in one regulated scene. It is obvious that as a signature means almost everything in the physical world of paper-based business, some kind of the instrument that could ensure security, trust and functionality of E-Business, should be introduced. This issue is considered the core category of any national and international regulation in digital economy – the answer lies with introducing electronic signature equivalence with a hand-written signature no matter what type of information technology is in use.

Electronic Signature as the Core Category in Digital Economy

Background

For E-Business of any kind (private or public sector) to grow, businesses must implement the use of electronic signatures correctly, and legally. With the advent of electronic signatures, E-Business is changing the way we sign and store documents. Thus, any business that wants to succeed in the digital economy must deal with electronic signatures. It is considered an everyday activity whenever a law or other arrangement requires a signature of a person. A signature is needed as a medium for authentication in order to identify the person (the signer), to indicate the person's approval of the information communicated and, to be legally applicable.

Whether captured on paper or electronically, a signature has a specific legal definition and purpose. The Commercial Codes (the laws adopted by most countries to govern commercial transactions) defines a document that is "signed" as one that includes any name, word, mark, or symbol executed or adopted by a party with the present intention to authenticate the writing. A signature usually serves several purposes, including authentication and attribution of a document to its signer, a reminder of the significance of the document, evidence that the signer intended the signed document to have legal effect, and an indication that the signed document was intended to be the final version.

In today's digital economy environment, establishing a framework for the authentication of computer-based information requires a familiarity with concepts and professional skills from both the legal and computer security fields. Combining these two disciplines is not an easy task. Concepts from the information security field often correspond only loosely to concepts from the legal field, even in situations where the terminology is similar.

The historical legal concept of signature is broader. It recognizes any mark made with the intention of authenticating the marked document. In a digital setting, today's broad legal concept of signature may well include markings as diverse as digitized images of paper signatures, typed notations, or even addressing notations, such as electronic mail origination headers. A signature is not part of the substance of a transaction, but rather of its representation or form. Signing writings serve the following general purposes:

- *Evidence:* A signature authenticates a writing by identifying the signer with the signed document. When the signer makes a mark in a distinctive manner, the writing becomes attributable to the signer.

- *Ceremony:* The act of signing a document calls to the signer's attention the legal significance of the signer's act, and thereby helps prevent "inconsiderate engagements."

- *Approval:* A signature expresses the signer's approval or authorization of the writing, or the signer's intention that it has legal effect.

- *Efficiency:* A signature on a written document often imparts a sense of clarity and finality to the transaction and may lessen the subsequent need to inquire beyond the face of a document.

To achieve the basic purposes of signatures outlined above, a signature must have the following attributes:

- *Signer authentication:* A signature should indicate *who signed* a document, message or record, and should be difficult for another person to produce without authorization.

- *Document authentication:* A signature should identify *what is signed*, making it impracticable to falsify or alter either the signed matter or the signature without detection.

Signer authentication and document authentication are tools used to exclude impersonators and forgers and are essential ingredients of what is often called a non-repudiation service. A non-repudiation service provides assurance of the origin or delivery of data in order to protect the sender against false denial by the recipient that the data has been received, or to protect the recipient against false denial by the sender that the data has been sent. Thus, a non-repudiation service provides evidence to prevent a person from unilaterally modifying or terminating legal obligations arising out of a transaction effected by computer-based means.

Traditional methods, however, are undergoing fundamental changes that are coming with the digital economy. Although digital media is in use, documents continue to be written on paper, but sometimes merely to satisfy the need for a legally recognized form. In many instances, the information exchanged to effect a transaction never takes paper form. Computer-based information can also be utilized differently than its paper counterpart. For example, computers can read digital information and transform the information or take programmable actions based on the information. Information stored in digital media rather than on paper can travel near the speed of light, may be duplicated without limit and with insignificant cost. Although the basic nature of transactions has not changed, the law has only begun to adapt to advances in technology. The legal and business communities must develop rules and practices, which use new information technology to achieve and surpass the effects historically expected from paper forms. Electronic signature technology generally surpasses paper technology in all these attributes.

Electronic Signature: Scope and Definition

The term *electronic signature* could be defined as a sound, symbol or process attached to or logically associated with an electronic record by a person (a signer) with the present intent to authenticate that record. Every downloading software activity from the Internet includes reading the licensing agreement and clicking "I accept," where a person is using some kind of an electronic signature (the click combined with a person self identification create the signature). If a person places a trade over the phone and verbally confirms that wants to buy or sell stock, the recording of a person's voice could be considered as an electronic signature. Digital signatures and images of handwritten signatures also constitute electronic signatures. A handwritten signature signals intent to agree with the terms of a document, and it authenticates – at least in theory – the identity of the signer.

Handwritten signatures don't have an exact parallel online. In the electronic world, a person may end up doing the same things in a different way. The authentication may be done up front and the signal of intent may be done later. Authentication, the act of making sure that signers are who they say they are, can be handled online in several ways. A signer can use a digital certificate or smart card, take a fingerprint or retina scan, answer additional questions regarding personal identification. A signal of intent may be created online by clicking an "I accept" button, by signing one's name on an electronic signature pad or by appending a signature image to a document.

Hence, the foregoing definition of electronic signature within most national legislation is a generic, technology-neutral definition, which recognizes that there are many different methods by which a person can sign an electronic record. In all cases, electronic signatures are represented digitally, but they can take many forms, and can be created by many different technologies. Examples of electronic signatures include:

- A name typed at the end of an e-mail message by the sender;

- A digitized image of a handwritten signature that is attached to an electronic document (sometimes created via a biometrics-based technology called signature dynamics);

- A secret code, password, or PIN to identify the sender to the recipient (such as that used with phone cards and credit cards);

- A unique biometrics-based identifier, such as a fingerprint, voice print, or a retinal scan;

- A mouse click (such as on an "I accept" button);

- A sound (or voice) attempting to issue a meaning to agree);

- A digital signature (created through the use of public key cryptography).

There are other ways of signing an electronic document, and presumably many more will be developed in the future. However, all forms of electronic signature must satisfy the three requirements:

- there must be a *digitally mediated* symbol, or process,

- digitally mediated symbol, or process must be *logically associated* with an electronic record, and

- digitally mediated symbol, or process must be made *with the intent of a person* (a signer) to sign the electronic record.

Forms of Electronic Signature Technology

In an E-Business environment and networked economy, the terms of authentication and identification of parties are vital elements of functionality, operability and security. We should also underline the distinction between authentication and identification.

Authentication refers to the authentication or verification of a claimed identity. In other words, the user wishes to log on to a network or service, or undertake an online transaction and claims to be a certain person. The authentication process seeks to verify this claim via the provision of a characteristic (PIN/password/token/biometrics or other information), or multiple characteristics, known to be associated with the claimed identity. There is therefore a one-to-one matching process involved, as the characteristic in question is matched against the reference associated with the claimed identity, according to predefined threshold criteria in the case of biometrics.

Identification seeks to identify a user from within a population of possible users, according to a characteristic, or multiple characteristics that can be reliably associated with a particular individual, without an identity being explicitly claimed by the user. There is therefore a one-to-many matching process involved against a database of relevant data. We should perhaps make a further distinction between identifying an individual from within a known population using relevant characteristics (PIN/password/token/biometrics, etc.) and seeking to identify an individual via connectivity address information. In the latter case, we may correctly identify an address and the name that is registered in association with it, but that does not necessarily guarantee that the same individual undertook a specific transaction (unless robust biometrics have been used across multiple processes).

While the rapid development of new information technologies has improved the ease of access and use of digital information, it has also led to fears that consumer protection, intellectual property rights, privacy and related issues could be eroded by the illegal copying and redistribution of digital media. Mechanisms to protect digital content are seen as a necessary step towards the creation of global business and commercial information infrastructure. While equipment capable of copying digital content exists in any E-Business environment, some technologies of electronic signatures are emerging to provide organizations with the desired degree of protection, and to act as a disincentive to information piracy. These technologies are relating to:

- *Watermarking:* A technique for embedding hidden data that attaches copyright protection information to a digital object and provides an indication of ownership of object signed by watermark

- *Fingerprinting:* A technique that identifies the recipient of a digital object and its owner, and acts as a deterrent to illegal redistribution by enabling the owner of digital object to identify the original user of the redistributed copy.

E-Business users are not confident enough in the security of online systems to believe that a hacker can't break in and steal credentials there. Password lists and credit card lists are stolen regularly from online servers and can just as easily be lifted from unsuspecting users' machines by malicious software. For instance, the "Love Bug" virus was designed to collect user credentials and mail them out. So shared secret systems, including passwords and biometrics, are inappropriate for use directly as electronic signatures, but we will find that they still have an important indirect role. What we need are credentials that don't have to be given away to prove an identity or to create a verifiable electronic signature. Fortunately, proven technology that solves these problems is available through the Public Key Infrastructure environment.

Public Key Infrastructure

Security is always a concern with any electronic signature technology. An electronic signature based on asymmetric cryptography (digital signature) is considered superior to a handwritten signature in that it attests to the contents of a message as well as to the identity of the signer. As long as a secure hash function is used, there is almost no chance of taking someone's signature from one document and attaching it to another, or of altering a signed message in any way. The slightest change in a signed document will cause the digital signature verification process to fail. Thus, public key authentication allows people to check the integrity of signed documents. If a signature verification fails, however, it will generally be difficult to determine whether there was an attempted forgery or simply a transmission error.

Within a Public Key Infrastructure technology environment, an electronic signature is accompanied by the term digital signature – a data item that vouches for the origin and integrity of a document or message (Forno & Feinbloom, 2001). *Digital signature* is a mechanism employed within Public Key Cryptosystem that enables the originator of an digital object to generate a signature using encipherment in order to provide the recipient with the proof of the authenticity of the digital object's originator (author).

Public Key Infrastructure uses a digital signature as one type of electronic signature. It is made by asymmetric encryption in order to authenticate the contents of a document, secure its integrity and confidentiality, and attribute it to a particular signatory. When a digital signature is used by Public Key Infrastructure, the document is finalized, encrypted using a private key, and then sealed by attaching a numerical hash file reflecting the contents of the document. Any changes in the document result in a numerical hash file that does not match that of the original document.

Figure 1. View of the digital certificate

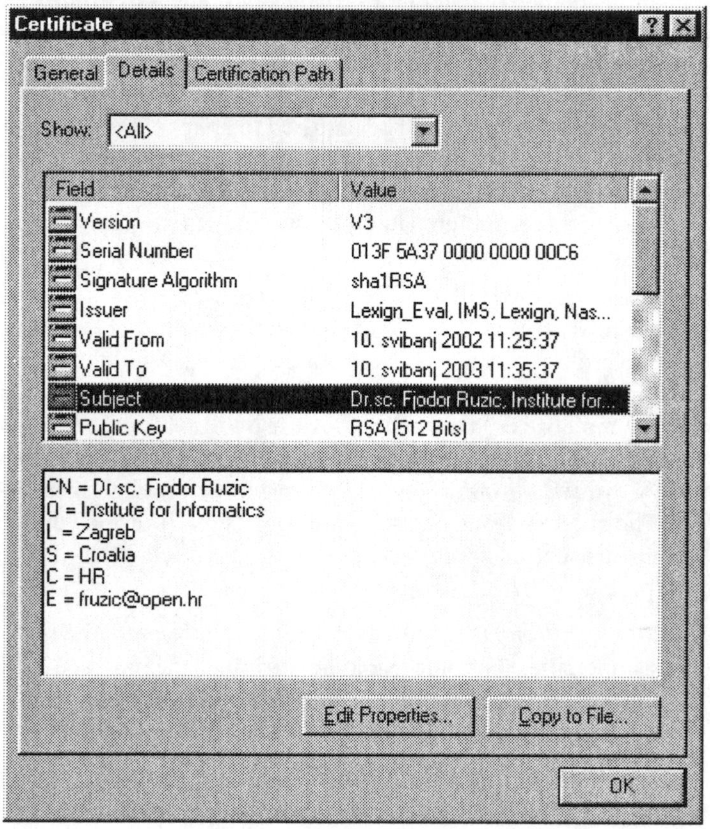

Within Public Key Infrastructure, the encrypted document is usually transferred through a third party known as a Certification Authority. The Certification Authority may assist in encrypting the document and in creating the numerical hash file, as well as authenticate the identities of one or more of the parties through the digital certificate, keep a record of the digitally signed document's unique numerical hash file, and maintain the public key that permits decryption of the document. Taken together, this multistep process constitutes the digital signature.

A digital certificate can be issued by the organization initiating the approval process or by a Certification Authority. A certificate usually contains the holder's name, a serial number, expiration dates, a private key that signs documents and messages through encryption, and a public key that the recipient uses to decrypt the message. Cryptography binds the digital signature to a document. If someone changes the terms and conditions or prices in that electronic document, the signature will become invalid.

Although digital signatures and the assistance of Certification Authorities can be costly, they provide worthwhile safeguards against electronic document tampering, deception, fraud, and unwanted disclosure, particularly when the stakes are high. Most people consider digital signatures to be the most robust technology available. But the strength of a digital signature depends on the rigor of its registration process. In some cases, a Certification Authority may register new private key holders by simply asking users to type in their email addresses. In other cases, the Certification Authority asks registrants for several pieces of private information, such as Social Security numbers, the last four digits of their driver licenses or the amount of the last check they wrote. If even greater security is called for, registrants could be required to appear in person at the certificate authority's premises with multiple forms of identification. When this last term is used, the electronic signatures made with assistance of the digital signature is taken as equivalent to handwriting signatures in most national legislation regarding electronic business and electronic commerce.

Public Key Infrastructure strength is a new issue at the signer side – users (signers) must keep their private keys private. That private key is on a computer or on a smart card and the user has got to protect it, otherwise someone could get a hold of it and sign with it. Because Electronic Signatures within Public Key Infrastructure environment are created and verified by asymmetric cryptography, they use public-key cryptography, where one key is for creating a digital signature and another key is for verifying a digital signature. These two keys (which forms a key pair) are collectively termed as asymmetric cryptosystem. The processes of creating a electronic signature and verifying it through the Public Key Infrastructure accomplish the essential effects desired of a signature for many legal purposes:

- *Signer authentication*: If a public and private key pair is associated with an identified signer, the electronic signature attributes the message to the signer. The electronic signature cannot be forged, unless the signer loses control of the private key, such as losing the media or device in which it is contained.

- *Message authentication*: The electronic signature also identifies the signed message, typically with far greater certainty and precision than paper signatures. Verification reveals any tampering, since the comparison of the hash results (one made at signing and the other made at verifying) shows whether the message is the same as when signed.

- *Affirmative act*: Creating an electronic signature requires the signer to use the signer's private key. This act can perform the ceremonial function of alerting the signer to the fact that the signer is consummating a transaction with legal consequences.

- *Efficiency*: The processes of creating and verifying an electronic signature provide a high level of assurance that the electronic signature is genuinely the signer's. Compared to paper methods (such as checking specimen signature cards - methods so tedious and labor-intensive that they are rarely actually used in practice) digital signatures yield a high degree of assurance without adding greatly to the resources required for processing.

Digital signatures are a reversal of public-key cryptography – data encrypted using a sender's private key can only be decrypted using the sender's public key. By obtaining the sender's public key to decrypt the digital signature, the recipient ensures that the digital signature was generated by the sender's private key. Anyone with access to the

Figure 2. Digital signature verification

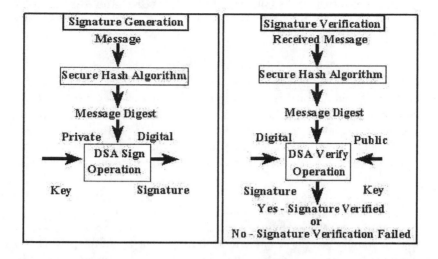

sender's public key can verify the digital signature. By comparing the hash values generated from the data by the sender and the recipient, the recipient ensures that the data did not change during the transfer.

Can a digital signature be forged? Not likely. It is protected by several layers of highly complex encryption. We like to think that a handwritten signature is unique to the signer and to the pieces of paper which hold it. What if someone produces a good likeness of your handwritten signature? Or, what if on a long contract, someone changes the text of the pages previous to the signature page? In these instances, the signature is valid, but the document has been altered. With digital signatures, forgery is next to impossible – much more difficult than forging a handwritten signature. First, a digital signature is more of a process than just affixing a signature. For example, when the document is "digitally signed," the digital software scans the document and creates a calculation which represents the document. This calculation becomes part of the "digital signature." When the recipient authenticates the signature, a similar process is carried out. The sender's and the receiver's calculations are then compared. If the results are the same, the signature is valid. If they are different, the signature is not valid.

Figure 3. Signed document flow within PKI environment

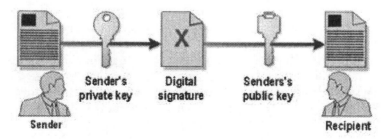

The process of creating a digital signature in E-Business communication is accomplished by the sender. The verification of the digital signature is performed by the receiver of the digital signature. The writing and sending a check example, illustrates how digital signature technology works.

Digital Signature Creation

- *Sign:* To begin the process, a check must be created. In order to create a digital signature with the check, a process known as hash function, must occur. A hash function is a mathematical algorithm that creates a digital representation or fingerprint in the form of message digest. The hash function generally consists of a standard length that is usually much smaller than the message but nevertheless substantially unique to it. Hash functions ensure that there has been no modification to the check (message) since it was digitally signed. The next step is to encrypt the check and signature. The sender's digital signature software transforms the hash result into a digital signature using the sender's private key. The resulting digital signature is thus unique to both the message and the private key used to create it. Typically, a digital signature is appended to its message and stored or transmitted with its message. However, it may also be sent or stored as a separate data element, so long as it maintains a reliable association with its message. Since a digital signature is unique to its message, it is useless if wholly disassociated from its message.

- *Seal:* Since public-key algorithms can be slow to transmit, the next step is to encrypt this information. The check is encrypted with a fast symmetric key (uniquely generated for this occasion) and then the symmetric key is encrypted with the receiver's public key. Now only the private key of the receiver can recover the symmetric key, and thus decrypt the check. A digital version of the envelope has been created.

- *Deliver:* At this point, the digital envelope is electronically sent to the receiver and the verification process begins.

Digital Signature Verification

- *Accept:* The encrypted digital envelope arrives at the destination.

- *Open:* The receiver of the check decrypts the one-time symmetric key by using the receiver's private key. Then the check is decrypted using the one-time symmetric key. Once this has been completed, the verification process begins.

- *Verify:* Verification of a digital signature is accomplished by computing a new hash result of the original message. Then, using the sender's public key and the new hash result, the verifier checks: 1) whether the digital signature was created using the corresponding private key; and 2) whether the newly computed hash result matches the original hash result. The software will confirm the digital signature as verified – the sender's private key was used to digitally sign the message and the message was unaltered. If the verification cannot be made, the software will identify that verification has failed.

An electronic signature is a convenient, timesaving, and secure way of signing electronic documents. An electronic document is any document that is generated or stored on a computer, such as a letter, a contract, or a will. In addition, an electronic document can be an image, such as a blueprint, a survey plat, a drawing, or even a photograph. and an electronic signature can be used to sign these documents. It means that the authenticity of any electronic document can be verified by an e-signature, but only if the document originally was "signed" using an e-signature program (software). Although this sounds complicated., it is a simple process and may vary slightly in the software in use, and e-signature software does all the work. The signer selects the signature option, then selects the document, and finally enters a secret Authorization Code. Everything is accomplished electronically. In the PKI environment, a digital certificate is added to the signed document, thus making verification available at any time after the document is signed.

Unfortunately, nobody can actually see the signers' handwritten signature, and there is no relationship to the signer's handwritten signature. While there's more to it behind the scenes, the visible portion of the digital signature is the signer's name, title and firm name, along with the certificate serial number and the Certification Authority name.

Digital signatures still face some cultural hurdles, such as convincing users to accept a line of hash code instead of a penned name. Several software solutions cover both ideologies by combining a PKI-based digital signature and a pictorial representation of the handwritten signature.

Visible Electronic Signature Protocol is a digital electronic signature protocol that allows the recipient of a secure electronic document to visually confirm the signature of the author and the authenticity of the document, just as with a paper document. A signature image, such as a seal or a written signature, is presented to the end user for verification. This intuitive approach to the digital signature process allows for extremely high confidence in the security and privacy of the encryption-decryption process, and

Figure 4. Verifying graphically presented e-signature; if the document is changed or used certificate is not valid, the cross-circled mark is presented to the reader

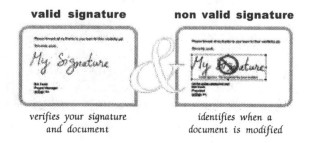

provides for a tamper-resistant way to transmit documents which must remain secure, such as e-commerce orders, contracts, blueprints, surveys, drawings, or photographs. the protocol works by encrypting the signature image.

As E-Business searches for more secure authentication methods for user access, e-commerce, and other security applications, it should be noticed that the security field uses three different types of authentication:

- *something user knows* - a password, PIN, or piece of personal information

- *something user has* - a card key, smart card, or token

- *something user is* - a biometrics

If an E-Business system is carefully constructed, almost any of these technologies could provide industrial-strength e-signatures with a number of additional tools that are not available yet:

Smart Cards

With a digital certificate or smart card protected by a password, there is a two-factor authentication - something owner knows and something owner has—and that makes e-signature protection stronger. Smart cards have finally entered the public domain and are used in a variety of applications, sometimes without the user being aware that they are actually using a smart card. The smart card itself is simply a plastic card with an integral embedded chip. This provides a degree of tamper resistance and security for the information held within the card. Smart cards may be categorized into two primary types, memory cards or microprocessor cards. Memory cards simply store data and allow that data to be subsequently read from the card. Microprocessor cards on the other hand, allow for additions and deletions to the data, as well as various manipulations and processing of the data. The smart cards may be further categorized into contact or contactless cards. Contact cards required the card to be physically inserted into a smart card reader. Contactless cards enable the card to be read without physical contact via a radio frequency link with an antenna embedded into the card. There is in fact another

Figure 5.: Smart card occurrences – contact and contactless

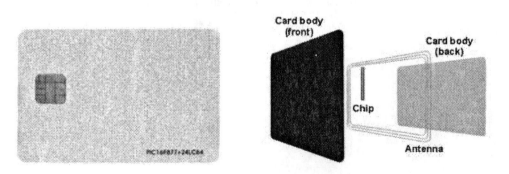

type of card called a combination card that combines both contact and contactless technology. This allows for the card to be read by either type of card reader, alternatively, to be read by both techniques at the same time, enabling a higher degree of security.

Smart cards support our contemporary networked society via a variety of applications, including network access control, secure payment systems, health care applications, ticketing applications, loyalty and other areas. They may also be used to store digital certificates and passwords and can encrypt sensitive data. Perhaps one of the most visible applications is that of SIM cards used for mobile phones. SIM stands for Subscriber Identification Module and the SIM cards store subscriber information which allows phones to be instantly personalized as well as providing roaming across different networks and devices. The mobile phone SIM card also provides for a variety of value-added services to be provided by the telecommunication companies as appropriate. An often referred to aspect of smart card technology is the potential for the multi-application card. The idea of multiple applications via the use of a single card is an attractive one. However, for this to be possible there needs to be a degree of interoperability between cards and applications. This interoperability has so far been rather weak, although there are now various initiatives with the aim of improving this vital aspect of smart card technology. There is of course an ISO standard for smart cards (7816 parts 1-10), although other different industry sectors have tended to create their own proprietary versions based around the ISO generic standard. There have also been related initiatives such as the Microsoft PC/SC standard, which was originally for Windows-based systems only, although this has now been opened up to be an across-platform initiative. Indeed, the PC/SC initiative boasts an impressive membership of several distinguished companies from the computer and telecommunications market place.

Another initiative called OpenCard has similar ambitions to provide interoperability across applications. Perhaps most interesting development of all in this context is Java Card (Wenderoth, 2001). Java card provides the potential for Java applets to run right on the card itself, a very interesting capability for those seeking to develop smart card applications. Smart cards are a valuable addition to this world because they interface seamlessly with smart devices and intelligent systems, giving people convenient and direct access to relevant information stored on powerful networks. The portable credentials on the smart card can securely identify and authenticate its owner, across the range of smart devices, providing a consistent means of authorization and digital signature for E-Business transactions. With embedded applications, these reloadable personal data carriers also allow users to tailor applications to fit personal needs. Smart cards are becoming crucial components of the E-Business economy and contribute to the realization of E-Business anytime, anywhere.

Public key cryptography is critical element in contactless systems. Traditionally, contactless systems have employed little-to-no security, due in large part to the very constrained nature (i.e., size or space limitations) of the token or card. To date, the majority of the security leveraged has been password-based technology, symmetric cryptography for authentication and/or confidentiality services or, in some very limited situations, legacy public key algorithms like RSA. It is clear that no security at all is unacceptable and that password-based systems have very well known management issues and security vulnerabilities.

Currently, the choice for strong security is between symmetric and public key cryptography. Symmetric key cryptography is characterized by the use of a single key to perform both the encryption and decryption of data. The primary weakness of symmetric key cryptography is referred to as the key management problem. Since the same key is used for encryption and decryption, it must be kept secure. Symmetric key cryptography transforms the problem of transmitting messages securely into that of transmitting keys securely. Ensuring that the sender and receiver are using the same key and that potential adversaries do not know this key remains a major stumbling block for symmetric key cryptography. In addition, when a new application is added to a symmetric key-based system, it must be permitted the same level of trust as the existing applications. If this new application (or any other trusted element of a symmetric key system) is compromised, so too is the entire system. In a contactless system that has tens of thousands of tokens or tags, the ramifications of this compromise can be catastrophic.

Public key cryptography overcomes the key management problem by using different encryption and decryption key pairs. This presents a significant advantage because two users can communicate securely without exchanging secret keys (Kozlov & Reyzin, 2003). The portable credentials on the smart card can securely identify and authenticate its owner, across the range of smart devices, providing a consistent means of authorization and digital signature for E-Business transactions. With embedded applications, these reloadable personal data carriers also allow users to tailor applications to fit personal needs. Smart cards are becoming crucial components of the E-Business economy and contribute to the realization of E-Business anytime, anywhere.

Signature Pads

This is a strong way of signaling signer intent because the person is signing in a traditional way. It's hard for persons (signers) to argue that they didn't know what they were doing – a signature pad also offers a biometric signature, so it is used to authenticate

Figure 6. Example of electronic pad system accepting written signature for digitalization process in electronic signature-based applications

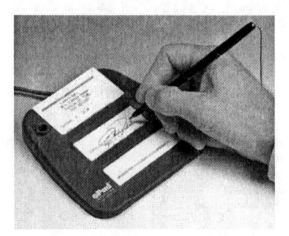

the signature as well. It is helpful for E-Business to let customers sign applications in their homes electronically. E-signature pads are used too, as the biometrics mechanism for verifying a hand-written signature with the holder of a pen.

Biometrics refers to the automatic identification of a person based on his/her physiological or behavioral characteristics. This technology of identification is preferred over traditional methods involving passwords and PINs (Personal Identification Numbers) for various reasons: the person to be identified is required to be physically present at the point of identification, and there is no need to remember a password/PIN or carry a token. At the same time, biometrics technology can potentially prevent unauthorized access to or fraudulent use of computer networks and information appliances connected to the E-Business environment. PINs and passwords may be forgotten, and tokens may be forged, stolen or lost. Thus biometrics technology is used in two basic ways – as an authentication systems or as an identification   system. It is worthy to note that although biometrics technology provides stronger identification, a biometric identification system based solely on a single identification identifier (fingerprints, faces, voice or another object) is not able to meet high performance requirements – thus, identification based on multiple biometrics represents an emerging trend.

Security systems use biometrics for two basic purposes: to verify or to identify users (Nanavati, Thieme & Nanavati, 2002). Biometrics measures individuals' unique physical or behavioral characteristics to recognize or authenticate their identity. Common physical biometrics includes fingerprints; hand or palm geometry; and retina, iris, or facial characteristics. E-commerce developers are exploring the use of biometrics and smart cards to more accurately verify a trading party's identity. For example, many banks are interested in this combination to better authenticate customers and ensure non-repudiation of online banking, trading, and purchasing transactions. Point-of-sales (POS) system vendors are working on the cardholder verification method, which would enlist smart cards and biometrics to replace signature verification (Schaechter, 2002). MasterCard estimates that adding smart-card-based biometrics authentication to a POS credit card payment will decrease fraud by 80 percent.

In the smart card – biometrics convergence process, the biometric information could be represented by a fingerprint (Struif, 2001). During the enrollment phase, a fingerprint template of the user is stored in a secure environment (smart card). For integrity and authenticity purposes, the (hashed) fingerprint is then inserted in an "attribute certificate" and the same smart card also stores an X.509 certificate of the user, which will be used to digitally sign electronic documents. In order to validate the fingerprint-identity pair, two important pieces of information are added to the attribute certificate:

a)   *the serial number of the smart card* - in this way the fingerprint can only be used with that smart card

b)   *the serial number of the X.509 user digital certificate* - in this way, the fingerprint can only be used together with its owner

Since fingerprints cannot be lost, duplicated, stolen or forgotten, a smart-card-fingerprint reader is providing a more reliable and convenient solution than traditional security devices. Security is improved further by storing the fingerprint templates inside a SIM card instead of the computer. This not only provides a more secure environment but it

Figure 7: Visual presentation of the smart card – biometrics integration smart card/ fingerprint reader (identification and verification unit for e-signature utilization)

also enhances portability and eliminates privacy concerns. What is more, it gives users the flexibility of being able to carry their fingerprint template with them, safe in the knowledge that no one else can use their smart card should it become lost or stolen. Such devices enhance smart card and PKI security by requiring a fingerprint instead of a PIN or password, and the credentials (digital certificate, etc.) are kept securely on portable smart card.

Typical applications for such devices are remote electronic voting, secure home-banking, secure e-commerce, secure e-finance.

Summary of Purposes of Electronic Signatures

The processes of creating an electronic signature and verifying it using Public Key Infrastructure accomplishes the essential effects that a handwritten signature does today for many legal purposes:

- *Signer authentication*: If a public and private key is associated with an identified signer, the digital signature attributes the message to the signer. The digital signature cannot be forged, unless the signer loses control of the private key;

- *Message authentication*: The digital signature also identifies the signed message, typically with far greater certainty and precision than paper signatures. Verification reveals any tampering, since the comparison of the hash results shows whether the message is the same as when signed;

- *Non-Repudiation*: Creating a digital signature requires the signer to use the signer's private key. This act can alert the signer to the fact that they are consummating a transaction with legal consequences;

- *Integrity*: The processes of creating and verifying a digital signature provide a high level of assurance that the digital signature is genuinely the signer's. Compared to paper methods, such as checking signature cards, methods that are tedious and labor-intensive, digital signatures yield a high degree of assurance without adding greatly to the resources required for processing.

Current Legislation and E-Signature Infrastructure

It is difficult to compare national approaches to electronic authentication legislation because so few countries have conceived of the purpose of such legislation in quite the same way. Some countries focused only on the technical standards for the operation of one technology – Public Key Infrastructure. Others have spanned the entire range of issues associated with the legal effect of electronic signatures, the legal framework for the operation of a Public Key Infrastructure, and the establishment of a regulatory apparatus to oversee Certification Authorities. In practice, there are several Legislative Models that are confronted with the issues of the tension between Technological Neutrality and Legal Specificity. Any legislative approach to electronic authentication must accommodate the inherent tension between the goal of technological neutrality and the goal of prescribing specific legal consequences for the use of electronic authentication systems. To the extent that legislation seeks to enable the use of diverse electronic authentication techniques, including some that are not yet even conceived, it becomes progressively more difficult to accord specific and meaningful legal consequences to their use. The reason for this inverse relationship is fairly straightforward – legislators' confidence in the security and reliability of known electronic authentication mechanisms allows them to grant greater legal benefits and presumptions to the use of those techniques. They may be less willing to grant the same level of legal benefits to as yet unknown techniques or to technologies that bear no imprimatur beyond recognition and acceptance in the marketplace. This conundrum is the inevitable consequence of legislating against a backdrop of rapid technological change.

Prior legislative initiatives began to emerge worldwide, and the use of asymmetric cryptography as a means of creating digital signatures was widely perceived as the nearly-universal foundation for all electronic authentication. One of the most complicated issues surrounding the creation of a Public Key Infrastructure is the extent to which the law should define or limit the liabilities of the three main parties to a secure electronic transaction, that is, the person who digitally signs a message, the person who receives the message and who may rely on its validity, and the Certification Authority that vouches for the identity or some other attribute of the sender. In a purely open networked transaction - that is, one in which the parties have not previously defined their respective rights and duties by contract - there are several major faults of liability. Most importantly, the Certification Authority may be liable to the recipient of the message for any inaccuracies or misrepresentations contained in the certificate, or for the failure of the Certification Authority to revoke an invalid certificate.

More recently, however, there has been growing recognition that other means of electronic authentication, including biometrics and dynamic signature analysis, will take on equal or greater importance in the years ahead. In fact, some of these techniques - and particularly those that are based on biometric features - may prove to be more reliable and less susceptible to compromise than digital signatures based on Public Key Infrastructure.

Thus, no single technology will prevail as the sole means of electronic authentication. Different technologies will likely be used in different settings and for different purposes. This diversity of authentication techniques, while generally promoting the expansion of electronic business, nonetheless poses a significant challenge for legislators, because not all technologies necessarily require the same legal infrastructure or may be accorded the same presumption of security and integrity. It is obvious that the widespread use of Public Key Infrastructure-based digital signatures require a legally established trust infrastructure, that defines the rights and obligations of the parties to an authenticated transaction, including the potential liability of Certification Authorities to third parties. Other technologies, such as voice authentication, may not require the same type of legally-defined trust infrastructure, although it is very hard to predict how any of these technologies will be used in widespread commercial practice and what their specific legal requirements will be.

For those legislators and policymakers who believe that the continued expansion of electronic business requires a known and reliable authentication mechanism with established legal consequences, the preference is usually to enact legislation that specifically addresses the use of digital signatures, and to save the issues raised by other authentication techniques for another day. At the same time, legislators and policymakers naturally fear that any attempt to codify a known authentication mechanism runs the risk of stunting the development of other authentication mechanisms, or at least of giving undue benefits to a technology that is itself only in the earliest stages of commercial use. Apart from these concerns and the general desire to avoid the rapid obsolescence of new legislation, there is also a concern among national legislators and policymakers that premature endorsement of a particular technology will set the country outside of the mainstream of technological and legislative developments internationally. For these reasons, technological neutrality in electronic authentication legislation has become an increasingly prevalent objective.

The manner in which legislators and policymakers have sought to accommodate the conflicting concerns largely defines the typology of existing and proposed electronic authentication legislation. Until the beginning of first decade of 21st century, the most common approach has been to ignore authentication mechanisms other than those based on digital signatures. These legislative initiatives are among the countries whose electronic signature legislation activities started before 2000. More recent initiatives, whether in the form of proposed legislation or reports by national experts groups, have increasingly focused on the need to accommodate emerging and even unforeseen technologies.

The second approach to electronic authentication legislation, accepts all or most electronic authentication mechanisms on a technologically-neutral basis, and grants these mechanisms a basic set of legal benefits. For example, technologies that are accepted at the first level might satisfy writing and form requirements, but would not be entitled to any presumptions concerning the signer's identity or intent. At the second level, the legislation creates a class of approved technologies whose use is invested with a broader array of legal benefits and obligations. The legislation may define these technologies – sometimes referred to as *secure* or *qualified* technologies – by reference to general criteria, by reference to the specific techniques of asymmetric cryptography, or by reference to a schedule of technologies approved by statute or regulation.

Documents that are authenticated by one of these methods are typically entitled to a more robust set of legal entitlements, for example, a presumption concerning the identity of the signer and the integrity of the document's contents. At this second level, the legislation also states requirements to address issues that are specifically associated with the operation of a Public Key Infrastructure, such as the operational requirements and liabilities of Certification Authorities.

This approach achieves the goal of technological neutrality by granting a minimum level of legal recognition to all or most authentication techniques, mostly with regard to satisfying form and writing requirements. At the same time, it affords greater legal certainty and benefits to those authentication mechanisms whose security and reliability permit greater confidence in their use. This approach also recognizes that some authentication mechanisms, and particularly those that are used in open systems, require a better-defined legal environment, while not depriving legal recognition to those authentication mechanisms that do not require a significant external legal framework. The most elemental objective of any electronic authentication legislation is to ensure that electronic signatures are accorded appropriate legal recognition. Virtually every jurisdiction has laws that require that certain types of documents be *signed*, or "*in writing*" or any one of countless other formulations that could be construed to require a physical document or hand-written signature.

The recent trend in legislation considering electronic signature utilization is for broad enabling legislation. When dealing with a technology that is new, it seems premature to draw up specific technology-related legislation. This could hamper innovation. Most countries define both electronic and digital signature, that are defined as:

- *Electronic signature:* Any letters, characters, or symbols manifested by electronic or similar means, executed or adopted by a party with the intent to authenticate a writing. A writing is electronically signed if an electronic signature is logically associated with such writing;

- *Digital signature:* A type of electronic signature that transforms a message using an asymmetric cryptosystem (public and private key capability) such that a person having the initial message and the signer's public key can accurately determine whether the transformation was created using the private key that corresponds to the signer's public key, and whether the initial message has been altered since the transformation was made.

A digital signature, that corresponds to advanced electronic signature in European Union, is intended by the party using it to have the same force and effect as the use of a manual signature, and it is unique to the party using it with capability of verification under the sole control of the party using it. It is also linked to data in such a manner that it is invalidated if the data is changed, and it is in conformity with rules that state a Certification Authority obligations and functionality.

This notion provides that unless otherwise provided by law, an electronic signature may be used to sign a writing and shall have the same force and effect as a written signature. It also provides that electronic signatures will be given the same force and effect as manual signatures, but also recognizes digital signatures. The validity of electronic signatures is not dependent on a licensed Certification Authority or other regulator, however, provision is made for licensure and regulation of certification authorities.

Most of countries within G4 (USA, Canada, Japan, and EU) have enacted legislation that would legalize digital technology for both the private and public sector. Some of them have restricted the technology to just state government business applications. One of the primary goals of most states is to promote electronic business, electronic commerce and online government and to ensure the security and reliability of electronic communications and records. At the same time, many countries adopted Public Key Infrastructure modeling schema and enacted legislation needed for the process of licensing Certification Authorities that would be issuing qualified certificate of electronic signatures.

The formal requirements for legal transactions, including the need for signatures, vary in different legal systems, and also vary with the passage of time. There is also variance in the legal consequences of failure to cast the transaction in a required form. The statute of frauds of the common law tradition, for example, does not render a transaction invalid for lack of a writing signed by the party to be charged, but rather makes it unenforceable in court. During the last decade, most legal systems have reduced formal requirements, or at least have minimized the consequences of failure to satisfy formal requirements. Nevertheless, sound practice still calls for transactions to be formalized in a manner which assures the parties of their validity and enforceability. In current practice, formalization usually involves documenting the transaction on paper and signing or authenticating the paper.

The legislation in many countries adopts slowly, but evidently in progressive way, along the general rule of validity of an electronic signature that is recognized as the essential, core category of the digital economy legislation. The general rule of validity is that a signature, contract, or other record related to any transaction in or affecting interstate or foreign electronic business may not be denied legal effect, validity, or enforceability solely because it is in electronic form.

When we sign a document, we become accountable. Our signature indicates our agreement, acceptance and authorization to act and move forward. Our business processes rely on the signatures of customers, managers, suppliers and business partners to keep work flowing. Patients sign consent forms, judges approve warrants, mortgage lenders need a signature for a loan, engineers stamp drawings, insurance providers can not proceed without a signature on an application. These acts of signing are critical to an organization's operation and success.

E-Business needs uniformity of e-signature in electronic transactions. Despite E-Business efforts to implement lawful e-signatures in electronic transactions, the worldwide digital economy still suffers from a substantial lack of uniformity. This lack creates substantial doubt in the minds of those wanting to sell goods and services over the Internet and definitely impedes e-commerce. Non-uniformity also makes parties more likely to specifically designate the law governing a transaction consummated electronically. In the same time, the Internet allows remote parties to enter into and perform contracts through systems that span multiple jurisdictions and may not depend on the physical location of either party. Conflict-of-law principles that apply when the parties fail to designate the governing law are complicated, archaic, and were certainly never written with electronic transactions in mind. In light of such uncertainty, many online brokerage firms and financial institutions are reluctant to open brokerage and bank agreements with electronic signatures via the Internet.

Remarks for E-Business

Any testimonial law provides that a signature, contract, or other record relating to such transaction may not be denied legal effect, validity, or enforceability solely because it is in electronic form. Moreover, a contract may not be denied legal effect, validity or enforceability solely because an electronic signature or electronic record was used in its formation. These straightforward provisions outlaw discrimination against electronic formats, and bring the fundamental for E-Business activities. To the extent that contracting parties do not understand proposed electronic formats, they can just say "no" to electronic agreements and signatures, but the result of saying "no" to electronic transaction can result in efficiency losses and missed opportunities to participate in global electronic business.

With low-value items, merchants may be willing to ship goods with just credit card information and without a legally binding contract. More sophisticated transactions, however, require a contract to create an enforceable agreement, and the entire process can take one to several days. Contrary, the acceptance of electronic signatures streamlines the whole process. An E-Business firm can expedite and simplify the entire processes by having the consumer sign and return the contract electronically. Electronic signatures greatly reduce the time to process the transaction, the consumer receives his goods faster, and the E-Business firm is legally entitled to receive payment prior to the shipment of goods.

Today, many organizations are interested in replacing paper-based systems with automated electronic systems. One of the inhibitors to the increasing use of electronic commercial transactions has been the concern for the risks of forgery over unsecured networks. This focus has brought about the need for a reliable, cost-effective way to replace a handwritten signature with an electronic signature. Like a handwritten signature, an electronic signature can be used to identify and authenticate the originator of the information. It can also be used to verify that information has not been altered after it is signed. Electronic signatures play a key role in enabling electronic business by helping to ensure that electronic documents are unaltered and have not been forged.

Companies considering the use of electronic signatures should evaluate their paper-based processes to determine where the risks are acceptable. The assessment requires a partnership between the Information Communications Technology people, the business people and the company's attorneys to establish what's possible, what makes sense accordingly to the risk and capital investment prepositions. In deciding which documents and processes require which types of electronic signatures, companies have to weigh the value of the underlying transaction and the confidentiality of the information. Does anybody have a motive to change the document after it's been signed? It may turn out that vacation requests that have always required a handwritten signature could be handled without any type of signature, but a million-dollar purchase order would clearly require strong authentication and signal of intent.

For any E-Business firm, there is a need to determine its overall business needs and time-frames. It should establish focus groups to identify business processes that would be enhanced or require the use of any electronic signature technology. The requirements from these business processes should be determined. A working group should be established to accomplish these goals. Both program staff and agency legal staff should be included.

At the same time, there are numerous applications that the entire government and public administration bodies (agencies) could use electronic signatures for, ranging from driver's license applications, vendor contracts, bids, purchase orders, employee applications, and voter registration to state employee time sheets. Again, when considering business requirements, consider any document requiring a signature that could be transmitted or filed electronically to be a candidate for the technology.

In the paper world, paper is the lowest common denominator, but in the digital world, there is no one common file format. To make e-signatures useful to the overall business community, the E-Business company shouldn't have to convert one format to a certain representation just for the sake of signing.

Transacting business remotely means making sure the receiving party can interpret the entire e-signature and trust the digital certificate behind it (Skrbek, 2003). Vendor interoperability is a problem, although not necessarily a technological one since almost all PKI certificates are based on the universal X509 standard, so interoperability is more a matter of business trust than of technology.

In the scope of e-signature standardization development, there is an open platform that could solve most of the interoperability problems. This platform is under the term XML-Signature Syntax and Processing standard (XML Signature) that is being incorporated into new products and services dealing with e-signature utilization. XML Signature is designed to work with existing XML (Extensible Markup Language) software, making it easier for modern software developers to incorporate the signature verification technology into new programs they develop. XML is the generation of Web-based software designed to make publishing data on the Web more flexible and adaptable than the fixed coding used in HTML, the programming language on which most Web sites are still based. By virtue of using the structured data formatting of XML software, users can apply their digital signature to distinct parts of an XML document. Most existing electronic signatures treat documents as single indivisible documents.

This is important for electronic documents that pass through multiple intermediaries, allowing the information to be open, read and then retransmitted while preserving the validity of the electronic signature embedded in the information (Onieva, Zhou, Carbonell & Lopez, 2003). Thus users may choose to sign portions of an electronic document but leave other parts unauthorized. Commercial applications can be sent through a series of intermediaries, with each party validating those portions of the document relevant to them. A mortgage applicant could sign an electronic form and forward it to a broker who would open it, process it, sign it and forward it on to a bank for final action. At the same time, the standard can be used to verify the authenticity not simply of text, but also of graphics and images stored in standard data compress formats such as "bitmaps" and "jpegs" used to transmit data-intensive images and other digital media.

For e-commerce to grow, businesses must implement the use of electronic signatures correctly and legally. Electronic commerce has changed the way we buy books, sell, and pay bills. Now, with the advent of electronic signatures, e-commerce is changing the way we sign and store documents. Eventually, any business that wants to succeed in e-commerce must deal with electronic signatures. Thus, any E-Business manager needs to understand

- what a signature is legally, and when it is needed,

- the various electronic-signature standards,

- current electronic-signature legislation, and

- some basics about electronic-signature technology.

Although the commercial world bases its need for "signed" documents on pre-Internet legal principles, this need is even more important today with remote buyers and sellers agreeing to exchange consideration for goods or services. Web sites that embrace electronic signatures and incorporate new document preparation and signature technologies will decrease transaction processing time and transaction non-fulfillment. More importantly, buyers and sellers using those Web sites will have more certainty of transaction fulfillment, creating participant loyalty to those Web sites, which in turn will create more usage and a more defensible market-share position.

Accordingly to the most often found statement, the electronic purchase of goods of greater value cannot be enforced in the absence of a signed contract. In contrast, with low-value items merchants are willing to ship goods with just credit card information and without a legally binding contract. More sophisticated transactions, however, require a contract to create an enforceable agreement. For example, Dell Financial Services requires a user to print an agreement, physically sign it, and return it by fax to Dell Financial Services when a consumer finances the purchase of a Dell computer or leases a Dell computer. This entire process can take two or three days. The acceptance of electronic signatures streamlines the whole process. A Web site operator can expedite and simplify the entire process by having the consumer sign and return the contract electronically. Electronic signatures greatly reduce the time to process the transaction, the consumer receives his goods faster, and the Web site operator is legally entitled to receive payment prior to the shipment of goods.

First-generation e-signature solutions are focused on platform-and application-specific solutions. Since then, many second-generation e-signature solutions are being implemented using open standards. These second-generation products and services will better integrate with corporate databases and security mechanisms, including biometrics. This is a perfect time to assess current business processes that require signatures. No industry is immune from the e-signature challenge. There are some big paybacks for implementing e-signature technology – especially for big-ticket transactions in the consumer market place and in business-to-business processes. In particular, there is the idea of using an e-signature to simplify auto and home loan processes and to speed up supply-chain operations.

Yet, you will now have to determine what changes you'll need to make to support e-signatures. More important, carefully examine available e-signature solutions and watch where they are going. Choose solutions and services that are platform and application agnostic. And look for those that will best integrate with the rest of your data and your security strategy.

E-signatures require businesses to obtain consent before sending information electronically, and to confirm that consumers can access the electronic form to be used. (For example, if a document were sent as a PDF, an end-user would need software with which to open it, such as Adobe Acrobat.) Anecdotal evidence suggests this provision can be a deterrent to e-commerce. Even if someone opens a trading account with an online broker at a storefront office, and asks for electronic account statements, that individual would also need to confirm the request electronically. The consumer consent provision can create headaches for companies if they change their electronic formats for users. A company using PDFs may decide to switch to a different format in a couple years, but when that happens they must receive new confirmations from all consumers to ensure they have access. Otherwise, the company can no longer send the information electronically.

As advice to E-Business, it is functional to start in applying electronic signatures to low-value transactions, and gradually work your way up to higher security. As businesses work up to more important and secure processes and documents, it is preferable to make sure you have the flexibility to migrate to a more secure solution such as Public Key Infrastructure combined with smart cards. It is slowly but surely becoming possible to conduct secure, legally binding transactions online. Forward-thinking companies are finding ways to make electronic signatures easy for customers to use and simple for the company to manage. Each business process has its own unique challenges, so there are few one-size-fits-all approaches. Aside from the reduced paperwork and faster processing, many business say they are happiest with the level of security and verification provided by the electronic signature utilization.

The Future of Electronic Signatures – Small businesses will be a significant driver to the growth of the business-to-business market. According to real business activity, Internet penetration among small businesses will steadily increase, reaching over 80 percent by 2004, and small businesses will generate 35 -40 percent of worldwide Internet commerce revenue by 2004. The entry of multiple small businesses into online marketplaces will decrease the overall credibility and credit worthiness of Internet market participants. This decrease will cause other participants to demand legally binding agreements based on an electronic signature to support online transactions prior to shipping goods.

Another driver to electronic signatures will be financial institutions. As small businesses increase their purchases via the Internet, it will encourage financial institutions to provide online financing and participate in this explosive growth. Already, Citibank NA has formed an online market in Asia, and First Union Corp. (another US financial institution) recently announced that it is building a business-to-business Internet market targeted at its 700,000 small businesses. Financial institutions have significant lobbying power and can cause the government and various states to initiate uniformity in electronic signature laws.

A third driver to electronic signatures is developing procedures for accepting signatures in digital or other electronic form with a goal of having at least 80 percent of all state tax and information returns filed electronically. As consumers grow more comfortable with electronic signatures, their use and popularity will increase.

E-Signature Utilization in a Real World

Loans – USA Funds Supports E-Signature

The electronic-signature process reduces paperwork, speeds the delivery of funds, and simplifies the education-loan process for schools, lenders and borrowers. USA Funds® provides functional ways of supporting e-signature utilization in loan processes. By July 1, 2002, or by the date they subsequently adopt e-signature usage, lenders must provide to USA Funds® a general explanation of each of their e-signature processes. The description must include an overview of the steps that borrowers must follow in completing that lender's e-signature process. If the lender uses multiple processes, the description also must outline how to identify which process was used for each loan. After providing this initial summary, lenders also must notify USA Funds of any significant changes in their e-signature processes. In addition, lenders must retain detailed documentation of the e-signature processes that they use, as well as documentation of any changes to their e-signature processes, including the effective date of these changes. This documentation should clearly describe the process under which individual notes are endorsed. Unless the lender follows guidelines established in the U.S. Department of Education's Safe Harbor policy for e-signatures, loans are not insured if deemed by a court to be legally unenforceable because of the e-signature process in use at the time the note was endorsed. If, however, a borrower who signed a promissory note through the electronic-signature process offered by USA Funds later challenges the validity of the promissory note, or the U.S. Department of Education determines that the loan is ineligible for reinsurance, because the note was executed using the electronic-signature process offered by USA Funds, USA Funds will not require the lender to repurchase the loan.

Federally subsidized Perkins and Stafford loans are the need-based loans available to students. To apply for Federal Stafford Loan, all first-time borrowers must complete a Master Promissory Note (MPN). To complete an MPN online, a candidate would fill out Apply for a Loan. Before selecting the "Sign electronically using my US Department of Education PIN" option, candidate should be sure that she/he has already obtained a PIN. AES is required to ask for consent in order to complete this electronic transaction, so a candidate will need to give her/his consent prior to proceeding. This process is active in the online environment and with e-signature utilization it gives more credibility and security to lenders and borrowers.

The standards provide that if a lender or holder's processes used for electronic signatures and related documents satisfy the standards set forth, those lenders or holders, "will be protected from the loss of Federal benefits on a loan if the loan is determined to be legally unenforceable by a court based solely on the processes used for the e-signature or related records." If the holder or lender does not follow the procedure set forth, "the Secretary will determine on a case-by-case basis whether Federal benefits should not be denied or repaid."

The online application process is guided through three steps:

1.   Student logs in, selects school and lender. (Student's name and address data are pre-populated using data from their log-in account.)

2.   Student selects one of the following options:

  •   Print at their printer.

  •   Have AES print it and mail it to them.

  •   Save the form for completion at a later date.

  •   Sign electronically using their USDE PIN.

3.   After the signed process, the student gives consent to complete the Stafford MPN process electronically.

Figure 8: Selection window to submit application including e-signature option

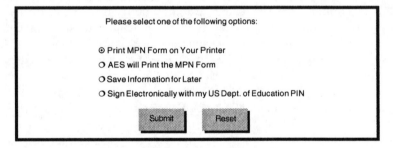

Figure 9: Consent-giving window to approve signing electronically

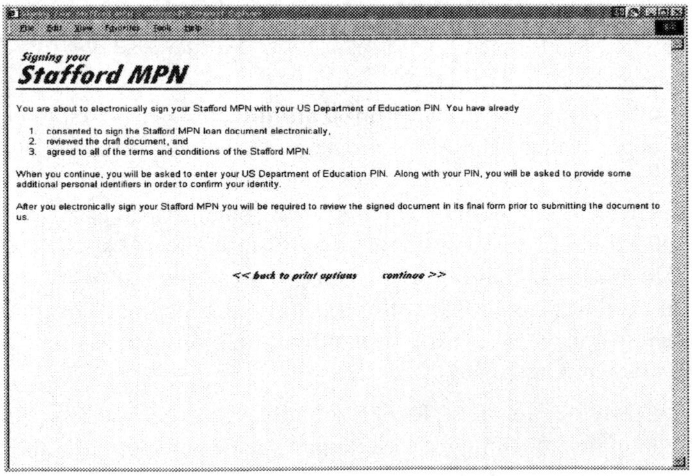

The student is informed of impending signature, MPN data and clicks are stored. Thus, the overall application process is done electronically saving time, money and organizational procedures.

Production – Ford Credit Introduced Electronic Signature

Interlink Electronics, Inc. and Ford Credit, a subsidiary of Ford Motor Company, are introducing in second half of 2003 Interlink's ePad handwritten electronic signature solution at thousands of dealerships throughout the US. ePad implementation will utilize electronic signatures to automate processing of some of its lease end documents, as the organizational solution for a system-wide transition from paper lease end documents to electronic lease end documents. The processing of thousands of lease end documents yearly will reduce operations costs by providing a handwritten electronic signature that is understood and accepted by the consumer, easy to use, and legally binding. Electronic signature solutions, like that software, are being deployed by larger companies to enable customer hand-signing of electronic forms and applications. Motivated by sharp reductions in processing costs and transaction times, companies are leveraging their investment in information systems to carry more revenue directly to the bottom line. ePad solution captures the handwritten signature converting it to a biometrically -secure e-signature for use in electronic forms and transactions. By providing user-intuitive electronic signatures, ePad enables enhanced workflow, reduced operations costs and faster document processing times. ePad e-signatures may be permanently bound into office-based digital files, Internet documents, and many proprietary forms and transactions, and it is used to authenticate the identity of the signer.

Healthcare – E-signature at Hospital Registration

At hospital registration, patients are normally required to sign a wide range of pre-printed forms and documents, with each generating a hard-copy duplicate that must be processed and filed in a document storage area in the medical records department. With e-Signature products, hospitals are able to secure a legally acceptable patient signatures without generating paperwork. In an e-Signature-enabled environment, patients complete a set of admissions forms as usual, but each document is now placed on an Access e-Signature tablet before signature. As the patient signs the paper document, the signature is simultaneously captured by the e-Signature tablet, encrypted, and bonded to an electronic version of that same document, which resides in, and is managed by, the hospital's database. In this scenario, there is only one set of hard-copy forms, which is given to the patient for his or her own records. No duplicate copies are left behind in registration for filing, allowing for a paperless registration process. As needed, registration staff can, with a single keystroke, digitally distribute the completed form to outputs such as document imaging systems, faxes, e-mail boxes, wireless messaging devices, or printers throughout the hospital.

The e-Signature devices are supported by a software application that ensures tamper-proof encryption and authentication of digital signatures and their associated source documents. e-Signature devices and software prevent encrypted signatures from being printed separately from their original source documents, thus making it virtually impossible for captured digital signatures to be stolen, falsified, or re-applied to fraudulent documents. To further increase security, e-Signature also uses proprietary technology to encrypt signatures with their uniquely identifiable biometric characteristics. With each signature, Access' technology captures specific information including speed, stroke, and pressure and digitally encodes this information to the document to ensure legal verification.

References

Ang, L., Dubelaar, C. and Lee, B. (2001). To trust or not to trust? A model of Internet from the Customer's point of view. *Proceedings of the 14th Bled Electronic Commerce Conference.*

Castells, M. (2000). *The Rise of the Network Society* (2nd ed.). Oxford: Blackwell.

Conte, R. and Castelfranchi, C. (1995). *Cognitive and Social Action.* London: UCL Press.

Forno, R. and Feinbloom, W. (2001). PKI: A question of trust and value. *Communications of the ACM, 44*(6).

Jones, S. and Wilikens, M. (2000). Trust requirements in E-business. *Communications of the ACM, 43*(12).

Kozlov, A. and Reyzin, L. (2003). Forward-Secure Signatures with Fast Key Update (2002). In S. Cimato, C. Galdi & G. Persiano (Eds.), *Security in Communication Networks* (pp. 241-256). London: Springer.

Nanavati, S., Thieme, M. and Nanavati, R. (2002). *Biometrics: Identity Verification in a Networked World.* New York: John Wiley & Sons.

Onieva, A., Zhou, J., Carbonell, M. and Lopez (2003). Multi-Party Non-Repudiation Protocol for Exchange of Different Messages. In D. Gritzalis (Ed.), *Security and Privacy in the Age of Uncertainty* (pp. 37-48). London: Kluwer.

Sang-Ro, K. (2002). Liability of On-line Service Provider for Copyrights. *Commercial laws Review, 21*(1).

Schaechter, A. (2002). Issues in Electronic Banking: An Overview. IMF Policy Discussion Paper, No. 02/6 Washington, D.C.: International Monetary Fund.

Skrbek, M. (2003). Signature Dynamics on a Mobile Electronic Signature Platform. In U. Grimm, H. Keller & K. Rannenberg (Eds.), *Sicherheit - Schutz und Zuverlässigkeit* (pp. 329-332). Frankfurt: GI.

Struif, B. (2001). Use of Biometrics for User Verification in Electronic Signature Smartcards. In I. Attali & T. Jensen (Eds.), *Smart Card Programming and Security.* Amsterdam: Springer.

Volti, R. (2001). *Society and technological change.* New York: Worth.

Wenderoth, D. (2001). Development of an European-Wide Citizen Javacard to Support Administrative Processes by the Use of the Electronic Signature and the Biometric Fingerprint Sensor. In B. Schmid, K. Stanoevska-Slabeva & V. Tschammer (Eds.), *Towards The E-Society: E-Commerce, E-Business, and E-Government* (pp . 817-830). London: Kluwer.

Zoellick, B. (2001). *CyberRegs: A Business Guide to Web Property, Privacy and Patents*. Boston, MA: Addison Wesley.

Chapter VII

Impacts of the Digital Economy:
The Shift to Consumer-Driven Competition and Life-Span Products

Simon Mowatt
Auckland University of Technology, New Zealand

Abstract

This chapter examines changes in innovation and competition made possible in two traditional industries by the adoption of integrated information and communication technologies. Using empirical interview-based research the chapter highlights the importance of consumer-driven innovation. The development of complex innovation networks to supply consumer needs is demonstrated using two example sectors, the UK magazine publishing and grocery retailing industries. The innovation process is outlined in detail and the importance of linkages to the end-consumer and market experts is acknowledged. In addition, this chapter offers the concept of "life-span" goods as those developed from the outset as having a short life dependent on changing consumer tastes and fashions. Within this environment firms act more as project orchestrators, using core skills in developing innovation teams based on a deep knowledge of consumer activities. Finally the chapter concludes by examining the challenge to economic analysis and to the theory of the firm provided by shifting and temporary alliances.

Introduction

The adoption and use of digital technologies by firms has created both many new industries and opportunities for existing firms to enter new markets. In addition to this, a key aspect of the use of digital and communications technologies based around those of the Internet has been to allow firms to reorganise their internal operations. This chapter provides an examination of the organizational responses to technological change made by firms in two industries transformed by the use of the "integrated information channels" (Nicol, 2001) which characterize the digital economy. Whilst the focus of many studies examining the impact of new digital technologies has been on high technology sectors, the adoption of digital communications technologies has also led to new competitive pressures in industries that could be characterized as low technology (Cox, Frenz and Preveezer, 2002). Firms in traditional industries have been able to gather more detailed information about the requirements of consumers, and the factors of competitive success have moved toward the ability to innovate the products and services which fulfill customer needs. An important aspect of organization and competition in the digital economy is therefore the process and management of innovation itself. This chapter argues that a key feature of competition in the digital age is that there has been a significant shift in competitive advantage toward the consumer-facing firms which are best placed to use details of consumer preferences to drive innovation, and that they are increasingly able to do this through the use of complex network arrangements. The balance of power between manufacturers and downstream companies has been shifting as a result of these changes, and the consequent reconfiguration of existing industries has important consequences for our understanding of economic analysis, particularly of organization, innovation, competition and industrial structure.

Background

The two industries that are the focus of this chapter are the food retailing and the magazine publishing sectors in the UK. Although distinctly different in character, both of these activities have been transformed from ones where competition was driven primarily by economies of scale in production to sectors where competitive success is conditioned by the ability to engage in continuous innovation driven by customer needs. In both examples the greatest impact of the digital revolution has been the changes in organizational structure within and between firms in the value-chain, although this may not readily be apparent. The temptation in these industries is to focus exclusively as to how the digital age has reduced the importance of "bricks and mortar" delivery relative to "clicks" and Internet delivery. Magazine publishers, for example, deal with an information product whose composition has become potentially purely digital. With the possibility of scale-free delivery on the Internet many industry observers predicted the end of paper-based magazines. Not only has this markedly failed to occur, with many magazine companies such as EMAP which invested heavily in digital brands and delivery scaling back their investment after losses in the early 2000s, but the range of paper-based magazines has proliferated hugely in the last decade (PIRA, 2002). Similarly, supermarkets have established their dominance as a retailing format by concentrating a large range of products in a specific outlet—often a large out-of-town shop. With the well publicised move to Internet-based ordering and home delivery, the significance of the wider changes to the industry conditioned by new technology may be overlooked. To date, for example, the vaunted benefits expected to accrue from online shopping have also proved to be elusive (Hughes, 2002). The leading exponent of this approach in Britain, Tesco plc, now holds 60% of the UK internet grocery provision market, with annual sales currently valued at £365 million (Tesco, 2002). Whilst this amount is larger than the entire European market for online grocery sales (Keynote, 2002), it nevertheless represents only 1.7% of Tesco's UK sales turnover. Rather, it has been the responses to customer preferences made possible by the application of digital technologies to other parts of their operations which Britain's supermarkets have used for competitive advantage.

By exploiting information gathered directly from and about their customers via scanning technology, inventory management software systems, data warehousing and mining, and consumer participation in online groups and surveys, supermarkets and magazine companies have been able to benefit directly from a strategy of new product development based on these requirements. Further to this, by engaging in innovation these consumer-facing firms have created a web of inter and intra-firm alliances and networks that have served to transform relationships within the industry's value system.

The interesting aspect to the transformation of these industries is that in many respects they appear much as they always have in terms of concentration ratios, the composition and identities of the largest firms, and superficially in the nature of activities undertaken. In the publishing industry the UK's two long-running dominant firms, EMAP and IPC, are still the largest consumer magazine publishing companies. The food manufacturing and retailing industry is still comprised of large multinational food manufacturers and large, mainly national retail groups. In the UK the top five supermarkets continue to control the grocery market. However, close empirical study reveals that the competitive dynamics within these two industries has changed substantially, with the balance of power shifting from firms engaged in production to those in closest proximity and control over information about the end consumer. Conventional measures of industrial structure such as concentration ratios fail to adequately depict the changes in activities undertaken by firms and fail to reflect the importance of the large number of small suppliers who are critical to the performance and operation of flexible business networks.

The detailed descriptions of the operation of the industries and the innovation processes described in this chapter are based on a four-year empirical investigation completed in December 2002 and a review of published sources. The study of the magazine publishing industry was undertaken by a programme of 28 semi-structured interviews in the consumer sector with senior managers who had an overview of both editorial and business functions, typically publishers or publishing directors (in the US this function is often referred to as the magazine general manager), printing firms and distribution companies. The particular sub-sectors used as vehicles to explore consumer-responsive innovation were the men's lifestyle, computer gaming and cycling segments. In support of the interview-based research we also undertook a census questionnaire survey of 246 publishing firms in the entire magazine publishing sector. A response rate of 23% was obtained from a statistically representative sample, comparison being made with a random selection of firms in the industry (Cox, Mowatt and Young, 2003). The retail industry was researched with a similar interview based programme, concentrating on the innovation network, suppliers and distributors to a leading supermarket, which we name here SuperCo for reasons of confidentiality.

This chapter illustrates the issues outlined above in the following manner: the next section examines the shift to consumer-driven competition in the two focus industries, with a focus on the importance of innovation. Following this the concept of "life-span" products is offered as a hallmark of the change in products to those characterised by consumer-driven pressures. The chapter then proceeds to examine in detail the innovation networks employed within the two exemplar industries. From this a review is offered as to how these issues may affect our understanding of innovation and the use of conventional economic approaches to analysing firms in the digital age. Finally the chapter concludes.

The Shift to Consumer-Driven Competition

The magazine market has changed markedly since the introduction of digital technologies. The market has shifted from being dominated by few publishing firms whose main activity was publishing largely undifferentiated established weekly magazines to a market characterised by a large number of often transient high-quality monthly niche titles. These titles are targeted towards narrow interest groups and publishing firms need to be able to both find information about target markets and be able to create new titles. The initial benefit to publishing firms is that consumers are willing to pay high prices for magazines that are based on their special interests. In the food retailing industry a similar shift has occurred from supermarkets vying to supply branded basic good at low price produced by the large manufacturers, to quality-based competition whereby firms sell products that consumers want. If food manufacturers do not supply these products the supermarkets have used their own brands to develop, procure and supply new products. This section reviews these changes before the next section examines how publishing and grocery retail firms innovate and supply new products.

The Magazine Publishing Industry

Before the adoption of digital technologies, competitive advantage in the food retailing and magazine sectors was held largely by the firms engaged in production and manufacture. Manufacturing firms could produce generally undifferentiated products at large scale and gain an advantage over competitors with the ability to offer lower prices. The change in the competitive process away from this paradigm within the magazine publishing industry is well illustrated by the change in industrial logic that has governed the fate of the UK's dominant firm in the sector. IPC Magazines was formed by the agglomeration of several publishing and printing firms by the Mirror Newspaper group in 1958 and later acquired by the publishing company Reed International in 1970. The driving force behind the creation of IPC and its acquisition by Reed was economics of production — economies of bulk buying of paper, the benefits of concentration allowing predatory pricing and the ownership of high-speed printing presses as decisive strategic assets (Price Commission, 1978; Mowatt, 2002). The nature of the product also was favourable to vertical integration. A paper-based magazine had to be laid out mechanically; a laboriously labour-intensive process where the product had to move physically from copy editors to the printing press and the distribution system to reach consumers (Bannard, 1990; Reed, 1997). Revenues at IPC were derived jointly from copy sales and through advertising sales. Copy sales were at a low cover price to deter competitors (and IPC was subject to Price Commission investigations concerning predatory pricing in the late 1970s) and large print runs kept costs down. Advertising was at a premium. As an example of this the largest magazine segment in 1977 (20%) was women's interest and IPC controlled 79% of this market with four titles. Even though IPC published 70 titles in total, 52% of its revenue was derived from these four titles alone, and 59% of *that* revenue was from advertising (Price Commission, 1978; BRAD data). With the widespread introduction of computers into editorial offices in the mid-1980s magazines could be created as "soft copies," and design, layout and composition became "virtual" rather than craft-based activities (Mowatt, 2002). The activity of printing therefore was stripped of these value-adding tasks, and became a residual function in the magazine publishing industry. By the 1990s our survey indicated that all printing was outsourced to external printing firms (Cox, Mowatt and Young, 2003). Desk Top Publishing systems (DTP) therefore removed much of the basis for vertical integration in the industry, although the rigid system of labour union control initially made it difficult for publishing firms to reorganise in response to technological change.

The change in technology not only changed the industrial logic of the dominance of few producers in publishing, but allowed both small firms and individuals to create their own "magazines" based on their special interests — at least on their own computers. Vertical disintegration and the dissolution of union power that had hampered the introduction of early digital technologies (Royal Commission on the Press, 1962) in the printing industry provided a channel for low-cost printing which potential publishers could access in order to join the industry. The early and mid-1980s witnessed an explosion of small publishing companies in the UK, such as Dennis and Future Publishing, whose founders initially saw opportunities for magazines catering for new market niches, often starting out as one-man operations working from a home office. The growing computing and gaming industry was one such area where many small publishers saw the chance to launch new titles into markets that the dominant printing firms were still too inflexible to enter quickly. Table 1 shows that although IPC has been able to retain its enduring position as top company in the women's weekly market (White, 1970), its total market share has been eroded from 79% in 1977 to 32% in 2002 by the entry of other low-cost producer firms in the weekly market (Mintel, 2002a; 2002b).

The monthly market, and new magazine segments established in the mid-1990s such as the men's lifestyle market, are contested by a much broader range of specialist publishers who are able to compete with larger companies head to head based on their ability to

Table 1. Magazine publishers' market shares of women's and men's interest market, 2000 (Mintel, 2002a; 2002b)

Publisher	Women's weekly Market share (%)	Women's monthly Market share (%)	Men's monthly Market share (%)
IPC Media	32	26	19
Bauer	24		
Northern & Shell	17		
Hello!	12		
EMAP Elan	3	24	32
DC Thomson	7		
National Magazines	5	34	3
The Lady	1		
Conde Nast		7	6
Attic Futura		6	
Dennis Publishing			15
Rodale Press			9
Cabal Communications			7
Others		3	10
Total	**100**	**100**	**100**

respond to consumer needs. IPC and EMAP as dominant producers were able in the late 1990s to reorganise around consumer market groups and to recognise the potential for reorganisation afforded by technology. The following section on innovation networks examines this process. The shift to digital composition also had one further significant impact on the magazine industry. Coupled with regulatory changes governing foreign ownership of the media, large-scale, low-cost producers of magazines could not only use existing competencies to enter the weekly market, but do so internationally. Large-scale European publishers such as Bauer were able to enter the UK market. The market therefore split between monthly magazines targeted at narrow markets and weekly magazines where low production cost and cover prices was still a key feature.

The ability of magazine publishing firms to become consumer-driven has been demonstrated by the increase in the number of magazine titles, from 2,000 consumer titles in the mid-1990s to over 3,000 titles in 2002. The UK is now arguably the leading player in the global magazine industry, easily outstripping countries such as the USA, Germany and France in terms of number of titles sold per million population (Pira International, 2002: Figures 8.12 and 9.2). The dual ability of existing firms such as IPC to restructure to consumer responsive media firms engaged in innovating new titles for the monthly high value-added market along with the entry of many niche publishers has fueled this growth.

In 2001 IPC, now IPC Media, was bought by the multinational media conglomerate AOL-Time-Warner. The reason for this acquisition was not based on the economics of production, but was justified in terms of the ownership of knowledge. Cross-media content sharing was seen as the key to competitive advantage. Titles, and increasingly services, could be supplied across different media formats charged at premium prices to narrowly targeted consumer segments. Whilst the logic of this approach has yet to be established as a viable business model across a media conglomerate, the advantage of a flexible publishing firm to use knowledge as a key strategic asset can be examined in the innovation section.

The Food Retailing Industry

The rise of powerful retailers such as the supermarkets in the UK and Wal-Mart in the US has demonstrated how effectively firms close to consumers can use their control of information management systems to not only gain advantage over competitors but to also exert pressure on manufacturers with monopoly power. Competition authorities are beginning to recognise that they need not only to concentrate on the power of manufacturers but that retailers' buying power can be significant in the modern age (Graham and Steele, 1997). Both Wal-Mart and British retailers have ruthlessly exploited their supply-chain management and category management systems in order to drive down supplier costs and decrease the costs of warehousing and prices paid to branded and own-label suppliers (Fernie and Sparks, 1998). The UK Competition authority recently delivered its verdict on the activities of the leading British supermarkets (Competition Commission, 2002). Concentrating on the use of buyer power the report presented evidence of supplier relationships with great differences in power between retailers and suppliers, but also gave contrary evidence of very close trust-based relationships between small suppliers and retailers. From the market power perspective, this proved problematic for the conclusive findings of the report, but can be explained by the shift to consumer-driven innovation networks. The ability to gain effective control of the supply chain has been decisive for retailers to not only challenge the dominance of branded manufacturers and squeeze supplier revenues, but to also respond more effectively to consumers. Information systems enable network hubs — the retailers in this case — to identify the value-adding activities in the value-chain, and the ability to use complex networks allows them to control these activities directly without ownership. The value-adding activities are those that drive innovation: consumer knowledge, controlled closely by the retailer, and the ability to create new batch-driven products quickly, offered by small suppliers. Where consumer responsiveness and flexibility are important, trust and cooperation rather than price-based relations will be central. The next section elaborates on this process, and the later section on innovation examines trust within the innovation process.

British supermarkets built their capacity to both source and supply novel products in three stages. First, their control of the supply-chain allowed British supermarkets to build up a detailed picture of suppliers operations and cost structures. Although retailers controlled distribution only *from* secondary consolidation points, the information management systems they employed enabled retailers to effectively control the entire supply-chain. Manufacturers and independent logistics companies have been manoeuvred into acting as agents in the supply-chain, picking up deliveries from small suppliers to feed into the retailers' distribution system. Second, the move in the late 1990s to replenishment-based logistics and to strategic inventory management in the early 2000s gave retailers the ability to supply retail stores with small deliveries — a few items per store for short-shelf-life products. Third, this ability to control the supply chain from small suppliers to batch deliveries enabled many suppliers too small to find independent distribution into the industry's value-system, and often as own-brand contractors. In this way the total number of firms engaged in the value-creating chain in the grocery sector has dramatically increased.

Supermarkets increasingly try to supply novel products to consumers based on customer desires. Retailers can supply these products to stores in a customer responsive fashion due to their mastery of the supply-chain. Information about consumer needs is obtained through a variety of channels: by analysing consumer information captured with loyalty cards at point of sale, with data mining and strategic ordering systems in dedicated data warehouses, with qualitative information as to consumer requirements gathered from customer feedback and focus groups, from Internet order histories, observing changing social trends (such as shifts in restaurant trends), and by consulting experts from past moving consumer areas such as those represented by "celebrity" chefs. Whilst increasing buyer power and category management techniques allows supermarket to offer cheaply produced own-*label* low cost versions of branded goods — sometimes manufactured by the branded producers themselves — knowledge of customer trends is also allowing them to out-compete manufacturers in high-value-added market segments by using innovation networks to create and produce their distinct own-*brand* products — although they neither own nor operate the production process.

The process of creating new magazine titles and novel own-brand products is the subject of the section on innovation networks. A key feature of these products however is that they are designed from the outset as short-life products and this attribute is the subject of the following section.

From Life-Cycle to Life-Span Products

The use of digital technology in publishing has removed many of the entry barriers to the industry. Competition in the high-value segments (i.e., monthly magazines) is therefore about addressing consumer needs — and consumer needs often change in line with current fashions, trends and new technologies—rather than printing costs. Magazine publishers and small independent entrants are able to use their detailed knowledge of "lifestyle" areas to offer specialist magazines. Consumer-driven innovation is not however about identifying one key product — a "killer app" — that will enable the producer to gain a competitive edge through an efficient scale of production to support low costs and moderate margins. Rather it is about the ability to manage a continuous process of development and innovation based on supplying products for changing consumer needs. The magazine publishers who identify fans of TV series such as "Buffy the Vampire Slayer" or a new computer gaming platform such as the X-Box do not expect that magazines targeted at these audiences will have more than a limited life-span. In the same way competition between the vertical networks supporting retailer's own-brands is enacted though the constant supply of products. Innovation for life-span goods is about managing constant innovation.

The publishing industry questionnaire responses showed that consumer magazine companies have extended their activities to exploit their knowledge of consumer markets by supplying new titles and also other products and services. Television stations, shows and radio programmes based on magazine brands (such as KaRang! TV for heavy metal music fans), licensing for foreign distribution, Internet advertising, event sponsorship, fairs, exhibitions and direct activity with consumers are all ways in which consumer knowledge has been exploited (for a detailed review of the questionnaire results, see Cox, Mowatt and Young, 2003). Consumer firms can get very close to consumers. In the mountain biking segment for instance riders may meet the editors of mountain biking magazines on public trails and also on trails actually sponsored and created by magazines. One magazine in the segment, *MBUK*, has an extremely active Internet chat room and forum with hundreds of discussion threads generated by mountain bikers per week. The magazines editorial staff not only engages in the sport themselves, and observe reader's activities directly, but also interact through the Internet: for example, six *MBUK* readers who had complained about the magazine online in a discussion were brought into the magazine company to work for a week and this later became the basis for a story — and continued dialogue on the forum. It is the speed, quality and depth of this interaction that characterises consumer-responsive firms in the digital age. This interaction allows firms to explore new niche markets and service, for example launching a new magazine to capture emerging trends in the sport and launch spin-off, single edition or special edition titles.

In the supermarket the chilled ready-meals story in the UK provides a compelling example of the transformation from producer to consumer-driven competition and the shift to life-span products in the food retailing industry. Chilled ready-meals are the prime example of retailers' ability to differentiate quality own-brands, and are high value-added premium convenience products, which have displayed consistent rapid growth from the 1990s to date. They are ready-prepared, short-shelf-life, complete meals which are chilled, not frozen, for freshness. Unlike frozen ready-meals, where four branded manufacturers still control 50% of the market, 95% of the chilled market is controlled by supermarket own-brands, supplied through innovation networks comprised largely of small firms (Cox and Mowatt, 2004). The appeal of the sector lies not only in its convenience, but also as a substitute for takeaway and restaurant meals, and retailers therefore need to be able to offer their customers an expanding and changing range of high quality products in line with fashionable eating trends. SuperCo offered a total of 141 different chilled ready-meals in 2000, having introduced some 44 new products in 1999 alone. Retailers tend to source the inputs for chilled ready-meals from a great number of suppliers (180 in 2000) in order to respond quickly to new restaurant trends with new recipes, exploiting the flexibility of small suppliers. The process of innovation is examined in the following section.

Innovation Networks for Life-Span Products

Publishing Firms

Publishing companies are able to use innovation networks to supply new titles and services to customers willing to pay high prices for quality magazines. People with expert knowledge of a special interest can take advantage of the low entry barriers in the industry to originate their own magazine titles — something that was possible before the digital age but very rare (the launch of an independent high-value monthly in the early 1980s such as *the Face* was exceptional). It is more usual that actors with experience in the publishing industry develop their network of expert contacts in order to create new titles. For example, publishers within large production-orientated firms that were until recently operating in the old paradigm had developed linkages with consumer experts across several market areas, and within the firm and through their personal contacts in the industry a network of technical and editorial people. Publishers and editors who identified new opportunities often either left their company to form their own start-ups or themselves launched a new title pilot to demonstrate the potential to the company. A typical story from one publisher detailed how he and his editor on a style magazine received a lot of feedback from readers concerning a feature on celebrity diets. The publisher was able to put together an informal team comprised from his personal networks to develop a spin-off title to cater to this market at this own personal initiative. In the last few years large magazine publishers have begun to realize that they are repositories of expert knowledge that can be used not only to publish existing magazines but to see their activity as coordinators of networks that can be flexibly rearranged to generate new titles quickly in response to consumer trends. For organisations this had meant re-forming around consumer interest groups, and using an essentially project-based approach to spin off new titles and products.

The small publishers formed in the first wave of digitization in the mid and late 1980s have also grown on this principle — using experts to inform the company about new opportunities and to put together a project-based team to develop a new title. This process relies on contributions from external actors (contract journalists and experts commissioned for work) which has greatly increased the scope of the production system coordinated but not internalized by firms. The digitization of publishing has occurred simultaneously with the externalization not only of printing, but also of journalism and copy-based tasks (Stanworth and Stanworth, 1988). For consumer-driven areas it is vital that these informants, who may compose copy, send reports or be brought in as technical advisors, journalists or editors, are authentically connected to consumer trends — which is one reason why a flexible external network rather than in-house journalists is a feature of project-based networks. On publisher described how he worked with people on a surfing magazine. The credibility of being informed by "real" surfers enabled the magazine to appeal to readers. The publisher noticed that surfers were increasingly riding mountain bikes after surfing, and snowboarding in winter — at a time when these sports were less well-known in the UK. He was able to develop new informants from these sports

Table 2: How publishing firms receive copy from external and contact staff

Method of Supply	Two Years Ago	Now
Physically (e.g., Film by post/couriers)	40	31
By EDI or Integrated Network Linkages	9	43
Electronically through the Internet	4	23
Only Electronically	4	26
Total Respondents	44	57

and put together magazine teams from his technical network to exploit these opportunities. These external experts and actors can be coordinated remotely by e-mail and Internet-based communications technologies, something increasing apparent from the response to our questionnaire (see Table 2), and again this flexibility allows a far faster and wider contribution to firms. In the innovation networks employed by magazine publishing firms the value-adding activities are those which provide quality to consumers — in terms of content (through expert contribution), layout and style. DTP allows editorial teams complete control over these key design processes with only a small staff per title. Supporting activities such as advertising sales can be centralized across consumer groups, rather than tied to a changing array of specialist titles. A final story illustrates the changing flexible nature of the magazine publishing firm: Roger (name changed) worked for a large magazine house as editor to a specialist water sports title. He left the company in 1994 and founded his own rival title using his trusted expert contacts from both the sport and the publishing world. From this he established several spin off titles, including one in the men's interest sector — competing head-to-head with international firms such as EMAP and IPC. From one title in the mid-1990s, he has established a portfolio of seven titles by 2002, having opened and closed four others. His main activity is now looking for new niches — those far from the related areas of lifestyle and sport. His competitive advantage is speed in developing new titles, a low-cost and low-risk process with current technology for specialist rather than weekly mass market titles. The UK has a very established magazine distribution system, with multiple magazine outlets such as WHSmith stocking a large number of tiles in each store (usually with a list of over 2,000) so it has been relatively simple to gain access to consumer points of sale (although retail pressures are beginning to change this). Roger's comment was that, "It is simple finding local experts to develop your copy once you have found a market."

Innovation in Food Retailing

In this section we examine the operation of SuperCo's innovation network to understand how life-span products are created through flexible innovation networks of firms in loose strategic alliances. SuperCo's innovation network evolved from its initial development of own-label specifications through internal hygiene and later product development departments for its own-brand goods (Fernie, 1997; Hughes and Merton, 1996; Senker, 1986, 1988). The consumer information which SuperCo collects is considered in conjunction with strategic alliance partners, whose activity is act in a co-ordinated way is possible because of the retailer's control of the supply-chain. SuperCo accepts that, "Many new product ideas come from our suppliers and we work very closely with some of the top chefs … so we follow those consumer trends which are very fashionable." In this sector the relationships engaged in are best understood as inter-organisational networks whereby manufacturers and packaging firms develop new products in conjunction with retailers. SuperCo claims to have "very long-term relationships" with some suppliers and accepts that trust within long-term relationships is critical (Lane and Bachmann, 1998), especially as SuperCo has no capital stake in suppliers and there are few formal contracts between retailers and food suppliers in the chilled ready-meal sector. Relations essentially take the form of a "gentleman's agreement" and this is made possible by the structure of the industry created by the innovation network itself. SuperCo uses many small suppliers to ensure it has access to a large variety of recipes, but relies on a key supplier for 50% of its ready-meals by sales volume. This firm, with a turnover of over £750m in 2002, has grown principally as a supplier to the supermarket sector and has a dedicated factory for SuperCo, guaranteeing confidentiality and exclusivity. This trust has enabled SuperCo to move from business plans of typically three years to longer terms of five years, and implement joint investment plans. These plans range from non-contractually based agreements in which SuperCo agrees to "deliver a volume of business to a manufacturer for five years and the manufacturer invests in a dedicated factory," to arrangements to supply small firms with technical assistance in return for access to new recipes. For this process to be effective the retailer must ensure that its quality standards and processes are adopted and integrated with its packaging and, crucially, own-brand marketing strategy. Information needs to be passed between the partners in this network. The "relationships in this sector are different than when you are working with the big branded suppliers as we work very closely with ready-meal suppliers and the confidences that we tell them we wouldn't do on the branded side." This is especially significant for small-scale suppliers where the retailer is their sole client. This series of very close relations binds the network firms into mutual dependencies. In the case of large manufacturers the relationship centers on negotiation over exclusivity agreements, the use and development of dedicated manufacturing centers, and the co-ordination of new hygiene technologies and processes, such as the development of specific packaging systems. Relations with smaller firms were characterized more by an exchange of hygiene technician staff to co-ordinate basic standards and to transfer technological information, especially information about production systems from manufacturers, from the retailer to small producers.

Knowledge is developed and disseminated throughout the innovation network. The *process* of working in a network is itself important knowledge. Relations in the innovation network are "fluid and dynamic" within and between firms. SuperCo's chilled ready-meal innovation unit is part of the fresh foods division and incorporates buyers responsible for recipe development and has a permanent team of 26 people. SuperCo staff and supplier staff spend around 50% of their time in each other's firms and meet in other locations. Flexibility and face-to-face contact are important when "some of the factories now are like large hotel kitchens, because it has become more and more specialized and the runs have become smaller." Far from the picture of adversarial price-based negotiation between suppliers and retailers which was partially responsible for the Competition

Commission enquiry into the activities of supermarkets in the UK, network relationships where complimentary assets (consumer information for new product; the ability to flexibly supply new quality recipes) are mutually beneficial to both firms and vital for the supply of life-span goods.

The Extension of Innovation Networks

In the preceding two sections we have examined how firms in two distinct sectors have been able to use innovation networks to produce and supply high-value niche products. A key element of this strategy has been for firms to be able to identify end-consumer desires. The ability to assemble project-based teams to source, design, manufacture and deliver products is in itself a key element of competitive success in the digital era. This flexibility has also enabled firms to be able to extend innovation networks, exploiting key consumer knowledge by offering additional products and services. In the example of the magazine industry, the spread of services from magazine production into supplying services to consumers was acknowledged. Similar observations can be made in the supermarket sector. Some supermarkets, for example, have exploited their proximity to consumers and their ability to innovate branded products through contractors to enter the magazine market. The retailer J. Sainsbury, for example, uses its contract publisher New Crane to offer *The Sainsbury's Magazine*. This magazine had a circulation of 278,043 copies in the first half 2003 (ABC data) and although only sold in Sainsbury's supermarkets, it competes directly with magazines offered by mainstream publishers. In this way coordinators of consumer-critical information are able to compete across industrial and market areas outside of their usual line of business. This underlines the complexity of competition in the contemporary period.

Shift to Consumer-Driven Life-Span Competition in Analytical Context

The ability of the firms in these two industries to leverage critical consumer information to drive innovation through the use of networks presents challenges for our understanding of innovation and organisation in the digital age. It has been suggested that the role of knowledge in the digital economy has led to "New Innovation Regimes" (Windrum, 2000) in seeking to explain innovation in "knowledge-intensive services." This perspective demonstrates that Schumpeterian approaches to innovation, first concentrating on the role of the individual in the innovation process (entrepreneurial capitalism) and later conceptualised in terms of the action of large firms upon innovation and the ownership of knowledge by big business, is limited in dealing with firms in the digital economy. From the evidence presented in this chapter it should be clear that rather than acquiring innovative capacity by internalising entrepreneurs as predicted by Schumpeter, firms are increasingly able to coordinate and control innovation through networks. The networks described are not only inter-organisational but bring in individuals and the end-consumer. A key feature of these networks is that the central hub firms co-ordinating information and innovation — magazine publishing firms and supermarket retailers — are managing many simultaneous networks with large numbers of suppliers. The analysis of these collaborative relationships is problematic for a transactions-cost approach to the organisation, with its central concerns of establishing the legal boundaries of the firm, make or buy decisions in production, bounded rationality and opportunism (Williamson, 1995), in attempting to understand the operation of these firms and competition between them.

Ekinsmyth (2002) has argued that the magazine publishing industry is project-based, and although this analysis focused on the operation of single magazine titles, our findings have borne this out. I argue that many new consumer-sector, project-based organizations are essentially concerned with life-span products, with a necessary focus on temporary and shifting patterns of alliances in production. From an analytical economic perspective recourse to a legal-ownership definition of the firm as recently argued by Foss (2002) does not further our understanding of production systems — surely the purpose of firm's activities — where due to the transient nature of activities internalization is unlikely.

The digital age has made new systems of innovation possible which are neither within nor outside of the legal definition of the firm, but managed through complex network arrangements. From this perspective the boundaries of firms are less important than the information flows that the firm controls. An approach to the analysis of firms offered by Casson (1997) allows us to conceive how resources outside of the ownership of the firm are potential strategic assets providing that firms can control them. Digital economy project-based, life-span firms as examined in this chapter are also problematic for conventional analysis as they are based on generic technologies. Unlike traditional R&D in manufacturing, where the focus is on the development of idiosyncratic assets developed through bespoke design, many features of the innovation systems that we are examining here are based on generic systems and even in some cases freely available software. For the "pervasive technologies" of the digital age (Cantwell and Noonan, 2001) their value rests not in their uniqueness, but conversely, in their availability to all partners in the value-chain (Nicol, 2001).

Network study approaches have attempted to move beyond a simple transactions-cost framework (see Ebers, 1997, for a review) and incorporate conceptualizations of the trust relationships that are important in innovation networks (Lane and Bachman, 1998, provide an overview). However, the value-chain and innovation systems in the industries illustrated also incorporate information directly from end-consumers, and few analysis of consumer-driven innovation to date treats the *final* consumer in these "edge" markets (White, 2002), as the majority of transactions within an industrial economy are those between firms involved in intermediate forms of production and related services (the customer is often taken to be another supplier or firm in the value chain). However, the communication potential of current technology allows firms to greatly increase their information reach. Consumer-driven competition makes it more likely that firms will extend their innovation networks to final consumers, and that the features described in these industries may be generalized across the economy more widely. Network analysis also often attempts to describe long-term or embedded social relationships rather than the dynamic short-term ones that characterize innovation networks for life-span goods. The challenge for economic analysis is to explain empirical realities with theories that can deal with the complex nature of firms and production systems in the digital economy.

Conclusions

This chapter has examined how two distinctly different "low-tech" industries have been able to embrace new forms of information management and complex network forms of organization in response to the use of new digital technologies. The common themes in examining the innovation process in both sectors is the importance of firms being able control and observe information flows through the use of information systems to engage in consumer-driven innovation. The key driver of innovation is the ability of firms to transform the critical information about consumers into knowledge about consumer preferences coupled with the ability to supply these needs through network arrangements. The products offered are more likely to have a short life-span, and this will be recognized from the outset.

This ability has transformed competitive pressures within traditional industries from those conditioned by the economics of production to the ability to engage in consumer-driven innovation. In the food industry the large retailers in the UK have successfully challenged the dominance of food manufactures in several key product areas and founded several new, highly profitable, own-brand-dominated product markets such as that represented by chilled ready-meals. The manufacturing in this case is undertaken not by the food manufacturers or the retailers but by many small flexible companies encompassed by the retailer's innovation network. In the publishing industry the advantage held by magazine companies whose competitive success had been founded on the ownership of production evaporated with the advent of DTP and ICTs. Competitive advantage in this industry shifted from economies of scale in production to firms able to innovate new magazines and services desired by end customers. Large incumbent firms have found that they can refocus their activities around consumer-driven innovation and establish a competency in managing knowledge leveraged through extensive networks of contract journalists and specialists. In both cases external experts and suppliers are crucial in supplying the information that the core firms in the network can transform into knowledge about consumer requirements.

Traditional economic approaches to analyzing the operations of firms find temporary and trust-based networks challenging. The focus on ownership and boundaries is of limited utility for understanding innovation networks. A key challenge for the firms in the digital economy is for firms to determine how to control the crucial, consumer-based information that drives the innovation of new products and services. Firms that offer little in the way of value-adding activities may find that they are unable to prevent firms from squeezing their margins. Firms far from sources of consumer information may find that they are increasingly beholden to retailers for distribution. Participation by small suppliers and contractors in innovation networks provides new opportunities for access distribution and growth through collaborative partnerships. The systems described in this chapter present new challenges for competition authorities and our understanding of the theory of the firm, which should seek to extend network-based analysis. Further detailed study is needed into other empirical examples of new and existing industries characterized by consumer-driven, life-span products.

Acknowledgments

The empirical work for this project was supported by a Leverhulme Trust Institutional grant. The research itself is indebted to the managers who were interviewed for this project. The analysis of the work also owes great thanks to Howard Cox who has co-authored several papers on networks and business history with the author, and Stuart Young who has analysed the questionnaire results with the author and Howard Cox.

References

Abernathy, F.H., Dunlop, J., Hammond, J. and Weil, D. (1999). *A Stitch in Time: Lean Retailing and the Transformation of Manufacturing - Lessons from the Apparel and Textile Industries*. New York: Oxford University Press.

Baker, S. (2003). Calm after the brainstorm. *Media Guardian*, August 4, 8.

Bannard, M. (1990). *Magazine and Journal Production*. London: Chapman & Hall.

Cantwell, J. and Noonan, C. (2001). Technology Relatedness and Corporate Diversification 1890-1995. Paper presented at the Nelson Winter Conference, Denmark, June 12-15 2001. Retrieved October 17, 2002 from the World Wide Web: http://www.druid.dk/conferences/nw/paper1/cantwell_noonan.pdf.

Competition Commission. (2002). Supermarkets: A report on the supply of groceries from multiple stores in the United Kingdom. London, HMSO. Retrieved July 17, 2002 from the World Wide Web: http://www.competition-commission.org.uk/reports/446super.htm.

Cox, H. and Mowatt, S. (2004). New Product Development and Product Supply within a Network Setting: the Chilled-Ready Meal Industry in the UK. *Qualitative Market Research, 7*(1), 9-20.

Cox, H., Frenz, M. and Prevezer, M. (2002). Patterns of Innovation in UK Industry: Exploring the CIS Data to Contrast High and Low Technology Industries. *Journal of Interdisciplinary Economics, 13*(1), 267-304.

Cox, H., Mowatt, S. and Prevezer, M. (2002). The Firm in the Information Age: Organizational Responses to Technological Change in the Processed Foods Sector. *Industrial and Corporate Change, 11*(1), 135-158.

Cox, H., Mowatt, S. and Young, S. (2003). Innovation and Organisation in the UK Magazine Print Publishing Industry: A Survey. In D. Kantarelis (Ed.), *Global Business and Economics Review - Anthology 2003*. Selected papers of the Business and Economics Society International Conference, San Francisco, July 2003. (forthcoming).

Delafons, A. (1965). *The Structure of the Printing Industry*. London: MacDonald.

Driver, S. and Gillespie, A. (1993). Information and Communication Technologies and the Geography of Magazine Print Publishing. *Regional Studies, 27*(1), 53-64.

Ekinsmyth, C. (2002). Project Organization, Embeddedness and Risk in Magazine Publishing. *Regional Studies, 36*(3), 229-243.

Ekstedt, E., Lundin, R.A., Söderholm, A. and Wirdenius, H. (1999). *Neo-Industrial Organising: Renewal by Action and Knowledge Formation in a Project-Intensive Economy*. London: Routledge.

Fernie, J. and Sparks, L. (1998). *Logistics and Retail Management*. London: Kogan Page.

Graham, M. and Steele, A. (1997). The Assessment of Profitability by Competition Authorities. Office of Fair Trading, Research Paper 10. London: Office of Fair Trading.

Guidone, L. (2000). The Magazine at the Millennium: Integrating the Internet. *Publishing Research Quarterly, 16*(2), 14-33.

Henry, H. (1986). *The Dynamics of the British Press 1961-1984: Patterns of Circulation and Cover Prices*. London: Advertising Association.

Hobday, M. (2000). The Project-Based Organisation: An Ideal Form for Managing Complex Products and Systems? *Research Policy, 29*(7-8), 871-893.

Ietto-Gillies, G. (2002). *Transnational Corporations: Fragmentation amidst Integration*. London, Routledge.

Key Note Report. (2001). Consumer Magazines, ICM.

Key Note Report. (2002). Publishing, ICM.

Lane, C. and Bachmann, R. (Eds.). (1998). *Trust Within and Between Organizations: Conceptual Issues and Empirical Applications*. Oxford: Oxford University Press.

Mowatt, S. (2002). Technology and Industrial Change: The Shift from Production to Knowledge-Based Business in the Magazine Print Publishing Industry. In D. Kantarelis (Ed.), *Global Business and Economics Review - Anthology 2002*. Selected papers of the Business and Economics Society International Conference, Montreal, July 2002, 282-296.

Murray, F. and Willmott, H. (1997). Putting Information Technology in its Place: Towards Flexible Integration in the Network Age? In B.P. Bloomfield, R. Coombs, D. Knights and D. Littler (Eds.), *Information Technology and Organizations: Strategies, Networks, and Integration*. Oxford: Oxford University Press.

Nicol, R. (2001). Standardization: The Philosophers Stone of the Information Age. In A. L. Haberman (Ed.), *Twenty Five Years Behind Bars*. London: Harvard University Press, 56-73.

Pira International. (2002). *Publishing in the Knowledge Economy: Competitive Analysis of the UK Publishing Media Sector*. London: DTI/PIRA.

Price Commission. (1978). *IPC Magazines Limited Increases in Cover Prices*. London: HMSO.

Reed, D. (1997). *The Popular Magazine in Britain and the United States of America, 1880-1960*. London: British Library.

Royal Commission on the Press. (1962). Report, 1961/62. London: HMSO.

Stanworth, C. and Stanworth, J. (1988). Reluctant Entrepreneurs and Their Clients - the Case of Self-Employed Freelance Workers in the British Book Publishing Industry. *International Small Business Journal, 16*(1), 58-73.

White, C. (1970). *Women's Magazines*. London: Michael Joseph.

Windrum, P. (2000). Knowledge Pools and Innovation Networks in e-Commerce: the Integrating Role of Knowledge Intensive Services. Paper presented at the SIEN workshop, January 2000. Retrieved January 6, 2003 from the World Wide Web: http://www.uni-bielefeld.de/iwt/sein/kibslond.pdf.

Chapter VIII

Digital Products on the Web:
Pricing Issues and Revenue Models

Gary P. Schneider
University of San Diego, USA

Abstract

Products that exist in digital form can be bought, sold, and, in some cases, delivered, online. The pricing issues that arise in the sale of these products are different from those that sellers face when pricing physical goods and can lead to interesting opportunities for devising revenue models. The success of revenue models for companies that sell digital products depend on the nature of the product, the characteristics of the buyers, and the traditional practices in the industry. This chapter examines the nature of digital products, their pricing issues, and the efficacy of various revenue models that have been implemented by companies that deal in digital products.

Digital Products

Some products exist only in digital form, such as software and certain types of information databases. Many more types of products exist in physical form, but can be digitized.

These products include many forms of intellectual property such as text, pictures, photographs, architectural drawings, choreography notes, sound recordings, and video recordings. In some cases, digital products arise from the transmission of other digital products, as in the case of telephone and fax transmissions.

Defining Digital Products

Krishnamurthy (2003) defines a digital product as anything that can be digitized and includes such items as "advertisements" and "financial assets" such as stocks or bonds. This overly broad definition contrasts with Choi and Whinston's (2000) definitions of knowledge-based and knowledge-enhanced products. Choi and Whinston (2000) include "information, knowledge, news, databases, software, literature, arts, and other forms of human creation" in their definition of knowledge-based products and any products that can be "enhanced by knowledge, networked, and customized" in their definition of knowledge-enhanced products. Note that these "goods" as defined can include sales of what might have been called "services" in the past.

Ease of use of digital products can be affected by changes in the underlying technologies used to transport, deliver, or provide the end-user experience associated with the product. In some cases, the underlying technology can create a digital product from a traditional physical product or service. Some examples of traditional physical products that have been converted in this manner include:

- Newspapers converted to news Web sites (Krumenaker, 2003)

- Magazines and journals delivered on Web sites (Barsh, Kramer, Maue and Zuckerman, 2001)

- Computer games presented as online experiences (Moon, 2001)

- Audio recordings of music or spoken words (for example, lectures) presented on Web sites (Manjoo, 2003)

- Financial market reports converted to financial information Web sites or Internet-delivered information feeds using, for example, technologies such as Really Simple Syndication (Gillmor, 2003)

Characteristics of Digital Products

Most digital products have common characteristics that identify them as digital products. These characteristics distinguish them from physical products or intangible products without a digital existence, such as financial instruments. These characteristics include:

- High fixed cost to produce the first unit, but low marginal costs to produce subsequent units,

- Quality is difficult to judge without actually experiencing the product,

- Capacity constraints do not limit production output in any significant way, and

- Storage, retrieval, and forwarding the product is easy and inexpensive to do.

One consequence of these characteristics is that unauthorized use by purchasers of the product (including the forwarding of the digital product to other parties who have not paid for the product) can be difficult or impossible to control. A second consequence is that sellers of such products must adopt different strategies from those used by sellers of physical products to ensure that a revenue stream flows from the continuing use of the digital product.

Many digital products are, in their essence, things that are experienced by customers. They often have no meaningful physical existence separate from the experience. Krishnamurthy (2003) discusses this characteristic of digital products as being either experience or credence goods. Unlike an item of clothing, which can be examined before purchase in a physical store, an experience good requires that the customer be exposed to the product before determining its quality. An artwork or performance is an experience good because the customer cannot judge its quality without experiencing it. A credence product is even more complex. A customer often cannot judge the quality of a credence good even after experiencing it. For example, the quality of a physician's services could be difficult for a person without medical training to judge even after the services have been rendered. Purchasers rely on third-party reviews of experience and credence goods for pre-purchase information.

Changing Technologies and Digital Products

Providers of digital products must maintain a current knowledge of underlying technologies that are used or could be used in the future for delivery of their products. One serious case of vendors' failure to keep up with delivery and transmission technologies is the music recording industry, which grossly underestimated the impact of file-size compression technologies and increasingly inexpensive Internet bandwidth (Christman, 2002; Dahl, 2003; Lee and Capell, 2003). The ability of customers to adapt and reformat digital products is also an essential characteristic of digital products—a characteristic that can be affected by changes in technologies, as well.

Pricing and Distribution of Digital Products

Issues regarding pricing and distribution control of digital products arose before the Internet and the World Wide Web (Web) became prevalent. However, the availability of an inexpensive and near-immediate electronic transmission medium has added new issues and complicated existing issues. These pricing and distribution issues affect the nature, quantity, and quality of competition in markets for these products.

Digital products require an approach to pricing that differs from that used for physical products. Some digital products are made available at no charge, thus, an alternative revenue stream that is somehow related to the product must be devised. Some digital products are bundled with other products (digital or physical) to avoid some of the problems inherent in the pricing of digital products alone. Another pricing strategy is to create an artificial distinction within a subset of digital products and use differential pricing to extract the highest revenue possible from each set of customers for the product. Perhaps the most common pricing method is to use a licensing approach of one kind or another.

On the Web, combinations of all these pricing methods are often seen. For example, Web sites often make free content available and charge for other, related content. This is a combination of the "no charge" approach with the differential pricing approach.

Although a number of studies (Bailey, 1998; Bakos, 1997; Brynjolfsson and Smith, 2000; Lee, 1998) have been published regarding pricing on the Internet, these studies consider the Internet as a part of the marketing and pricing mechanism in a general way for all types of goods sold on the Internet. They do not address the specific issues that arise when selling digital products on the Internet. Although these general analyses of the impact of the Internet on marketing channels do conclude that in many cases the transaction costs in the channel are reduced, the studies are less conclusive on the question of which parties in the channel are able to reap the benefits of those transaction cost reductions (Schneider, 2004). For most digital products, however, the real effect on pricing and distribution strategy does not derive from the introduction of the Internet into the marketing channel, but from the products' very nature as digital products. In this section, specific pricing and distribution strategies for digital products are outlined.

Low Price or Barter Strategies

Many digital products are offered on the Internet in a way that makes them appear to be free. In almost all cases, however, there is a low price exacted. In general, this price is non-monetary. In some cases, the site visitor obtains the digital product in exchange for personal information, which the site is then able to use for marketing or other purposes. In other cases, the site visitor agrees to have advertising appear in his or her Web browser window. In effect, the customer is bartering personal information or time spent viewing advertisements in exchange for the digital good.

Examples of these types of digital products and services include sites such as *The New York Times*. The Times provides news stories in exchange for a site visitor's registration, which discloses a small amount of personal information, and for the visitor's willingness to view advertisements that are included on the Web pages that display the digital product (the news stories). Many other newspapers, magazines, news services, and other online information portals use this pricing and distribution strategy to sell their digital products.

Another example of a low-price or barter strategy is the offering of "free" e-mail accounts. Companies such as Yahoo! and Microsoft (through its Hotmail business) offer a limited personal e-mail service. The companies do not charge for the service, but do collect personal information that they use for marketing purposes. The e-mail service is provided on Web pages that include targeted advertising. The advertising is targeted based on the personal information collected.

In most cases, the barter transaction is fully disclosed. In some cases, however, companies offer "free" information or software services but include in the software a feature that collects information from the customer's computer and reports it back to the seller for as long as the software is installed. This type of software is called stealthware or spyware because it often installs the reporting feature in a way that makes it difficult for the customer to detect its operation (Hagerty and Berman, 2003; Metz, 2003).

Sometimes, a digital product is given away so that customers can try it before purchasing it. Sites that sell information by subscription often offer a 30-day free trial period. Software is often sold this way. Called "shareware," the software is provided for download and can be used for a limited time. After the trail period expires, the software will either disable itself or launch periodic reminders (called nag boxes) to register and pay for the software. Some shareware does not include any type of disabling code or programmed reminders. The vendors simply ask users who like the product to contribute money. This has not been a terribly effective way to market digital products, but it was widely used in the early days of the Internet and it does still continue today as a distribution model for some software products (Liao-Troth and Griffith, 2002).

Subscription Strategies

In a subscription arrangement, the customer agrees to pay for access to content or the use of a digital service over time. Companies that offer free e-mail services, such as Yahoo!, often also offer additional services such as increased disk storage space or the right to send and receive larger sized e-mail messages or attachments on a paid subscription basis.

Some newspapers and magazines also offer paid subscriptions to Web site content. This Web content is distinguished from the content that is offered at no charge by either being additional content not available to non-subscriber site visitors, or it is content that is offered free of the advertising messages that accompany free content on the site.

Subscriptions are attractive to sellers because they reduce the administrative costs associated with tracking and billing individual consumption of digital products. Subscriptions can also appeal to customers because they provide a simple pricing arrangement that has a known and certain price (Fishburn and Odlyzko, 1999). In some cases, such as AOL's adoption of a fixed subscription price in 1996, the known and certain price can lead customers to consume greater quantities of what they perceive to be free digital goods. Once they have paid the subscription fee, their marginal cost of consuming additional units of the goods is near zero (Roth, 1998).

Differential Price Strategies

Each person wanting to buy a product has a maximum price that he or she is willing to pay for it. This price, often called a reservation price, is known to the buyer but not to the seller. Much of the seller's pricing task is to estimate potential purchasers' reservation prices and set the price of the product low enough to attract a large number of purchases, but no lower than necessary (Edwards, 1942).

One way for a seller to extract the highest possible reservation prices from a diverse group of potential purchasers is to segregate them into multiple categories and then charge a different price to purchasers in each category (Bichler and Loebbecke, 2000; Forsyth, Lavoie and McGuire, 2000). For example, some manufacturers sell their products primarily to wholesalers and retail stores, but also sell direct to end-user customers from time to time. These manufacturers typically charge a lower price to their wholesale customers than to their end-user customers. If sellers can identify any reasonable basis for discriminating in their pricing, they will optimize their profits if they can charge different prices to different customers.

The ultimate in price discrimination is charging a different price to every single customer (Peppers and Rogers, 1997). The Web, with its ability to identify site visitors and customize the shopping experience, makes this not only feasible, but relatively easy to accomplish (Godin and Peppers, 1999).

Some countries, such as the United States, have laws that prohibit certain types of price discrimination (*Purchasing Law Report*, 2001). However, most price discrimination is legal throughout the world. The ethics of price discrimination are open to debate (Campbell, 1999) and companies such as Amazon.com have faced highly critical customer reactions and press coverage when they have been identified as engaging in price discrimination (Adamy, 2000; Cox, 2001).

One form of price discrimination that works very well with digital products is versioning (Krishnamurthy, 2003). Information content on the Web can be versioned by:

*   Offering a version of the product without advertising or with a smaller amount of advertising or advertising in forms that are less obtrusive. The low-advertisement content version is sold for a higher price or made available only to subscribers.

*   More current information offered to customers who pay higher prices or who subscribe. Those paying lower prices or not subscribing to the site receive information after a time delay.

*   A more complete feature set is offered at a higher price. For example, a news site might include streaming video for subscribers.

*   Varying the quality of the offering. Many sites that sell or lease graphics for use on Web pages or in print applications offer a small, low-resolution picture on the Web site at no cost or at a very low price. This graphic might also include a visible mark that reduces the value of the image. For a higher price, customers can buy a higher resolution version of the graphic.

These versioning strategies do not work well if the content can be converted readily. That is, if a low-price version of the digital product can be converted to the high-price version easily, customers will not see any reason for the price differential and will object to it (Shapiro and Varian, 1998).

Product Bundling Strategies

Some products can be offered in combinations, or bundles. For example, a music CD is a bundle of individual song recordings. A newspaper is a bundle of stories and advertisements. A software suite is a bundle of individual programs. Research (Venkatesh and Mahajan, 1993) has shown that if customer preferences are not homogeneous, the prices of the individual items in the bundle are not close to each other, and a significant proportion of customers are indifferent to a large number of the products in the bundle, a mandatory bundling of products can yield greater profits than offering the products separately (Estalami, 1999).

If the individual products function better as a bundle, as might occur with software programs offered as a suite, the seller can even charge a premium for the bundle (Estelami, 1999). Companies offering digital products on the Web can easily bundle products and services (Sieber and Sabatier, 2003) and can charge premiums for complementary products in different amounts to different customers, thus combining the product-bundling strategy with the price discrimination strategy described above (Venkatesh and Kamakura, 2003).

Revenue Models for Digital Products

Companies have combined the basic pricing and distribution strategies described in the preceding section into a number of different revenue models that they are currently using to sell digital products on the Internet. These include subscription-based models, advertising-supported models, per-item sales models, and a variety of mixed models (Schneider, 2003). This section discusses specific industries that sell digital products and provides a brief description of how each industry is using various revenue models. According to Cohan (2001), Internet business models must be based on selling one or more of four digital product elements to customers. These four elements include: charging for access to content, charging for copies of content, charging to transmit messages to current or potential customers, and charging for transactions that result from exposure to or consumption of content.

Newspaper and Magazine Sites

Many newspapers and an increasing number of magazines publish all or part of their print content on the Web. It is unclear whether a newspaper's presence on the Web helps or hurts the newspaper's business as a whole. Choi (2003) argues that the reputation of an old product (the print newspaper, in this case) can carry over to a new product (the news Web site, in this case) if the products are bundled. However, other researchers, such as Cripps and Schmidt (1996) have argued that the reputation transfer is unpredictable.

Advertising Revenue Model

Although news Web sites can provide greater exposure for newspapers' names and can provide larger audiences for the advertising that the newspapers carry, they can also cannibalize sales from print editions. Like retailers or distributors whose online sales lead to cannibalization of their brick-and-mortar sales, publishers also can experience sales losses as a result of online distribution. Newspapers and other publishers worry about these sales losses, because they are very difficult to measure. Some publishers have conducted surveys in which they ask people whether they have stopped buying the newspaper because the content they want to see is available online. In addition to the concern about lost sales of print editions, most newspaper publishers have found that the cost of operating their Web sites cannot be covered by the revenue they can generate from selling advertising on the site. Thus, many newspaper publishers have experimented with various other ways of generating revenue from their Web sites.

The advertising revenue model is used by network television in the United States. Broadcasters provide free programming to an audience along with advertising messages. The advertising revenue is sufficient to support the operations of the network and the creation or purchase of the programs. Many observers of the Web in its early growth period believed that the potential for Internet advertising was tremendous. Web advertising had grown from essentially zero in 1994 to $2 billion in 1998 (Sharples, 1999). However, Web advertising has been flat or declining from 2000 until quite recently. In 2002, Web advertising revenues began to increase again, but at a fraction of their former growth rate (Tynan and Gilbert, 2003). After some years of experience in trying to develop profitable advertising revenue models without the growth rates of the early years of the Web, many companies are less optimistic about the potential for advertising as the sole basis for revenue generation.

The success of Web advertising has been hampered by two major problems. First, no consensus has emerged on how to measure and charge for site-visitor views. Since the Web allows multiple measurements, such as number of visitors, number of unique visitors, number of click-throughs, and other attributes of visitor behavior, it has been difficult for Web advertisers to develop a standard for advertising charges. In addition to the number of visitors or page views, stickiness is a critical element to creating a presence that will attract advertisers. The stickiness of a Web site is its ability to keep visitors at the site and to attract repeat visitors. People spend more time at a sticky Web site and are thus exposed to more advertising.

The second problem is that very few Web sites have sufficient numbers of visitors to interest large advertisers. Most successful advertising on the Web is targeted to very specific groups. The characteristics that marketers use to group visitors is called demographic information, and includes such things as address, age, gender, income level, type of job held, hobbies, and religion. It can be difficult to determine whether a given Web site is attracting a specific market segment unless that site collects demographic information from its visitors, which is information that visitors are increasingly reluctant to provide because of privacy concerns.

Subscription Revenue Model

One alternative to a pure advertising revenue model is to add the sale of subscriptions to the information content of the Web site. Few newspaper or magazine publishers use a pure subscription model. Most of these businesses that sell subscription access to their sites use a combination of advertising and subscription revenues, much as print newspapers and magazines do. Consumers Union, the publisher of the monthly product evaluations and ratings magazine *Consumer Reports*, is an exception to this rule. It does operate a Web site that relies heavily on subscriptions. Consumers Union is a not-for-profit organization that does not accept advertising as a matter of policy (because it might appear to influence its testing and research results for the products of its advertisers or their advertisers' competitors). Therefore, the site is supported by a combination of subscription revenue and some donations. The Web site does offer some free information as a way to attract subscribers and to fulfill its organizational mission of encouraging improvements in product safety, but this is not a revenue generator for the organization.

Advertising-Subscription Combination Model

In the advertising-subscription combined revenue model used by most online newspapers and magazines, subscribers pay a fee and accept some level of advertising. On Web sites that use the advertising-subscription revenue model, subscribers are typically subjected to much less advertising than they are on advertising-supported sites. Firms have had varying levels of success in applying this model and a number of companies have moved to or from this model over their lifetimes.

Two leading newspapers, *The New York Times* and *The Wall Street Journal*, use a combined advertising-subscription model. *The New York Times* version is mostly advertising-supported with a small subscription fee for visitors who want full access to enhanced online versions of the newspaper's crossword puzzles. *The New York Times* also provides a searchable archive of past articles and charges a small fee for access to non-current articles. *The Wall Street Journal*'s combination model is weighted more heavily to subscription revenue. The site allows non-subscriber visitors to view the classified ads and certain stories from the newspaper, but most of the content is reserved for subscribers who pay an annual fee for access to the site. Visitors who already subscribe to the print edition are offered a reduced rate on subscriptions to the online edition.

Note that both of these newspapers use one version of this revenue model for their print edition and another version for their online editions. Increasingly, newspapers and magazines are finding that they need to use different revenue models for their print and online editions. Other newspapers, including *The Washington Post* and the *Los Angeles Times*, use another variation of the combination revenue model. These newspapers do not charge any subscription fees for access to their Web sites. Instead, they offer current stories free of charge on their Web sites, but require payment for older articles.

Business Week offers yet another combination revenue variation. It offers some free content at its *Business Week* online site, but requires the purchase of a subscription to the *Business Week* print magazine if visitors want to gain access the entire site. Subscribers who want to read archived articles that are more than five years old are levied an additional charge per article. *Business Week* does place content in the subscriber section of its Web site before the magazine appears on the newsstands or is delivered to subscribers.

Sports fans visit the ESPN site for all types of sports-related information. Leveraging its brand name from its cable television businesses, ESPN is one of the most visited sites on the Web. It sells advertising and offers a vast amount of free information, but serious sports fans can subscribe to its Insider service to obtain access to even more sports information. Thus, ESPN uses a revenue model that includes advertising and subscription revenue, but it only collects the subscription revenue from Insider subscribers, who are a small percentage of site visitors.

Classified Advertising Sites: An Advertising Revenue Model

Although attempts to create general-interest Web sites that generate sufficient advertising revenue to be profitable have met with mixed results, sites that target niche markets have been more successful. For newspapers, classified advertising is very profitable. Thus, Web sites that specialize in providing only classified advertising do have profit potential. This is especially true if they can reach a narrow target market and charge higher rates because the advertising reaches the right audience.

One implementation of the advertising-supported revenue model that does appear to be successful is Web employment advertising. As the number of people using the Web increases, these businesses will be able to move out of their current focus on technology and higher-level jobs and include advertising for all kinds of positions. These sites can use the same approach that search-engine sites use to offer advertisers target markets. When a visitor specifies an interest in, for example, engineering jobs in Dallas, the results page can include a targeted banner ad for which an advertiser will pay more, because it is directed at a specific segment of the audience.

Employment ad sites can also target specific categories of job seekers by including short articles on topics of interest. These articles increase the site's stickiness and it helps draw people to the site who are not necessarily looking for a job. This is a good tactic because people who are not looking for a job are often the candidates most highly sought by employers. Classified employment advertising site Monster.com includes links to articles, reports, a message board, and chat sessions that might interest employees at various levels. It also offers a variety of newsletters tailored to employees at various levels in their current positions.

Another type of classified advertising Web site that can generate sufficient revenue to be profitable is the "used vehicle" site. Trader Publishing has printed advertising newspapers for many years and now operates a number of vehicle classified advertising sites under names such as AutoTrader.com, CycleTrader.com, BoatTrader.com, and AeroTrader.com. These sites accept paid advertising from individuals and companies that want to sell cars, motorcycles, boats, and airplanes. Trader Publishing charges a fee for each listing and gives the seller the option of running the ad on the Web site only or on the Web and in the print version of the advertising newspaper. If the product has a dedicated following, this type of site can be successful by catering to small audiences. For example, the VetteFinders site sells classified ads for Corvette automobiles only.

In 2002, another classified advertising category emerged, the dating services and personal ads sector. This category yielded more than $87 million in sales revenue in 2002 and is expected to continue growing rapidly (Smith, 2003).

Information Providers: Subscription Revenue Models

Some companies that own intellectual property or the rights to such property have begun using the Internet as an important distribution channel for selling intellectual property rights as digital products. For example, LexisNexis began as a legal research tool that has been available as an online product for years. Today, LexisNexis offers a variety of information services, including legal information, corporate information, government information, news, and resources for academic libraries (*Electronic Information Report*, 2001). The original legal information product exists on the Web today as Lexis.com and provides full-text search of court cases, laws, patent databases, and tax regulations. In the past, law firms had to subscribe and install expensive dedicated computer systems to obtain access to this information.

The Web has given LexisNexis customers much more flexibility in how they purchase information. Through the Lexis.com Web site, law firms can subscribe to several versions of the service that are customized for different firm sizes and usage patterns. The Web site even offers a credit card charge option for infrequent users who do not want a subscription. LexisNexis has used the Web to improve the delivery and variety of its existing product line and has been able to devise new products that take advantage of the Web's features. Chung and Rao (2003) outline a general model for using product bundling in market segmentation applications such as the LexisNexis example.

ProQuest, a Web site that sells digital copies of published documents, has its roots in two businesses: the former Bell and Howell learning materials business and University Microfilms International (UMI). These firms had acquired reproduction rights to a variety of published and unpublished materials (Hane, 1999). For example, UMI had contracts with most North American universities to publish all doctoral dissertations and masters theses on demand. ProQuest offers digital versions of these documents for sale, along with a number of newspapers, journals, and other specialized academic publications. Many schools and libraries have subscriptions to ProQuest. Other companies, such as SilverPlatter Information and EBSCO Information Services sell subscriptions to digital versions of journals and books to corporate and university libraries. These companies also sell access to bibliographic databases and electronic journals to individuals, schools, companies, and libraries.

Dow Jones is a major business publisher that has sold subscriptions to digitized newspaper, magazine, and journal content for a number of years. The company offered a customized digital clipping service that provided subscribers with a daily e-mail message of news on topics of interest to them (O'Leary, 1998). Dow Jones and Reuters, a British company, joined in 2002 to create an online content management and integration service called Factiva. Factiva now provides the same types of services that Dow Jones had provided, but also gives companies the ability to integrate their existing content (such as a corporate library) with Dow Jones and Reuters news sources (Conhaim, 2002).

One of the first academic organizations to use Internet distribution was the Association for Computer Machinery (ACM) with its ACM Digital Library. This Web site offers subscriptions to electronic versions of ACM journals to its members and to library and institutional subscribers (White, 2001). Academic publishing has always been a business with thin margins because the number of potential subscribers is much smaller than more mainstream publications. Even the most highly regarded academic journals often have fewer than 2,000 subscribers. However, the fixed costs of publishing remained very much the same for all publishers, both large and small. To break even, academic journals often must charge hundreds or even thousands of dollars for a one-year subscription (Parks, 2002). Electronic publishing eliminates the high costs of paper, printing, and delivery, and makes dissemination of research results less expensive and more timely.

As was the case for other technologies, such as VCRs and subscription cable television, many of the early commercial users of Web technology were dealers in adult-themed entertainment material. Many of the first profitable sites on the Web were sellers of adult digital content (Simons, 1996). These sites pioneered the processing of credit card payment transactions on the Internet and many different digital video technologies that are now used by all types of businesses on the Web.

Online Games: Subscription and Combination Revenue Models

Computer and video games have become a huge industry, with revenue now exceeding that of the film industry. An increasing portion of the industry's revenue is generated online. In the past, many sites that offered games relied on advertising revenue. A growing number of these sites now include subscription and fee-for-play games. Some sites sell software that gamers must buy and download to play the games, others require payment of a subscription fee to enter the fee-for-play games area on the site. Microsoft's MSN Games, Sony's Station.com, Electronic Arts' EA.com, and RealNetworks' RealOne Arcade are among the leading game sites that include subscription game services. For example, Sony's EverQuest adventure game has drawn more than 400,000 players who have purchased a $40 software package and pay $10 per month to continue playing the game (Kushner, 2002). Most of the game sites charge a monthly subscription of between $5 and $20 for access to all their fee-based, games offerings. The Interactive Digital Software Association estimates that about 170 million people in the United States alone are regular game players, a number that is growing about 17 percent each year (McLaughlin, 2001).

Concerts and Films: Subscription Revenue Models

As more households obtain broadband access to the Internet, an increasing number of companies will provide streaming video of concerts and films to paying subscribers. With a revenue model patterned after cable television companies, firms such as Intertainer and RealNetworks are selling subscriptions for delivery of video content to computers and other devices through cable modem and DSL connections.

The main technological limitation these companies face is that each additional customer who downloads a video stream requires that the provider purchase additional bandwidth from its ISP. Television broadcasters, on the other hand, need only pay the fixed cost of a transmitter because the airwaves are free and carry the transmission to an unlimited number of viewers at no additional cost. In contrast, as the number of an Internet-based provider's subscribers increases, the cost of the provider's Internet connection increases. However, if these Web entertainment companies can charge a high enough monthly fee, they should be able to cover the additional costs of technology upgrades and still make a profit.

Revenue Models in Transition

Many companies have gone through transitions in their revenue models for digital products. As more people use the Web and as their behavior changes, some companies have altered their revenue models to meet their customers' needs. This section describes the revenue model transitions undertaken by five different companies as they gained experience in the online world and as they faced the changes that occurred in that world. These and other companies might well face the need to make further adjustments to their revenue models in the future.

Transition: Subscription to Advertising

Microsoft created an online magazine, Slate, to provide news and current events information. Slate included experienced writers and editors on its staff and industry observers expected the magazine to be a success. Microsoft felt that the magazine had a high value, too. At a time when most online magazines were using an advertising-supported revenue model, Slate charged an annual subscription fee after a limited free introductory period.

Although Slate drew a wide readership and received acclaim for its quality reporting and writing, it was unable to draw a sufficient number of paid subscribers. At its peak, Slate had about 27,000 subscribers generating annual revenue of $500,000, which was far less than the cost of creating the content and maintaining the Web site (Sanderfoot and Jenkins, 2001).

Slate is now operated as an advertising-supported site. Because it is a part of Microsoft, Slate does not report detailed profit numbers, but the magazine announced that it was profitable as of April 2003 on revenues of $7 million (Carr, 2003). Microsoft maintains the Slate site as part of its MSN portal, so it is likely that Slate increases the stickiness of the portal, which is an additional benefit to Microsoft not reflected in the accounting determination of unit profits for Slate.

Transition: Pure Advertising to Combination Revenue

Another online magazine, Salon.com, that has also received acclaim for its content, has moved its revenue model in a direction opposite to that of Slate. After operating for several years as an advertising-supported site, Salon.com now offers an optional subscription version of its site. The subscription offering was motivated by the company's inability to raise the additional money from investors that it needed to continue operations (Sanderfoot and Jenkins, 2001).

Subscribers pay $30 per year for access rights to a version of the magazine called Salon Premium that is free of advertising and that can be downloaded for storage and later offline reading on the subscriber's computer. Premium subscribers also gain access to additional content such as downloadable music, e-books, and audio books.

Transition: Advertising to Fee-for-Services

Xdrive Technologies opened its original advertising-supported Web site in 1999. Xdrive offered free disk storage space online to users. The users would see advertising on each page and had to provide personal information that would allow Xdrive to send targeted e-mail advertising to them. Its offering was very attractive to Web users who had begun to accumulate large files, such as MP3 music files, and who wanted to access those files from several computers in different locations (Schwarz, 2001).

After two years of offering free disk storage space, Xdrive found that it was unable to pay the costs of providing the service with the advertising revenue it had been able to generate. It switched to a subscription-supported model and began selling the service to business users as well as individuals. The amount of the monthly subscription is based on the amount of disk space reserved for the user and on the number of people who have access to the disk space (Schuchart, 2003).

Transition: Advertising to Subscription

Northern Light was founded in 1995 as a search engine with a twist. In addition to searching the Web, it searched its own database of journal articles and other publications to which it had acquired reproduction rights. When a user ran a search, Northern Light would return a results page that included links to Web sites and to abstracts of the items in its own database. Users could then follow the links to Web sites, which were free, or could purchase access to the database items (Kalin, 1997).

Thus, Northern Light's revenue model was a combination of the advertising-supported model used by most other Web search engines plus a fee-based information access service similar to the subscription services offered by ProQuest and EBSCO mentioned earlier in this chapter. The difference in the Northern Light model was that users could pay for just one or two articles (the cost was typically between one and five dollars per article) instead of paying a large amount of money for unlimited access to its database on an annual subscription basis. Northern Light did also offer subscription access to most of its database to companies, schools, and libraries, however.

In January 2002, Northern Light decided that the advertising revenue it was earning from the ads it sold on search results pages was insufficient to justify continuing to offer that service. It stopped offering public access to its search engine and converted to a new revenue model that is primarily subscription-supported (Kontzer, 2002).

Multiple Transitions

Encyclopedia Britannica is a company that transferred its existing reputation for high quality to the Web (Schneider, 2004). The Encyclopedia Britannica has developed a very respected brand name in research and education over its many years in print publishing. Britannica began in the late 1700s when a group of academics collected notes they had made while conducting research and decided to publish them as a series of articles. After more than 200 years of successful print publications, Britannica moved to electronic distribution with a CD offering in the mid-1990s (Ferris, 1996).

About the same time, Britannica launched its online presence with two Web offerings. The Britannica Internet Guide was a free Web navigation aid that classified and rated information-laden Web sites. It featured reviews written by Britannica editors who also selected and indexed the sites. The company's other Web site, Encyclopedia Britannica Online, was available for a subscription fee or as part of its Encyclopedia Britannica CD package. Britannica used the free site to attract users to the paid subscription site (Conhaim, 2001).

In 1999, disappointed by low subscription sales, Britannica converted to a free, adver-tiser-supported site (Schneider, 2004). The first day the new site, Britannica.com, became available at no cost to the public, it had over 15 million visitors, forcing Britannica to shut down for two weeks to upgrade its servers (Book Publishing Report, 1999). The Britannica.com site offered the full content of the print edition in searchable form, plus access to the Merriam-Webster's Collegiate Dictionary and the Britannica Book of the Year. One of the most successful aspects of the site was the way it integrated the Britannica Internet Guide Web-rating service with its print content. The Britannica Store sold the CD version of the encyclopedia along with other educational and scientific products to help generate revenue.

After two years of trying to generate a profit using advertising to generate revenue, Britannica succumbed to its insufficient advertising revenues (Schneider, 2004). In 2001, Britannica returned to a combination model in which it offered free summaries of encyclopedia articles and access to the Merriam-Webster's Collegiate Dictionary on the Web, but placed the full text of the encyclopedia in a restricted part of their Web site. Full text access was available for a subscription fee of $50 per year or $5 per month (DiSabatino, 2001).

Schneider (2004) notes that Britannica has undergone four major revenue model transitions, from being a print publisher to a seller of information on the Web to an advertising revenue-supported Web site to a combination advertising subscription model, in just a few short years. The main thing that Britannica sells is its reputation and the expertise of its editors, contributors, and advisors. Britannica has decided that the best way to capitalize on that reputation and expertise is through a combined format of subscriptions and advertising support.

The Future of Digital Product Sales: Web Services

A key element in the delivery of digital products is the ability to communicate and send products across organizational boundaries: from one company to another, or from a company to an individual consumer. Web services hold the hope of providing this capability in the near future (Homan, 2002).

Web services are combination of software tools that let application software in one organization communicate with other applications over a network by using a specific set of standard protocols. Web services can be described as self-contained, modular units of application logic that provide some business functionality to other applications through an Internet connection (Ismail, Patil, and Saigal, 2002). A growing number of companies are using Web services today to improve customer service and reduce costs of operations within their enterprises.

Web services allow programs written in different languages on different platforms to communicate with each other and accomplish transaction processing and other business tasks. The common format of this machine-to-machine communication was originally HTML, however, most newer Web services implementations use XML.

Development of Web Services

The first Web services were information sources that programmers incorporated into software applications. For example, a company that wanted to collect all of its financial management information into one spreadsheet might use Web services to obtain bank account and loan balances, stock portfolio holdings, and current interest rates on financial instruments. If this information is available through Web services, the spreadsheet program can use those services to update itself automatically. Some of the information might be available as a Web service at no cost. Other information access might require a subscription. But Web services can make automated access of the information much easier (Fingar, 2002).

A more advanced example is a purchasing software application that could use Web services to obtain price information from a variety of vendors. After a purchasing agent reviews the price and delivery information and authorizes the purchase, the software can submit the order and track it until the shipment is received. On the other side of this transaction, the vendor's software can use Web services (in addition to providing price and delivery information) to check the buyer's credit and contract with a freight company to handle the shipment (Dyck, 2002).

Current Applications of Web Services

J.P. Morgan Chase & Co., a major investment bank, uses Web services in its investment information portal to pull information such as economic forecasts, analyses of specific companies, industry forecasts, and current securities trading markets results into online reports that customers can access on the company's customer portal site. The bank's customers could each obtain all of this information independently, but the bank's aggregation provides a service to its customers. Another example is CUNA Mutual Group, which sells services such as check clearing and construction management to credit union customers throughout the United States. CUNA provides many of these services by running programs on its legacy systems. Instead of reprogramming everything so it could be accessible on the Web, CUNA uses Web services to take information from the legacy systems and generate Web pages that it makes accessible to its customers (Pallatto, 2002).

Dollar Rent-a-Car developed a Web services implementation, built with XML, that connects its reservation system to Southwest Airline' system. This allows current information about availability and pricing to be automatically transferred to the Southwest system that runs its reservations Web site. Customers who buy a Southwest airline ticket can book a rental car on the Southwest site. The transaction is automatically transmitted back through a Web services connection to Dollar, where the inventory control and accounting systems are updated in real time (Choi and Whinston, 2002).

The Promise of Web Services

For years, the IT industry has been driven by vendors who promoted proprietary programming languages and systems that could not communicate with each other easily. Large companies have been forced to hire substantial programming staffs or consulting firms to create middleware that could integrate their hodgepodge of programs for order entry, financial management, inventory control, marketing, and other functions. Since the idea of successfully and easily connecting software within an organization is still an unachieved goal in many organizations, connecting software across organizational boundaries is revolutionary.

Software has been traditionally sold as a product. Web services allow software and related knowledge-based products to be sold as a service. This gives sellers more flexibility to use bundling, versioning, and price-differentiation strategies to increase profits.

The promise of easy integration (Choi and Whinston, 2002) provides a significant benefit to customers. Web services built with XML can give organizations the ability to adapt to changing software environments, as well (Dyck, 2002). However, many companies are concerned about managing Web services given that the standards are evolving, no quality-of-service monitoring function has been included in the standards, and the security of Web services has yet to be tested by a concerted attack (Hall, 2003).

Conclusions

This chapter defined digital products, described their characteristics, and outlined the environment in which they are offered for sale on the Web. The chapter analyzed pricing and distribution options for digital products in an online environment and provided examples of how companies are combining those options into viable revenue models. The chapter concluded with an analysis of the promises and risks of a combined–delivery, digital-product medium, Web services.

References

Adamy, J. (2000, September 26). E-tailer price tailoring may be wave of future. *Chicago Tribune*, 4.

Bailey, J. (1998). Intermediation and electronic markets: aggregation and pricing in internet commerce. Ph.D. dissertation. Cambridge, MA: Massachusetts Institute of Technology.

Bakos, J. (1997). Reducing buyer search costs: implications for electronic marketplaces. *Management Science, 43*(12), 1676-1692.

Barsh, J., Kramer, E., Maue, D. & Zuckerman, N. (2001). Magazines' home companion. *McKinsey Quarterly, 2*, 83-91.

Bichler, M. & Loebbecke, C. (2000). Pricing strategies and technologies for on-line delivered content. *Journal of End User Computing, 12*(2), 4-10.

Book Publishing Report. (1999). Britannica's online move signals critical point for reference market, *24*(44), 4-5.

Brynjolfsson, E. & Smith, M. (2000). Frictionless commerce? a comparison of Internet and conventional retailers. *Management Science, 46*(4), 563-585.

Buyer and seller liability for price discrimination. (2001, September). *Purchasing Law Report*, 2-5.

Campbell, M. (1999). Perceptions of price unfairness: antecedents and consequences. *Journal of Marketing Research*, *36*(2), 187-199.

Choi, J. (2003). Bundling new products with old to signal quality, with application to the sequencing of new products. *International Journal of Industrial Organization*, *21*(8), 1179-1200.

Choi, S.Y. & Whinston, A. (2000). *The Internet economy: technology and practice.* Austin: SmartEcon.

Choi, S.Y. & Whinston, A. (2002). Web services: laying down the infrastructure for the digital economy. SmartEcon.com. Retrieved from the World Wide Web: http://www.smartecon.com/articles/web_services.asp.

Chung, J. & Rao, V. (2003). A general choice model for bundles with multiple-category products: application to market segmentation and optimal pricing for bundles. *Journal of Marketing Research*, *40*(2), 115-130.

Cohan, P. (2001). Considerations for profitable business models. *eContent*, 60-61.

Cox, J. (2001). Can differential prices be fair? *Journal of Product & Brand Management*, *10*(5), 264-275.

Cripps, M. & Schmidt, K. (1996). Reputation in perturbed repeated games. *Journal of Economic Theory*, *69*(2), 387-410.

Christman, E. (2002, June). Wishful Thinking. *Billboard*, *114*(23), C 1-2.

Conhaim, W. (2001). Encyclopedia Britannica makes some changes. *Link-Up*, *18*(4), 1-2.

Conhaim, W. (2002). Upgrading from Dow Jones Interactive to Factiva.com. *Link-Up*, *19*(4), 2-3.

Dahl, E. (2003). Online music: new hits and misses. *PC World*, *21*(9), 119-123.

DiSabatino, J. (2001). From fee to free to fee again: Britannica.com restructures. *Computerworld*, *35*(12), 16.

Dyck, T. (2002). Web services impact. *eWeek*, September 16, 39-51.

Edwards, C. (1942). Types of differential pricing. *Journal of Marketing*, *6*(4), 156-167.

Electronic Information Report. (2001). LexisNexis counterpunches competitors with product launch, *22*(22), 1-2.

Estalami, A. (1999). Consumer savings in complementary product bundles. *Journal of Marketing Theory and Practice, 7*(3), 107-115.

Fingar, P. (2002, January 21). Web services among peers. *Internet World*.

Fishburn, P. and Odlyzko, A. (1999). Competitive pricing of information goods: subscription pricing versus pay-per-use. *Economic Theory*, *13*(2), 447-470.

Forsyth, J., Lavoie, J. & McGuire, T. (2000). Segmenting the e-market. *The McKinsey Quarterly*, 4. Retrieved from the World Wide Web: http://mckinseyquarterly.com/article_page.asp?tk=302016:939:24&ar=939&L2=24&L3=44.

Gillmor, D. (2003). RSS starting to catch on. *Computerworld*, *37*(30), 19.

Godin, S. & Peppers, D. (1999). *Permission Marketing: Turning Strangers into Friends, and Friends into Customers*. New York: Simon & Schuster.

Hagerty, J. & Berman, D. (2003, August 27). New battleground over Web privacy: ads that snoop. *The Wall Street Journal*, A1-A2.

Hall, M. (2003). Web services' sharp edge. *Computerworld*, *37*(20), 34.

Hane, P. (1999). UMI's new identity. *Information Today*, *16*(5), 1-4.

Homan, D. (2002, August 26). Look past products to Web services' true promise. *InformationWeek*, 44–45.

Ismail, A., Patil, S. & Saigal, S. (2002). When computers learn to talk: a web services primer. *McKinsey Quarterly*, 70–78.

Jones, R. (2001). Factiva.com launched at SLA. *Information Today*, *18*(7), 1-2.

Kalin, S. (1997). Northern Light search engine finds more than web pages. *InfoWorld*, *19*(33), 56.

Kontzer, T. (2002, January 28). In Search Of Business Data. *InformationWeek*, 63-64.

Krishnamurthy, S. (2003). *E-Commerce Management: Text and Cases*. Mason, OH: South-Western.

Krumenaker, L. (2003). Tribunes and tribulation. *Searcher*, *11*(7), 28-30.

Kushner, D. (2002, July 11). Multiplayer game servers provide worlds of fun. *The New York Times*. Retrieved from the World Wide Web: http://www.nytimes.com/2002/07/11/technology/circuits/11HOWW.html.

Lee, H. (1998). Do electronic marketplaces lower the price of goods? *Communications of the ACM*, *41*(1), 73-80.

Lee, L. & Capell, K. (2003, June 23). Taps form music retailers? *Business Week*, 40.

Liao-Troth, M. & Griffith, T. (2002). Software, shareware and freeware: multiplex commitment to an electronic social exchange system. *Journal of Organizational Behavior*, *33*(5), 635-653.

Manjoo, F. (2003, April 29). I have seen the future of music and its name is i-tunes. *Salon.com*. Retrieved from the World Wide Web: http://www.salon.com/tech/feature/2003/04/29/itunes/index.html.

McLaughlin, K. (2001, March 21). Real makes gaming play: hopes its customer base will pay for online diversions. *Business 2.0*. Retrieved from the World Wide Web: http://www.business2.com/ebusiness/2001/03/28783.htm.

Metz, C. (2003, April 22). Just how rampant is spyware? *PC Magazine*, M7-M8.

Moon, I. (2001, July 23). The champs in online games. *Business Week*, 51.

O'Leary, M. (1998). Dow Jones interactive rounds out Dow Jones web migration. *Information Today*, *15*(1).

Pallatto, J. (2002). Web services deliver, *Internet World*, *8*(10).

Parks, R. (2002). The Faustian grip of academic publishing. *Journal of Economic Methodology*, *9*(3), 317-335.

Peppers, D. & Rogers, M. (1997). *The One to One Future: Building Relationships One Customer at a Time*. New York: Currency Books.

Roth, D. (1998, April 6). Well connected. *Forbes, 161*(7), 44.

Sanderfoot, A. & Jenkins, C. (2001). Content sites pursue fee-based model. *Folio: The Magazine for Magazine Management, 30*(6), 15-16.

Schneider, G. (2004). *Electronic Commerce*. (5th ed.). Boston, MA: Course Technology.

Schuchart, S. (2003, February 20). Xdrive revitalizes file sharing, *Network Computing, 14*(3), 32-33.

Schwartz, E. (2001). Next frontier: storage. *InfoWorld, 23*(22), 91.

Shapiro, C. & Varian, H. (1998). *Information rules: A strategic guide to the network economy*. Cambridge, MA: Harvard Business School Press.

Sharples, H. (1999). Internet advertising spending is projected to rise sharply. *Graphic Arts Monthly, 71*(11), 86.

Sieber, S. & Sabatier, J. (2003). Market bundling strategies in the horizontal portal industry. *International Journal of Electronic Commerce, 7*(4), 37-54.

Simons, J. (1996). The Web's dirty secret. *U.S. News & World Report, 121*(7), 51-52.

Smith, S. (2003). Content plus: what's selling online. *eContent, 26*(4), 40.

Tynan, D. & Gilbert, J. (2003). Web ads on the rebound? *Sales & Marketing Management, 155*(2), 17-18.

Venkatesh, R. & Kamakura, W. (2003). Optimal bundling and pricing under a monopoly: contrasting complements and substitutes from independently valued products. *Journal of Business, 76*(2), 211-231.

Venkatesh, R. & Mahajan, V., (1993). A probabilistic approach to pricing a bundle of products. *Journal of Marketing Research, 30*(4), 494-508.

White, J. (2001). ACM opens portal to computing literature. *Communications of the ACM, 44*(7), 14-17.

Chapter IX

On Software Piracy*

Sougata Poddar
National University of Singapore (NUS), Singapore

Abstract

The pervasiveness of the illegal copying of software is indeed a worldwide phenomenon. Economists argue that when the piracy takes place at the end-users' level, the original software developer finds it profitable to allow limited piracy when the effect of network externality is reasonably strong in the users market. We argue when the piracy is of retail in nature, the same logic cannot be extended as the reason for piracy and show that it is always optimal for the original software developer to protect its software even when the effect of network externality is strong in the end-users' market. We suggest that piracy depends on more fundamental issues like demand environment, market structure, nature of piracy and nature of competition. The other issue we cover here is the economic impact of piracy on the welfare of a society. We discuss various policy implications on regulating piracy in developing as well as developed markets.

Introduction

In this age of digital technology, the heavy use of computer-related jobs using various software packages in our day-to-day activity has become a rule rather than exception. With the advent of digital technology and the popular usage of software packages, one thing that is also making headlines at the same time is software piracy. The pervasiveness of the illegal copying of software is indeed a worldwide phenomenon. It is not only having a profound effect on the users of the software, but also on the software industry as a whole. It is also having a tremendous effect on the development of digital intellectual properties and technologies. Software piracy is rampant because of the very nature of the product. Software production incurs large development costs, but once developed, the manufacturing costs of fabricating a copy of the software program are almost negligible. In other words, replicated copies of the original software incur zero costs and this is precisely why software piracy presents such a lucrative and effective option for those who are out to make a quick profit.[1] This implies a huge loss of potential customers of original software buyers, which directly translates into revenue losses for the software industry. Software manufacturers, through their trade organizations, have been asserting the huge damage inflicted on their businesses by the illegal use of software. In 1995, the Business Software Alliance (BSA) claimed that the industry lost "$13 billion per year," "$35 million per day," and "$407 per second" from software piracy. The *1998 Global Software Piracy Report* released (in May 1999) by the BSA and the Software & Information Industry Association (SIIA), the two leading trade associations for the software industry, estimates that of the 615 million new business software applications installed worldwide during 1998, 231 million – or 38% – were pirated. In other words, one out of every three software applications installed worldwide was pirated! In 2001, the corresponding figure remains at 40%.[2] Revenue losses to the global software industry due to piracy were estimated at $13.08 billion in 2002. Asia, North America, and Western Europe accounted for the majority of world revenue losses. In 2002, the combined total losses for these regions stood over $10.5 billion, and within that Asia alone accounted for a loss over $5 billion. These losses not only pose a serious constraint on the growth of the software industry but also adversely affect investment decisions and limit the development of new software products. At the same time, rampant piracy inhibits job creation and government revenue contributions. As a matter of fact, PricewaterhouseCoopers (1998) estimated that if world governments had reduced software piracy rates to benchmark levels[3], direct and indirect employment would have increased by 521,663 jobs and tax revenues by as much as $13.7 billion in 1996/97 alone for the non-U.S. economy. For the U.S. economy, reducing piracy would have generated an additional 130,000 jobs and nearly $1.0 billion in tax revenues in 1996. And this problem of software piracy only gets bigger with the revolution and intensification of the Internet. "What Do You Want To Pirate Today?" reads a banner at one of the many sites that can be found by any user doing a basic Internet search for the word "warez" – the online term for unlicensed programs. The emergence of the "Web" has added a new dimension to software piracy by permitting electronic sales and transmissions of illegal software on a grand scale.

Given this, conventional wisdom suggests the need for the legal software firms and governments to take a harsh approach on piracy of software. Interestingly, a group of economists would ask the question, in reality, is the original software developer or the government or the controlling authority seriously interested to stop piracy? In their recent work they actually show that the answer is not necessarily positive. This strand of literature (Conner and Rumelt (1991), Takeyama (1994), Slive and Bernhardt (1998), Shy and Thisse (1999)) provides us with the unconventional wisdom on the issue of software piracy. It shows that in some situations even the original software developer may not necessarily want to clamp down on piracy – even when it has the means to do so. In other words, it is actually profitable for the original software developer to allow limited piracy. The arguments to establish this basically stand on the feature of network externality that is observed in the software user market.[4] It is true that the occurrence of network externality is a very prevalent feature in the software market and the existence of it plays a central role for this (piracy) phenomenon. But, in this chapter, we argue that all these unconventional results cannot be accepted as a general explanation for the existence of software piracy in the real world. To prove the point, the chapter comes up with a model where its shows that even in the presence of strong effect of network externality, protection as opposed to allowing piracy is always optimal for the original software developer. It also shows that the incentive to protect is even higher with the presence of network externality as opposed to the case without any network externality. Therefore, to understand the real reason for existence of software piracy, one needs to have a closer look to the more fundamental economic issues that lie behind this phenomenon. The main message is whether piracy is profitable or not to the original developer depends on the market structure, demand environment and the nature of the competition.

The whole chapter will be done in three parts. In the first part (part I), we begin following the existing literature, why network externality could be a reason for the existence of software piracy in certain situations. After that a game-theoretic model of price competition between an original software developer and a pirate will be studied and analyzed in detail to see the effect of network externality on piracy. In this part, we will assume that both of the competitors move *simultaneously,* i.e., choose their strategies for operation simultaneously. In the second part (part II), a game of *sequential* moves will be focused, where the original firm acts as a leader and the pirate as the follower. The mode of piracy that will be considered in both of these analyses is retail piracy. A retail piracy takes place when a pirate (just like another firm) competes with the original software developer by producing a copy which may not be as reliable as the original product, but comes with a cheaper price. In the third part (part III) of the chapter, a complete welfare analysis will be done by assuming (i) when a pirate is present in the market, and (ii) when the pirate is absent. The question we ask, if there is a social planner (say, the government) whose objective is to maximize society's welfare, then what would be the policy recommendation with respect to piracy? In other words, the question is whether allowing piracy is welfare improving or welfare reducing from the society's point of view. In this part, a rigorous analysis will be done on this issue. This will be followed by a general discussion on the welfare aspects of software piracy in a wider perspective. Towards the end, we highlight the contribution of this chapter to the academic as well as business practitioners, like managers and entrepreneurs. Finally, we conclude the chapter with a brief summary of the main findings and by pointing out some future directions of research.

The whole study that will be done here is a theoretical analysis. Tools of economic theory and game theory are used to model various economic situations. It will develop analytical models in order to explain and understand the important economic issues of software piracy. The study will also provide testable hypotheses for empirical and applied work.

Before concluding the introduction, we would like to say a few words on game theory and the aspect of network externality that we consider here. Firstly, for those readers who are not that familiar with game theory (some reading material is listed in bibliography), game theory is a formalization of strategic thinking. It is useful in a situation where the number of players (e.g., firms, economic agents) is not very large. In a situation like this every player thinks strategically to maximize his/her payoff knowing about the fact that every other player is doing the same. In such a situation, the payoff to one player not only depends on his/her action (strategy), but it also depends on other players' actions (strategies) as well. In real life, in industries where there are only a few firms operating, game theory could be a useful tool to analyze the strategic behaviour of firms. Examples of such industries are: airline, pharmaceutical, telecommunication, banking, computer (hardware and software) and so on.

The second issue is pertaining to the feature of network externality that we have already talked about. We would like to emphasize that when we talk about network externality, we are not limiting ourselves to the physical internal or external network among users, but a network in much broader sense. All possible users (whether or not they are physically connected by some network) of particular software or generally an operating system (e.g., Windows, Linux, etc.) potentially form a group/network, where they can gain much by sharing information/files among themselves. Naturally, the greater the number of users in the network, the higher the gain from sharing, hence, the higher the utility to the individual user.[5] As we will see, this aspect of network externality is going to play a major role in our forthcoming analysis.

Part I

Network Externality – A Reason for Piracy

We start with the assumption that consumers' willingness to pay for software increases with the total number of consumers who use (legally or illegally) the same software. That is, the presence of network externalities reflects the fact that software users place a high value on compatibility and file sharing. Suppose now that software is protected, and let us assume that installed protective devices make it prohibitively costly for any consumer to pirate the software. In this case, some consumers buy the software, whereas all others simply do not use any software. Notice that if firms keep prices fixed, legal users have all the incentives in the world to give this software for free to non-users, thereby increasing the compatibility value of the software. However, legal users are prevented from sharing their software by the protective devices installed into the software. If, however, firms would remove protection from the software, then some consumers may be willing to pay a higher price since the value of the software increases with the total number of legal and illegal users. This is the core of the argument developed in the section.

In particular, Takeyama (1994) considers a model of unauthorized reproduction of intellectual property in the presence of demand network externalities and shows that unauthorized copying can induce greater profits to the original firm. She considered a discreet demand model with two groups of consumers who have different valuations for a good. She analyzed the situations when copying is easily possible by the users and when cost of copying is prohibitively high, hence copying is not possible. In these two contrasting situations, she showed that if the network effect is sufficiently large, profits for the firm are higher with copying than without copying. The result follows from the fact that unauthorized copying can be relatively efficient means of increasing network size. In effect, unauthorized copying allows the firm to price-discriminate among different classes of consumers. With copying, large network size can be achieved by the existence of marginal consumers who make reproductions (at zero cost to the firm), while infra-marginal consumers purchase originals at a price that may largely appropriate the externality of increased network size created by copiers. Without copying, the same network size may only be obtained at a possibly lower price on all existing units. Increase in network size increases the value of the product unambiguously to all consumers therefore enabling firms to raise price to those who buy it from the firm. In other papers, Conner and Rumelt (1991) and Slive and Berhardt (1998) come up with a similar finding explaining why a software manufacturer may permit limited piracy of its product. These studies concentrated in a situation where there is only one original manufacturer, in other words, a monopolistic industry. On the other hand a strategic approach to software piracy is found in Shy and Thisse (1999). They show that there is a strategic reason why software firms have followed consumers' desire to drop software protection. They analyze software protection policies in a price-setting duopoly software industry selling differentiated software packages, where also consumers' preference for particular software is affected by the number of other consumers who (legally or illegally) use the same software. Their results show when firms protect their software a low-price equilibrium emerges if network effects are strong, whereas a high-price equilibrium arises under weak network effects. Therefore, all firms are better off with software protection when network effects are weak. In contrasts, firms prefer not to protect their software when network effects are strong. In another set of results which deals with a market situation where firms choose to protect or not, prior to price competition they found that for very weak network effects, both firms choose to protect their software because the impact of piracy on sales is insignificant. For the intermediate value of the network effects, one firm chooses to protect whereas the other does not. This is because the network effects are now strong enough to induce one firm not to protect, thereby benefiting from the larger network size, whereas these effects are still too low for the other firm to be able to afford to do it. Furthermore, the non-protecting firm earns a higher profit than the protecting firm. Finally, when network effects are sufficiently strong, both firms choose non-protection.

Hence, all these studies unambiguously try to make a point that the existence of strong demand network externalities is the central reason for the existence of piracy. In the following section, we lay out a model of software piracy with the feature of network externality and show that above arguments are not generally valid.

Network Externality – A Reason for Protection

The Model

Consider an original software firm and a pirate software firm. The pirate has the technology to copy the original software. In reality, we know that the cost of copying software is negligible, hence we assume the cost of copying is zero for the pirate. The probability that a pirated software works is q, $q \in (0,1)$ and this probability is common knowledge. Therefore q serves as a proxy for the quality of the pirated software. Usually pirated copies does not come with the supporting services, so one can think even if the pirated software is exactly same as the original one (because of digital coping), but the lack of supporting service does not allow the user to get the full value of the pirated software, hence quality of the pirated software q can also be interpreted like this. For simplicity, we also assume that the marginal costs of software production (i.e., making copies) are nil for both firms.[6]

There is a continuum of consumers indexed by X, $X \in [0,1]$. A consumer's willingness to pay for the software depends on how much he/she values it – measured by X. A high value of X means higher valuation for the software and low value of X means lower valuation for the software. Therefore, one consumer differs from another on the basis of his valuation for the particular software. Valuations are uniformly distributed over the interval [0,1] and the size of the market is normalized to 1.

A consumer's utility function is given as:

$$
U = \begin{cases} X - P_O & \text{if buys original software} \\ q\,X - P_P{}^{[7]} & \text{if buys pirated software} \\ 0 & \text{if buys none} \end{cases}
$$

There is no way a consumer can get pirated software which has a defect replaced, since there is no warranty for it.[8] Hence, the consumer enjoys the benefit of the pirated software only with probability q. In the event that the pirated software purchased does not work at all, the loss to the consumer is the price paid for it. The original software is fully guaranteed to work. P_O and P_P are the prices of the original and pirated software respectively. It must be true that $P_O > P_P$. $P_O - P_P$ can be viewed as the premium a consumer pays for buying "guaranteed-to-work" software.

In our model, just as before, network externality implies that the value of a particular piece of software for a consumer increases as more and more consumers use it. With the presence of a pirate, and due to lower price of the pirated software, more people tend to buy the software, which in turn increases the number of software users in the society.

This intensifies the network effect, and as a result, this increases the value of that software for any potential buyers (both legal and illegal). Under this, we will consider two cases in turn. First, where the original developer protects its software, and secondly, where the original developer does not protect.[9]

Software Protection (No Piracy)

Without piracy, consumers would choose only between either buying the original one or not buying, depending on their valuation of the software.

Thus a consumer's utility in the presence of network externality is given by:

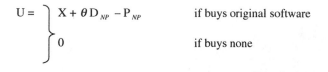

$$U = \begin{cases} X + \theta D_{NP} - P_{NP} & \text{if buys original software} \\ 0 & \text{if buys none} \end{cases}$$

D_{NP} denotes the total demand of the software under protection (i.e., no piracy)[10] and P_{NP} denotes the price. Now $\theta \in [0, \frac{1}{2}]$[11] is a coefficient which measures the importance of network size to the software user. It can be viewed as the degree of network externalities. For example, if θ is close to $\frac{1}{2}$, it implies the stronger effect of network externality and when θ is close to zero, there is almost no effect of any network externality at all.

Figure 1. Distribution of buyers (case of protection)

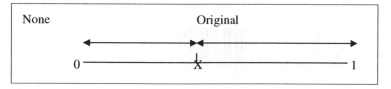

X is the marginal consumer who is indifferent between buying the original software and not buying any software at all:

$$X + \theta D_{NP} - P_{NP} = 0$$

$$X = P_{NP} - \theta D_{NP}$$

Demand for the original software is:

$$D_{NP} = 1 - X = 1 - P_{NP} + \theta D_{NP}$$

$$\Rightarrow D_{NP} = \frac{1 - P_{NP}}{1 - \theta}$$

The monopolist's profit is:

$$\pi_{NP} = P_{NP} \cdot D_{NP}$$

$$= P_{NP} \cdot \frac{1 - P_{NP}}{1 - \theta}$$

Solving for the profit-maximizing monopolist price, we get:

$$P^*_{NP} = \frac{1}{2} \qquad\qquad (1)$$

And demand is:

$$D^*_{NP} = \frac{1}{2(1 - \theta)} \qquad\qquad (2)$$

Note that when $\theta = \frac{1}{2}$, $D^*_{NP} = 1$, i.e., the full market is served.
Hence, the profit of the monopolist software firm in the case is:

$$\pi^*_{NP} = \frac{1}{4(1 - \theta)} \qquad\qquad (3)$$

No Software Protection (Piracy)

This time, a consumer's utility is given by:

$$U = \begin{cases} X + \theta D_O + q\theta \, D_P - P_O \,^{12} & \text{if buys original software} \\ q X + q\theta \, D_O + q^2 \, \theta \, D_P - P_P \,^{13} & \text{if buys pirated software} \\ 0 & \text{if buys none} \end{cases}$$

D_O, P_O and D_P, P_P are the demand and prices for the original and pirated software respectively.

As mentioned earlier, q is the probability that the pirated software works. This time, though, the loss to the consumer if the pirated software does not work is comprised of the price paid for the illegal software and the intangible cost which arises from not being able to enjoy the positive network externality.

Figure 2. Distribution of buyers (case of non-protection)

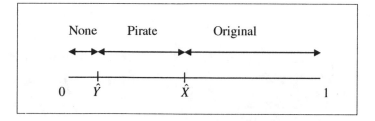

Like before, the marginal consumer, $\hat{X}$, who is indifferent between buying the original software and the pirated version is given by:

$$\hat{X} + \theta D_O + q\theta D_P - P_O = q\,\hat{X} + q\theta D_O + q^2\theta D_P - P_P$$

$$\hat{X} = \frac{P_O - P_P}{1-q} - \theta(D_O + qD_P)$$

The marginal consumer, $\hat{Y}$, who is indifferent between buying the pirated software and not buying any software at all is given by:

$$q\,\hat{Y} + q\theta D_O + q^2\theta D_P - P_P = 0$$

$$\hat{Y} = \frac{P_P}{q} - \theta(D_O + qD_P)$$

The demand for original software is given by:

$$D_O = 1 - \hat{X}$$

$$\Rightarrow D_O = \frac{(1-q)+\theta(qP_O-P_P)-(P_O-P_P)}{(1-q)(1-\theta)}$$

and the demand for pirated software is given by:

$$D_P = \hat{X} - \hat{Y}$$

$$\Rightarrow D_P = \frac{qP_O - P_P}{q(1-q)}$$

The original firm and the pirate compete by choosing price strategically. The respective reaction functions are given by:

$$P_O(P_P) = \frac{1-q+P_P(1-\theta)}{2(1-\theta q)}$$

$$P_P(P_O) = \frac{qP_O}{2}$$

Hence, Nash Equilibrium prices are:

$$P^*{}_O = \frac{2(1-q)}{4-q-3\theta q} \tag{4}$$

$$P^*{}_P = \frac{q(1-q)}{4-q-3\theta q} \tag{5}$$

Equilibrium demands are:

$$D^*_O = \frac{1}{1-\theta}\left[\frac{2-2\theta q}{4-q-3\theta q}\right] \tag{6}$$

$$D^*_P = \frac{1}{4-q-3\theta q} \tag{7}$$

The profit of the original software firm is:

$$\pi_O^{**} = \frac{4(1-q)(1-\theta q)}{(1-\theta)(4-q-3\theta q)^2} \qquad (8)$$

and that of the pirate is:

$$\pi_P^{**} = \frac{q(1-q)}{(4-q-3\theta q)^2} \qquad (9)$$

The following result summarizes the impact of the presence of the pirate in the market under network externality.

Proposition 1

In the presence of network externality, when the pirate is present in the market, the demand for the original firm is higher than its demand under protection, while price under piracy is lower than under protection. Formally:

$$D_O^* > D_{NP}^* \text{ and } P_O^* < P_{NP}^*.$$

Proof: Follows after comparing (and simplifying) (2) with (6) and (1) with (4) respectively. Q.E.D.

So under network externality, the presence of the pirate has a positive effect on the original firm's demand as expected, but a dampening effect on the price due to competition. Under this, we are interested to see how these two opposing effects combine and what would be a more profitable situation for the original firm between piracy and protection.

Protection versus Non-Protection

We compare between the profits of the original software firm under protection and non-protection.

Proposition 2

In the presence of network externality given a choice between employing protection and non-protection, it is always profitable for the original software developer to protect its software.

Proof: To show that $\pi^*_{NP} - \pi^{**}_{o} \geq 0$

Observe that:

$$\pi^*_{NP} - \pi^{**}_{o} = \frac{1}{(1-\theta)}\left[\frac{1}{4} - \frac{4(1-q)(1-\theta q)}{(4-q-3\theta q)^2}\right]$$

$$= \frac{q^2 - 8q\theta - 10\theta q^2 + 8q + 9\theta^2 q^2}{4(1-\theta)(4-q-3\theta q)^2}$$

The denominator of the above expression is non-negative. We have to show that the numerator is non-negative for all θ and q.

Simplifying the numerator, we get $(1-\theta)[8q - q^2(9\theta - 1)]$, to make it positive we must

have $\theta \leq \frac{8+q}{9q}$ which is always true for all $q \in (0.1)$ and $\theta \in \left[0, \frac{1}{2}\right]$. Note that $\frac{8+q}{9q}$ is

decreasing in q.   Q.E.D.

This result is interesting since under network externality, when the pirate is present in the market, even if there is a positive effect on the demand of the original firm, yet the more profitable situation for the firm, is to protect.

Proposition 3

The original software developer has got higher incentive to protect its product in the presence of network externality as oppose to the case of without any network externality.

Proof: It is easy to see that the incentive to protect increases with the degree of network

externality. Gain from protection under network externality is $\frac{q(8+q-9q\theta)}{4(4-q-3\theta q)^2} = G$ (say).

Observe that G is an increasing function of θ.   Q.E.D.

Discussion

In this part, we tried to argue that the prevalence of network externality in the software user market cannot generally be held as a reason for software piracy. We showed that in some situations, even with very strong network effect, protection instead of allowing piracy, is the optimal measure for the original software developer. To this end one might argue that in our model since deterring the pirate (or protection) is costless to the original software firm, the original firm will always deter the pirate and enjoy the monopoly market simply because monopoly profit is always higher than duopoly profit. To this end, readers would also like to notice that the presence of the pirate increases the demand of the original firm through network effect compared to the full protection case. Thus, this is clearly a positive effect of allowing piracy. Although there exists the dampening effect on the price under piracy due to competition, but a priori it is not quite clear which effect dominates and eventually which situation would be more profitable to the original firm.

Digging a little bit deeper and contrasting with previous results in the literature (discussed earlier), we realize that the market structure, the nature of competition and the demand structure play a very crucial role to drive these results. For example, when the market structure is monopolistic with two types of consumers, software piracy allows price-discrimination among the different classes consumers (see Conner and Rumelt, 1991; Takeyama, 1994; Slive and Bernhardt, 1998).[14] On the other hand, when the market structure is duopolistic (or strategic in general), the results regarding the existence (or not) of software piracy very much depends on the nature of competition between the competing firms. For example, when competition takes place between two *symmetric* firms (both are original software developer, while their products are differentiated) (see Shy and Thisse (1999)), then allowing software piracy by one group (typically low-valued users) of software users could be supported as a non-cooperative equilibrium under strong network effect. At the same time, when the competition takes place between two *asymmetric* firms, i.e., one firm is the original software developer and the other is just a pirate (as in this case), then allowing piracy (by the pirate) is not a profitable outcome to the original firm. Therefore, protection remains the only profitable option to the original developer.

One important distinction that we would like the readers to notice here is that our study is based on retail piracy (i.e., one single pirate does all the piracy and sells to others),[15] while most of the studies (except Banerjee 2003) discussed in the literature (see section 2 and above) so far, are mainly based on end-user piracy (i.e., consumers pirate copies mainly for their own use). So there is a distinct difference in the act of coping. Hence, whether the nature of piracy actually leads to alternative outcomes that remain to be seen. A future research along this will line would be desirable.

Part II

The Case of Sequential Move

So far we have considered a simultaneous move game between the original developer and the pirate. Now we are going to consider a sequential move game where the original firm acts as a leader and the pirate as the follower. We believe this market structure is also very common in many real life situations, where the original producer is an established firm in the business and is the market leader. In such situation if any pirate comes to operate, it naturally becomes the follower. An analysis of the leader-follower game also gives us the opportunity to compare the outcomes of the simultaneous move game scenario, which we had studied in the previous part, with the sequential version of the game. This also makes our analysis on software piracy in a strategic framework rather complete.

The Leader-Follower Game of Piracy

Given the distribution of the buyers which we have discussed earlier (see section 3.3), the profit function of the pirate (follower) is given by:

$$\pi^F_P = D_P \cdot P_P$$

$$= P_P \cdot [\frac{qP_O - P_P}{q(1-q)}] \text{ (For the expression } D_P \text{ see section 3.3)}$$

Thus, the reaction function is given by: $P^F_P (P_O) = \frac{qP_O}{2}$

The profit function of the original firm (leader) is:

$$\pi_O = D_O \cdot P_O$$

$$= P_O \cdot [\frac{(1-q)+\theta(qP_O - P_P)-(P_O - P_P)}{(1-q)(1-\theta)}] \text{ (for } D_O \text{ see 3.3)}$$

Plugging in the reaction function of the follower in the above expression, we solve for (subgame perfect) equilibrium prices:

$$P_O^L = \frac{1-q}{2-q-\theta q}; P_P^F = \frac{q(1-q)}{2(2-q-q\theta)} \tag{10}$$

Equilibrium demands are given by:

$$D_O^L = \frac{1}{2(1-\theta)} ; D_P^F = \frac{1}{2(2-q-\theta q)} \tag{11}$$

The profit of the original software firm is given by:

$$\pi_O^{L*} = \frac{(1-q)}{2(1-\theta)(2-q-\theta q)} \tag{12}$$

and that of the pirate is:

$$\pi_P^{F*} = \frac{q(1-q)}{4(2-q-\theta q)^2} \tag{13}$$

Comparison between Simultaneous and Sequential Move Game

When we compare the equilibrium expressions in the leader-follower game with the simultaneous move game, we get the following results.

Proposition 4

(i)   *In the leader-follower game, the prices of the original firm and the pirate are higher compared to the simultaneous move game. Formally, $P_O^L \geq P_O^*$ and $P_O^F \geq P_P^*$.*

(ii) *The demand of the original firm becomes lower while the demand of the pirate becomes higher in the leader-follower game compared to the simultaneous move game. Formally, $D_O^L < D_O^*$ and $D_P^F \geq D_P^*$.*

Proof: (i) Follows after comparing (10) with (4) and (10) with (5) respectively.

(ii) Follows after comparing (11) with (6) and (11) with (7) respectively.

Proposition 5

(i)   *The profits for both the leader and the follower are higher than respective simultaneous Bertrand profits. Formally, $\pi_O^{L*} \geq \pi_O^{**}$ and $\pi_P^{F*} \geq \pi_P^{**}$.*

(ii) *The original firm (leader) gets a higher profit than the pirate (follower). Formally, $\pi_O^{L*} \geq \pi_P^{F*}$.*

Proof: (i) Follows after comparing (12) with (8) and (13) with (9) respectively.

(ii) Follows after comparing (12) with (13).

Note that point (ii) needs some attention. Usually, if the strategies are strategic complements between the competitors (which is the case here), then the follower gets higher profit than the leader. Here, that is not happening since the products are vertically differentiated. The leader is selling the high quality product and the follower is selling the low quality product. The former is true when the products are horizontally differentiated.

Now, we compare between the profits of the original software firm under protection and non-protection.

Protection versus Non-Protection

We begin with the following interesting observation:

$$D_O^L = \frac{1}{2(1-\theta)} = D_{NP}^*,$$

where D_{NP}^* is the demand under protection.
Also:

$$P_O^{L*} = \frac{1-q}{2-q-\theta q} < \frac{1}{2} = P_{NP}^*,$$

where P_{NP}^* is the monopoly price under protection.
Hence, we have the following result.

Proposition 6

In this leader-follower case with the presence of network externality, presence of the pirate does not make any difference to the demand of the original firm. It remains exactly the same as it was under protection, yet the price is reduced due to competition.

This implies total profit of the original firm under the leader-follower game must be less than the total profit under protection. Thus, we arrive at the main result for this part.

Proposition 7

In the presence of network externality given a choice between employing protection and non-protection, it is always profitable for the original software developer to protect its software, even when it is the market leader.

Proposition 8

The ranking of profits of the original firm in three different regimes (i.e., (i) simultaneous move under no protection, (ii) sequential move under no protection, and (iii) protection) respectively is as follows: $\pi_O^{**} < \pi_O^{L*} < \pi_{NP}^*$.

Thus, moving from a simultaneous move game to a sequential move game as a leader improves the original firm's profit, yet the improved profit is still lower than the profit under protection. Hence, protection remains the optimal policy to the original developer under all circumstances.

Like the simultaneous case, the following result is also true in the sequential game.

Proposition 9

The original software developer has a greater incentive to protect its product in the presence of network externality as oppose to the case without any network externality.

Proof: As before, the incentive to protect increases with the degree of network externality. Gain from protection under network externality is:

$$\frac{q^2(1-q)}{2(1-\theta)(2-q-\theta q)(4-q-3\theta q)^2} = G^1 \text{ (say)}.$$

Observe that G^1 is an increasing function of θ.   Q.E.D.

Part III

Welfare Analysis

Now we are ready to do some welfare analysis. Assume that in the set up, that is, discussed in previous two parts (I and II), there is a social planner (say, the government) whose objective is to maximize society's welfare. What would be the policy recommendation with respect to piracy? In other words, the question is, whether allowing piracy is welfare improving or welfare reducing from the society's point of view. To analyze that, first we list the consumer surplus and the social welfare under various cases.

Software Protection (No Piracy)

$$CS_1 = \frac{1}{8(1-\theta)^2} \tag{14}$$

$$W_1 = \frac{1}{8(1-\theta)^2} + \frac{1}{4(1-\theta)} = \frac{3-2\theta}{8(1-\theta)^2} \tag{15}$$

No Software Protection (Piracy) - The Simultaneous Game

$$CS_2 = \frac{8\theta^2 q^2 + \theta^2 q - 14\theta q + 5q - 4\theta q^2 + 4}{2(1-\theta)^2(4-q-3\theta q)^2} \tag{16}$$

$$W_2 = \frac{12 - 8\theta - q - 18\theta q + 11\theta^2 q + 8\theta q^2 - 2\theta^2 q^2 - 2q^2}{2(1-\theta)^2(4-q-3\theta q)^2} \tag{17}$$

Comparisons

Comparing between (15) and (17), we get the following result.

Proposition 10

Under network externality, the society is better off with the pirate. Formally:

$$W_2 > W_1.$$

Proof: It can be shown that W_2 is increasing in q for all $\theta \in (0, \frac{1}{2})$. It is also true that $W_1(\theta) = W_2(\theta)\big|_{q=0}$. Thus, combining these two we get the result.

No Software Protection (Piracy) - The Sequential Game

Here again, we list the consumer surplus and the welfare for the case when the original developer is the leader in the market, while the pirate is the follower.

$$CS_3 = \frac{3\theta^2 q^2 + 2\theta q^2 + \theta^2 q - 10\theta q + q - q^2 + 4}{8(1-\theta)^2(2-q-\theta q)^2} \tag{18}$$

$$W_3 = \frac{12 - 8\theta - 9q - 6\theta q + 7\theta^2 q + q^2 + 6\theta q^2 - 3\theta^2 q^2}{8(1-\theta)^2(2-q-\theta q)^2} \tag{19}$$

Comparisons

Comparing between (15) and (19), we get the following result.

Proposition 11

The society is better off with the pirate under network externality, i.e.:

$$W_3 > W_1.$$

Proof: Like before, it can be shown that W_3 is increasing in q for all $\theta \in (0, \frac{1}{2})$. It is also true that $W_1(\theta) = W_3(\theta)\big|_{q=0}$. Thus, combining these two, we get the result.

Discussion

Thus, in our models, we find that the existence of the pirate is always better for the society. This is true for both the simultaneous and sequential version of the game under network externality. But at the same time, we would like to warn our readers to be more careful in order to generalize this result in other situations. First of all, here we only capture a situation of retail piracy in a particular demand environment. Generally, the impact of piracy on social welfare is a far more complex issue than we captured here. For that matter, we would like to draw the readers' attention on a comprehensive study by Chen and Png (2003) on copyright enforcement and pricing of information goods and welfare aspects. Software is one of the information goods that we are interested here. Chen and Png deal with general information goods, where the primary question was – how should the government use its various policy instruments – penalties, taxes, and subsidies – in the market for information good? This question is especially difficult because the government, in setting policy, must consider how legitimate producers will adjust their pricing and enforcement in response to government policy. So the study addresses the impact of government policy on the software publisher's price and detection expenditure and then analyzes the consequences for social welfare. One distinct difference from their study to our study here is that in their study the pirates are end-users (consumers) and there is no retail piracy. The main findings from the study can be summarized as follows. While the publisher may consider a price reduction and an increase in detection as simply two alternative ways to boost legitimate demand, the two changes have qualitatively different welfare effects. Society prefers the publisher to manage piracy through lower prices rather than increased enforcement. Lower prices allow more people to use software, which in turn increase consumer surplus and welfare. Second, a tax on the copying medium is welfare superior to a penalty for copyright violations. Compared to the penalty, the tax has less effect on the legitimate price and leads the publisher to reduce rather than raise spending on detection. Reducing spending on detection always has a positive effect on welfare, since the cost of detection is somewhat wasteful. Lastly, it is optimal to subsidize legitimate purchases. Here also subsidy leads to reduced spending on detection. On the other hand, it is generally true that the government policies that focus only on penalties will never be an optimal choice from society's welfare point of view. So the other policy instruments available turn out to be crucial in enhancing society's overall welfare under the existence of software piracy.

Contribution of the Study to Researchers/Instructors and Managers/Entrepreneurs

Academic Purpose for Researchers and Instructors

Up until now, the literature on the economics of software piracy is scattered in various directions and sometimes even with several conflicting results. This chapter puts an order to this scattered literature and connects one research agenda with the other. It explains why some results are in conflict with other results. In doing so, the study provides an in-depth analysis of certain important issues raised in the literature of software piracy. We believe the chapter will be a useful guide to an academic researcher as well as to the instructor who plans to teach a course on the economics of software piracy. Further readings on the issue of software piracy are listed in the bibliography.

Business Purpose for Managers and Entrepreneurs

We also believe this study will give some new insights to the business practitioners who are involved in the software industry. Every year software piracy is costing billions of dollars to the industry. So the conventional wisdom would suggest to stop piracy at any cost to save the industry. But at the same time, the legal software products are almost beyond the purchasing capability of the average software users in the developing world. So piracy remains the only way out in those regions. It is also true that easy availability of the software products in a developing country's markets increases the know-how and the usage of software products. This in turn helps the software companies to sell their products in those markets more successfully. When the scenario is like this, it is important to the managers and entrepreneurs in the industry to come up with innovative business strategies, which are feasible as well as profitable. We believe this study will help them to formulate such business strategies.

Another issue is that in the present business world, e-business and e-commerce are gradually taking the center stage, and it is needless to say that the behaviour of the software industry will have a profound effect on them as well. Managers and entrepreneurs will try to understand this impact in great detail in order to find profitable business solutions. The analysis done in this chapter will be a good starting point to see how the software industry behaviour and industry growth are actually going to affect e-business and e-commerce over time.

Concluding Thoughts

In this chapter, we argued that the presence of consumer network externality cannot be generally held as the prime reason for piracy in all situations. We emphasize the fact that whether network externality can be a possible reason for allowing piracy by the original producer depends on the market structure, demand environment and the nature of competition. We also identify that the policy recommendations on the issue of software piracy could be very complicated, and in many cases, the effect on overall welfare is ambiguous. We believe one policy recommendation that is unambiguous is: the government's incentive to enforce laws against piracy increases with the size of the domestic software industry. In other words, this means, for small and developing domestic software industries, allowing limited piracy does give a solid impetus for a rapid development of the domestic software market in terms of usage and know-how. In order to facilitate this, the growth of the industry attaining a critical market size is absolutely essential. But this stance usually changes, once the domestic software industry becomes relatively developed. Then to foster new innovations and in order to keep a steady growth of the industry, a strong copyright protection law is vital. It clearly appears that piracy can have positive social effects in the short run, provided it does not provoke a market breakdown. In the long run, piracy is unambiguously detrimental because it limits the potential development of new products by software sellers.

Lastly, we would like to point out that there are certain limitations with the models that we described in this chapter. We always assumed stopping piracy is costless to the original firm, but in reality this may not be the case. Actually, in most of the cases, it is not a costless operation. To stop piracy or at least to limit the activity of the pirate, the original developer has to do something which is costly. For example, to stop piracy, the original firm may wish to set up an operation in order to monitor the market for piracy. Now this is definitely a costly operation, which has to be borne by the original firm in order to check the pirate. In general, monitoring also raises the cost of piracy to the pirate mainly because if the pirate gets caught, he or she has to pay some kind of penalty. One can capture this notion by assuming that the pirate's cost of producing a copy increases with the monitoring effort of the original developer. So higher the monitoring level, higher the cost of producing pirated copies. Hence, overall piracy becomes costly with the degree of monitoring arrangement made by the original firm. Secondly, instead of monitoring or in addition to monitoring, the original firm can invest in R & D, so that it can develop a technology (like putting a protective chip inside the software), which increases the cost of copying the software. Now to develop such technology, costly R&D must be undertaken before. So the idea is that the original firm can increase the cost of the pirate's activity by investing in something before the pirate starts it operation. Since the investment is costly, the question that naturally arises is whether the original firm will actually undertake such operation or not. And if it undertakes such operation, under what circumstances it will be effective? We believe these are some important issues that need a great deal of attention. For future research in this area, this would be a good starting point.

Endnotes

*   First of all, I would like to thank the editor of the book, Dr. H. S. Kehal for the encouragement and giving me the support to write this chapter and anonymous reviewers for the most helpful comments. I also thank the seminar participants at the Department of Economics at NUS, and the conference participants at Australian Economic Society Meeting (2002) in Adelaide for useful helpful comments and suggestions. All possible remaining errors are mine.

    This chapter is a part of the research work done under the research project titled "Economics of Software Piracy" (2002). Financial support from NUS in the form of research grant (R-122-000-040-112) for the project is gratefully acknowledged.

[1]   With advanced and sophisticated technological methods, pirated software copies or even copies of copies become almost if not perfectly identical to an original one.

[2]   In Vietnam only 5% software is legitimate; while in U.S. 23% software is pirated (Source: BSA 2003).

[3]   Benchmark levels vary from country to country and from one software category to another. For PC business software, benchmark levels of 23% (the rate currently experienced in the U.S.) were used for most countries, and a rate of 0% was used for the United States.

[4]   The idea of network externality stems from the work of Katz and Shapiro (1985). See also Rohlfs (1974), Gandal (1994) and Shy (1996). Generally, the idea is that the utility that a given user derives from some products depends upon the number of other users who consume the same products. In other words, consumers' preferences are said to exhibit network externality if the utility of each consumer increases with the cumulative number of other consumers purchasing the same brand. When this is the case, each additional purchase raises the value to existing users as well as the expected value to future adopters. A classic example of a product that exhibits such a characteristic is found in the telephone network.

[5]   We would like to emphasize that in this study we do not deal with network security issues or any such technical matter.

[6]   Presumably, the original developer had incurred some fixed cost (like R&D to develop the software) which is sunk now. The cost of making a copy of the software is negligible.

[7] $q\,X - P_p = q\,(X - P_p) + (1 - q)(-P_p)$. If the pirated software is not working, consumer does not derive any benefit from the software and instead only incurs a loss equivalent to the amount paid for the pirated software.

[8]   In most market pirates operate using some makeshift arrangement. If the pirated software turns out to be a defect product, there is no chance of getting software replaced.

[9]   The effects of installing protection into software in the market for software as well as monitoring piracy have been analyzed in Chen and Png (2003) and Banerjee (2003) among others.

[10]   Using notation "NP" in the subscript for no piracy.

[11]   Network effect is bounded by ½; because $\theta = $ ½ is enough to serve the full market under monopoly.

[12]   Since the consumer buys original software, he gets to enjoy the benefit X and the network externality generated by those who also buy original software with certainty. However, he only gets to enjoy the network created by those who buy pirated software with probability q, since only there is only a q chance that it works.

[13]   Since this consumer buys pirated software, he gets to enjoy the benefit and the network effect created by both legal and illegal users if and only if his software works.

[14]   Although, recently King and Lampe (2002) argued that allowing piracy cannot raise profits if the monopoly producer itself can directly price discriminate between potential consumers who pirate and other consumers who buy original product.

[15]   Retail piracy is more prevalent in the poor and developing countries, where the laws against piracy or in general copyright violations are rather weak, and sometimes even more difficult to enforce because of corruptions.

References

Banerjee, D. S. (2003). Software Piracy: A Strategic Analysis and Policy Instruments. *International Journal of industrial Organization, 21*(1), 97-127.

Chen, Y, and Png, I. (2003). Information Goods Pricing and Copyright Enforcement: Welfare Analysis. *Information Systems Research, 14*(1), 107-123.

Conner, K.R., and Rumelt, R.P. (1991). Software Piracy: An Analysis of Protection Strategies. *Management Science, 37*(2), 125-139.

Gandal, N. (1994). Hedonic Price Indexes for Spreadsheets and an Empirical Test of Network Externalities Hypothesis. *Rand Journal of Economics, 25*, 160-170.

Katz, M. and Shapiro, C. (1985). Network Externalities, Competition and Compatibility. *American Economic Review, 75*(2), 424-440.

King, P. S. and Lampe, R. (2002). *Network Externalities, Price Discrimination and Profitable Piracy*. Mimeo: University of Melbourne.

PricewaterhouseCoopers for Business Software Alliance. (1998). Contributions of the Packaged Software Industry to the Global Economy. Washington, D.C.

Rohlfs, J. (1974). A Theory of Interdependent Demand for a Communication Service. *Bell Journal of Economics, 8*, 16-37.

Shy, O. (1995). *Industrial Organization: Theory and Applications*. Cambridge: MIT Press.

Shy, O. and Thisse, J. F. (1999). A Strategic Approach to Software Protection. *Journal of Economics and Management Science, 8*(2), 163-190.

Slive, J. and Bernhardt, D. (1998). Pirated for profit. *Canadian Journal of Economics, 31*(4), 886-899.

Takeyama, L. N. (1994). The Welfare Implications of Unauthorized Reproduction of Intellectual Property in the Presence of Demand Network Externalities. *Journal of Industrial Economics, 2*, 155-165.

Takeyama, L.N. (1997). The Intertemporal Consequences of Unauthorized Reproduction of Intellectual Property. *Journal of Law and Economics, 40*(2), 511-522.

Internet Sources

1998, 2000, 2002, 2003 Global Software Piracy Report. Retrieved from the World Wide Web: http://www.bsa.org.

Further Readings on Software Piracy

Low, L. (2000). *Economics of Information Technology and the Media*. Singapore, New Jersey, London, Hong Kong: Singapore University Press and World Scientific Publishing Co. Pte. Ltd.

Mowery, D. C. (1996). *The International Computer Software Industry*. New York and Oxford: Oxford University Press.

Poddar, S. (2002). "Economics of Software Piracy" – Project Report 2002. NUS. (Project supported by NUS research grant R-122-000-040112.)

Steven C., Jr. (2002). *Copycat: The Effects of Software Piracy on the Global Economy. Retrieved from the World Wide Web:* http://www.stanford.edu/class/e297c/new/trade_environment/growing_pains/schew.htm.

Watt, R. (2000). *Copyright And Economic Theory: Friends or Foes?* Northampton, MA: Edward Elgar.

Readings in Game Theory

Fudenberg, D. and Tirole, J. (1991). *Game Theory*. Cambridge, MA: MIT Press.

Gibbons, R. (1992). *A Primer in Game Theory*. New York: Harvester Wheatsheaf.

Rasmusen, E. (1994). *Games and Information: An Introduction to Game Theory*. (2nd Edition) Oxford: Blackwell.

Romp, G. (1997). *Game Theory: Introduction and Applications*. Oxford: Oxford University Press.

Chapter X

An E-Classification of the World's Capital Cities:
URL References to Web Sites

Stanley D. Brunn
University of Kentucky, USA

Abstract

The world's capital cities perform various political functions for their populations, contain embassies, consulates, and missions of other governments, and serve as headquarters for major corporations, cultural, and humanitarian organizations. While social scientists have classified major cities based on population size, number of corporate headquarters, banks, and airline connections, the emergence of ICTs suggests additional criteria. I use the number of URL references to Web sites listed in the Google search engine for 199 world capitals and classify them into five distinct categories. Small, prosperous city-states and major capitals in Western Europe and North America have the most hyperlinks. The fewest are for capitals in poor, rural Sub-Saharan Africa and Southeast Asia. Capitals with multiple government offices, strong ICT economies and dominant tourist economies have the most hyperlinks per capita. These are mostly in wealthy Europe and North America. The lowest values are among African and Asian capitals in poor countries and those with repressive regimes. Major news items, embassy, financial, and tourism information are major themes on web pages. Additional research topics are suggested.

The emerging worlds of digital economies or e-commerce present challenges and opportunities for scholars in the social and policy sciences who are interested in the information that is available about individual cities and their linkages with other cities in a region (Brunn, 2003b). Valuable and insightful contributions into these new worlds of geography, economics, management, sociology, and politics have come from scholars in a number of fields including geography (*Geographical Review*, 1997; Janelle and Hodge, 2000; Wilson and Corey, 2000; Leinbach and Brunn, 2001; *Tijdschrift voor Economische en Sociale Geografie*, 2002; *Environment and Planning A*, 2003), sociology (Barnett, 2001; Castells, 2001; Hargittai and Centeno, 2001; Kick and Davis, 2001; Sassen, 2001), organizational science and management (Sacks, Ventresca and Uzzi, 2001). Cities, urban regions, and networks have also been a focus of disciplinary and interdisciplinary research initiatives (Castells, 2002; Van der Wusten, 2002). Among the topics addressed are telecommunications and the changing structures of cities (Graham and Marvin, 1996; Wheeler, Aoyama and Warf, 2000; Brunn and Ghose, 2003), the changing geographies of the Internet (Zook, 2001; Kellerman, 2002), the most and least linked regions (Saad, House and Brunn, 2002), the changing infrastructure of international Internet-based cities (Townsend, 2001), the changing dynamics of airline networks (Smith and Timberlake, 2001), and salient features of globally networked cities (GaWC Study and Network).

One feature of the contemporary urban world that has not been investigated to date is a classification of the world's capital cities, in particular, based on how much and what kinds of information are available using major search engines. Classifying the world's largest cities or urban areas has long been of interest among social scientists, including geographers, sociologists, and economists, because of their political, economic, and cultural significance. One of the major themes has been classifying world or global cities by using a number of indices, including population sizes, international sports venues, number of major corporations, head offices of major banks, stock agencies, advertising agencies, airline passengers, networks and freight volume, and cultural events (Brunn, Williams and Zeigler, 2003; Friedman, 1986, 1995; Short et al., 1995; Short and Kim, 1999; Knox, 1994; Knox and Taylor, 1995; Knox and Pinch, 2000; Hall 1966, 1984, 2001; Lo and Marcotullio, 2001; GaWC Study and Network; Smith and Timberlake, 2001; Wagenaar, Mamadouh and Dijkink, 2000). These studies are valuable in suggesting subsequent studies on specific types of cities or city systems using new databases and perspectives.

National Capitals

National capitals represent a major category of important cities. They are not only significant political, economic, and cultural nodes for the state in which they are located, but they are also significant for the roles they play and influences they have elsewhere. Capital cities are networked to rural areas and small towns within their state, as well as the major centers of commerce, industry, research and development, and learning. As the major administrative center for the country's central government, the capital city is the place where national decisions are made regarding the lives of those within its borders, including educational funding and the content of school curricula, economic development initiatives, social welfare policy, and environmental regulations. Capital cities often are the sites of not only the executive branches of the national government, but the national legislative chambers, the highest courts, and military/defense and law enforcement offices, as well. Many national capitals also are places where the embassies, consulates, and missions of other countries are located as well as the headquarters for IGOs and NGOs. Thus capital cities, in short, perform a variety of functions and roles, not just to those living within its borders, but also to those in neighboring states, and those in distant states.

Classifying a National Capital's Importance

Missing from the disciplinary and interdisciplinary literature on city functions are examinations into the amounts and varieties of data from electronic databases that are available about individual cities within a country, the world's largest cities, and specific types of cities. The latter would include capital cities, major university cities, medical centers, tourist destinations, and high tech clusters. This chapter is an initial inquiry into the amounts of information that are available about a specific category of cities, viz., capital cities of the world's states, and using the references to Web sites in major electronic search engines as a database.

There are a number of criteria one might utilize to describe, rank and classify a capital city's importance on a regional or global scale. These would include population size, although in many countries, the capital is not the largest city, such as Brazil, Canada, Australia, South Africa, India, Switzerland, Nigeria, Turkey, and Morocco. Capital cities also include a number of embassies and consulates, offices of interregional and international agencies, organizations and programs (United Nations or European Union). The sizes of the international professional labor force (diplomats, diplomatic staff, students, translators, program officers, bankers, consultants, lobbyists, health care and environmental professionals) vary as do the number and variety of cultural (music and theater performances, museum exhibitions, sporting events, and public lectures) events that take place during a year, including international and regional conferences and conventions. Capital cities are frequently also the sites of visits by international heads of states or heads of various state programs (environment, trade and investment, education, children, and health care). Transportation and communication linkages to and from the capital cities are also important, including direct road and rail connections to other capitals, airline connections as well as the volume of phone, mail (letters and packages), and fax traffic, the exchanges of information among members of diplomatic staff and print and visual journalists for various news organizations, and the volume of monies or credit transferred for investment, developmental assistance, and personal use. (Many of these information exchanges are already performed electronically.) Also we could use the frequencies with which cities have appeared in major international newspapers or on global TV networks (CNN, Skylab, etc.) and discuss their importance in a regional or global context. An additional data source we could use is the amount of information provided in an electronic database. Search engines provide access to materials specialists and generalists use to learn about specific subjects, in this case, capital cities and distinctive features of those cities, including their histories, economies, cultures, tourist sites, restaurants, and weather. URL references or hyperlinks provide access to Web addresses for the desired information. We could utilize this information from search engines to measure the importance of a capital city in an electronic world. That is, a high hyperlink per capita rating for a capital city will inform us of the quantity, not necessarily the quality, of information available electronically. A low volume will inform us that there is little electronic information available. The number of electronic references also provides a useful measure with which to compare world capitals.

One might picture what a set or volume of network maps might look like for the capital cities of the world's nearly 200 political units. These could be maps of each city individually or networks of other capitals. Whether one uses absolute data, such as the number of diplomatic staff, or international conferences held each year, or network data (airline connections), or the number of diplomatic visits per year from a neighboring state, geographic variations would surface. That is, some capitals would rank high using these or other criteria, others would rank very low.

Digital Technologies

To assess the position of the world's capital cities on the current world political map, I use the number or volume of URL references to Web sites for each capital city. Each URL reference or hyperlink gives a reference to a web address. That address provides electronically available information. This information may be about population numbers, investment opportunities, health and social well-being data, tourist sites, hotels, or some combination of the above. This information may be in the form of narratives, graphs, tables, photos, or maps. A capital city with few URLs is one with little electronically available information compared to another capital city with thousands or hundreds of thousands of references available about a city's economy, history, culture, entertainment, and government.

When we examine data on the number of URL references or hyperlinks per capita, we obtain an additional measure of that city's regional and global importance, at least in an electronic or wired world. Capital cities with low per capita ratings are cities where we find little information available electronically. Values of 1.00 or higher are cities that have more hyperlinks than number of residents, that is, there are many more references to web pages than residents.

Below I address the following questions:

- What capital cities have the most URL references or hyperlinks, and which have the fewest? How might we classify them?

- Are the most "wired" capital cities, or those with most electronic addresses, located in the richest countries? And, correspondingly, are the least wired in the poorest regions?

- What capital cities have the highest and lowest hyperlinks per capita? Are they the same as those cities with the most URLs?

- Are there any commonalities among those capital cities with lowest and highest hyperlinks per capita? Are they the poorest and the smallest in populations? Are they new states on the world political map? Do they have specialized economies?

- Are there any differences in the content of the Web sites of the cities with the most and fewest URL references?

In the following section I describe the database and methodology, followed by a presentation and discussion of the results. The findings are examined in regards to the total number of URLs for each capital city, hyperlinks (or URL references) per capita, and subject content of selected capital cities' information on Web pages. I also discuss these findings within a regional context, as I am interested in discerning whether capital cities in some regions have significantly more or fewer addresses than others. The presentation below is supported by several tables and graphics.

Data and Methodology

To ascertain the number of URLs or hyperlinks for each capital city, I used the Google Search Engine. While there are other search engines one might use, including MetaCrawler, Yahoo, DogPile, and AltaVista, I used Google because it has one of the largest and most comprehensive electronic databases (more than 3 billion Web sites as of July 2003) and because it contains international and multilingual entries. During several weeks in June and July 2003, I collected information on the number of URL references for each capital city. In the appropriate "box" on the screen, I typed in the name of the capital city and the country, for example, Tegucigalpa+Honduras, Khartoum+Sudan, Rome+Italy, Washington, D.C. Within seconds I was given the total number of URL references or hyperlinks for that city.

I used the above procedure to identify the number of URL references for 199 capital cities. I included the capital cities of large countries, as well as small island states and political units in the Caribbean (Dominica, Curaçao, and Guadeloupe); South Indian Ocean (Mauritius and Seychelles); and Pacific Basin (Nauru, Tonga, and New Caledonia). Data on the population sizes of these cities are available from a number of sources, including statistical abstracts, world almanacs and capital city Web sites. The analyses below are discussed in three sections: first, absolute numbers of references, and second, the URL references or hyperlinks per capita, and third, the content of the first Web pages for selected cities.

There are three additional points regarding the data set that merit mention. First, most of the entries in the Google Search Engine are in English. While English is the unofficial language of the Internet, there are doubtless many additional information items available about these capital cities, even electronically available, that are not listed in this search engine. Thus any data count on electronic entries from a major search engine will be incomplete as someone has to place the information on the Web. Second, the number of references for any given city is subject to change quickly, even within a 24-hour period or from week to week. New entries appear and others disappear. This feature applies just as much to very large capital cities as it does to small capitals. Third, the existence of a given URL reference to a web address reveals nothing about the quality of that information to the potential user, only that it is electronically available information. The reference may be an official government document, an intergovernmental report, information from an investment group, publicity by an indigenous or outside tourist bureau or a private report or a webcam site prepared by a former resident, recent traveler, student or exile. Sometimes brief descriptions accompany the URL. Thus examining in detail the content of a single URL reference may result in the city only mentioned within a table or a small section of a report or it could be devoted to an extensive discussion about that city's history, economy, and culture. In short, URL references contain a wide variety of electronic information, and the quality and utility of that information will vary depending on the source. That same generalization could be made about the printed materials available in many public libraries.

To understand the kinds of information available on the WWW about capital cities, I examined the sites listed on the first screen ("page") listing URL references for a group of individual capital cities. Google provides a PageLink for each site accessed. It describes this metric as "an indicator of an individual page's value" (www.google.com). It looks at the links between each Web page and every other Web page. Thus the rank is not based solely on volume of votes or links a page has, but at the pages that "vote" or rank the page. This search engine, in describing this ranking, notes that "votes" cast by pages that are themselves "important" weigh more heavily and help to make other pages "important." In the discussion below, I examined the first pages on the screen of the 27 capital cities with the most URL references and those five capitals with the fewest.

Results

Absolute Totals

The 199 capital cities had a combined total of nearly 120 million hyperlinks or URL references (Table 1). There was very wide variation from 6.6 million URL references for Singapore to 3,550 for Yaren (capital of Nauru). I divided the countries and their respective capitals into 19 major regions, adopting those used in a university world geography textbook (Pulsipher and Pulsipher, 2002). The capitals in Western Europe had the most hyperlinks (16.6 million) followed by Southern Europe (13.2 million), and Central America (12.2 million) (Table 1). These three regions had 13, 11, and 10% respectively of the total. By contrast, the regions with capital cities having the fewest hyperlinks were Southern Africa (603,000) and the Pacific Islands (only 470,000). Together these regions had less than 1% of all capital city references.

Table 1. Total number of URL references or hyperlinks for capital cities in major world regions (number of capital cities in the region in parenthesis)

Region	Number	% of total
United States and Canada (2)	7,260,000	6.1
Europe – North (10)	10,637,000	9.0
Europe – South	13,241,700	11.1
Europe – East (10)	6,875,000	5.8
Europe – West (9)	15,230,000	13.0
South America (13)	5,783,900	4.9
Central America (8)	12,279.000	10.3
Caribbean (18)	6,664,000	5.6
Africa – West (16)	2,891,000	2.4
Africa – Central (9)	2,293,000	1.9
Africa – Southern (5)	603,000	.5
Africa – North (5)	1,229,000	1.0
Africa – East (18)	3,275,000	2.7
Asia – East (6)	5,769,000	4.9
Asia – South & Central (14)	4,065,000	3.4
Asia – Southeast (11)	11,182,000	9.4
Asia – Southwest (17)	6,273,000	5.3
Pacific Islands (11)	410,000	.3
Australia and New Zealand (2)	2,840,000	2.4
TOTAL	118,799,000	100.0

Classifying the World's Capitals

Fifteen capitals had more than 2 million hyperlinks, led by Singapore, a city-state that is among the world's leaders in ICT development and e-commerce (Corey, 2000). Washington, D.C. was a distant second (Table 2). Several with more than 2 million references each are "global cities," such as, London, Paris, and Tokyo. Others are major continental cities, including Rome, Berlin, and Madrid in Europe, and Mexico City in Central America.

Table 2. Leading capital cities in number of URL references or hyperlinks in thousands

City	Country	Hyperlinks
Singapore	Singapore	6,640
Washington, D.C.	U.S.	5,120
Mexico City	Mexico	4,210
Luxembourg	Luxembourg	3,400
Paris	France	3,370
Panama	Panama	3,170
Tokyo	Japan	2,450
Monaco	Monaco	2,410
Madrid	Spain	2,310
Berlin	Germany	2,250
Rome	Italy	2,200
London	United Kingdom	2,170
Ottawa	Canada	2,140
San Salvador	El Salvador	2,140
Guatemala City	Guatemala	2,020
Dublin	Ireland	1,970
Kuwait City	Kuwait	1,890
Moscow	Russia	1,890
San Marino	San Marino	1,800
Vienna	Austria	1,750
Beijing	China	1,690
Buenos Aires	Argentina	1,670
Stockholm	Sweden	1,630
Auckland	New Zealand	1,570
Athens	Greece	1,550
Bangkok	Thailand	1,540
Delhi	India	1,510

The top 15 capitals, with 46 million references, had 31% of the all capital city references. The top 27 capitals had 66 million or 56% of the total. Some of the cities with high rankings are mentioned frequently in the international news as places with major military conflicts, a natural disaster, or disease outbreak. Examples include Kabul, Baghdad, and Djibouti. Cities with the most hyperlinks in a region are not always the largest political capital. For example, Djibouti had the most in East Africa, Kingston in the Caribbean, and Bissau in West Africa.

Figure 1. Total number of URL references or hyperlinks of capital cities in the world's political states

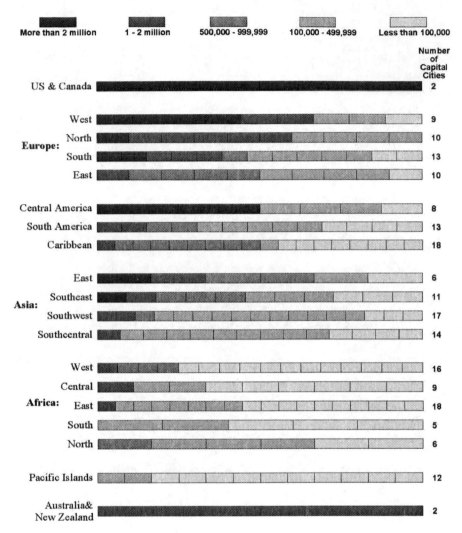

Each of the 24 capitals in the second category had between 1.0-1.9 million references (Figure 1). It included a mix of cities in different parts of the world, but especially in Europe. Vienna, Brussels, Stockholm, and Dublin were included, as were Kuwait City, Baghdad, and Djibouti. In this category were also Beijing, Moscow, Bangkok, and Canberra, as well as Buenos Aires, Auckland, San Marino, the Vatican, and Bissau.

The third category included 22 capitals which had between 500,000-999,999 hyperlinks each. Most of these cities were in the Caribbean, including Kingston, Santo Domingo, Havana, Port au Prince, and Port of Spain. Another cluster was in eastern Europe: Prague, Budapest, Warsaw, and Kiev. Lisbon was the only southern European city in this category and Cairo the only one in Africa. Seoul, Jakarta, and Kuala Lumpur were also in this category.

Category four included 67 cities which had between 100,000-499,000 references. There were capitals in most world regions, but most notably in Southwest Asia (Damascus, Doha, Beirut, Tbilisi, and Dubai), South Central Asia (Kathmandu, Colombo, Tashkent, and Karachi), and East Africa (Dar es Salaam, Nairobi, Addis Ababa, and Lusaka).

The fifth category included those 71 capitals, each with fewer than 100,000 hyperlinks. There were cities in more than a dozen regions, with most being in West Africa (12), the Pacific Islands (10), East Africa (10), and the Caribbean (eight). Examples of cities were: Niamey, Freetown, Ouagadougou, Conarky, and Nouckehott in West Africa; Yaren, Palikir, and Apia in the Pacific; Maputo (Mozambique), Asmara (Eritrea), Moroni (Comoros), Lilongwe (Malawi), and Mogadishu (Somalia) in East Africa; and Castries (St. Lucia), Willemstad (Curaçao), St. George's (Grenada), and Plymouth in the Caribbean. Thirteen national capitals had fewer than 15,000 references. Five had fewer than 6,000 each: Thimpu (Bhutan) 5,290, Palikir (Micronesia) 4,110, Nuku'alofa (Tonga) 3,940, Port Louis (Mauritius) 3,860, and Yaren (Nauru) 3,550.

Additional insights into the importance of capital cities in an electronic world are gained by examining the absolute number of URL references of some cities compared to the combined totals of other cities or entire regions. For example, Singapore, with more than 6.6 million hyperlinks, had a higher total than all capital cities in Western, Central, and North Africa combined. The nine capital cities in Western Europe (15.2 million total hyperlinks) had almost as many as the combined number of those 13 capitals in South America and eight in Central America. The combined totals of Washington, D.C. and Ottawa (7.2 million) were more than all capital cities in West, Central, Southern, and Northern Africa. The combined total of all the 12 capital cities in the island Pacific (the region with the fewest capital city references) was less than the total number of references for Sofia, Nairobi, San José, Hanoi, or Ankara. Moscow's total was similar to that of Kuwait City (about 1.9 million). Auckland, New Delhi, Athens, and Bangkok had about the same number (1.5 million references).

Hyperlinks Per Capita

In regards to the number of hyperlinks per capita for the world's capital city residents, there was also wide variation. They ranged from 1,629 per capita for the Vatican City to .012 for Abidjan, Côte d'Ivoire, .016 for Ulan Bator, Mongolia and .017 for Dhaka, Bangladesh (Figure 2). There were 48 capital cities with more hyperlinks than residents, including 18 with more than five hyperlinks per capita. The highest figures were for highly specialized small city states with dominant economies including: finance (Vaduz, Liechtenstein), telecommunications and communications (Singapore), religious head-quarters (Vatican City), administration (Brussels, Belgium; Luxembourg, Luxembourg; Washington, D.C., Canberra, and Ottawa), and tourism (Monaco; Yaren, Nauru; Valletta, Malta; Plymouth, Montserrat, and Victoria, Seychelles).

The *first* category of 48 capitals includes those with .01 - .09 hyperlinks per capita (Figure 2). In the main, these were capitals in very poor countries and those with closed or

Figure 2. URL references per capita for the world's capital cities

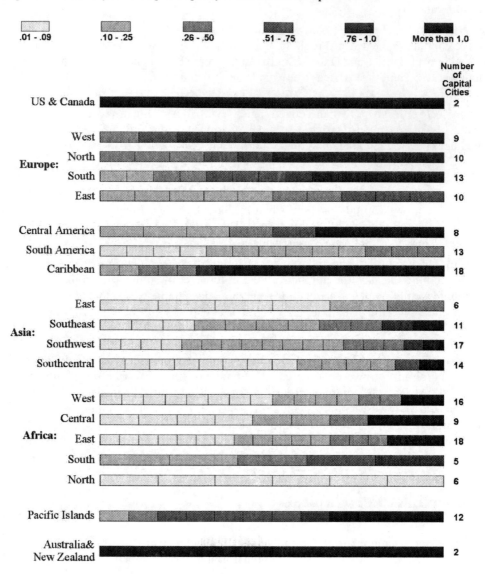

repressive (not open to heavy computer usage) regimes. The capitals in this group were concentrated in South and Central Asia, West, East, and North Africa. These capitals have the fewest number of electronic materials available per city. These six capitals had .02 hyperlinks per capita: Yangon, Myanmur; Yaoundé, Cameroon, N'Djamena, and Sana'a. Also some very large cities had few electronic references per capita; these include Tokyo, Seoul, Jakarta, Cairo, Rabat, Riyadh, and Lima. The *second* category includes 49 capital cities, mostly in Southwest Asia, East Europe, East and West Africa, and South America that have .10 - .25 hyperlinks per capita. Examples of capitals in this category include Beijing, Moscow, Mexico City, Buenos Aires, Delhi, Kabul, Freetown, and Baghdad. The *third* category has 29 cities with .26 - .50 hyperlinks per capita. These are a number of capitals in large countries and mini-states in Europe, Asia and Africa. Examples of cities include London, Paris, Luanda, Gaborone, Tel Aviv, Doha, Dubai, Havana, and San José. The *fourth* category includes 16 capitals with .51 - .75 hyperlinks per capita. These are mostly in southern and eastern Europe and in the Pacific. Examples of cities include Prague, Ljubljana, Budapest, as well as Port Moresby, Honiara, Nouméa, and Suva. The *fifth* category includes nine cities with .76 - .99 hyperlinks per capita. Most of these are capitals of mini-states, of large and wealthy European states, or political hotspots. Examples include Copenhagen, Nicosia, The Hague, Rome, Vienna, Dili, and Windhoek. The *sixth* category includes those 48 states with more than one hyperlink per person. These were mostly Caribbean and Pacific Island capitals with strong tourist economies, capitals with major concentrations of government offices (Canberra, Ottawa, and Washington, D.C.), and those with a single dominant service economy (Vaduz, Luxembourg, and Singapore).

Content of First Web Pages of Capitals with Most and Fewest Hyperlinks

I used the URL references listed on the first "screen page" of the 27 capital cities with more than 1.5 million hyperlinks to identify materials on their Web pages. I identified nearly three dozen categories of information. The first pages usually contained six to eight web addresses; nearly all also contained three or four current news items at the lead item. The contents of these pages included information provided by embassies, local travel and tourism information, degree programs at major universities or institutes to specific sites with city maps, investment opportunities, and local time (probably for potential tourists). The major categories were addresses to Web sites for U.S. embassies, embassies other than the U.S., weather, news and newspapers, travel and tourism (Figure 3). Nineteen capitals had sites with information from U.S. embassies; other counties with embassy sites were India in Berlin, Pakistan in Tokyo, Australia in Beijing, Brazil in San Salvador, the Netherlands in Delhi, and Switzerland and Indonesia in London. The popular travel information site Expedia.com was another major content item. The *CIA Factbook* was listed for Panama, Monaco, and San Marino. Aside from the generic travel and tourism sites in these capital cities, there were Web sites by The Lonely Planet for Panama and San Salvador, a site promoting the Olympic 2008 games in Beijing, festivals in Berlin, and museums in Washington, D.C. and Paris. Webcam sites were provided for Moscow, Auckland, and Luxembourg. Business directories were provided for Guatemala City and San Marino and stock market updates for Singapore and Madrid. While most of these first pages were in English, there were also Spanish sites for Madrid and Mexico City, French sites for Paris, German for Berlin, and Chinese for Beijing.

The Web page contents of the five capitals with fewer than 6,000 URL references were different than the largest capitals (Figure 3). These were small states; four were islands, and three were in the Pacific Basin. Their use of the web to promote tourism was noted; tourism sites, hotels and associated activities were prominent; many listed more than one hotel web address or tourist/vacation opportunity. Local time was another first page

Figure 3. Content analysis of first pages of Web sites: Capital cities with most and least URLs or hyperlinks

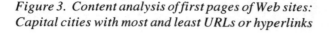

item, perhaps to acquaint potential visitors with where they are coming from vs. what the time would be when they arrive.

Discussion

The Google search engine provides an additional data source from which to classify and rank the world's cities. The results, not surprisingly, are different from scholars who used airline connections or passenger volume or a combination of economic and cultural data to rank world cities. The results also demonstrate there are wide discrepancies in the amount of electronically available information about the world's capitals. In using the volume of URL references or number of hyperlinks, we discover there are clearly some capitals in which the amount of information electronically available using the World Wide Web is substantial. These places produce or have produced for them huge amounts of reference materials for Web sites. And that volume of electronic information increases weekly, and in many cases daily. While many of these high-volume capital cities are in advanced or core economic and wealthy states in Europe and North America, there are others that are also well served by having much web material, including small city states such as Singapore. Evidence of this observation is apparent in Table 2, which also identifies some capital cities that have strong tourism/recreation (including sports and gambling) economies on the world scale or are major capitals with the most regional and international offices of financial firms, NGOs, and IGOs. Second, there are clearly marginal capitals on the world map, as measured by volume of URL references or hyperlinks alone, especially in parts of the developing world in Africa and Asia. These have far fewer links and might be termed "semiperipheral capitals." Many of these are primate cities in countries with rural economies and large rural populations. In a sense they represent another tier of capital cities being less connected to the electronic world, thereby having less electronic information available. The third observation, not surprisingly, identifies those capitals that are in a peripheral category. There is just little information available electronically about them, as measured by web addresses. These peripheral capital cities are in some of the smallest, poorest and least accessible (measured by transportation and communication networks to the rest of the world) states in Sub-Saharan Africa and Southeast Asia. A fourth observation is that physical location on the world political map is not in itself a good determinant of a state's volume of electronic information being available. Some of the microstates in the Caribbean and Pacific Islands have as many URL references or hyperlinks per capita as those in the traditional economic core regions of the developed world. Their external economies, supported in large part by tourism, have facilitated their entry into worlds where electronic information is vital for their raison d'être.

Research Directions

This initial study into classifying the world's capital cities using the number of URL references suggests a number of additional topics that merit investigation by social and policy scientists. I mention four. *First*, it would seem most appropriate to follow up this study on the number of URL references or hyperlinks to specifically examine the number of linkages or pairs of hyperlinks between and among the world's capital cities, that is, between each capital and every other capital. We could construct a 199x199 matrix to examine the number of linkages between each pair of cities. For example, how many linkages are there between Cairo and Pretoria, Cairo and Paris, Cairo and Beijing, etc.? Or between the capital cities in Southeast Asia, South America or Europe? This investigation would identify those capitals with the fewest and the most linkages, and the most and fewest links with what other capitals and which major regions. (See Brunn (2003a) for an initial inquiry into the paired hyperlinks between four major Eurasian capitals.) A similar "linkage" study was done by Brunn and Dodge (2001) on the "export" and "import" of the world's states. Saad, House and Brunn (2002) did the same for the most and least linked states. A *second* study would examine the number of actual linkages a capital city has with other large, medium, and small cities within its own country. This study might be especially insightful where the capital city is not the largest, for example, Ottawa in Canada, Canberra in Australia, and Brasilia in Brazil. A *third* study would undertake a content analysis of Web pages of capital cities in a given region to discern if there are any commonalities or major themes. For example, are the Caribbean and Pacific Island regions mostly promoting tourism? Are investment Web sites more common in

Europe than South Asia? Also are the contents of Web sites similar for large and small states and those with similar socioeconomic standing? A *fourth* would look at the number of linkages each world capital has with New York, the site of the United Nations, and also with Geneva and Vienna, which have U.N. offices. Also it would merit measuring the number of linkages between existing and potentially new European Union member capitals with Brussels and Strasbourg. In carrying out these and other studies that use data from major search engines, we will learn more about individual capitals, information that is becoming of increased importance to scholars, the commercial sector and governments. We also learn more about capital cities in major world regions and their place in contemporary and future worlds (Brunn and Ghose, 2003; Castells, 2002; Van der Wusten, 2002).

References

Barnett, G.A. (2001). A Longitudinal Analysis of the International Telecommunications Network, 1978-1996. *American Behavioral Scientist, 44*(10), 1638-1655.

Brunn, S.D. (2003a). A Note on the Hyperlinks of Major Eurasian Cities. *Eurasian Geography and Economics, 44*(4), 321-324.

Brunn, S.D. (2003b). The New Worlds of Electronic Geography. *GeoTropico, 1*(1). Retrieved from the World Wide Web: www.geotropico.org/Actual.

Brunn, S.D. and Dodge, M. (2001). Mapping the "Worlds" of the World Wide Web: (Re)Structuring Global Commerce Through Hyperlinks. *American Behavioral Scientist, 44*(10), 1717-1739.

Brunn, S.D. and Ghose, R. (2003). Cities of the Future. In S.D. Brunn, J.F. Williams & D.J. Zeigler (Eds.), *Cities of the World: World Regional Urban Geography*. Lanham, MD: Rowman and Littlefield, pp. 489-519.

Brunn, S. D., Williams, J.F. and Zeigler, D.J. (Eds.). (2003). *Cities of the World: World Regional Urban Geography*. Lanham, MD: Rowman and Littlefield.

Castells, M. (2001). *The Internet Galaxy: Reflections on the Internet, Business and Society*. New York: Oxford University Press.

Castells, M. (2002). Local and Global: Cities in the Network Society. *Tijdschrift voor Economische en Sociale Geografie, 93*(5), 548-558.

Corey, K.E. (2000). Electronic space: creating cyber communities in Southeast Asia. In M.I. Wilson & K.E. Corey (Eds.), *Information Tectonics: Space, Place and Technology in an Electronic Age*. New York: Wiley, pp. 135-164.

Environment and Planning A (2003). The Dialectics of Geographic and Virtual Space, 1143-1286.

Friedman, J. (1986). The World City Hypothesis. *Development and Change, 17*, 69-84.

Friedman, J. (1995). Where We Stand: A Decade of World City Research. In P.L. Knox & P.J. Taylor (Eds.), *World Cities in a World System*. New York: Cambridge University Press, pp. 21-47.

GaWC (Global and World Cities) Study and Network. Loughborough University, United Kingdom. Retrieved from the World Wide Web: www.lboro.ac.uk/gawc.

Geographical Review. (1997).Cyberspace, 87(2), 139-307.

Google Technology Home Page. Retrieved from the World Wide Web: www.google.com.

Graham, S.M. and Marvin, S. (1996). Telecommunications and the City: Electronic Spaces, Urban Places. New York and London: Routledge.

Hall, P.G. (1966). World Cities. New York: McGraw-Hill.

Hall, P.G. (1998). Cities in Civilization. New York: Pantheon.

Hargittai, E. and Centeno, M.A. (2001). Developing a Global Geography. American Behavioral Scientist, 44(10), 1541-1544.

Janelle, D.G. and Hodge, D.C. (Eds.) (2000). Information, Place and Cyberspace. Berlin and New York: Springer-Verlag.

Kellerman, A. (2002). The Internet on Earth: A Geography of Information. New York: Wiley.

Kick, E. L. and Davis, B.L. (2001). World-System Structure and Change. American Behavioral Scientist, 44(10), 1561-1578.

Knox, P.L. (1994). Urbanization: An Introduction to Urban Geography. Englewood Cliffs, NJ: Prentice-Hall.

Knox, P.L. and Pinch, S. (2000). Urban Social Geography. Harlow, UK: Pearson Education.

Knox, P.L. and Taylor, P.J. (1995). World Cities in a World System. New York: Columbia University Press.

Leinbach, T.R. and Brunn, S.D. (Eds.) (2001). World of E-Commerce: Economic, Geographical, and Social. New York: John Wiley.

Lo, F.C. and Marcotullio, P.J. (Eds.) (2001). Globalization and the Sustainability of Cities in the Asia Pacific Region. Tokyo: United Nations University Press.

Pulsipher, L. and Pulsipher, A. (2002). World Regional Geography: Global Patterns, Local Lives. New York: Freeman.

Saad, T., House, J. and Brunn, S.D. (2002, Nov/Dec). The Weakest Links: A Hyperlink Index Map of Country to Country Internet Linkages. FP Foreign Policy, p. 101.

Sacks, A. M., Ventresca, M.J. and Uzzi, B. (2001). The Global 500: Mapping the World Economy at Century's End. American Behavioral Scientist, 44(10), 1602-1615.

Sassen, S. (Ed.) (2001). The Global City: New York, London, Tokyo. Princeton: Princeton University Press.

Short, J.R. and Kim, J. (1998). Globalization and the City. New York: Addison Wesley Longman.

Short, J.R., Kim, J. and Wells, H. (1996). The Dirty Little Secret of World Cities Research: Data Problems in Comparative Analysis. International Journal of Urban and Regional Research, 20(4), 697-717.

Smith, D.A. and Timberlake, M.F. (2001). World City Networks and Hierarchies, 1977-1997: An Empirical Analysis of Global Air Travel Links. *American Behavioral Scientist, 44*(10), 1656-1578.

Tijdschrift voor Economische en Sociale Geografie. (2002). The Geography of E-Commerce, 93(5), 484-547. T. R. Leinbach and S. D. Brunn (Eds).

Townsend, A.M. (2001). Network Cities and the Global Structure of the Internet. *American Behavioral Scientist, 44*(10), 1697-1716.

Van der Wusten, H. (2002). Comment on Manuel Castells' Paper in This Issue: Local and Global: Cities in the Network Society. *Tijdschrift voor Economische en Sociale Geografie, 93*(5), 549-562.

Wagenaar, M., Mamadouh, V. and Dijkink, G. (Eds.) (2000). Special Issue on European Capital Cities. *GeoJournal, 51*(1-2), 1-133.

Wheeler, J.O., Aoyama, Y. and Warf, B. (Eds.) (2000). *Cities in the Telecommunications Age.* New York: Routledge.

Wilson, M.I. and Corey, K.E. (Eds.) (2000). *Information Tectonics. Space, Place, and Technology in an Electronic Age.* New York: John Wiley.

Zook, M.A. (2001). Old Hierarchies or New Networks of Centrality? The Global Geography of the Internet Content Market. *American Behavioral Scientist, 44*(10), 1679-1716.

Chapter XI

Online Services and Regional Web Portals:
Exploring the Social and Economic Impacts[1]

Helen Thompson
University of Ballarat, Australia

Abstract

This chapter examines community empowerment, economic and business development, and equity of service as the issue of success and decline in regional and rural communities is explored with a particular focus on community informatics initiatives (CI). In Australia, there has been a vision for online services to be used to open up regional communities to the rest of the world. Government support has been seen as enhancing the competence levels of local communities so they become strong enough to deal equitably in an increasingly open marketplace. But how effective have regional portals and other online initiatives been? This chapter explores whether economic and social benefits are generated via establishing and sustaining regional CI initiatives. Theory relevant to online communities is introduced to provide a context for the presentation of two case studies. The dissemination of the critical learning from these cases can inform others about the diverse factors which impact on the effectiveness and long-term sustainability of regional CI initiatives.

Introduction

Information communications technology (ICT) has been identified as a key enabler in the achievement of regional and rural success, particularly in terms of economic and business development. The potential for achieving equity of service through improved communications infrastructure and enhanced access to government, health, education and other services has been identified. ICT has also been linked to the aspiration of community empowerment where dimensions include revitalising a sense of community, building regional capacity, enhancing democracy and increasing social capital.

There has been strong support for the view that the information economy will play a seminal role in the growth of regional and rural Australia. Online capabilities and services have been promoted on the basis that they can build stronger and more viable regional communities with enhanced investment, employment and skills, and improved quality and convenience of life. ICT has also been identified as providing opportunities to "level the playing field" with access increasingly being seen as critical for both economic and social well-being. Benefits have been espoused in terms of "location independence" and the end of the "tyranny of distance" (Department for Information Technology and the Arts, 1998; Department of Communications Information Technology and the Arts, 2000; Department of Communications Information Technology and the Arts and National Office for the Information Economy, 2000). In terms of enhancing community well-being, it has been argued that online capabilities can help to stimulate and reinvigorate geographic communities and communities of interest.

There has been considerable interest in promoting ICT and e-commerce uptake for small and medium enterprises (SMEs) with the role of local government in promoting SME uptake receiving consideration (Surridge, 2000; Romm and Taylor, 2001; SkillsNet Association Co-operative Limited, 2001; Jakobs, 2002). Summary case studies have been presented to demonstrate how individual businesses have adopted and benefited from ICT and e-commerce (Department of Communications and the Arts and AUSe.NET Australian Electronic Business Network, 1998; Papandrea, 1998; National Office for the Information Economy, 2000; Papandrea and Wade, 2000; Ernst & Young and Multimedia Victoria, 2002). These are, however, generally very brief accounts which lack detail in terms of the processes, the challenges, the evaluation approach and actual outcomes (both expected and unexpected). In terms of community informatics literature, the focus tends to be either on discrete ICT initiatives or on telecentres. There is scant literature which explores how communities can establish web-based services which support local community goals, whether they are social, economic or environmental.

A raft of government policies and programs has been launched and reports published and disseminated, based around the theme of ICT and online capabilities. However, a range of barriers continues to impede uptake, particularly in regional and rural areas. Issues which have been explored include the "digital divide" and "equity of access." While it is has been argued that regional and rural communities require first class infrastructure to harness the power of ICT (Victorian Government, 2002), others, perhaps more realistically, state that the goal of true equity of access may never be achieved (Hunter, 1999; Fong, 2001). Hunter, for example, believes that regional Australia must stop "talking down" its ability to participate in the new global economy (Hunter, 1999, p.3). Supply and demand and economies of scale "will always ensure technology and therefore services will be rolled out in metropolitan areas long before they are even considered for regional areas" (Hunter, 1999, p.1). "If we wait for equity of access, we will wait forever" (Hunter, 1999, p.3).

Calls continue for regional communities to join the globalised, online world. These are supported by the view that success today is based less and less on natural resource wealth, labour costs and relative exchange rates and more and more on individual knowledge, skills and innovation. But how can regional communities "grab their share of this wealth" and use it to strengthen local communities (Simpson, 1999, p.6)? Should communities be moving, as Porter (2001, p.18) recommends (for business), away from the rhetoric about "Internet industries," "e-business strategies" and the "new economy" to see the Internet for what it is: "an enabling technology – a powerful set of tools that can be used, wisely or unwisely, in almost any industry and as part of almost any strategy?"

Recent Australian literature (particularly government literature) does indeed demonstrate somewhat of a shift in terms of the expectations of ICT and e-commerce (National Office for the Information Economy, 2001; Multimedia Victoria, 2002; National Office for the Information Economy, 2002). Consistent with reflections on international industry experience, there is now a greater emphasis on identifying locally appropriate initiatives, exploring opportunities for improving existing communication and service quality and for using the Internet and ICT to support more efficient community processes and relationships (Hunter, 1999; Municipal Association of Victoria and ETC Electronic Trading Concepts Pty Ltd, 2000; National Office for the Information Economy, 2002).

In spite of a context where ICT and online capabilities are promoted as critical elements of potential regional and rural success, few attempts have been made to draw together various intellectual streams of research with examples of community practice to gain a clear understanding of their contribution. Goggin (2001) identifies the need to redress apparent oversights in the literature dealing with online technologies and regional development. Denison et al. (2002) recognise the need for research which clarifies many of the assumptions and unspoken expectations about how electronic tools can be used by groups and organisations. Black et al. (2000) make a specific call for research to be instigated to collect case studies that demonstrate how community-based Internet services can be established for socially and economically beneficial purposes.

This chapter makes a contribution by investigating factors which affect the success of community informatics initiatives. It also examines impacts in terms of promoting community empowerment, economic and business development, and equity of services. Two case studies are presented. Both initiatives were premised on an understanding that well-developed and well-implemented online services could make a positive contribution to the future of regional and rural communities. These cases provide a focus for examining the benefits and challenges of establishing and sustaining community informatics initiatives in a regional and rural context.

Policy Vision

With the proliferation of information and Web sites, it becomes increasingly difficult to find relevant information via the Internet. Web portals have developed to facilitate the location of online information. Examples include: community portals, geographical or interest-based; business portals, internally or externally focused; and government portals, for particular groups such as businesses, young people, women or regional communities. In most cases, the objectives include providing efficient access to information, resources and services, reaching a larger audience, and providing "anytime, anywhere" service, 24 hours a day, seven days a week (Hunter, 1999; Thompson, 1999; Gill, 2000; McGrath and More, 2002; Telstra Country Wide, 2002).

In Australia, there has been a vision for online services to be used to open up regional communities to the rest of the world. Government support has been seen "as enhancing the competence levels of local economies and communities so they become strong enough to deal equitably in an increasingly open marketplace" (McGrath and More, 2002, p.40). Two Federal Government programs managed by the National Office for the Information Economy (NOIE) provide examples of the support which has been available. The Information Technology Online (ITOL) program aims to accelerate Australian adoption of business-to-business e-commerce and encourage collaborative industry-based projects (McGrath and More, 2002). The complementary, five-year $464 million program, Networking the Nation (NTN), was designed to help bridge the gap in the level of telecommunications services, access, and costs between urban and non-urban Australia. Both programs have provided a funding source for initiatives, variously termed as portals, online communities, comprehensive gateways and regional Web sites (Department Communications Information Technology and the Arts, 2001). Funding priority has been given to projects that offer regional aggregation of business, government and community services and provide interactive services to clients both within and external to a region (Commonwealth of Australia, 2001).

While no formal evaluation of the NTN program has been published, a recent evaluation of the ITOL program explores the notion of online communities and reports on portal projects funded through that program. Findings indicate that most ITOL-funded projects are not fully meeting original objectives. Unforeseen challenges during the course of project implementation have included: technological problems, delays in legal agreements, slowness of industry and/or project beneficiaries to respond to the e-commerce initiative, and an underestimation of the time and effort required. For most, the plan to provide full online e-commerce capabilities (for example, online ordering and payments) will not be achieved (McGrath and More, 2002).

McGrath and More (2002, p.67) observe that these potential online communities are "evolving rather than having arrived." Further, despite the rise of interest in online communities, these alliances are not "magic bullets or quick-fix solutions for SMEs or even larger organisations, communities, or industries." They however observe that "where commitment, compatibility, [and] shared strategic intent are at the heart of collaborative relationships, success and learning is much more likely to occur" (McGrath and More, 2002, p.68).

Centre for Electronic Commerce and Communications

The University of Ballarat (UoB) is a distinctive, dual-sector regional institution pre-eminently serving the Australian communities of the Central Highlands and Wimmera regions of Victoria.   The UoB vision is to be a regional university of international standing, highly regarded by the communities it serves. UoB provides clear educational pathways between TAFE and Higher Education and offers a broad range of courses to meet the diverse educational and training needs of the region. The University also has a growing national and international focus. A key objective of the University is to provide leadership for the uptake of ICT in industries, local government and within and among regional groups. Through its activities UoB also seeks to contribute to the educational, social, economic and cultural well-being of the region.

The Centre for Electronic Commerce and Communications (CECC) contributes to these objectives by promoting the advancement of e-commerce, particularly in its practical application in regional and rural Australia. Since being established in 1998 CECC has built extensive partnerships and strategic alliances within and beyond the University region and developed and implemented a range of projects utilising information communication technologies. Different education and training strategies have been used by CECC to foster learning and to build social capital through ICT and e-commerce.

Through the implementation of a $409,000 NTN-funded regional portal project (www.mainstreet.net.au) during the period from 1999 to 2001, CECC gained an enhanced understanding of regional ICT needs. CECC also established significant capabilities in developing, replicating and customising online services capable of meeting the specific needs of regional communities, groups and organisations. Diverse groups and communities now access online services through CECC. These include local governments, town-based communities, membership-based organisations, industry groups and small and medium enterprises. In almost all cases the Web sites, online communities and/or Web portals are meeting or exceeding the initial client objectives. Clients have strong ownership of their online activities, maintain their own web-based information and are committed to investing annually to maintain the shared infrastructure and services they access. The first of two case studies is presented. These case studies help in analysing the complex and dynamic relationship between technological innovations and changing social relations.

Ararat Online

Over the past two decades Ararat and district, like many Australian regions, has been subjected to the consequences of economic rationalisation and restructuring. Population has reduced from 8,336 in 1981 to 7,052 as of the last census of population in 2001 (Department of Infrastructure Research Unit, 1999; Australian Bureau of Statistics, 2003).

Declining commodity prices, changing farm practices, reducing family size and changes in government policy have variously impacted on the Ararat region. Since 1990, the closures of the Aradale Psychiatric Hospital and the regional rail yards have created a direct loss of more than 700 jobs. Following the withdrawal of these two key employers, the Ararat region experienced rapid decline with multiple impacts including: closure of support industries, falling school enrolments, the loss of skilled workers, the withdrawal of State and Commonwealth Government offices and services, and declining housing prices (Surridge, 2000).

Ararat Rural City came into existence in 1996 as a result of the amalgamation of the Shire of Ararat (rural area) and the Ararat City Council (city area). Prior to amalgamation "there was a sense of belonging to either a rural municipality or a city municipality." A "them and us mentality" was apparent (Nicholson and Surridge, 2002, p.10). Since amalgamation, this strong competitive environment has largely continued with residents from outlying areas wary of city-centric decisions and resource allocations. Addressing this perception has been a priority for the region. Increasing the uptake of ICT and e-commerce has been another significant priority.

The Ararat Municipal E-Commerce Strategy was first presented at the Ararat Council Management Group meeting in March of 2000 (Surridge, 2000). This report outlined how the Ararat Rural City was seeking to facilitate an increase in the uptake of ICT and e-commerce across the range of business and service organisations operating in Ararat and district. Council's activities were premised on a belief that the competitiveness of the municipality would be enhanced by the earliest possible adoption of ICT and e-commerce because it was "no longer a question of whether or not to start using the powerful technology of the Internet. It was more a question of *how*" (Surridge, 2000, p.1). The E-Commerce Strategy identified that a "bottom-up approach" would be adopted to empower local businesses and individuals by providing them with opportunities to become more ICT literate and to generate awareness and familiarisation with available technologies.

In 2000, Ararat Rural City partnered with the University of Ballarat to redevelop Ararat Online (www.ararat.asn.au). Ararat Online (Stage 1) had evolved from a partnership between Ararat Rural City and the Ararat Community College. Students had in early 1999 developed simple web pages for local businesses and community groups. But there were some limitations. There was a lack of site consistency, no searching capabilities, some quality problems, and an inability to easily update sites.

The project to upgrade Ararat Online included a range of elements. The site structure and design was completely revamped and new toolsets were incorporated. These included news building tools, a community events calendar, a searchable business directory, online registration and payment system and a community discussion forum. Comprehensive training was provided to the local project team so that future workshops, content development, and the ongoing maintenance of Ararat Online could be managed locally. More than 80 business and community groups directly benefited from an upgrade of their web presence. Each organisation was provided with the opportunity to undertake training to gain the skills to manage their own site.

Victoria's Minister for Regional Development, John Brumby, officially relaunched Ararat Online on August 4, 2000. The Ararat Online Web site was identified as "a first in Victoria because it uses unique ASP software providing easy and affordable community owner-ship, access and input" (*Wimmera Mail Times*, 2000). Businesses and organisations could therefore manage and update their Web sites from their business or home PCs without the need for third-party expert involvement or additional costs to business.

The new site generated immediate benefits through the efficient linking of Internet-based information and services. The region could now more effectively promote local busi-nesses, tourism and regional events. The project also generated significant learning opportunities for community members.

Reflecting on the project, the City's Economic Development Manager identified that the quality of the outcomes could not have been achieved without access to the project management, web development, and training services provided by the University of Ballarat. The project had enabled the community to access tools, technical services and resources that were not previously available. The resultant functionality exceeded original expectations. Three other areas of benefit were: reductions in recurrent operating costs, enhancements in terms of accuracy of information and the achievement of increased community participation.

The Ararat Online project has provided the catalyst for a range of complementary projects. These have included:

1. E-commerce mentoring project for six businesses (2000).

2. Establishment of web services to promote Ararat Tourism (Late 2000).

3. Establishment of a Web site for the Rural City of Ararat (July 2001 version 1 and March 2003 version 2).

4. Launch of web-based services to support the annual regional business awards (2001 and ongoing).

5. Internet access point established in six small communities (Late 2001).

6. Development of web-based infrastructure to record and house information on the skills of residents and groups in Ararat's surrounding towns (2002 and ongoing).

7. A project which surveyed 500 businesses in conjunction with Council's property valuation process (2002 and ongoing).

8. A project to develop and launch township Web sites for six small towns in the region (2002).

9. Further upgrades to Ararat Online with enhanced functionality, opportunities for interaction and information sharing (2002 and 2003).

10. Appointment of staff with specific responsibilities for supporting further develop-ment of Ararat Online and associated community-building activities (2003).

While many similar-sized towns and regions have yet to start their journey, the Ararat region has progressively advanced its uptake of electronic commerce and improved its online service delivery with Ararat Online, a critical component of the region's efforts. Ararat Online has been recognised as an exemplar online community, which demon-strates how regional development approaches and online technologies can come together. According to the SkillsNet Association (SkillsNet Association Co-operative

Figure 1. Ararat Online, September 2003

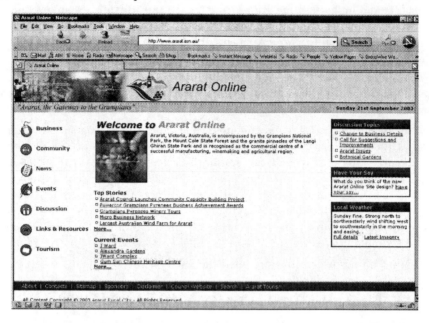

Limited, 2001, p.9), there are only a limited number of landmark implementations in e-commerce which have been encouraged by local government. "The Ararat Online Project, a community and business partnership project, with an online portal for the whole of the Ararat community, and one which includes a mentoring component" is one of these.

The Ararat Online case study acts as a powerful mechanism for promoting online service adoption. This is particularly effective when the Ararat Online "story" is linked with a series of visual images (predominately screen grabs) gathered at regular intervals between 1999 to the present. The presentation of this type of information helps community groups and other regional organisations identify the "big picture" that they can work toward.

The progressive adoption and expansion of online services in Ararat has been achieved through a staged approach with regular local government investment to enhance the ICT infrastructure and a continuing effort and commitment from individuals in the community and in local government to renew, sustain and enhance the information accessible through Ararat Online. The business directory has, for example, recently been redeveloped with the number of participating businesses expanded from approximately 100 to 500. The most recent redevelopment of Ararat Online (launched May 2003) has more closely aligned its services with the wider business and community building efforts in the region.

Figure 2. Site statistics, Ararat Online, June 2002-August 2003

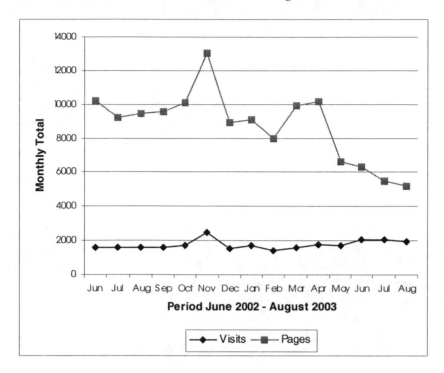

Site statistics provide one measure of utilisation. From June 2002 to August 2003 the site received 24,805 visits, provided users with 125,394 pages of information and recorded a total of 325,970 hits. Figure 2 illustrates utilisation on a monthly basis. Usage peaked in the lead up to the Christmas holiday period. While site visits have been relatively steady, there has been a reduction in utilisation of the site in recent months, as measured by page views. This may indicate that a review of the site content and services should be conducted to ensure that these continue to meet the needs of online visitors.

The Ararat Online case illustrates benefits in terms of expanded local capabilities and confidence, the fostering of business innovation, the provision of new education and training opportunities and the establishment of improved communications services. For the University of Ballarat, the partnership with Ararat Rural City has provided many opportunities to develop and pilot services which promote the advancement of e-commerce. This has assisted the University in developing a replicable portal framework and a suite of scaleable and customisable applications, which are used to establish geographical portals and other forms of online services to meet the needs of SMEs, regional groups, local government and other regional initiatives.

The learning achieved through the Ararat Online project is being very effectively transferred to other Australian communities as the University of Ballarat continues to work with geographic and interest-based communities to identify their online service needs and then to customise, develop and deliver relevant functionality and locally appropriate web services (See Appendix 1 for web addresses). The case of the Young Australian Rural Network is presented in the following section. This case demonstrates how online services can be established to leverage the activities of a community of interest.

Young Australian Rural Network

The Young Australian Rural Network (YARN) (www.yarn.gov.au) is an initiative of the Commonwealth Department of Agriculture, Fisheries and Forestry – Australia (AFFA). YARN is an interactive online community, "a vehicle" for young people working in rural industries "to communicate directly with AFFA and with each other" and to "keep in touch, collaborate, share ideas and strengthen networks" (Downie [AFFA], 2002). The University of Ballarat was invited to submit a proposal for the development of YARN in June 2002 after AFFA identified the University's involvement in projects including Ararat Online, the MainStreet Regional Portal project (www.mainstreet.net.au) and Moorabool Online (www.mconline.com.au).

The establishment of YARN was supported by research undertaken during 2001 which sought to better inform AFFA about young people 18-35 years who represented one-third of all people working in rural industries. The research outcomes were subsequently communicated through a publication entitled, *Guidelines for Reaching our Clients – Young People*, which was launched in May 2002 (Department of Agriculture Fisheries & Forestry Australia, 2002). This guide was designed to help AFFA staff members recognise opportunities to include young people in their work. In introducing the guide, Michael Taylor, the Department Secretary, highlighted the importance of including young people in AFFA's decision-making:

> *Our research tells us that this significant group is impatient with prevailing timeframes for government and industry policy development; is not enthusiastic about agro-political structures and decision-making; communicates differently; is more likely to be positive about the future of agriculture and their own future than their older peers; and, importantly, wants to roll up its collective sleeves and get the job done...This client group must be effectively engaged in our work because not only have they inherited our current agriculture, fisheries and forestry environments and the well-being of rural communities, they determine the immediate future of rural and regional Australia* (Department of Agriculture Fisheries & Forestry Australia, 2002, p.2).

The research conducted for AFFA confirmed that the Internet represented a powerful communication channel for reaching young people. Of the 350 young people surveyed, 67 percent had access to the Internet with 50 percent using it at least weekly. Email was the preferred medium for communicating, but Web sites were identified as a more useful way of accessing information, "particularly for keeping up with industry information"

(Department of Agriculture Fisheries & Forestry Australia, 2002). The extensive use of links to other relevant sites would be most likely to draw young people back to a site but "out-of-date Web sites were unlikely to get a second chance." In terms of designing Internet communications, the need for interactivity was confirmed. There was also the continuing requirement to be mindful of slow download times in some areas (Department of Agriculture Fisheries & Forestry Australia, 2002, p.15).

In June 2002 AFFA recruited a person who would have the primary responsibility of researching and overseeing the establishment and ongoing development of an online community where "ownership" would be shared between AFFA and young people in rural industries. The project objectives for the Young Australian Rural Network project (YARN) would include:

1. Promoting and supporting further networking amongst graduates of the various Young People in Rural Industries programs coordinated by AFFA.

2. Providing a two-way communication tool as a conduit for information flow between AFFA and its stakeholders, with communication ideally being equally initiated at both ends.

3. Serving as an information "hub" for young people in rural industries to find further information on non-government organisations, networks and groups, particularly by providing a facility for non-government youth networks to post information about their organisation on the site.

4. Serving also as a general dissemination tool for the Young People in Rural Industries program (YPIRI program), in conjunction with the existing AFFA Web site (www.affa.gov.au).

While the intention was for AFFA to establish and maintain the site, graduates from various elements of the YPIRI program would determine the content, and as far as possible, the structure and facilities. AFFA clearly understood that functionality could be created (discussion forums, event calendars, web page building facilities, member listings, etc.) but that an online community would not exist unless its members were actively involved and interacting with each other.

The framework for the online community would be developed by University of Ballarat. It was proposed that the core functionality would include six key elements as detailed in Table 1.

A key objective was to actively engage graduates of the YPIRI program in the initial and ongoing development of YARN. Approximately 100 YPIRI graduates were contacted via email on July 7, 2002 and asked to contribute to an online survey that would gather their opinions on the features of an online community that they would find most useful. The results would inform the development of YARN, confirm whether AFFA's vision was appropriate and also test the level of responsiveness and interest which was generated from graduates. Three music gift voucher prizes were offered as an incentive to encourage participation. One email reminder was sent during the two-week collection period. Results were collated, prize winners were announced and detailed feedback provided to all graduates on 25 July 2002. Table 2 summarises the responses which were

Table 1. Proposed functionality for YARN

Functionality	Description
Discussion Forum	Have your say, share information, ask questions, or just find out what people are talking about.
Event Calendar	Check out what events are available nationwide, promote your events and get free publicity on YARN.
News Page	Where you can submit news that you would like young people to know about.
People Listing	Look up who has been involved in AFFA's YPIRI program, and get in contact with them.
Have Your Say	Respond to draft policy posted on the site, or post information for consultation and feedback by young people.
Free Web Page	Promote non-government organisations for young people in agriculture, fisheries, forestry, food and natural resource management.

Table 2. Web site survey results for YARN

Type of Functionality	Very Useful %	Somewh at Useful %	Neutral, or unsure %	Not particularly useful %
Events calendar	81	14	5	0
Member listing	69	31	0	0
Discussion forum	63	28	5	4
Document library	54	28	13	5
Site builder for NGOs	46	36	9	9

Source: www.affa.gov.au/content/ind_dev/youthsurvey.cfm

communicated to graduates via email and to others by making the result available on the AFFA Web site.

Strategies of "engage early" and "communicate innovatively" were embraced by AFFA in implementing the YARN project (Department of Agriculture Fisheries & Forestry Australia, 2002). The response from graduates supported findings from earlier research which identified the benefit of getting young people involved early in a project:

> *Young women and men are likely to give new approaches and mediums a go.*
> *They are more inclined to get involved if they can play a role in the direction*
> *setting/planning stage, rather than if they are simply invited to participate at*
> *the consultative stage. That is, they want to be part of driving direction rather*
> *than reacting to it* (Department of Agriculture Fisheries & Forestry Australia, 2002, p.16).

When the survey results were disseminated, graduates were thanked for their participation and advised that AFFA would contact them during the next week to seek contributions for content for the site. Graduates were assured that submitting content would not be a complex process. Publishing information on the events calendar, news section, or providing information about the rural networks or organisations they were involved in, would be no more difficult than the online survey they had participated in.

Regular communication with graduates continued throughout the very short development period for the YARN project. Graduates were, for example, provided with access to the development site and asked for feedback on its design, navigation and functionality. They each received individual user names and passwords and were given instructions on how to access the graduates' area of the Web site and how to begin submitting content in the lead-up to its official launch on the 27 August 2002.

Initial publicity associated with the launch of YARN included the issuing of a press release, direct email notification to key people such as the presidents and/or convenors of organisations for young people, and a front-page link and news story on the Federal Government entry point at www.fed.gov.au. The key message was for young people to "get online and get involved," to "take pride" in their views, ideas and achievements and to "watch the awareness grow amongst government and industry" of their valuable contributions (Truss, 2002, p.1).

Longer-term promotion has been achieved through the fortnightly e-newsletter of the Rural Industries Leadership Section of AFFA and by and providing all new graduates of the YPIRI program with publishing and member access on YARN. Organisations that use the "site builder" tool also promote YARN through their web address (see, for example, the Bush Capital Club at www.yarn.gov.au/sites/BCC).

A key strategy has also been to ensure that site visitors are actively engaged when they visit the site. This is being achieved by providing multiple opportunities for participation and involvement, for example, by contribution or starting an online discussion, building a site, adding a link, publishing events or suggesting new items.

During the 12 months since its official launch, YARN has received over 237,000 hits, 18,900 unique visits and provided users with more than 53,500 page views. Figure 4

Figure 3: YARN – August 2002

illustrates how visits fell from the initial levels experienced at the time of the site launch. Visitation statistics began to gradually increase in the early months of 2003. Significant increases were then experienced during April and May.

This increase in site visitation coincided with the launch of GATEway, an opportunities reference database which has been incorporated into the existing Web site and promotional activities such as the issuing of a press release by the Federal Minister for AFFA. The reference tool provides young people with a centrally housed information database of relevant government and non-government programs, awards, events and training opportunities. The initial database content was contributed by members of the Young People in Rural Industries Working Group, but since the GATEway application has gone "live," other agencies and organisations have been invited to publish information.

While the application design is very functional, it is simple to enter information and users are able to interrogate the database in a number of ways, for example, by using key terms or by entering one or more qualifiers to narrow their search as required. Selections can then be collated and printed in PDF quality format. The increase in site utilisation as measured by page views indicates that site visitors were exploring more areas of the site. In the months of June and July there has been some reduction in the levels of site utilisation from the peak experienced in May 2003.

The next upgrade for YARN is currently in the planning stage. Objectives and outcomes, graduate and visitor feedback, site statistics and other available information will continue to be regularly reviewed to identify further opportunities for enhancement to better ensure that YARN can meet the information and communication needs of AFFA and young people in rural industries.

Figure 4. Usage statistics for YARN August 2002–2003

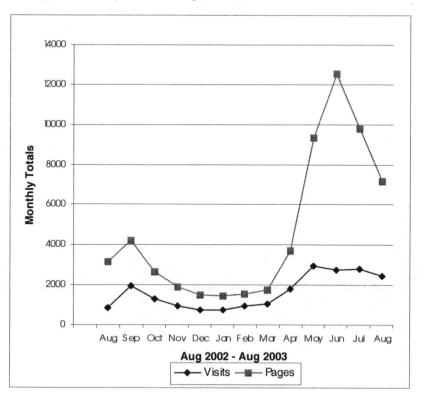

Conclusions

The case studies for Ararat Online and YARN have highlighted a number of factors that have impacted and influenced their development. Collaboration with a regional University has also been an important factor in the renewal and growth of each of these portal initiatives. In terms of infrastructure, challenges have been reduced by the availability of a comprehensive portal platform and toolset, which has been specifically designed to meet regional and rural needs, particularly the skills and infrastructure gaps which often exist. Initiatives have then been sustained by putting community members in charge of the management of their online services. Through this model, local ownership and the sustainability of infrastructure and technical support services have been achieved by effectively aggregating demand for CI services.

Key factors in sustaining regional CI initiatives appear to be directly related to the level of ownership that can be provided to stakeholders and site users, the ability for multiple users to contribute, publish and maintain the web-based information, and finally the degree to which web-based applications are tailored to meet the particular business or community purpose. These finding are consistent with findings in the business-to-business context. For example the report entitled, *B2B E-Commerce Capturing Value Online* identified that "ultimately, the point of success is where industry can see the broad-based business case...and then take initiatives forward" (National Office for the Information Economy, 2001).

Communities, however, just like businesses, require assistance in identifying the most appropriate online services for their particular circumstances. Policies which encourage communities to enter collaborative partnerships, which leverage existing infrastructure, knowledge and learning should thus be seen as preferable to the funding of discrete stand-alone initiatives. Well-developed and well-implemented online services can make a positive contribution to the future of regional and rural communities. Case studies, such as those presented in this chapter, are effective in illustrating the impacts, influences and challenges that can be experienced in operationalizing and sustaining regional community informatics initiatives.

Endnote

[1]   The author acknowledges Dr. Brian West from the University of Ballarat who has been generous in the provision of advice and encouragement that greatly assisted in the preparation of this work.

References

Australian Bureau of Statistics. (2003). 2001 Census of Population and Housing 2016.2 Selected Characteristics for Urban Centres and Localities: Victoria. Canberra, ABS.

Black et al. (2000). Rural Communities and Rural Social Issues: Priorities for Research, A Report for the Rural Industries Research and Development Corporation. RIRDC Publication No. 00/130.

Commonwealth of Australia. (2001). Government Response to the House of Representatives Standing Committee on Primary Industries and Regional Services - Report of the Inquiry into Infrastructure and the Development of Australia's Regional Areas - Time Running Out: Shaping Regional Australia's Future. Canberra: Commonwealth Government.

Department of Agriculture Fisheries & Forestry Australia. (2002). Guidelines for Reaching our Clients - Young People. Canberra, Commonwealth of Australia. Retrieved 16 May 2003 from the World Wide Web: <http://www.affa.gov.au/content/publications.cfm?Category=Young%People%in%Rural%Industries& ObjectID=71BF31EA-F44A-45B0-8702F253C31E31B3>.

Department of Communications and the Arts and AUSe.NET Australian Electronic Business Network. (1998). Where to Go? How to Get There. Guide to Electronic Commerce for Small Business. Canberra: Commonwealth of Australia.

Department of Infrastructure Research Unit. (1999). Towns in Time Analysis: Population Changes in Victoria's Towns and Rural Areas, 1981-96. Melbourne: Department of Infrastructure.

Ernst & Young and Multimedia Victoria. (2002). Victoria's E-commerce Advantage: E-commerce Case Studies. Melbourne: Government of Victoria.

Fong, G. (2001). Electronic Communities - Problems and Potential. *Proceedings of the Inaugural Telstra Consumer Consultative Council Annual Forum*, Sydney, 14 November 2001, Telstra.

Gill, J. (2000). *Portal Power - Online Communities Development and the Emergence of the 'New' Community.* Perth: HarvestRoad.

Goggin, G. (2001). "Pump Up the Volume": Telecommunications and the Reinvention of Regional Communities. Telstra Consumer Consultative Council Annual Forum, Sydney, 14 November 2001, Telstra.

Hunter, A. (1999). Opportunities Through Communications Technology for Regional Australia. Regional Australia Summit, Canberra.

Jakobs, G. (2002, September). Building Online Community Capacity - The Challenges and Opportunities. Institute for Regional and Rural Research Forum. Ballarat: University of Ballarat.

McGrath, M. and More, E. (2002). Forging and Managing Online Collaboration: The ITOL Experience. Canberra: National Office for the Information Economy and Macquarie University.

Multimedia Victoria. (2002). Connecting Victoria: A Progress Report 1999-2002. Melbourne: State Government of Victoria.

Municipal Association of Victoria and ETC Electronic Trading Concepts Pty Ltd. (2000). Local Government - Integrated Online Service Delivery Strategy and Implementation Plan, Executive Summary - Final. Melbourne: Municipal Association of Victoria.

National Office for the Information Economy. (2000). Where to Go? How to Get There 2000. A Guide to Electronic Commerce for Small to Medium Businesses. Canberra: Commonwealth of Australia.

National Office for the Information Economy. (2001). B2B E-Commerce: Capturing Value Online. Canberra: Commonwealth of Australia.

National Office for the Information Economy. (2002). The Benefits of Doing Business Electronically - eBusiness. Canberra: Commonwealth Government.

National Office for the Information Economy. (2002). Guide to Successful eBusiness Collaboration. Canberra: Commonwealth of Australia.

Nicholson, D. and Surridge, I. (2002). Final Report to VicHealth - ABCD Project Ararat Rural City. Ararat: Ararat Rural City.

Papandrea, F. (1998). *An Introduction to Electronic Commerce in Tasmanian Business*. Launceston: Learning Media Services.

Papandrea, F. and Wade, M. (2000). E-commerce in Rural Areas - Case Studies. Canberra: Rural Industries Research and Development Corporation.

Porter, M. E. (2001, April). Strategy After the Net. *BOSS*, 17-23.

Romm, C. T. and Taylor, W. (2001). The Role of Local Government in Community Informatics Success Prospects: The Autonomy/Harmony Model. *34th Hawaii International Conference on System Sciences*, Hawaii.

Simpson, R. (1999). Brave New Regions. Regional Australia Summit. Canberra: Australia.

SkillsNet Association Co-operative Limited. (2001). E-Barriers, E-Benefits, E-Business Bridging the Digital Divide for Small and Medium Enterprises: An Investigation of Benefits and Inhibitors for Small and Medium Business Use of E-Commerce and Electronic Service Delivery. Melbourne: SkillsNet Association Co-operative Limited.

Surridge, I. (2002). Municipal E-Commerce Strategy. Ararat: Ararat Rural City Council Management Group.

Telstra Country Wide. (2002). Our Community Online. Letter and Brochure Distributed to Local Government Conference Delegates 31 October 2002, Telstra Corporation Limited.

Thompson, H. (1999). Victoria's Golden West Portal Project Business Case. Ballarat: Centre for Electronic Commerce and Communications, University of Ballarat.

Truss, W. (2002). 'Media Release', Rural Young People YARN Online. Canberra: Department of Agriculture, Fisheries and Forestry-Australia. Retrieved 12 May 2003 from the World Wide Web: <http://www.affa.gov.au/ministers/truss/releases/02/02210wt.html>.

Victorian Government. (2002). Victorian Government Business Statement: Building Tomorrow's Businesses Today, Competitive, Innovative, Connected. Melbourne: State Government of Victoria.

Appendix 1

University of Ballarat URLs

University of Ballarat   www.ballarat.edu.au
CECC   www.cecc.com.au

MainStreet portal URL

Mainstreet.net.au   www.mainstreet.net.au

Geographical portal URLs examples

Ararat Online   www.ararat.asn.au
Moorabool Online   www.mconline.com.au
Pyrenees Online   www.pyreneesonline.com.au

Membership based communities URLs examples

Birchip Cropping Group   www.bcg.org.au
Young Australian Rural Network   www.yarn.gov.au
Rural Regional Research Network   www.cecc.com.au/rrrn
Pyrenees Hay Processors   www.exporthay.com
Central Highlands Exporters   www.growexport.com

Comprehensive Web site URLs examples

Ballarat A Learning City   www.ballaratlearningcity.com.au
Central Highlands Area Consultative
Committee   www.chacc.com.au
Pyrenees Shire   www.pyrenees.vic.gov.au
Regional Connectivity Project   www.regionalconnectivity.org

Chapter XII

ICT Growth and Diffusion:
Concepts, Impacts and Policy Issues in the Indian Experience with Reference to the International Digital Divide

Saundarjya Borbora
Indian Institute of Technology Guwahati, India

Abstract

This chapter examines the role of technology in economic and social development in developing countries, with a particular emphasis on India as an example. The concepts of ICT growth and ICT diffusion are examined. From this the chapter reviews the Indian government's successful policies encouraging ICT Growth through the support of the export-oriented service industry. This industry has witnessed long-term growth primarily as the result of the increasing tradability and consequent internationalisation made possible by changes in ICTs. However, the export focus policy has created enclaves within the Indian economy without significant forward and backward linkages. Evidence suggests that the International Digital Divide may be increasing. This chapter suggests that in order to maintain its relative technological position and to increase its comparative advantage in the IT sector, government policy should focus on domestic ICT Diffusion. The chapter reviews several local public, private, and public-private initiatives to spread the use of ICT throughout Indian regions that have been successful and may serve to offer examples for future development. We conclude that ICT-driven development may be achieved with supportive central government policies, lessening the International Digital Divide.

Introduction

Today Information and Communication Technologies (ICTs) pervade almost all human activities. In both developed and developing countries there is an intense debate concerning the contribution of these technologies towards economic development and, consequently, human welfare. In relation to the economic benefits, several cross-country studies in recent years have indicated that the return on investment in information technology created by increasing productivity and growth is substantial (Kraemer and Dedrick, 2001; Pohjola, 2001). According to Pohjola's study, the output elasticity of IT capital was found to be 0.31 for a sample of 39 countries, which is quite high, and a figure of 0.23 in the OECD sub-sample. Another cross-country study by the IMF (2001) also provides a similar conclusion. Country-specific studies, of Singapore for example, have concluded that the net return to IT capital is 37.9 percent compared to 14.6 percent for non-IT capital, which is about two and a half times higher (Wong, 2001). These studies also highlight that IT-induced productivity, and thereby economic development, is still concentrated in developed countries and the developing countries are yet to gain the same order of benefits as their counterparts in developed economies.

This leads us to the ongoing debate over the International Digital Divide. Examining the present unequal access to ICT, it may be stated that new technologies reinforce the disparities between developed societies and developing societies. Several studies supplement this view. OECD (2000) stated that affluent states at the cutting edge of technological advantage have reinforced their lead in the knowledge economy. The benefits enjoyed by the most technologically advanced economies have not yet trickled down to their neighbors. Many European countries are still behind the most advanced countries, not to speak of poor countries in the Sub-Saharan Africa, Latin America or South East Asia that are much further behind. Similarly, UNDP (1999) argues that productivity gains from ICT may actually widen the gulf between the developed economies and those that lack the skills, resources, and infrastructure to invest in ICT.

The impact of ICT can be seen from the perspective of two inter-related issues: ICT growth and ICT diffusion. ICT growth refers to the growth of IT-related industries and services and their effect on employment, export earnings, and the outsourcing of activities. ICT diffusion refers to IT-induced development, which increases productivity, competitiveness, economic growth, and human welfare from the use of the technology by different sectors of the economy. Until now, India has mainly benefited from ICT growth through a series of institutional innovations and policy measures, although it would not be correct to say that the importance of ICT diffusion has not been recognized.

For example, the software policy of 1986 explicitly recognized the importance of the balanced development of the software industry both for export and domestic use. But of late emphasis has been given to the diffusion of new technology and ICT-induced development. Therefore, in the Indian context, the often-cited success of the IT sector has not been achieved by the harnessing of new technology to increase efficiency and productivity, but mainly derived from earning foreign exchange by exporting IT-enabled goods and services. India's export performance in this sector is noteworthy in comparison with other producers of exports, not only in terms of its growth rates but also in terms of its stability.

The current chapter will focus on the direct benefits of ICT growth, paying special attention to the service sector. We argue that the role of IT in economic development has not received adequate attention. The purpose of the chapter is to highlight the contemporary economic realities and to suggest that the ICT development should be the focus of research and policymaking in India. We propose to undertake this both on the basis of empirical facts and on the basis of the arguments regarding the International Digital Divide. The central message of this chapter is that although ICT growth is important for developing countries such as India, it is time to shift the focus towards ICT-induced development. The following section subjects these issues to analytical and empirical scrutiny within the limits of data availability.

The Digital Divide

The concept of the Digital Divide is a complex one that manifests itself in different ways in different countries. This leads us to accept that there is no single definition of the Digital Divide, although it is clear that there are growing disparities between the "haves" and "have-nots," and to conclude that the potential impact on society will be exacerbated by technology. This divide poses both practical and policy challenges. It is also evident that solutions that work in developed countries cannot simply be transplanted to a developing country's environment. Solutions must be based on an understanding of local needs and conditions.

Broadly, we can examine both International and Domestic Digital Divides. Real disparities exist both in the access to and the use of information and communication technology between countries (the International Digital Divide) and between groups within countries (the Domestic Digital Divide). The concept of the Digital Divide is grounded in substantial empirical research (Norris, 2001) and the extent of the Divide can be suggested with some statistics: "In the entire continent of Africa, there are a mere 14 million phone lines – fewer than in either Manhattan or Tokyo. Wealthy nations comprise some 16 percent of the world's population, but command 90 percent of Internet host computers. Of all the Internet users worldwide, 60 percent reside in North America, where a mere five percent of world's population reside" (Nkrumah, 2000). In addition to this, even the positive outlook adopted by the Economist (2000) accepted that "One in two Americans is online, compared with only one in 250 Africans. In Bangladesh a computer costs the equivalent of eight years' average pay." From such studies and statistics, the following patterns emerge:

There is a trend of growing ICT disparities between and within countries:

- All countries are increasing their access to and use of ICT. But those countries that are the "information haves" are increasing their access and use at such an exponential rate that, in effect, the divide between countries is actually growing.

- Within countries, all groups are increasing access to ICT. But the "information haves" are increasing access and use at such an exponential rate that the division within countries is actually growing.

ICT Diffusion

The Digital Divide is not a simple phenomenon, but a complicated overlapping set of issues created by varying levels of ICT access, basic ICT usage, and the patterns of ICT applications among countries and peoples. Developing countries may have to achieve higher levels of *per capita* income in order to support the level of IT dissemination throughout society that is a precondition for ICT-induced development. However, due to the characteristics of ICTs, the leapfrogging of stages of development is possible as long as supportive government policies are in place. In fact it can be argued that there is an advantage in not having the problems associated with obsolete IT infrastructures and legacy systems typical in early investing countries for late entrants. Investment made in new technologies also complements investments already made in communication technologies such as satellites, telephone, and cable networks. Again newly developed technologies like the "wireless in local loop" (WILL) can significantly reduce the cost of last-mile connectivity, making it possible to connect remote villages cost-effectively (Planning Commission, 2001). Many new computer technologies are essentially multi-user by nature and there is scope for Internet kiosks, community Internet centers and hubs to provide access for many users. As previously indicated, late entrants such as India have the advantage of access to frontline technologies and cost-effective infrastructure development without the sunk costs in extant systems carried by many more developed countries (Planning Commission, 2001). There exists real opportunities for promoting ICT diffusion through the involvement of both the public and private sectors, NGOs and other stakeholders (Mansell, 1999).

The new technologies are mostly supply-driven and provide a greater scope for diffusion agents to influence the technology diffusion process. There are a large number of organizations involved in developing country's ICT development and adoption. This multi-institutional stakeholder network should be in the forefront of diffusion of ICT in developing countries. In India recently there have been a number of ICT diffusion initiatives undertaken by the government, the private sector, and NGOs for economic development and to provide services to citizens. Some of the initiatives are in the initial stages, but acceptance by local communities has the potential to transform technological usage in rural areas of the country.

Bridging the Digital Divide: Selected Experiments from Indian States

The following section details some of the government initiatives that are underpinning technological change in Indian regions. This does not seek to be a comprehensive survey, but rather to present a selection of initiatives to give a feel for the type of development plans currently being undertaken. The first example examines an initiative in the state of Andhra Pradesh, which includes 23 districts, 1,125 mandals, 295 assembly constituencies and 28,245 revenue villages. This area has been digitized to a certain extent by a state-wide area network (SWAN) called APSWAN. With this SWAN the state is in a position to provide government-to-citizen services. Agricultural market yards have been computerized and connected with state headquarters, providing the prices of commodities and arrival times to markets and other important information to agriculturists. This process has the aim of eliminating middlemen and, in policy terms, the exploitation of farmers. This digital connectivity also brings transparency and efficiency to the functioning of government. Other states are also trying to undertake similar projects.

The second example considers the Gyandoot Dotcom project in Madhya Pradesh, which has demonstrated the feasibility of universal access to information. The Dhar district has been connected by 21 centers situated in 30 villages using locally made servers and multimedia kits in a cost-effective way. Villagers are required to pay a nominal charge for services such as accessing land records and for regular market updates. Each of these centers has a potential clientele of around half a million inhabitants in the Dhar district. The success has emphasized the social and economic benefits of mass empowerment. The potential of this project has been recognized internationally for introducing a new paradigm in the use of IT in bringing about social transformation.

In addition, the region of Uttar Pradesh provides more examples of central and state government-initiated ICT service-based projects. Initiatives such Internet kiosks providing e-mail and access to computer education programmes are common. In eastern Up, for example, Kashika Telecom has established a presence in low-cost dhabas (computer kiosks) financed through bank loans. Such initiatives can be seen in Karnataka, Tamil Nadu as well in the North Eastern States of India.

The private sector also has been responsible for developing new IT initiatives. The Zee Interactive Learning System Project, for example, provides interactive multimedia learning using satellite, video, Internet, and a cable network for delivery at several "ZED point" kiosks. This is directed towards educating rural children by constructing "knowledge building communities" at an affordable cost even to the rural population. With a continuing focus on education, the Intel Corporation has taken the initiative to set up teacher training laboratories to train 100,000 schoolteachers in India. At the time of this writing, Intel also envisages operating a "cyber school on wheels" project also targeted toward educating rural masses.

Despite the initiatives outlined above, there is no specific central government policy for ICT diffusion in India. However, the current evidence suggests that there has been some degree of ICT diffusion created by both the activities of industry and discrete public and private initiatives. Within India, computers for accounting and management functions are widespread, especially in private enterprises (as in Table 1). With regard to Internet use, some industries are ahead of others. Evidence shows, in this time of liberalization and globalization, that some firms are using technology to increase their productivity and competitiveness. Some degree of ICT diffusion has been taking place, although it may be mostly confined to the manufacturing sectors of the economy, even though this has been a low central government political priority.

Table 1. Indicators of IT use in India's industrial sector, 1997

Industries	Total no. of Factories	Percent of Factories with:			
		Computers in office	Network	Internet	Robots or computer in production
Food products	14,695	13.01	0.84	1.39	0.29
Other food products	8,109	24.17	1.38	2.01	1.64
Beverages, tobacco, etc.	8,669	47.81	0.36	0.28	0.14
Cotton textiles	9,227	22.28	0.54	1.87	1.37
Wool/silk textiles	3,989	49.76	1.25	2.28	0.25
Jute/other fibre textiles	503	16.70	0.40	3.78	0.60
Textile incl. apparel	5,409	51.32	3.18	11.31	2.09
Wood and wood products	3,787	8.98	0.40	0.95	0.24
Paper and paper products	6,304	38.50	1.84	3.73	4.71
Leather products	1,742	37.60	1.89	7.18	0.29
Basic chemicals/related	9,357	50.69	2.91	5.58	2.56
Rubber/plastic/coal	7,597	42.57	2.80	4.01	1.59
Non met. mineral product	11,376	13.37	0.41	0.95	1.09
Basic metal/alloys	6,915	41.94	0.93	3.69	1.72
Metal products	8,243	31.68	0.92	2.86	1.01
Machinery/equipment	8,203	44.46	2.12	5.63	2.66
Electric machinery	5,743	55.77	3.53	10.92	4.89
Transport equipment	3,999	46.96	1.63	7.15	2.58
Scientific equipment	2,243	48.02	4.01	14.00	3.97
Repair of capital goods	2,240	25.89	0.80	1.96	0.36
Electricity	3,644	64.71	0.93	3.10	3.24
Gas and steam	80	75.00	2.50	3.75	5.00
Water works and supply	293	10.58	0.68	1.02	0.68
Non-conventional energy	4	25.00	25.00	25.00	0.00
Storage and warehousing	1,078	0.37	0.37	0.09	0.00
Sanitation	102	0.00	0.00	0.00	0.00
Motion pictures, etc.	51	7.84	7.84	27.45	0.00
Laundry and others	94	0.00	0.00	0.00	0.00
Repair services	1,966	2.59	2.59	1.12	0.00
All Industries	135,679	34.70	1.50	3.72	1.77

Source: Annual Survey of Industries (CSO), 1997.

ICT and the Service Sector

Economic globalization has facilitated the internationalization of the service sector and the advances in ICTs have made it possible for firms to provide novel services that are creating new forms of international trade. Service industries provide links between geographically dispersed economic activities and play an important role in the growing interdependence of markets and production activities across nations. As technology develops, it further reduces communication costs, stimulating the faster growth of the international trade in services.

For developing countries such as India, the internationalization of services and the development of the ICT sector have provided an opportunity as well as a challenge. The opportunity has been in terms of the potential exports of services and of service-related foreign investments and trade. The challenges are for designing appropriate regulatory environments for the service sector as it is an important factor influencing productivity and competitiveness, providing the necessary investments in the ICT sector and adapting the education system in line with the requirements of the Information Age.

Until recently economists characterized the service sector as generally non-tradable activities whose growth was perceived to be a by-product of expansion of the primary and secondary sectors. The changes in the service sector driven by development in ICTs have changed this conception and today service industries are regarded as a pre-condition of economic growth. The main growth in this area has been the rapid expansion of knowledge-intensive services (KIS), such as professional and technical services, advanced health care, education, banking, and insurance. The growing tradability of services has been a direct outcome of these changes, and many developing countries have benefited from the outsourcing of services by multi-national companies (MNCs) made possible by ICTs. Today service industries are important investors in IT throughout the world, and KISs that have high income elasticity are growing in both developed and developing economies. Technological innovation has expanded the opportunities for the provision of services, and electronic networks such as the Internet are a dynamic force for creating new possibilities for trade between distant areas. Technological developments in ICTs are driving not only the internationalization of services but also of manufacturing and primary industries, as technology blurs the boundaries between products and services. In the United States, for example, as much as 65 to 75 percent of employment in manufacturing may be associated with service-based activities (Braga, 1996). With falling communication costs the potential for international outsourcing in both the service and manufacturing industries has grown.

Service activities such as data entry, the analysis of income statements, the development of computer software and financial products are mostly exportable services. The impact of ICTs on the tradability of services is not only limited to international markets, but has facilitated the expansion of services within and between regions, from firms to final consumers. Even services in which consumer-provider interaction has been very high, such as education and health services, are today offered using high technology in ICT. Advances in computer-mediated technology make it possible to effectively gain the benefits in distance education and tele-medicine without relocating to provider locations. Trade in commercial services has been growing exponentially, and with the internationalization of services the flow of FDI to developing countries has increased faster than global trade and output. Services now represent a much higher share of FDI. The prospect for the continuing internationalization of services through FDI is bright as the demand for services is still in the growth phase. Developing countries are attracted to FDI in services as a means of obtaining the transfer of technical and professional skills and know-how.

As modern service industries are highly ICT-dependent they require human and financial capital input. Developing countries such as India are carving out areas of comparative advantage in IT-based services, and one of their key strengths is the ability to offer access to large numbers of highly trained and lower-cost IT professionals. This phenomenon not only acts to expand exports, but also helps domestic producers gain access to more efficient and diversified services in world markets. Efficient producer services are increasingly important in this outward-oriented development strategy.

Developing countries have much scope for the expansion of traditional service export areas. Data entry was one of the first services to be the subject of international outsourcing. Software programming is another activity that is increasingly traded internationally. India has taken a big lead in these areas and one estimate suggests that India has captured roughly 12 percent of the international market for customized software. Yet another area of strong comparative advantage is in "back office" service activities. For example, several US and UK-based insurance and accounting companies now send claims overseas for processing. In manufacturing, service activities such as logistics management, design, and customer services are being outsourced internationally. It may be difficult to estimate precisely the size of these markets, but from the perspective of developing countries the potential impact in terms of higher exports over the long term is significant. These important developments reveal that developing countries with large workforces and a modern technology infrastructure can successfully exploit the changing patterns of international production made possible by ICTs.

The Indian IT Export Scenario

The growth of IT exports from India over the last decade has been the subject of considerable interest to developed as well as developing economies. This attention has been stimulated by studies demonstrating that the spillover benefits and linkages with the rest of the economy from the IT sector are extensive (Joseph, 2002). The contribution made by Software Exports to India's Economy is shown in Table 2.

Table 2 illustrates the sustained growth of foreign exchange earnings represented by Software Exports to the Indian economy, and highlights the rapid increase made after the liberalization of the Indian economy to the international services sector began in 1991.

Whether the IT sector with its export-oriented growth strategy will generate significant spillovers and linkage effects with the rest of the economy is not the focus of this chapter, but on the basis of available data this seems unlikely. The Indian IT industry appears to be locked into activities such as low-level design, coding and maintenance with negligible linkages to rest of the economy (D'Costa, 2001). As these activities are

Table 2. India's software exports (gross foreign exchange earnings)

Year	Software Exports(US$m)	Export Growth (%)
1980	4.0	-
1981	6.8	70%
1982	13.5	99%
1983	18.2	35%
1984	25.3	39%
1985	27.7	9%
1986	38.9	40%
1987	54.1	38%
1988/89(Apr-Mar)	69.7	(29%)
1989/90	105.4	51%
1990/91	131.2	24%
1991/92	173.9	33%
1992/93	219.8	26%
1993/94	314.0	43%
1994/95	480.9	53%
1995/96	668.0	39%
1996/97	997.0	49%
1997/98	1650	65%
1998/99	2180	32%
1999/2000	3600	65%
2000/01	5300	47%
2001/02	6200	17%
2002/03	7800 (est.)	24%

Source: Heeks, 1999.

primarily driven by the export market, the growth of this sector remains an enclave of the general economy without many forward or backward linkages. In terms of the spatial location of the industry, approximately 90 percent of software development and export is confined to the four major metropolitan areas of Bangalore, Mumbai, Delhi and Chennai (as shown in Table 3), leading Mansell (1999) to perceive that export-oriented IT growth would seem to have generated marginal spillover benefits.

The IT sector export-based strategy has been successful in India primarily as a result of the outsourcing of services by the firms based in the developed economies. India has been the focus for many Western firms as its competitive advantage is based on technological agility, flexibility, cost control, time-to-market and quality. These advantages are rooted in the established education sector, and Indian technology institutes are acknowledged as world-leading institutions that select and train IT professionals. 115,000 Indian IT professionals graduate annually in a country with an English speaking population of around 1 billion people. There is expansion in the IT market with more than 3,000 Indian software exporting companies currently having export relationships with over 100 countries. Some of the leading Indian companies are registered with the NYSE or Nasdaq.

Table 3. Distribution of software sales and exports across major locations in India

Location	Sales %		Exports %	
	1997	1998	1997	1998
Bangalore	33.9	27.9	30.3	29.7
Mumbai	24.3	24.7	27.5	24.0
Delhi/Noida	15.9	20.3	15.3	18.5
Chennai	14.8	16.8	15.5	17.3
Hyderabad	4.2	5.4	5.3	6.3
Calcutta	3.3	2.3	1.5	1.3
Others	3.6	2.6	4.6	2.9

Source: Joseph, 2002:16.

It should be noted here that the IT sector is highly labour intensive, and one that employs mostly skilled labour, although the level of this varies with the nature of a firm's activities. Available empirical evidence suggests that the IT export boom of the last decade should be considered in the context of India's labour cost advantage (as shown in Table 4). The IT sector upswing has lead to increases in the demand for labour and also wage rates.

Table 4 reflects India's cost advantage in relation to skilled employable labour in the IT sector. More than this, off-shore IT work is also cheaper for MNCs than employing Indian

Table 4: IT labour costs across different countries in 1995 (Note: Figures are averages for 1995 and were likely to rise 5 to 10 percent approximately per annum, with rates being slightly higher in lower-income countries.)

	Switzer land	USA	Canada	UK	Ireland	Greece	India
			(US$ per annum)				
Project leader	74,000	54,000	39,000	39,000	43,000	24,000	23,000
Business analyst	74,000	38,000	36,000	37,000	36,000	28,000	21,000
System analyst	74,000	48,000	32,000	34,000	36,000	15,000	14,000
System designer	67,000	55,000	36,000	34,000	31,000	15,000	11,000
Development programmer	56,000	41,000	29,000	29,000	21,000	13,000	8,000
Support programmer	56,000	37,000	26,000	25,000	21,000	15,000	8,000
Network analyst/designer	67,000	49,000	32,000	31,000	26,000	15,000	14,000
Quality assurance specialist	71,000	50,000	28,000	33,000	29,000	15,000	14,000
Database data analyst	67,000	50,000	32,000	22,000	29,000	24,000	17,000
Metrics/process analyst	74,000	48,000	29,000	31,000	-	15,000	17,000
Documentation/training staff	59,000	36,000	26,000	21,000	-	15,000	8,000
Test engineer	59,000	47,000	25,000	24,000	-	13,000	8,000

Source: Heeks (1999), adapted from Rubin (1996).

IT labour onsite. For example, using data invoice processing as an example, onsite work at the client's site would cost US $8,000 (plus local taxes) as opposed to US $4,600 offsite in India (Heeks, 1999).

Policy Measures Supportive of IT Growth in the Indian Experience

The importance of promoting the software development industry has long been recognized in India by the Department of Electronics (DoE), and suitable supportive policies were in place as far back as in 1972 (Parthasarathi and Joseph, 2002). By 1982 the DoE had begun concentrating on software export promotion policies, and the Computer Policy of 1984 gave further thrust to the industry by underlining the need for institutional and policy support in key areas. The accelerated growth of the computer industry after 1984 created calls for the rationalization of the import policies and for additional export promotion. As a result of this, a new policy was announced in 1986 that identified software specifically as one of the key areas for export promotion and underlined the importance of an integrated approach to the development of software for both domestic and export markets. This policy had the following major objectives:

- To promote software exports to take a quantum leap and capture a sizeable share in international software markets;

- To promote the integrated development of the national software industry for both domestic and export markets;

- To simplify existing procedures allowing the software industry to grow faster;

- To establish a strong base for the national software industry in India;

- To promote the use of the computer as a decision-making tool, to increase work efficiency, and to promote appropriate applications in order to gain long-term benefits of computerization for the economy.

To achieve these objectives various commercial incentives were provided to software firms. These measures included tax holidays, income-tax exemption on software exports, and the subsidized and duty-free import of hardware and software used for export industries.

In 1991 the Indian government began to open the economy with a programme of market liberalization and economic reform. At that time the Indian government's assessment of the IT industry was that India had a comparative advantage in the software export market but not the hardware sector. Following this evaluation, the government consciously prioritized software exports and new policy measures were initiated to support this strategy, including the removal of entry barriers for foreign companies, the lifting of restrictions on foreign technology transfers, the participation of the private sector in policymaking, the provision of finance through equity and venture capital, reforms for faster and cheaper data communication facilities, and the rationalization of taxes and tariffs (Narayanmurthy, 2000).

In addition to these measures the Indian government also undertook a series of institutional reforms including the establishment of an integrated Ministry of Communications and Information Technology. One key development stemming from these reform was the establishment of Software Technology Parks (STP) to provide the necessary infrastructure for software exports. At the time of this writing, there are 18 STPs in India throughout the country and these play a significant role in exports. The total number of units registered with the STPs increased from 164 in 1991 to 5,582 in 1999, accounting for about 68 percent of all Indian IT Exports (Table 5). The facilities in these STPs include, amongst others, modern computers and communication networks that are beyond the reach of individual firms. In June 2000 a new STP consisting of a business support center and an India Infotech Center was set up in Silicon Valley to facilitate software exports by small and medium Indian firms to the US (Economic Times, 2000). The center also fosters business relationships by providing access to US financial institutions, venture capitalists and specialized trade bodies to promote partnership between the US and Indian ICT software and service companies.

The success of the aforementioned policies and of the STPs led to an appreciable growth of investment in ICT exports (Venkitesh, 1995). The growth of the sector outstripped that of the workforce, leading to eventual labour constraints (Schware, 1987; Sen, 1995). Traditionally the main source of ICT and software professionals was from Indian public-sector educational institutes such as the Indian Institutes of Technology (IITs), Industrial Training Institutes (ITIs) and engineering colleges, as well as additional public-sector institutions such as C-DAC and CMC, Ltd. engaged in training computer personnel. With the demand for skilled IT-sector labour increasing in the early 1980s, the Government permitted private investment in IT training. Today, there are private companies running training centers throughout the country through franchise networks offering many courses. These institutes primarily cater to the middle and lower-skill-level labour demand. In addition to this, seven Indian Institutes of Information Technologies (IIITs) were established to provide excellence in IT with the input of academics. Available estimates indicate that in 1999 there were over 1,832 educational institutions providing

Table 5: Trends in IT exports from units registered with software technology parks

Year	No. of units registered With STPs	Total exports from India (US$million)	Share of STP units in total exports
1991-92	164	164	na
1992-93	227	225	8
1993-94	269	330	12
1994-95	364	485	16
1995-96	521	734	29
1996-97	667	1085	46
1997-98	844	1750	54
1998-99	1196	2650	58
1999-2000	5582	3900	68

Source: Joseph, 2002.

training in IT to 67,785 professionals (Nasscom, 1999). The breakdown of the current labour pool indicates that holders of the three main awards relevant to the sector, B.Techs, diplomas and ITI certificates, account for some 70 percent of the total IT workforce in India.

Besides development of the infrastructure and labour pool for the IT sector, the Indian government has taken measures to address the problem of software piracy by including the protection of the computer software copyright within the established Indian Copyright Act of 1957, reinforcing active role of the state in promoting the industry. Other factors which have added to India's comparative advantage in this sector have been the availability of a highly skilled English speaking workforce and also the time difference between India and major export markets such as the USA.

It is clear that over the last decade the Indian IT sector has benefited enormously from a national system of innovation comprised of many actors working effectively together in order to develop international competitive advantage and credibility. This successful strategy has been the result of a focused state development strategy toward the promotion of the ICT software and service sector for foreign exchange earnings. This export-oriented strategy has so far overlooked the importance of ICT diffusion to the economy in general, such as improved efficiency, productivity, and competitiveness to domestic industries and services.

Concluding Remarks

Today there is an increasing realization that the benefits offered by IT for improvements to human welfare, economic productivity, and growth are mainly limited to the developed economies. Even though this International Digital Divide is a feature of the current global environment, there is potential to reducing the gap between the leading and developing countries with appropriate government policies. The development of such policies requires an integrated approach with the involvement of actors in counties across the public and private sectors. Sustained development requires both revenues from ICT-growth strategies and from improvements to the economy obtained through ICT diffusion. With reference to the Indian experience, we can observe that an export-oriented IT-growth strategy has deflected attention away from ICT diffusion at a time when a recent study by the IMF (2001) has reported that IT-using countries tend to benefit more than IT-producing countries. The disappointing welfare gains for IT producers have been attributed to the deterioration in the terms of trade between the producers and users. Despite the growth of the software industry, India is also among the losers. These finding underline the importance of the complementary roles of the domestic market in promoting innovation and exports and export-orientated, IT-induced productivity and growth. The policy implication for developing countries, and for India in particular, would suggest that ICT diffusion should be prioritized for economic development and growth.

The growth of the service sector has been one of the key drivers of economic development in both the developed and developing world in the last decades, underlining the fact that international competitive advantage will in the future be determined more by trade in intangibles rather than goods. Developing countries such as India can obtain the benefits resulting from the internationalization of services with the adoption of liberal trade and investment policies designed to support IT growth. However, in order to maximize the wider economic and social benefits, complimentary policies supporting national ICT diffusion cannot be overlooked, and should be the focus of future policy development.

Acknowledgments

I would like to express our gratitude to Professor K. J. Joseph (Jawaharlal Nehru University, India), Dr. Richard Heeks (University of Manchester, UK), and the information officer of Bridges.org for allowing the use of the duly acknowledged sources in the development of this chapter.

References

Arora, A., Arunachalam, V.S., Asundi, J. and Ronald, F. (2000). The Indian Software Services Industry. *Research Policy, 30*, 1267-1287.

Bedi, K., Singh, P.J. and Srivastava, S. (2001). *Government @ Net: New Governance Opportunities for India*. New Delhi: Sage Publications.

Braga, C.A.P. (1996). The Impact of the Internationalization of Services on Developing Countries. Retrieved February 17, 2002 from the World Wide Web: http://www.worldbank.org/fandd/English/0396/articles/070396.htm.

Bridges.org. (2001). Spanning the Digital Divide: Understanding and Tackling the Issues Retrieved February 17, 2002 from the World Wide Web: http://proto.bridges.org.za/spanning/pdf/SpanningTheDigitalDivide.pdf.

Compaine, B.M. (Ed.). (2001). *The Digital Divide: Facing a Crisis or Creating a Myth?* London: MIT Press.

D'Costa, A. (2001). *Export Growth and Path Dependence: The Locking in of Innovations in the Software Industry*. New Delhi: University of Pennsylvania Institute for the Advanced Study of India, Mimeo.

Economic Times. (2000). STPI Now Opens Office at Silicon Valley, USA. Special Supplement on Software Technology Parks of India, June 11, New Delhi, India.

The Economist. (2000). *Falling Through the Net?* Print Edition, September 21.

Government of India. (1972). Annual Report. New Delhi: Department of Electronics.

Government of India. (1982). Annual Report. New Delhi: Department of Electronics.

Government of India. (1985). New Computer Policy. *The Gazette of India*, August 31, 679-681.

Government of India. (1986). Policy on Computer Software Exports, Software Development and Training. New Delhi: Department of Electronics.

Government of India. (1996). Guide to Electronics Industry in India. New Delhi: Department of Electronics.

Heeks, R. (1996). India's Software Industry: State Policy, Liberalization and Industrial Development. New Delhi: Sage Publications.

Heeks, R. (1999). Indian Software Labour: Cost Breakdown and Comparison. Retrieved March 15, 2002 from the World Wide Web: http://idpm.man.ac.uk/rsc/is/isi/isicost.shtml.

IMF. (2001). World Economic Outlook: The Information Technology Revolution. Washington, D.C.: IMF.

Joseph, K.J. (1997). Industry Under Economic Liberalization: The Case of Indian Electronics. New Delhi: Sage Publications.

Joseph, K.J. (2001). IT Boom, the Economy and Labour. *Labour and Development, 7*(2), 1-36.

Joseph, K.J. (2002). Growth of ICT and ICT for Development: Realities and Myths of the Indian Experience. World Institute for Development Economics Research. Discussion paper No. 2002/78. Retrieved February 15, 2002 from the World Wide Web: http://www.wider.unu.edu/publications/dps/dps2002/dp2002-78.pdf.

Joseph, K.J. and Harilal, K.N. (2001). Structure and Growth of India's IT Exports: Implications of an Export-Oriented Growth Strategy. *Economic and Political Weekly, 36*(34), 3263-3270.

Kanungo, S. (1999). Making Information Technology Work. New Delhi: Sage Publications.

Kiely, R. and Marfleet, P. (Eds.). (1998). *Globalization and the Third World*. London: Routledge.

Kraemer, K.L. and Dedrick, J. (2001). Information Technology and Economic Development: Results and Policy Implications of Cross-Country Studies. In M. Pohjola (Ed.), *Information Technology, Productivity and Economic Growth*. Oxford: OUP.

Kumar, N. (2001). Indian Software Industry Development: International and National Perspective. *Economic and Political Weekly, 36*, 4278-4290.

Mansell, R. (1999). Global Access to Information Communication Technologies. Johannesburg and Canada: International Development Center.

Michie, J. and Smith, J.G. (Eds.). (1998). *Globalization, Growth and Governance: Creating an Innovative Economy*. Oxford: Oxford University Press.

Monen, P. (2001). International R&D Spillovers and Economic Growth. In Pahjola, M. (Ed.), *Information Technology, Productivity and Economic Growth*. Oxford: OUP.

Narayanamurthy, N.R. (2000). Making India a Significant IT Player in This Millennium. In Thapar, R. (Ed.). *India: Another Millennium*. New Delhi: Viking and Penguin Books.

Nasscom. (1999). *Directory of Indian Software and Service Companies.* New Delhi: Nasscom.

Nasscom. (1999). *The Software Industry in India: A Strategic Review.* New Delhi: Nasscom.

Nkrumah, G. (2000). Digital Divide. Al-Ahram Weekly, 27 July to 2 August. Retrieved August 25, 2000 from the World Wide Web: http://weekly.ahram.org.eg/2000/492/in3.htm.

Norris, P. (2001). *Digital Divide: Civic Engagement, Information Poverty and Internet Worldwide.* Cambridge: Cambridge University Press.

Oberoi, S.S. (1991). Software Technology Park: Concepts, Procedures and Status. *Electronics Information and Planning, 19*(3), 42-46.

OECD. (2000). *Information Technology Outlook.* Paris:OECD.

Parthasarathi, A. and Joseph, K.J. (2002). Limits to Innovation Set by Strong Export Orientation: The Experience of India's Information Communication Technology Sector. *Science, Technology and Society, 7*(1), 13-49.

Planning Commission. (2001). India Knowledge Super Power: Strategy for Transformation. New Delhi: Planning Commission.

Pohjola, M. (2001). Information Technology and Economic Growth: A Cross-Country Analysis. In M. Pohjola (Ed.), *Information Technology, Productivity and Economic Growth.* Oxford: OUP.

Rodrik, D. (1995). Trade and Industrial Policy Reform. In J. Behrman and T.N. Srinivasan (Eds.), *Handbook of Development Economics, Vol. III B.* New York: Elsevier.

Rubin et.al. (1996). *Worldwide Benchmark Project.* Pound Ridge, NY: Rubin Systems.

Schware, R. (1987). Software Industry in the Third World: Policy Guide Lines, Institutional Options and Constraints. *World Development, 15*(10/11), 1249-1267.

Schware, R. (1992). Software Entry Strategies for Developing Countries. *World Development, 20*(2), 143-164.

Sen, P. (1995). Indian Software Exports: An Assessment. *Economic and Political Weekly, 30*(7-8), 2053-2058.

UNDP. (1999). Human Development Report 1999. New York: Oxford University Press.

Venkitesh, P. (1995). India's Software Exports: A Study with Special Reference to Technology Parks. Trivandrum: Center for Development Studies, JNU. Unpublished M.Phil dissertation.

Wong, P.K. (2001). The Contribution of Information Technology to the Rapid Economic Growth of Singapore. In M, Pohjola (Ed.), *Information Technology, Productivity and Economic Growth.* Oxford: OUP.

Chapter XIII

Digital Technologies and the Cross-Border Expansion of South African Banks

Joanne Roberts
University of Durham, UK

Chipo Mukonoweshuro
University of Durham, UK

Abstract

This chapter explores the role of Information and Communication Technologies (ICTs) in the international development of South African banks. It is argued that South African banks derive important advantages from the use of ICTs in their expansion into neighbouring countries. Using Dunning's (1989, 1988) eclectic approach as a mechanism with which to assess the evidence supporting this argument, ICT is explored both as an ownership specific capacity, as a locational specific factor influencing the geographical pattern of international expansion, and as a facilitator of the internalization of cross-border banking networks. Through an investigation of the significance of digital technologies in the cross-border expansion of South African banks, including case studies of Stanbic and ABSA, this chapter highlights the opportunities and challenges confronting such organizations. In so doing, the chapter will contribute to the understanding of intra-African foreign direct investment in the banking sector and the emerging digital economy in developing countries.

Introduction

The financial sector is central to the economy. Economic activity must be financed, thus, as economies grow so to do their financial sectors. Indeed, developments in the economic, political and technological environment over the last 30 years have intensified the impact of financial-sector activity on the economy as a whole. For example, in the current era, financial market integration is a major aspect of the ongoing process of globalization (Held, McGrew, Goldblatt & Perraton, 1999). The increasing intensity of competition since the 1970s, together with deregulation of the financial markets and the internationalisation of financial services, has driven the application of digital technologies in the sector. In particular, innovations in the field of Information and Communication Technologies (ICTs) have fundamentally influenced the sector, especially in terms of the speed with which financial services may be produced and delivered (Strange, 1998). However, the impact of digital technologies combined with the deregulation of financial markets has led to a growing concentration of financial service activity in global cities, such as New York, London, and Tokyo (Sassen, 2001; Castells, 2000). Consequently, the enormous flows of capital circulating around the globe, including, for example, the daily foreign exchange market turnover, which amounted to US $1,500 billion in 1998 (BIS, 2002), largely by-pass the developing countries of Africa, including South Africa. Nevertheless, digital technologies do influence the financial services sectors in these countries, both in terms of the availability and cost of capital, consumer access to services and the organisational development of service providers. While digital technologies are having a significant impact on the global financial markets, this chapter focuses on the impact and role of ICTs in the expansion of financial services organisations in the developing countries of Africa and, in particular, on the international development of South African banking organisations.

To exploit the opportunities arising from the adoption of liberal economic policies and privatization of state-owned companies by many African countries, South African banking organizations have sought to extend their international networks throughout the continent. The aim of this chapter is to explore the role of digital technologies in facilitating this cross-border expansion of South African banking organizations. The rise of ICTs since the 1970s and, in particular, the growth of the Internet since the mid-1990s, has influenced the organization of economic activity (Castells, 2000). The banking sector has experienced significant organizational change resulting from the adoption of ICTs (Bryan, 1993; Jones, 1993). However, specific challenges do exist for financial-sector organizations operating in Africa. For example, compared to most other parts of the world, Africa has a poorly developed ICT infrastructure (Mansell & Wehn, 1998). Even so, it is argued here that South African banking organisations derive important advantages from the use of ICTs in their expansion into neighbouring countries.

Through an investigation of the significance of digital technologies in the cross-border expansion of South African banking organizations this chapter highlights the opportunities and challenges that confront such organizations. In so doing, the chapter will make a contribution to the understanding of intra-African foreign direct investment in the banking sector. Furthermore, by examining the use of ICTs by developing countries' multinational organizations this chapter will contribute to an understanding of the emerging digital economy in developing countries. The chapter will be of interest to policy-makers, academic researchers and business managers in developing countries seeking to appreciate the role of ICTs in the promotion of economic activity.

The use of digital technologies in the cross-border expansion of South African banking organizations is examined through a review of relevant literature and evidence. A number of case studies, elaborating on the cross-border expansion of South African banks, will be used to investigate the role of ICT in the internationalization of African banking organizations. Dunning's (1989, 1988) eclectic approach, which is one of the most widely used frameworks to analyse the international development of the firm, is applied as a mechanism with which to assess the evidence supporting the argument that the use of ICTs give South African banks an advantage over their regional competitors in the cross-border delivery of banking services. Within this analysis ICT is explored both as an ownership specific internal capacity, as a locational specific factor influencing the geographical pattern of international expansion, and as a facilitator of the internalization of cross-border banking networks. The chapter begins with a review of banking in Africa with particular attention focused on South Africa. This is followed by an analysis of the internationalization of South African banking organization. The use of digital technologies in the delivery of services and the organization of banking networks is then explored before their role in the South African banking organization networks is investigated. Finally, conclusions are drawn regarding the role of digital technologies in the international development of South African banks as well as the challenges facing these banks in their efforts to maintain a leadership position in the supply of banking services in Africa.

Banking in Africa

The colonization of Africa allowed countries like the United Kingdom, France, Germany, and Belgium to build up significant financial networks across the continent between 1880 and 1914 (Darroch, 1992; Jones, 1990). These financial networks were generally linked to domestic banking institutions in their home economies and focused on trade and the relatively undeveloped capital markets. The earliest indigenous African banks were established in the 1920s. Although initially plagued by failure, indigenous banks became more prolific in the 1940s and 1950s (Jones, 1993). From 1950, the indigenous banking sector experienced greater stability and continued to rise in prominence, particularly during the 1960s. The Second World War marked the end of the era of European dominance in Africa. Moves toward independence resulted in the growth of nationalist feelings, which brought about sweeping regulatory changes, the accelerated rise of indigenous banks and pressures for localization of ownership. Despite this, British banks retained their prominent positions in the domestic banking systems particularly in the Southern hemisphere. For example, in Southern and Central Africa British banks held more than 50% of the market share in 1971 while in South Africa, 73% of local deposits were still held by two British banks – Standard and Barclays (Jones, 1993).

Notwithstanding the radical changes seen in banking structures throughout the continent, colonial banks retain their influence today and a significant number of subsidiaries of large institutions such as Standard Chartered bank and Barclays still dominate. Nevertheless, indigenous African banks continue to increase in sophistication and expand their roles, even though in terms of Tier 1[1] capital and assets they remain small. According to The Banker, in 2001 the top 100 Sub-Saharan banks (excluding South Africa) had combined total assets of US$29.6 billion and total pre-tax profits of US$888 million, which amounts to a middle-size bank on the world stage ("Minnows still," 2001).

Despite the negative image of the African continent today, growth is starting to occur. While only a small number of African countries continue to be involved in civil conflicts, many others have undergone significant economic reform ("Minnows still," 2001). A number of countries are casting off their reputations for economic mismanagement, liberalizing their markets and promoting the private sector (Cockerill, 2000). Significant efforts are being made to improve national financial infrastructures because a sound and well-structured banking sector plays a key part in maintaining growth and stability. African countries adopting "structural adjustment" policies at the instigation of the International Monetary Fund (IMF) and World Bank have generated a great need for more rigorous financial standards ("Minnows still," 2001; Moore, 2000). In addition, the privatization of businesses and liberalization of markets arising from the adoption of such policies has resulted in the takeover of many local banks by foreign investors. Overall, the continent has seen vast improvements in services and accountability to a previously un-competitive, state subsidized, and heavily bureaucratic financial sector (Manson, 2002a).

A key factor in the development of the banking sector is profitability. International banks and investors claim that their African operations are extremely profitable. WPA Consulting (2002) confirms that the average return on equity in Sub-Saharan Africa is 15% compared the rest of the world at 7%. Not surprisingly then, more investors are crossing national borders to establish a presence in African countries. Today, domestic South African banks have emerged as the leading investors on the continent followed by a number of European groups. It is, then, to the international development of South African banks that our attention now turns.

The Rise of International South African Banking Organizations

In this section, Dunning's (1988, 1989) eclectic approach is used as a lens through which to view the international development of South African banks. The eclectic approach, which draws together three groups of advantages arising from Ownership, Location and Internalization (OLI approach), provides a useful framework with which to explore the existence and development of multinational firms. Ownership specific advantages include the firm's unique assets such as brands, technology, knowledge base, reputation, economies of scale and domestic market conditions that give the firm an advantage over foreign firms. Locational advantages relate to the characteristics of overseas locations including those that are specific to the market, the availability of resources and the general economic and political environment. Finally, internalization advantages arise from securing ownership advantages within the boundaries of the firm, for example, rather than licensing unique knowledge through contractual mechanisms the firm gains greater advantage by internalizing such assets within the firm. Originally developed to analyse the activities of manufacturing firms, Dunning (1989) later applied the approach to service firms. Although Dunning's eclectic approach has weaknesses,[2] it docs provide a useful framework with which to analyse the international development of service organizations, including banks.[3]

Despite enormous investment into South Africa in the period from the late 1800s to the 1960s, most foreign banks withdrew their investments in the South African economy during the apartheid era, resulting in the development of a strong domestic banking sector. Today the South African banking system is well developed, with a prudent regulatory and legal infrastructure and good accounting standards and disclosure practices. Due to South Africa's colonial history, many of the institutions have First World structures that would not normally be prevalent in an emerging market. The legal system is mature, contractual rights are enforceable and creditor rights are well recognized.

The South African banking sector is dominated by a few large groups, which are also the largest banks in Africa. They overshadow most segments of the banking market, except for resale and repurchase agreements, where some foreign banks or their branches have a significant share of the market. In 2000 South Africa dominated The Banker's list of the top 100 African banks with 76.5% of the total Tier 1 Capital of US$11.3 million and with seven South African banks among the top ten banks ("Minnows still," 2001), (Table 1).

Table 1. Largest banks in Africa

Rank	Bank	Tier 1 Capital US$ million
1.	Stanbic (SA)	2,333
2.	Nedcor (SA)	2,111
3.	ABSA Group (SA)	1,273
4.	First Rand Banking Group (SA)	1,222
5.	Investec Group (SA)	876
6.	BoE bank (SA)	582
7.	Mauritius Commercial Bank	234
8.	State Bank of Mauritius	171
9.	First Bank of Nigeria	150
10.	Saambou Bank (SA)	149

Source: Compiled from "Minnows Still" (2001, p.17)

Although South African financial institutions could not operate directly in neighbouring states during the apartheid years, today they have become the most important investors in Sub-Saharan Africa's financial sector (Odenthal, 2001). One motivation for the internationalization of South African banks is the rise of competition in the home market. Since 1994, at least 50 foreign banks have entered the country (KPMG, 2000). The demise of the siege economy fostered during isolation, rising competition in local markets, and the dismantling of protective tariffs at home have forced the biggest local companies to look abroad. Hence, South African banks are attracted by the locational advantages offered by other Sub-Saharan African countries. In particular, they can benefit from using their ownership advantages in terms of experience, size and strength as the banking markets develop in these other African countries.

There are several other motivations underlying internationalization. Firstly, most of the banks are fully diversified within the local economy. During the second half of the 1990s, average return on assets was not as high as that in other emerging markets, reflecting the maturity of the South African banking system. Interest margins are much smaller than those of some Eastern European countries and have been following a downward trend for a number of years. Operating costs remain high because of extensive branch networks and electronic banking infrastructures. Therefore, geographical expansion in terms of internationalization is necessary to sustain growth and profitability. Secondly, many banks have large reserves, which they were unable to invest when the economy was closed. These reserves provide an ownership advantage that the banks can exploit in other markets. Thirdly, Theobald (2002) declares that the huge profits to be made on the continent are a major attraction to financial investors. Hence, there are locational advantages that attract South African banks to invest in other African nations. Fourthly, evidence suggests that the banks are merely following their clients ("Standard Bearer," 1996). South African firms in sectors such as brewing, mining, hospitality and retailing are becoming international in scope, either in search of hitherto inaccessible resources or markets in Africa. Relationships with existing clients in the home market can be seen as an ownership advantage that the bank is able to take into another market when the client firm moves overseas. Certain countries will then have locational advantages because of the presence of existing clients. Fifthly, the banks may be seeking efficiency and economies of scale and scope. Here efficiency gains may arise from cheaper resources in other countries or through the more intensive use of existing resources such as ICT networks. Finally, African governments are more inclined to work with other Africans ("Standard Bearer," 1996), particularly with the more sophisticated South African banks. African identity is then another ownership advantage for South African banks. It is also a locational advantage in terms of the attractiveness of African markets for South African banks.

The key sources of ownership advantage for knowledge intensive service firms such as banks are intangible assets. These assets take time to develop, they are difficult to measure and value and importantly they are fragile and difficult to protect. They include reputation, brand name, technical/specialized expertise, knowledge of clients and relationships with them, global scope of the service firm's affiliate network, methodologies for producing services, knowledge of the market for the services and management skills (Aharoni, 2000; Grosse, 2000; Roberts, 1998). For banks, ownership advantages also arise from the use of ICT networks as well as the level of their reserves. Economies of scale arising from the size of the bank provide a source of ownership advantage as also does access to international capital and financial markets. Furthermore, financial institutions may acquire advantages from innovative activity. This type of advantage has become increasingly important with the application of technology to the delivery of financial services since the 1970s and the deregulation of the sector in many countries since the 1980s. Such innovative activity has given rise to many new financial products, including derivatives - the most important product innovation since the mid-1980s.[4]

Ownership advantages also arise from the home environment of multinational firms. For South African banks, this environment includes a well-developed banking system, including effective regulatory and legal structures, a superior telecommunication infrastructure and a technologically progressive environment. This environment gives South African banks advantages that are not available to the banks of other African nations. The strength, size and maturity of the South African banking sector would appear to be an ownership advantage for them arising from the historical development of the sector in their domestic market. South African banks are able to develop superior financial services in their home market, which they can then deliver to other African markets. Such services include the development and use of advanced technologies that improve service quality and efficiency of provision. Additionally, South African banks have knowledge and experience of operating in Africa giving them an important advantage compared to non-African banks. In a sense, South African banks have the opportunity to become first-movers in the delivery of banking services in other African markets.

The forces driving the internationalization of South African banks outlined above suggest that the nature of internationalization is largely market-oriented. Furthermore, psychic distance (Johanson & Wiedersheim-Paul, 1975) is a factor influencing the locational choice of South African banks. By investing in other African countries, South African banks are entering markets that are psychically close in the sense that their social, cultural, political and economic development has similarities with that of the banks' home market. Although the poor technological infrastructures available in African countries present many challenges, it also provides a locational advantage for South African banks giving them the opportunity to exploit their technological expertise.

Multinational banks generally demonstrate a preference for overseas expansion through wholly or majority-owned subsidiaries (Jones, 1993). This form of expansion allows banks to control their ownership advantages by internalizing them within the boundaries of the firm. South African banks have adopted two strategies to drive international expansion (Theobald, 2002). The first is to buy controlling stakes in African banks. The second is to take a minority stake, which increases profitability and directs business back to the head office. African banks choose whenever possible to internalize their ownership specific advantages in order to maintain control, which is particularly important in unstable environments. The establishment of wholly or majority-owned subsidiaries facilitates control over intangible assets that cannot be fully protected through formal contracts and intellectual property rights. This is especially important in locations where regulatory and legal systems are poorly developed, as in many African countries. Furthermore, the knowledge-intensive nature of the ownership advantages of banking firms discourages the exchange of such assets in the market. The transfer of knowledge through market exchange presents a number of difficulties including those explored by researchers studying the economics of information (Arrow, 1969, 1974; Stigler, 1961).[5]

Increasingly, control over intangible assets can be facilitated through the intensive monitoring of independent partners enabled by the use of joint information systems. In many sectors, such developments are leading to the evolution of networked enterprises (Castells, 2000). Clearly, internationally active banks are benefiting from the monitoring capacities of their international information systems. Nevertheless, control through ownership remains important in this sector.

Digital Technologies and the Delivery of Banking Services in Africa

The application of digital technologies to the production and delivery of financial services has fundamentally influenced the banking sector. As Dicken (2003, p.442) notes, *"information is both the process and the product of financial services"* (original emphasis). The primary essence of all financial transactions is the collection, analysis and dissemination of information. For this reason, the banking sector has experienced significant organizational change resulting from the adoption of ICTs (Bryan, 1993; Jones, 1993). Given the information intensiveness of banking services the effective use of information systems by multinational banking organizations can be an important source of competitive advantage (Kuljis, Macredie & Paul, 1998).

National and international interbanking transactions largely involve the flow of information. Consequently, advances in ICT have transformed the speed and efficiency with which such transactions are effected. For example, prior to 1977 the international settlement of accounts between banks was largely carried out by mail or telex with each bank having its own procedures. To increase the speed of these transactions groups of banks joined together to create standardized telecommunications networks such as SWIFT (Society for Worldwide Interbank Financial Telecommunications) (Wright & Pauli, 1987). SWIFT was one of a number of proprietary data networks developed in the 1970s by financial service firms. The rise of the Internet in the 1990s presented new opportunities for data networks and electronic payment systems. As an open network infrastructure, the Internet disconnects the network from the proprietary infrastructure. Moreover, with encryption technology highly secure environments can be created on public networks. Hence, banks can take advantage of the Internet to supplement their internal proprietary data networks and existing interbank networks to develop global reach in the provision of a range of new electronic financial services.

Internet banking, for example, includes a range of retail and wholesale banking services. Involving both individual and corporate clients, it includes bank transfers, payments and settlements, documentary collections and credits, corporate and household lending, card business and other activities (UNCTAD, 2002). According to UNCTAD (2002), Sub-Saharan Africa, apart from South Africa, is the region that is most seriously lagging behind in Internet banking. This is not surprising given that the continent of Africa, compared to most other parts of the world, has a poorly developed ICT infrastructure (United Nations Development Programme [UNDP], 2003; Mansell & Wehn, 1998). A major problem for the adoption of Internet banking and e-commerce in developing

Table 2. Access to communication technologies: A comparison between South African and various developed and developing regions

	Telephone mainlines (per 1,000 people)		Cellular subscribers (per 1,000 people)		Internet users (per 1,000 people)	
	1990	2001	1990	2001	1990	2001
South Africa	93	111	..	242	0.1*	64.9
Developing countries	21	87	..	75	..	26.5
Least developed countries	3	6	0	6	..	1.8
Arab States	35	76	..	58	..	15.6
East Asia and the Pacific	17	122	..	113	..	41.4
Latin America and the Caribbean	62	162	..	160	..	49.0
South Asia	7	38	..	7	..	6.3
Sub-Saharan Africa	11	15	..	28	..	7.8
Central and Eastern Europe and the CIS	124	224	..	120	..	42.8
OECD	392	523	10	539	2.8	332.0
High-income OECD	465	597	13	605	3.2	400.1
World	98	169	2	153	..	79.6

* data refer to 1991
.. not available

Source: Constructed from data presented in UNDP, (2003), Human Development Report 2003, United Nations: Geneva and New York.

countries is the lack of universal access. Table 2 compares the access to communications across groups of developed and developing countries. This disparity of access is referred to as the global digital divide (Castells, 2001), a divide that is often replicated within countries both developed and developing. There are, as Polikanov and Abramova (2003) note in their review of Africa and ICT, a number of initiatives to widen access to telecommunications and the Internet including RASCOM and *Africa One*. In the field of telecommunications, the RASCOM project aims to provide Africa with a regional system of satellite communications. Although initiated in 1992 this project has yet to make significant progress. *Africa One* aims to build an undersea fibre-optic cable circling the continent, which will connect African states to each other and to the global Internet backbone. In 2002, the first stage of *Africa One* linking West Africa to Asia via South Africa was inaugurated (Polikanov & Abramova, 2003). Despite such initiatives, Africa seriously lags behind other regions of the world, apart from the Middle East, in the numbers of Internet users. According to NUA online surveys (Nua Internet Surveys, 2003), in September 2002 there were some 605.60 million Internet users worldwide, distributed as follows: North America 30.16 %; Europe 31.52 %; Asia/Pacific 30.92 %; Latin America 5.51%; Middle East 0.85%; and, Africa 1.04 %, with most users being in South Africa.

Nevertheless, a study of the impact of information technology on the banking and insurance sector in Nigeria, (Ugwu, Oyebisi, Ilori & Adagunodo, 2000) identifies the following electronic application services employed in the banking industry: electronic fund transfer, electronic fund transfer at the point of sale, pass card, smart card and home banking. Just over 10% of Nigerian banks offer their customers electronic banking services (Manson, 2002b). Automatic Teller Machines (ATMs) and credit card payments are widely established in some African countries, particularly South Africa, Kenya and Zimbabwe. However, other African countries such as Tanzania and Uganda have limited use of these instruments. By utilizing new electronic banking systems, banks are tapping in to the continent's great potential for growth bypassing the underdeveloped infra-structure. For instance, Ghana was introduced to electronic banking in 2000 and, in June 2001, the co-operative bank of Kenya became one of four banks to launch a centralized banking system. Furthermore, as UNCTAD (2002) notes, where the telecommunications infrastructure is inadequate, technologies that allow the storage and transaction of value in proximity and offline are being adopted. For example, smart cards based on Visa Horizon proximity technologies are being introduced in Ghana and a number of other African countries.

At the local level, these developments are also greatly increasing the capacity of both banks and non-banks to access local and national markets without the high cost investments in traditional delivery systems. Consequently, the leap from low tech to latest tech is more marked in Africa than in almost any other part of the world (Melly & Marks, 2000).

Significant challenges, however, do exist for financial-sector organizations operating in Africa. For instance, merging banking operations into a single cross-border information system is a major feat in places without electricity supplies or telephone lines. A key challenge in Africa is to bringing the benefits of the formal first-world economy to the largely low-income population that depends heavily on local micro-credit and savings schemes which play an important role in the development process (Moore, 2000). Electronic banking has the potential to bridge the divide between the formal tax-paying economy and the dynamic informal economy of the rural areas and to replace expensive bricks and mortar with more cost-effective systems in a continent where 70% of the population is still unbanked (Paulson, 2000).

South Africa has a major advantage over other African countries in the area of Internet access. It has a developed telecommunications infrastructure, which was restructured in 1996, and although the commercialized Public Telecommunications Operator, Telkom, initially retained a monopoly in the provision of basic fixed telephony services, in an agreement with the World Trade Organization under the Agreement on Basic Telecommunications South Africa is bound to liberalize and privatize its telecommunications sector (Cogburn, 2003). The level of competition in the telecommunications sector is a key factor determining the price of access to the Internet. Effective competition brings price down and since most Internet access is through fixed telecommunication lines, allows for the successful development of Internet-based activity. This has been clearly demonstrated in relation to the uneven development of Internet activity in Europe (Waesche, 2003).

The South African government has sought to promote a digital economy and provide universal access to the Internet and basic telephony in order to redress the socio-economic ills created by apartheid. To widen access to the Internet in South Africa the Department of Communication has promoted a range of public access initiatives including the development of Multi-Purpose Community Information Centres, the Universal Service Agency and Public Information Terminals (Cogburn, 2003). Table 2 also includes data for South Africa from which it is evident that the country is advanced in its access to the Internet and telecommunications (including cellular access) compared to developing countries as a whole.

South Africa has a well-developed financial system, in which the South African Reserve Bank (SARB) has taken the lead on issues concerning e-payments. In 1998, for example, it developed the South African Multiple Option Settlement (SAMOS) system that allows real-time settlement between banks (Cogburn, 2003). Indeed, South Africa's top four banks are the largest consumers of telecommunication services (Cogburn & Nyaki Adeya, 2002). All major financial institutions have electronic networks that span the country, and the networks of the largest banks reach out into other nations. These institutions already engage in a significant level of e-commerce from web-based electronic banking, online bill presentation and payment, asset financing, mortgage applications and online share dealings to unit trusts, insurance product sales and insurance claims processing. The number of such transactions grew substantially between 1999 and 2000, and they are expected to continue to develop rapidly (Cogburn & Nyaki Adeya, 2002).

One innovative new application in Internet banking is Paycom express, a prepaid Internet account developed by a South African consortium. It combines a pre-paid credit with a user-identification and can be used to make electronic purchases over the Internet. More importantly, it is being used to dial into the Internet at a national network of Caltex petrol stations in order to buy fuel. This is extremely beneficial in remote areas where petrol stations often provide the only telecommunications link for miles.

Financial institutions in the developed world are already adopting wireless communication for the delivery of services (Yen & Chou, 2001). Given the poor development of the land-based telecommunications infrastructure in Africa, wireless communication would appear to offer great potential for the future development of the Internet and Internet-based services on the Continent. South African banks are already involved in wireless pilots of varying complexity ranging from basic banking services and SMS (Short Messaging Service) alerts, to full-blown payment, bill-payment, pre-paid cellular recharging and other services (Manson, 2002b). The future of mobile delivery has significant potential in African markets. Large sectors of the population still do not have access to the wired world and wireless technology has the ability to provide a range of innovative financial inquiry and payment services at relatively low cost to potential users. However, a major challenge for banks adopting wireless technologies relates to the proliferation of mobile telecommunication operators across Africa. These operators are using a variety of largely incompatible standards thereby increasing the costs for businesses wishing to supply services to users of mobile communications.

With a few exceptions, non-African investors in the banking sector tend to cater to large businesses and up-market personal customers who can make good use of technology and the foreign banks' capacity to provide investment advice, structure trade financings or deal in foreign exchange. Internet and other online services are well suited to this clientele. However, the lower end of the personal banking market together with the small, medium and micro enterprise market are not as attractive to non-African banks, consequently, they offer many opportunities for South African banks to exploit throughout the continent of Africa.

Digital Technologies in South African Banking Organization Networks

In this section, the role of digital technologies in South African banking organization networks is examined through case studies of Standard Bank of South Africa Limited (Stanbic) and the Amalgamated Banks of South Africa (ABSA). Both Stanbic and ABSA are among the top banks in South Africa and Africa (Table 1), as such they are leading investors in, and users of, ICT. An examination of the use of ICT by these two banking organizations will provide insights of relevance to the wider African banking community. However, before progressing further it is useful to review briefly the historical development of these two banks.

The Standard Bank of South Africa Limited (Stanbic) was formed in 1962 and registered as a South African company operating as a subsidiary of Standard Bank in London (subsequently to become Standard Chartered Bank plc.). However, in 1987 Standard Chartered sold its 39% stake in Stanbic, transferring complete ownership to the holding company in South Africa ("Global Sweep," 2002). In 1988, the group became international by opening a branch in Swaziland. In 1992, it established a bank in Botswana and acquired the long established Grindlays network in Botswana, Kenya, Uganda, Zaire, Zambia and

Zimbabwe, with minority holdings in Ghana and Nigeria. In 2002, the group acquired an interest in a bank in Malawi and established a representative office of an offshore banking unit in Mauritius. Although involved in retail banking, Stanbic's main emphasis has been on corporate banking. It taps into the competency of its London operation to provide project finance as well as commodity finance for trade. Today the group has the largest single network of banking services in Africa (Table 1) and made US$5.6 million before tax in Africa in 2001 (Theobald, 2002).

ABSA was formed more recently in 1991 by the merger of Allied Bank (Allied Building Society established in 1888), Volkskas Group (Volkskas Co-operative Limited established in 1934) and United Bank (United Building Society established in 1889). TrustBank (Federale Trust Limited established in 1954) joined the ABSA Group when Bankorp merged with ABSA in 1992. ABSA Group is the controlling company of the third largest banking and financial services group in Africa (Table 1). ABSA prefers to use its Johannesburg base to do deals in trade and structure finance as well as project finance. Consequently, it has limited African exposure to corporate banking. ABSA's African expansion is predominantly in the retail sector. The group purchased two major retail banks in privatization deals - Banco Austral in Mozambique and the Tanzanian National Bank of Commerce. It focuses on under-performing banks, which it then develops giving the group quick returns on capital. The bank plans to acquire at least one bank a year in selected African countries to improve efficiencies and to use them as channels for tried-and-tested retail products (Theobald, 2002).

South African banks are increasingly looking to technology to support their growth (Belford, 2003). Digital technologies have played a key role in facilitating the international organizational structures of international banks. For instance, organizational wide information systems facilitate the control over ownership advantages through the intensive monitoring of activities within the boundaries of the firm. Indeed, ABSA insists that control is mandatory and non-negotiable and abandoned a deal with the Diamond Bank of Nigeria, when the owner refused to surrender control. ABSA has connected the back offices of its two foreign banks via satellite to Johannesburg where full monitoring takes place. All 35 of its Tanzanian subsidiaries have direct online links to the head office in South Africa. Satellite dishes ensure that customers nationwide have real-time instant service (Melly & Marks, 2000).

More importantly, in Africa, digital technology is allowing banks to bypass the traditional bricks and mortar communications infrastructure with more cost-effective electronic systems. This is critical on a mostly undeveloped continent, which at the size of 12 million square miles, is almost as large as North America and Europe combined. For instance, Stanbic's network spans 17 other Sub-Saharan countries, extends to 20 countries on other continents and is connected by banking systems that link into the SWIFT international message system. Furthermore, satellite communications are being harnessed to reduce reliance on inadequate telecommunications systems throughout the Sub-Saharan region.

Clearly, access to global financial networks is an important ownership advantage for banks like Stanbic and ABSA. These banks are also generating further ownership advantage by investing heavily in pioneering new methods of electronic banking and the development of real-time communication networks (Ashurst, 1998). Johannesburg has emerged as a strategic locality for the development of a new standard for electronic cash transactions, giving South African banks further ownership advantages deriving from their home base.

One limiting factor in the issuing of credit cards is the costly and unreliable telecommunications infrastructure. To overcome this problem banks have distributed multifunction "chip" cards that track spending and support a pre-paid "electronic purse," thus severing the bond linking points of sale to mainframes. By 1997, both Stanbic and ABSA had issued conventional magnetic stripe debit cards developed by Mastercard, to be upgraded to "chip" cards for about 9 million clients[6], many of whom have never used chequebooks or ATMs. The new equipment includes GSM (Global Systems for Mobile) terminals, which rely on digital cellular telephony in areas where cable networks supporting landline telephony are unavailable. Indeed, ABSA was the first bank in South Africa to launch a mass-market mobile banking application in August 2000. The bank offers customers access to balance enquiries, mini-statements, transfers and third-party payments via cellular devices.

Stanbic aims to grow income and reduce costs through the use of mobile technologies (Manson, 2002a). The group offers its customers access to traditional banking products via cellular banking. It also offers subscribers to certain networks the ability to purchase pre-paid airtime via electronic channels, namely Interactive Voice Response (accessible directly from cell phones and landlines), and ATMs. In addition, Stanbic is using technology to help target low-income customers by developing low-cost distribution networks to service them. In 2001, Stanbic's AutoBank E in South Africa had 2.6m low-income customers, and almost all are people who "previously kept their money in biscuit tins or informal neighbourhood savings clubs" ("South African banking," 2000). Many were unable to meet minimum-balance requirements to open traditional bank accounts or to understand complex bank charges. AutoBank E allows almost anyone to open an account with a deposit of only 50 Rand ($8). Paperwork is kept to a minimum. Customers are given a cash-point card, and shown how to use it by employees who speak a variety of African languages. Simplicity is paramount, so all transactions occur through ATMs with a flat fee charged each time. Customers do not need a separate savings account because a "savings purse," into which money can be transferred, is attached to every account. Customers do not even have to be literate to use the service: many simply remember the sequence of buttons they need to press. Computerization makes it possible to lend money to people with no collateral and no formal address. The computer analyses a customer's savings history to decide whether he or she is creditworthy. Since there are no back-office staff and little paperwork, AutoBank E's costs are 30-40% lower than at traditional branches. Interest rates on deposits are low, but even those whose only income is a state pension can afford to bank with AutoBank E (Moore, 2000).

Most African banks have lost competitiveness because high costs and the lack of appropriately skilled labour have hindered their ability to maintain sophisticated systems. A major challenge for South African banks and other businesses highly dependent on ICT is the ability to recruit, train and retain a skilled workforce. Information technology skills are in demand across the globe, hence South African businesses must compete for these skills in the global market. Furthermore, the development of such skills in South Africa is inhibited by the vast inequality that exists within the country. A legacy of the

Table 3. The ownership, locational and internalization advantages of South African multinational banks investing in Africa

Ownership advantages	Locational Advantages	Internalization Advantages
• Existing client relations, access to transnational clients, foreigners abroad	• Person-to-person contact required therefore need to be close to clients	• Maintenance of quality through control
• Reputation, brand name and professional expertise	• Presence of existing clients	• Control over intangible assets, such as reputation and brand name
• Access to, and knowledge of, international capital and financial markets	• Government regulations	• Economies of scale and scope in the use of assets such as data networks
• Economies of scale and scope	• Growing markets for financial services	• Economies of coordinating capital flows
• Intrinsic value of reserve currencies	• Low levels of effective competition in African markets	• Importance of international arbitraging
• Substantial capital base	• Lower costs of foreign operations	• Protection against exchange/political risks
• Financial innovations	• Availability of skilled labour	• Need to pursue pan-African/global investment strategy
• Control over trans-border data/communication networks	• Low psychic distance, including African identity	
• Access to global financial networks	• African countries prefer investment from other African rather than non-African countries	
• Ability to invest in the latest information and communications technology	• Low technological competencies of indigenous banks	
• South African nationality/ African identity	• Availability of indigenous banks for acquisitions	
• Advantages arising from the home base including the regulatory and legal environment and the strong promotion of ICTs by government policies		

apartheid era is the continuing disparity in economic power between Blacks and Whites. The poorest 40% of the population earn less that 4% of the income, while the wealthiest 10% earn more than 51% (Marais, 2000; Cogburn and Nyaki Adeya, 2002). Such disparity limits the scope for growth and the development of a skilled workforce.

Banks need to upgrade software systems continually to keep them competitive. For banks using older versions of software, which software vendors no longer support, upgrading often involves the complete re-integration and re-customization of software, increasing costs dramatically (Vecchiatto, 2002). For a number of reasons African banks pay a premium for the customization of their software. Firstly, some deal in environments where people regularly exchange one currency for another local currency. Secondly, in some countries power failures are an everyday occurrence, so software and hardware must be robust, and banks must have adequate back-up facilities. Finally, African banks do not generally benefit from efficiencies of scale as they are operating from much smaller bases than Western incumbents are. However, the large size and economic strength of Stanbic and ABSA give them ownership advantages arising from economies of scale that are not available to smaller African banks. Internal competencies in the use and development of banking technology together with the external technological environment of their home country, in which digital technologies are highly developed relative to other African countries, provide these banks with significant ownership advantages in the use of ICTs. Table 3 provides a summary of the ownership, locational and internalization advantages from which South African banking organizations, including Stanbic and ABSA, benefit in their competition with non-African and indigenous banks in African markets. It is the desire to exploit these advantages that motivates South African banks to expand into other African markets.

Clearly, both Stanbic and ABSA are well endowed with ICTs and the necessary skills to apply them successfully to the banking sector in Africa. Their expertise in the use and development of technology is an important source of ownership advantage for these organizations when expanding into foreign markets. Combined with their emerging market specialization and experience with African conditions, their use of digital technologies provides them with the opportunity to dominate the banking sector in Africa.

Conclusions

The banking sector worldwide has experienced significant organizational change resulting from the adoption of ICTs. This chapter has examined the role of digital technologies in facilitating the cross-border development of African banking organizations by investigating the activities of a number of South African banks. In addition, the analysis explored ICT both as an ownership specific internal capacity, as a locational specific factor influencing the geographical pattern of international expansion, and as a facilitator of the internalization of cross-border banking networks.

Specific challenges exist for financial sector organizations operating in Africa. These arise from the low level of development and the weak ICT infrastructure. South African banks have several advantages beyond those available to other African banks and to non-African banks. Firstly, South African banks have the knowledge and experience of operating in Africa and have strong brands and reputations across the continent. Secondly, the size and maturity of the South African banking sector has promoted the strength and stability of these banks, which are amongst the largest in Africa. Thirdly, their origins in South Africa give them an advantage over non-African banks because African governments prefer to use African rather than non-African banks. Finally, South African banks have well-developed information systems and invest heavily in telecommunications and information technology in order to maintain their advantage arising from the use of digital technologies.

The locational advantages available to South African banks operating in Africa include the ability to exploit the increasingly stable and liberalized economic environments in these countries. National financial infrastructures are improving as countries adopt standards that are more rigorous. Foreign investment in Africa has increased significantly following these improvements. Furthermore, the technological weaknesses of many African countries allow South African banks to develop a leading position in the use of information systems.

South African banks also gain from the maintenance of control over ownership advantages which leads to internalization within the boundaries of the firm. In particular, ICT has played a key role in facilitating the control of assets through the organizational structures of international banks. For example, both ABSA and Stanbic use real-time communication networks to monitor activities in their subsidiaries.

This chapter has highlighted a number of issues regarding intra-African investment in the banking sector. In particular, the evidence presented above supports the argument that South African banks have an advantage over their regional competitors arising from their ability to apply ICTs successfully to the production and delivery of their services as well as to the operation of their organisational networks. Clearly, the technological leadership of South African banks derives from historical factors and the policies pursued by a government that is keen to promote the digital economy as a means to improve opportunities across the country. Important also has been the regulatory environment as it relates to both the banking and telecommunications sector and wider social issues in South Africa. The government has sought to maintain a stable economic environment, although the persistence of corruption and the AIDs epidemic present great challenges which must be faced if the country is to continue to progress.

South African banks currently have an advantage in the use and development of digital technologies. However, there is no guarantee that this technological leadership will persist. As noted, a major challenge for South African banks is the ability to recruit, train and retain a skilled workforce. There is then the danger that South African banks will not be able to sustain their advantages as they expand across Africa. This would allow non-African banks to takeover and build upon the foundations laid by South African banks.

Endnotes

[1]   Tier 1 capital is a measure of the strength of the bank and is defined as common equity, qualifying non-cumulative perpetual preferred stock, and minority interests, less goodwill.

[2]   For a critical discussion of Dunning's eclectic approach see, for example, Ietto-Gillies (1992), chapter 12, pp. 120-124.

[3]   For a detailed discussion of the application of Dunning's eclectic approach to the internationalisation of service firms see Roberts (1998).

[4]   See Dicken (2003, p. 446), for examples of product innovations in financial markets.

[5]   Briefly, difficulties arise because of the asymmetric distribution of information concerning the transaction between buyer and seller. The exchange of knowledge gives rise to problems of adverse selection and moral hazard that may prevent such transactions occurring in the open market. Adverse selection is an ex ante information problem referring to a situation in which one party in a potential transaction is better informed about a relevant variable in the transaction than the other party. Moral hazard is an ex post information problem referring to action which parties in a transaction may take after they have agreed to execute the transaction.

[6]   According to Ashurst (1998), the sheer scale of this project puts other e-cash projects in the world "in the shade."

References

Aharoni, Y. (2000). The role of reputation in global professional business services. In Y. Aharoni and L. Nachum (Eds.), *Globalization of Services: Some implications for theory and practice*. London: Routledge.

Arrow, K. J. (1969). Classificatory Notes on the Introduction and Transmission of Technical Knowledge. *American Economic Review, 59*, 29-35.

Arrow, K. J. (1974). *The Limits to Organizatian*. New York: W.W Norton.

Ashurst, M. (1998, October). South Africa's Banking Revolution. *The Banker, 148*(872) 102-104. Retrieved May 7, 2003, from EBESCO database.

Belford, D. (2003). African Banks' IT investment boom imminent, says Comparex Africa, *ITWeb (Johannesburg), Feburary 18*. Retrieved May 27, 2003 from the World Wide Web: http://www .allafrica.com/.

BIS. (2002). *BIS 72nd Annual Report*. Basel, July 8. Retrieved August 10, 2003 from the World Wide Web: http://www.bis.org/publ/ar2002e.htm.

Bryan, L. (1993, Spring). The forces reshaping global banking. *The McKinsey Quarterly, 2*, 59-72.

Castells, M. (2000). *The Rise of the Network Society.* Oxford: Blackwell.

Castells, M. (2001). *The Internet Galaxy: Reflections on the Internet, Business, and Society.* Oxford: Oxford University Press.

Cockerill, C. (2000, September). Big Risk, Big Profit. *Euromoney, 377,* 354-359.

Cogburn, D. L. (2003). Governing global information and communication policy: Emergent regime formation and the impact on Africa. *Telecommunications Policy, 27,* 135-153.

Cogburn, D. L. & Nyaki Adeya, C. (2002). Prospects for the Digital Economy in South Africa: Technology, Policy, People, and Strategies. *INTECH Institute for New Technologies Discussion Paper Series. 2002-2.* The United Nations University.

Darroch, J. (1992, July). Global competitiveness and public policy: the case of Canadian multinational banks. *Business History, 34*(3), 153-176.

Dicken, P. (2003). *Global Shift: Reshaping the Global Economic Map in the 21st Century* (4th Edition). London: Sage Publications.

Dunning, J.H. (1988, Spring/Summer). The eclectic paradigm of international production: a restatement and some possible extensions. *Journal of International Business Studies, 19,* 1-31.

Dunning, J. H. (1989). Multinational Enterprises and the Growth of Services: Some Conceptual and Theoretical Issues, *The Service Industries Journal, 9*(1), 5-39.

Global sweep and precise focus. (2002). *The Banker, 152*(920), 34. Retrieved July 18, 2003 from EBESCO database.

Grosse, R. (2000). Knowledge creation and transfer in global service firms. In Y. Aharoni & L. Nachum (Eds.), *Globalization of Services: Some implications for theory and practice.* London: Routledge.

Held, D., McGrew, A., Goldblatt, D. and Perraton, J. (1999). *Global Transformations: Politics, Economics and Culture.* Cambridge: Polity Press.

Ietto-Gillies, G. (1992). *International Production: Trends, Theories, Effects.* Cambridge: Polity Press.

Johanson, J. and Weidershein-Paul, F. (1975, October). The internationalization of the firm – four Swedish cases. *Journal of Management Studies,* 305-322.

Jones, G. (1990). *Banks as Multinationals.* New York: Routledge.

Jones, G. (1993). *British Multinational Banking.* Oxford: Clarendon Press.

KPMG. (2001). *Investment Banking,* Retrieved February 27, 2003 from the World Wide Web: http://www.kpmg.com/.

Kuljis, J., Macredie, R.D. and Paul, R.J. (1998). Information gathering problems in multinational banking. *Journal of Strategic Information Systems, 7,* 233-245.

Manson, H. (2002a). *Driving home value to banking customers.* Retrieved May 27, 2003 from the World Wide Web: http://www.mediatoolbox.co.za/.

Mansell, R. and Wehn, U. (Eds.). (1998). *Knowledge Societies: Information Technology for Sustainable Development.* Oxford: Oxford University Press.

Manson, H. (2002b), *The smart future of African banking.* Retrieved May 27, 2003 from the World Wide Web: http://www.mediatoolbox.co.za/.

Melly, P. and Marks, J. (2000, December). Stepping out of the shadows. *The Banker, 150*(i898), 67.

Minnows still. (2001, October). *The Banker, 151*(908), 17. Retrieved January 8, 2003, from EBESCO database.

Moore, D. (2000). Financial Services for everyone. *McKinsey Quarterly, 1,* 124–131.

Nua Internet Surveys. (2003). Retrieved July 13, 2003 from the World Wide Web: http://www.nua.ie/surveys/how_many_online/.

Odenthal, L. (2001). New Forms of Co-operation and integration in emerging Africa. *OECD Technical Paper No. 173.* Paris: OECD.

Paulson, J. (2000). Financial Services for the Urban Poor: South Africa's E Plan, *World Bank Working Paper Series,* No. 2016.

Polikanov, D. and Abramova, I. (2003). Africa and ICT: A Chance for Breakthrough? *Information, Communication & Society, 6*(1), 42-56.

Reshaping the face of banking. (1998, September). *The Banker, 148*(871), 18-20. Retrieved June 8, 2003 from EBESCO database.

Roberts, J. (1998). *Multinational Business Service Firms.* Aldershot: Ashgate.

Sassen, S. (2001). *Global Cities: New York, London, Tokyo.* 2nd Edition. Princeton and Oxford: Princeton University Press.

South African banking. (2000, March). *The Economist (US), 354*(8), 81.

South African Banking – Going IT alone. (2000, August). *The Economist (US), 356*(8185), 64.

Standard Bank of South Africa (Corporate Statement). Global sweep and precise focus. (2002, October). *The Banker, 152*(920), 34. Retrieved January 8, 2003 from EBESCO database.

Standard bearer: African banking. (1996). *The Economist (US), 339*(7970), 73-75. Retrieved January 8, 2003 from EBESCO database.

Stigler, G. J. (1961). The Economics of Information. *Journal of Political Economy, 69,* 213-225.

Strange, S. (1998). *Mad Money.* Manchester: Manchester University Press.

Technological innovation points to cashless society (1998, April). *The Banker, 148*(866), 72. Retrieved June 8, 2003 from EBESCO database.

Theobald, S. (2002). Waking up to Africa: the regenesis of the South African banking system has created banks that are in a strong position to dominate the continent. *The Banker, 152*(920), 13-15.

Ugwu, L.O., Oyebisi, T.O., Ilori, M.O. and Adagunodo, E.R. (2000). Organisational impact of information technology on the banking and insurance sector in Nigeria. *Technovation, 20,* 711-721.

UNCTAD. (2000). *World Investment Report 2000: Cross-border Mergers and Acquisitions and Development.* New York and Geneva: United Nations.

UNCTAD. (2002). *E-Commerce and Development Report 2002*. New York and Geneva: United Nations.

UNDP. (2003). *Human Development Report 2003*. Geneva and New York: United Nations.

Vecchiatto, P. (2002, December). African banks face costly upgrades, *ITWeb (Johannesburg)*. Retrieved July 8, 2003 from the World Wide Web: http://www.allafrica.com.

Waesche, N. M. (2003). *Internet Entrepreneurship in Europe: Venture Failure and the Timing of Telecommunications Reform*. Cheltenham, UK and Northampton, MA: Edward Elgar.

WPA Consulting. (2002). *African Banking*. Retrieved July 8, 2003 from the World Wide Web: http://www.africanbanking.com.

Wright, R. W. and Pauli, G. A. (1987). *The Second Wave: Japan's Global Assault on Financial Services*. London: Waterlow Publishers.

Yen, D.C. and Chou, D.C. (2001). Wireless communication: the next wave of Internet technology. *Technology in Society*, *23*, 217-226.

Chapter XIV

Technology and Culture: E-Commerce in China

Alev M. Efendioglu
University of San Francisco, USA

Vincent F. Yip
University of San Francisco, USA

Abstract

The number of Internet users around the world has been steadily growing and this growth has provided the impetus and the opportunities for global and regional e-commerce. However, as with the Internet, different characteristics (infrastructure and socio-economic) of the local environment have created a significant level of variation in the acceptance and growth of e-commerce in different regions of the world. Our research focuses on the impact of these infrastructure and socio-economic factors on e-commerce development in China and the findings provide insights into the role of culture in e-commerce, and the factors that may impact a broader acceptance and development of e-commerce in China. In this chapter, we present and discuss our findings, and propose some strategies for success for e-commerce in China.

Introduction

In this chapter, we will present and discuss our findings from a research study we conducted that focuses on culture and its implications on e-commerce development in China. To identify the current infrastructure and socio-economic influences on the development and growth of e-commerce in China, we developed a 20-question question-naire and pre-tested it by administering it to small group of participants. It was eventually administered to a total of 252 individuals that formed our study group. The study participants were located in Beijing, Shenzhen, Shanghai, Guangzhou, Wuhan, and Shandong during the time of the study, worked for different types of organizations (Joint Ventures, State Owned Enterprises, Multi-National Corporations, etc.), resided and worked in different regions in China, and had different educational levels, professions, and gender.

Over time, similar studies have been conducted in other countries and various models, by Zwass (1996), Wolcott et al. (2001), and Travica (2002), were developed to identify diffusion of e-commerce in different environments, with Travica's study being the only one that presented some discussion of the impact of social factors in e-commerce development, focusing on Costa Rica. These models have looked at "infrastructure" and "services" as the primary diffusion factors and we did incorporate some of the concepts and characteristics identified in these models into our questionnaire. However, in our study, we combined the "infrastructure" and "services" categories into a broader infrastructure group and focused on cultural issues more so than these models have incorporated in their studies. However, we do recognize the importance of infrastructure-related issues and have collected some information on these issues as well.

Based on similar previous research, we identified three primary infrastructure-related elements and two cultural issues that impact consumer participation in e-commerce in China. The infrastructure elements we identified are access to technology (computers, connectivity, and gateway to the Internet), payment systems for enabling transfer of funds (credit cards, bank transfers, etc.), and distribution systems for physical transfer of goods (physical delivery to consumers). The two cultural issues we consider to be most relevant and unique to China and that we focused on are: transaction trust (representations of the goods are accurate and true, purchased goods will be delivered and payment will be made) and attitudes towards debt (role and acceptance of debt in Chinese society). Previous studies have identified that Chinese rely on face-to-face contact and personal relationships ("*guanxi*") much more than other cultures (Davies and Lsung, 1995), and we consider this to be an element and manifestation of the importance of "transaction trust" in Chinese society and support our assumptions about the concept. Our questionnaire was designed to test the relative importance of these characteristics. As we present and discuss the responses of our participants on cultural issues, we will also present our infrastructure-related findings. However, in our opinion, the infrastructure issues, as important as they may be, are in a constant state of change and improvement, and we project that, in a relatively short time, they will cease to be a major constraint for e-commerce development in China. Whereas, the unique social and cultural characteristics of China and the concepts associated with off-site exchange systems, which are the foundations of e-commerce, will pose much greater challenges and will act as the major impediments.

The Research Study

Our objective was to find answers to three primary research questions and present some possible solutions.

1. What is the degree of e-commerce participation among Chinese consumers that have similar characteristics to participants in a consumer society such as the U.S. (compare and contrast the development and acceptance of e-commerce)?

2. What are some of the prevailing attitudes and cultural issues associated with e-commerce in China (identify and test the influence and impact of prominent Chinese cultural characteristics on e-commerce)?

3. What can domestic and foreign businesses do to facilitate e-commerce in China (present some short-and-long run recommendations and approaches to e-commerce development in China)?

Our study has some unique characteristics when compared with similar studies done in China. The survey questions, developed in English, were translated into and administered in Chinese. The translation was done by one of the co-authors, who is very proficient in English and Chinese, Internet and E-Commerce terminology, and has a profound understanding of cultural nuances of the Chinese language. This is important because of the possible danger of lost meanings and incorrect interpretations of what is being asked when questionnaires are developed in one language and administered in another language (especially in Chinese) to a culturally different population. The questionnaires were administered by one of the authors personally, increasing the validity of the study by minimizing contamination that may be inserted into mail or online surveys, increasing the participation rate, and decreasing the rejection of responses that were unclear or incomplete. The participants were asked to fill out the questionnaire without any inducements, such as prizes or money, as is the tradition in most of the mail in or electronic surveys conducted in China. The questionnaire contained questions designed to collect information on demographics, Internet usage, e-commerce activities (frequency of commerce and type of purchase, means used for purchase, transaction experience), and perceptions and attitudes towards e-commerce in China.

The study group (252 participants) was specifically selected to represent a group of e-commerce users that we identified and classified as "early adopters" and considered to be a close match to e-commerce users in developed countries. As researchers with previous research experience in China and knowing the degree of technological and economic development among the general populace, we selected these participants because we considered them to be the most likely users of e-commerce, with access to technology, significant purchasing power, exposure to concepts and practices outside China, and open to trying new/novel things. Since we wanted to focus on the "impact

Table 1. Organizational affiliation of study participants (n=252)

	MNC	Domestic Enterprises*	Joint Venture
Participants in Sample	53	160	39
% of Participants	21.03%	63.49%	15.48%
* Includes Private Enterprises, SOE, and University			

of culture," we wanted to get the opinions of actual participant/users of e-commerce and wanted to eliminate the infrastructure problems (payment transfer systems, access to computers, telecommunication infrastructure, access to Internet Service Providers, etc.) as much as possible. As such, our study population was not intended to be, and is not, a representative sample of the general populace in China.

Findings

Study Population Demographics

The study population (252 participants) consisted of 59.92% males and 40.08% females, 88.89% with a Bachelors degree or above (13.49% with graduate level degrees), 62.30% were between ages 26-35 years, with 75.40% between ages 26-40 years of age. There were also differences in the professions of the participants. The largest representative professions were 40.87% management, 29.76% IT (Information Technology), 5.56% service, and 5.56% consulting. These study population characteristics are very different than the overall characteristics of China's general populace and are also significantly different than other studies conducted to primarily identify the development and progress of Internet use in China. Among these studies is one semi-annual study, conducted by the China Internet Network Information Center (CCNIC), using the Internet to collect information. The demographics of their latest (*China Internet Network Information Center*, 2002) survey included 60.9% males, 35.7% between the ages of 25-40 years (with 53.5% younger than 20 years of age), and only 31.3% with college education (Bachelors degree or higher). Their study participants also had a much broader sample of professions and backgrounds, including those who checked categories such as "military," "peasants," "agriculture, forestry, fishery," real estate," "wholesale and retail," "culture and arts," and "sports," etc., professions which were not covered by our survey. However, since they conduct their surveys using the Internet and participants are self-selected, their population demographics, other than possibly the professions and backgrounds, do not necessarily truly represent China's general population, either.

Internet Usage

The responses to our questions related to Internet access and usage reinforced our primary premise in selecting this group to be the study participants. Overall, they had complete and easy access to Internet enabling technology (e.g., access to a PC and telecommunication connection to an ISP) and used the Internet regularly for multiple purposes/activities (e.g., email, web search, etc.). 37.70% of the respondents accessed both English and Chinese Internet sites and pages, while the remaining 62.30% used only Chinese language sites and pages. The three most popular Internet based activities were email, with 88.49% of respondents, reading news, with 80.95% of respondents, and search, with 58.33% of respondents. Other activity categories were downloads, chat, games, etc. The most popular Internet site accessed was sina.com (with 80.56% respondents) followed closely by sohu.com (with 54.76% respondents) and yahoo.com (with 39.29% of respondents). In the type of Internet usage, we found significant differences between our study participants and the latest CNNIC survey findings. The CNNIC (official Internet data collector for the Chinese government) survey data shows that 45.5% of their respondents engage in "online chatting" and 18.6% in "online games and entertainment," which may be attributable to their much younger (53.5% of them <24 year old) population with lower education level (42% being of high school and lower) and to the diversity of the professions (or lack of any profession) of their respondents, all of which are significantly different than our study group characteristics (China Internet Network Information Center, 2002).

E-Commerce Activity

The objective of the next set of questions (pervasiveness of e-commerce acceptance, choice of payment methods for electronic transactions, purchased items, and evaluation of their experiences by e-commerce participants) was to identify and clarify the culturally based behavioral patterns of the study participants, especially as they related to their attitudes towards "transaction trust" and "debt," which are among the most critical foundations of e-commerce. Chinese culture does not condemn piracy and copying, and the legal infrastructure is not sophisticated or organized enough to deal with some illegal activities, especially fraud. Counterfeiting and distribution of below par products is a major problem in China, which amplifies the prevailing lack of transactional trust between parties that do not know each other personally. As a result, Chinese rely on face-to-face contact more so than other cultures (strong individual relationship and long-term association between the parties, a concept described as "*guanxi*," which refers to a particular kind of social networking based on trust) and, to provide themselves with the necessary comfort level that they are making the right purchase and demand to have physical contact with the purchased good before they pay for it. Furthermore, the current Chinese banking system is primarily designed to accommodate businesses, especially SOEs, and banks are primarily owned and used as tools by the Chinese government to further its economic and social aims, and such a system does not provide an opportunity for the general public to easily acquire credit cards and use them in making purchases. Financial institutions have not yet developed, do not encourage or support consumer lending practices, and continue to reinforce the principle of "buy when you have cash to pay," make debt unavailable, unknown and unacceptable, and further perpetuate the "cash society" characteristics.

The first set of questions in this group were designed to determine the ability (access to type of medium used for payment) of the respondents to pay (possession of credit

Table 2. Sample population (n=252) vs. e-commerce participants (n=166)

	Male	Age <36 years	Education (BS-GRAD)	Have Credit Card	Purchase in 12-mo	Purchase in 6-Mo
All Respondents (%)	59.92%	79.37%	88.89%	86.51%	64.29%	65.88%
E-Commerce Participants (%)	55.42%	88.55%	88.55%	86.75%	97.59%	100.00%

cards) for e-commerce and whether or not they had purchased any goods/services, using e-commerce, within the previous 12-month period. The 166 respondents that indicated having purchased goods/services were further asked about the frequency of their transactions during the previous 12 and 6-month periods, the products/services they purchased, highest total value of their single purchase, and their payment method (credit cards and other commonly used methods of payment in China) for these purchases. They were also asked to list their primary reasons for utilizing e-commerce and rate their overall satisfaction with the activity, and to provide unstructured comments on what they considered to be impediments to the development of e-commerce in China and Chinese attitudes towards use technology as a means for commerce.

Of our 252 respondents, 65.88% had participated in e-commerce transactions. The ability to pay (access to credit cards) was not an impediment to e-commerce (86.51% of our study participants had credit cards, with 69.84% having two or more credit cards), and we do not consider this finding to be representative of China and attribute it to the deliberate composition of our study population. However, what was surprising was the percent of respondents participating in e-commerce, 53.01%, that had made more than six purchases during the previous 12 months and the 55.42% of respondents that had purchased goods/ services more than three times during the previous six months. These percentages are far greater than the findings of a recent Business Software Alliance survey, reporting around 38% of U.S. Internet users that say they purchase products fairly or very often using the Internet (*Business Software Association*, 2002). It was also quite surprising to find that our study respondents who possessed credit cards participated in e-commerce activity (86.75% of the credit card holders purchased goods/services via e-commerce) in rates similar to U.S. Internet users (with 93% of Internet users who have bought online). Furthermore, our study results show that younger age customers have a greater propensity to use e-commerce (88.55% of the e-commerce participants were 35 years or younger in age as compared to 79.35% of the study population). If we consider that the earning power increases with age, this finding is also somewhat surprising for China and might signal pervasiveness of technology acceptance among younger age groups that one normally finds in other societies. Based on consumer behaviors in the U.S., if we assume a positive correlation between ownership of increased number of credit cards and frequency of purchase patterns, our findings did not support this general rule. In our study, the respondents with four or more credit cards constituted 21.03% of total respondents and 21.69% of e-commerce participants, with other credit card ownership ranges having similar equal distributions between the study participants vs. e-commerce participants. We could not find comparable age, availability of credit cards, or frequency of purchases data in the CNNIC semi-annual survey that conducts studies of broader Chinese Internet user populations. However, the latest CNNIC survey showed that 68.8%

of the respondents had never made any online purchases, which is much higher than our findings that showed only a 34.12% non-participation rate (*China Internet Network Information Center*, 2002).

The value of single purchases ranged from less than RMB50 ($6.00) to over RMB1000 ($80.00), with the majority of the purchases (83.73%) ranging in value from RMB50 to RMB500 ($6.00-$60). The respondents paid for these purchases in four major ways: cash/check (travel-related purchases were paid at the time of use, e.g., hotel stay), C.O.D., credit card, and bank transfer. In our study group, contrary to purchases made in the U.S., a credit card was not the most common payment method. Chinese mentality and their traditions (reinforced by the prevailing operational characteristics of the financial institutions and the legal system) still adhere to a way of thinking that says debt is not good. Furthermore, the estimated RMB410billion (USD50billion) stashed away in savings and for future purchases provide some evidence that the credit system is not as popular and that China still is a cash society. Our findings also support this cultural characteristic. Even though 86.51% of our study group (218 respondents) had credit cards, only 19.28% of the e-commerce participants (32 out of 166 respondents) paid for their purchases using a credit card. Both authors, during their extensive travels in China, rarely encountered credit cards being used for any daily purchases, including some very expensive entertainment events hosted by high-level managers and individuals that have significant economic means, and, without any doubt, have multiple credit cards.

U.S. e-commerce vendors would require credit card information before accepting any requests for online purchases and have set up infrastructure (secure servers to collect credit card information) to accommodate and enable this payment methodology. However, lack of such infrastructure and a lack of broad availability of personal credit cards in China have created transaction payment systems that also utilize other payment methods, such as C.O.D, cash, and postal order (money order). This lack of infrastructure (payment systems), coupled with not-so-generous return policies of Chinese businesses, and the prevailing societal characteristics have made the Chinese cynical consumers and reinforced commerce systems where the customer must see and check the product and the seller must get paid in cash, without any ambiguities or collection problems that may accompany credit-based payment systems. When one looks at the findings of our study, it is easy to see that these attitudes are still prevalent and will continue to act as a major impediment to large-scale diffusion of e-commerce in China. Our 166 e-commerce participants used C.O.D. (39.16%) as their primary payment method, closely followed by Cash/Check (33.13%), with a Credit Card having the distinction of being the third highest (19.28%) further followed by the Bank Transfer (8.43%) method. The latest CNNIC survey shows the top three payment methods as cash and carry (33.1%), online payment (30.7 %), and post office transfer (30.0%) (*China Internet Network Information Center*, 2002). Both our findings (approximately 73% of e-commerce participants paid in cash) and the findings of CNNIC (approximately 63% paid in cash) clearly demonstrate and support our observation and classification of China as a "cash based society."

Even though some of our findings confirmed the cultural characteristics we had identified as the prevailing characteristics of the society, the responses to the questions related to the types of purchases presented findings contrary to some of the other characteristics associated by the Chinese consumers. When we asked what was bought online, the responses we received were in categories that were similar to purchases made by U.S. online customers and the findings of the latest CNNIC survey. Our respondents (166 e-commerce participants) indicated a total of 379 transactions over the previous 12-month period, with books as the most popular item (34.83% of respondents stated purchasing books), followed by video-CDs (26.39%), and travel (15.57%). In comparison, in the U.S., books and videos are the most common online purchases, followed by music CDs, clothing or accessories, and computer software or hardware. The top five online purchases in the CNNIC survey were books and magazines (37.0%), computer appliances (27.6%) and communication/AV equipment/electrical appliances, each ranging around 19.5%. The high preferences for online purchases of books and video-CDs were surprising findings in a country where normal, as well as pirated, books and video-CDs are sold in local markets for very low prices. Unfortunately, we did not have an opportunity to focus more on this preference by our respondents to determine possible reasons and explanations for this behavior seemingly contradictory to general and popular beliefs.

We also asked questions to determine the level of satisfaction e-commerce users experienced while making online purchases. Our scale used categories "very unsatisfactory," "unsatisfactory," "average," "satisfactory," and "very satisfactory" to solicit responses, without assigning any number value to each category. One of the most important attributes of the Chinese culture is for Chinese to act humbly and take the middle of the road and understate their ideas, as compared to taking a position that is clearly identifiable. Unfortunately, most of our respondents exhibited this cultural trait and selected "average" ("*Yi Ban*" in Chinese) as their response, reinforcing the fact that a complicated set of conditions are required to conduct any type of field research in China. Nevertheless, we had some responses that presented clear "satisfaction" or "dissatisfaction" with their online purchase experience.

Our findings show that frequent users of e-commerce were satisfied or very satisfied with their experience in larger numbers as compared to the least frequent users. Overall, the "unsatisfied" and "very unsatisfied" responses were selected in very low frequencies. We attribute this finding to the affinity of the user with technology and more experience with the online transaction process through increased usage. Except for the least frequent users, the transactional experiences during the most recent six months were more satisfying than the previous six-month period. Even though the vendors might have made changes in their presence and processes, this improvement most likely was the

Table 3. E-commerce transaction frequency & satisfaction (n=166)

	Frequency of Purchase (times)				
Satisfied/Very Satisfied	**<=3**	**4-6**	**7-9**	**9<**	**Study Group**
Purchases During Last 6months	24.32%	34.15%	50.00%	61.29%	36.75%
Purchase During Last 12months	24.32%	29.27%	18.18%	54.55%	36.75%
Very Unsatisfied/Unsatisfied	**<=3**	**4-6**	**7-9**	**9<**	**Study Group**
Purchases During Last 6months	1.20%	1.80%	0.00%	1.20%	4.22%
Purchase During Last 12months	1.20%	0.60%	0.60%	1.81%	4.22%

result of learning that came with repetition. Similarly, *Shenzhen Economics Daily* reported that the portion of Internet users who made online purchases rose to 31.67% while the overall dissatisfaction of online experience decreased from 52.8% to 21.04% (*Shenzhen Economics Daily*, 2002). Shenzhen population has characteristics similar to our study population, as it is one of the most prosperous cities in China (has the highest per capita income) and has the youngest average age population. Once again, these characteristics are significantly different than most of the other regions in China. No data was provided by the CNNIC survey (which has a wider geographic coverage) related to satisfaction with online transaction process/activity.

Convenience was identified as the most selected reason for conducting an online transaction, with price, delivery, and speed as being next three reasons with almost equal frequencies. Given that our study participants were all working adults, it is somewhat understandable to find "convenience" as the overwhelming choice within the study group, and this finding reflects similar findings in the U.S., where a large number of e-commerce participants work. However, it might seem as a surprising finding to see the fairly similar frequencies of choice among "price," "delivery," and "speed." We can explain this as another specific finding based on the composition of our sample group, working adults, with relatively good earnings, and in valued professions. Given our study group characteristics, it is no surprise that "delivery" and "speed" are as important (different types of convenience preferred by busy professionals) as "price" (high income level). Even a delivery charge of 10% for purchases up to RMB800 (USD100) for deliveries, with no charges for anything above this amount, did not seem to be a major concern for our participants, especially for C.O.D. payments. Even if for orders less than RMB100, the most common delivery charge of RMB5 (barely enough to buy a can of Coca Cola in the store) is easily affordable by most city residents of China. Given the Chinese consumers' culturally based behaviors (especially the need to physically evaluate the purchased product) that govern their purchases, we think the acceptance of this system and associated costs (delivery charge) are not unique to our study group and a similar acceptance will prevail among the general populace.

We also included a section for unstructured comments on the questionnaire and conducted brief interviews to identify perceptions on positive and negative aspects of e-commerce as it currently exits and its future in China, and any other issues that we might have neglected to categorize and include in our questionnaire. These comments, in some cases, provided additional information, and in others, reinforced the previous responses and strengthened the data we collected through other questions.

As we had assumed and previously identified as unique to our study group, the lack of credit cards or the deficiencies in payment mechanisms was not an issue for our respondents (even though they indicated that this is a major problem for the general public). Neither did the lack of brand name products or the quality of the products. The

Table 4. Reasons (multiple responses accepted) for using e-commerce & satisfaction

	Convenience	Price	Delivery	Speed	Selection	Privacy
Stated as Main Reason	128	96	75	65	18	9
Satisfied/Very Satisfied	39.06%	40.63%	33.33%	44.62%	33.33%	22.22%
Very Unsatisfied/Unsatisfied	2.34%	2.08%	4.00%	1.54%	11.11%	1.11%

primary obstacles (which support our "early adopters" classification of our sample size), in the order of importance, were "Internet security," "lack of feel-and-touch associated with online purchases," "problems in returning products," and "selection" (product breadth). In comparison, CNNIC survey identified the top five obstacles to be "Internet security," "inconvenient payment method," "quality of products and trustworthiness of merchant," "late delivery," and "unattractive price" (*China Internet Network Information Center*, 2002). As can be seen, there are some overlaps and some contradictions between our findings and the CNNIC's findings, which can be explained by the different study demographics.

Our study participants also identified some infrastructure and social issues that will impede and be obstacles to full development of e-commerce in China in the near future. Among the most identified and repeatedly mentioned issues were lack of credit cards (availability of them for the general public in China) and convenient payment means, poor distribution logistics, lack of specialized, trust-worthy online merchants of reasonable size (too many small players facing many bottlenecks and without necessary resources to set up e-commerce systems), an imperfect legal system, and the lack of large scale telecommunication transmission capability (broadband). Overall, however, the respondents were reasonably positive about the availability of hardware/software, government and industry support for IT in China.

Even though it was identified as a major infrastructure impediment, over the recent years access to technology in China dramatically increased and it is projected that 10.3 million PCs will be sold during 2002, making China the third largest market after the U.S. and Japan. About 30% of China's 1.3 billion people are currently wealthy enough to afford PCs, roughly corresponding to a market size equal to the population of the U.S. Furthermore, according to Nielsen/NetRatings (as reported by BBC News, 2002), China is now second only to the United States in the number of home Internet users with nearly 57 million people with web access at home, and Internet subscriptions are growing by 5-6% every month. In just three or four years, 25% of the population could have Internet access, translating to over 250 million people. Physical distribution was also identified as one of the impediments. Currently, multiple private courier companies, that already have operations in major cities, are providing physical distribution, with China's postal service that has contracts with dozens of merchants for regular or express delivery. Manpower for physical distribution is abundant and relatively cheap, and there are many inexpensive modes of transportation, including bicycles, motor scooters, and small trucks, that can be effectively used as alternates to large scale distribution in close geographical areas. As more efficiency (grouped deliveries, efficient modes of transportation, efficient routing systems, etc.) is incorporated into the system, this impediment will cease to be a major problem. Unfortunately, the problems associated with financial infrastructure (credit cards and credit-based transaction systems) require major action by the government and the financial institutions. To overcome this e-commerce constraint, Chinese government has to accelerate the banking reforms and the banks should reorient themselves to provide more services (credit cards and credit card payment clearing systems) to the general public and the average consumer. In their report titled Consumer E-Commerce in China, BDA-China argues that China has over 150 million bankcards, providing some evidence that support positive changes in this direction (Consumer E-Commerce in China, 2000). However, these cards are in the hands of very few consumers (in our study, 70.12% had two or more credit cards) and, as such, the existing card owners may not be large enough to sustain broad-based e-commerce in China, one that is available to large segments of the general populace.

Our study group was overwhelmingly less positive when asked if the Chinese culture "supports" the propagation of IT and e-commerce. The group thought the Chinese consumer society was not quite ready (lack of confidence in technology and off-site transactions, online culture, and overall sophistication of the general public) and the conditions were not "ripe" for e-commerce. Off-site transaction systems (like e-commerce, catalog sales, mail order systems) which require a trusting relationship (transaction trust) between the unseen vendor and the consumer requires a sophisticated consumer society, specific legal (consumer protection laws) and financial (consumer credit systems and social acceptance of credit cards as a payment mechanism) practices. Continuing lack of consumer protection laws and the prevalent business practices of the financial institutions contribute to and enhance the negative connotations associated with debt and reinforce cash-based transaction systems. Absence of these practices, coupled with inherent social and political characteristics of the Chinese society, have made Chinese cynical consumers and reinforced commerce systems where customer can see and check the product and the seller can get paid in cash, without any ambiguities or collection problems that may accompany credit-based payment systems. Furthermore, Chinese consumers see commerce as a social activity and value time-developed personal relationships with vendors that are local and have a physical presence. This is an attitude that is very contrary to e-commerce process/practices and, as a result, the cultural acceptance of online transactions (business foundations of e-commerce) will take much longer and will require major transformations in Chinese society. Similar transformations have taken place in other societies over extended time periods, by first becoming a true consumer society (a transition that took over four decades in the U.S.) and then eventually accepting e-commerce (a transition that has been taking place in the U.S. for the past decade). Even after years of being a consumer society and developing technological sophistication among the general populace (very high levels of penetration of computers at work, school and home, and over 55% of the population accessing the Internet from home), only around 38% of U.S. Internet users say they purchase products from the Net fairly or very often, and 55% buy occasionally. Fundamental changes, both in the way Chinese banks operate, and the way the Chinese society views consumerism and commercial activity need to be instituted over time to overcome these major barriers. However, as China opens up to the outside world and becomes a more integral part of the world community (evidenced by China's entry and full membership in WTO, 2008 Olympics in Beijing, and 2010 World Expo in Shanghai), changes will take place, starting with the banking reforms, which in return will promote fundamental cultural changes in the Chinese society.

Conclusions

While the infrastructural and cultural impediments identified above will get resolved over time, Chinese business establishments and their professional groups can play a significant role in providing interim solutions and services that address the infrastructure issues and help society in its efforts to become a truly consumer society, within which many different business models can develop and flourish, including e-commerce. One of these approaches is to utilize a combination (**virtual storefront and physical distribution center**) business model that can address many of the issues we have identified and may be the only way for businesses to participate in e-commerce in China in the short run. Chinese companies are socio-economic entities and not just pure economic ones and there is a strong individual relationship and long-term association between the parties (buyer and the seller), which provides a sense of community and enhances social bonding. Since most of the business is conducted through small enterprises and is local, the success of doing business in China depends heavily on the quality and sometimes the quantity (number of customers that have this special relationship with the business owner) of personal relationships. These local, smaller enterprises can use a system that is similar to the franchising system in the U.S. to exploit this characteristic in their efforts to transition to large-scale, e-commerce systems. Businesses that sell similar products can form alliances with businesses in other cities and towns, even establishing loosely aligned franchises, and utilize the services of existing Internet Service Providers (ISP), acting as intermediaries, to develop national electronic storefronts with local distribution systems. Through these alliances, they can provide credit (issue local or alliance-wide credit cards) or continue to provide "cash-and-carry" services to the consumers who prefer to pay cash (aversive to debt), overcome the local distribution problems (by transferring products among themselves) and surmount customer concerns related to the "touch-and-feel" issues (counterfeit and below par products, problems with product returns, online merchants are not trustworthy, and Internet is not secure). These newly formed e-commerce businesses can overcome some of these customer concerns by forming organizations that encourage, validate, and publicize establishments that have instituted product policies that condemn piracy and counterfeiting, and distribute quality products. Furthermore, these businesses can and should develop more consumer favorable return policies and extensively publicize their policies and efforts. These types of practices will give them additional competitive advantages while appealing to another cultural characteristic of the Chinese people, "moral obligation to return a favor." Chinese customers feel bad and think they have a "moral obligation" to buy again from the same merchant to make up for the "loss of face" on both sides, caused by the rejected purchase. These same recommendations apply to foreign firms, which are even at a greater cultural disadvantage, as they try to conduct domestic business. Foreign firms that want to participate in e-commerce in China will have to find ways to overcome the cultural barriers and will have to utilize similar approaches by creating a local presence (through associations with local vendors) and use the "*guanxi*" developed by these local businesses. However, they do have some competitive advantages, such as brand recognition and e-commerce infrastructure (web servers, computer-based transaction systems, and telecommunication infrastructure) which they can exploit and use to support local businesses.

References

Business Software Association: Most US Internet Users have bought online. (2002). Retrieved November 25, 2002 from the World Wide Web: http://www.nua.com.

China mulls E-Commerce. (1999, March). Retrieved November 2, 2002 from the World Wide Web: http://asia.internet.com/asia-news/print/0,,161_646921,00.html.

China's Home Web Use Soars. (2002, April 23). *BBC News.* Retrieved November 2, 2002 from the World Wide Web: http://news.bbc.co.uk/1/hi/world/asia-pacific/1945275.stm accessed on 11/2/2002.

Consumer E-Commerce in China (2000). BDA (China) Limited. Retrieved September 16, 2002 from the World Wide Web: http://www.bdaconnect.com.

Davies, H. and Lsung, H. (1995). The Benefits of Guanxi: The Value of Relationships. *Industrial Marketing Management,* 24, 207-213.

Internet Users in Shenzhen. (2002, October 8). *Shenzhen Economics Daily,* 1.

Semiannual Survey Report on the Development of China's Internet (1997-2002). (2002). *China Internet Network Information Center.* Retrieved September 11, 2002 from the World Wide Web: http://www.cnnic.net.ch/develst/2002-7e/5.shtml.

StatMarket: China has the second largest online population. Retrieved August 30, 2002 from the World Wide Web: http://www.nua.com.

Travica, B. (2002). Diffusion of electronic commerce in developing countries: The case of Costa Rica. *Journal of Global Information Technology Management,* 5(1), 4-24.

Wolcott, P., Press, L., McHenry, W., Goodman, S. E. & Foster, W. (2001). A framework for assessing the global diffusion of the Internet. *Journal of the Association for Information Systems,* 2(6).

Zwass, V. (1996). Electronic commerce: Structure and issues. *International Journal of Electronic Commerce,* 1(1), 3-23.

Chapter XV

Internet Economy of the Online Game Business in South Korea:
The Case of NCsoft's *Lineage*

Kyonghwan Park
University of Kentucky, USA

Abstract

This chapter attempts to lay the groundwork for in-depth discussions on the economic, social and cultural dimensions of the online game business as one of the most successful forms of the contemporary digital contents industry using the Internet. As a form of the digital economy, the online game has evolved both "through" and "within" the space of the Internet. I suggest that the broadband Internet infrastructure and the construction of the game users' community in cyberspace constitute two necessary conditions for the economic success of the online game business. Conceptualizing such a socio-cultural economy of the Internet business as the economy of a "third space," I argue that the online game business contains emerging forms of new economic space not only in-between the real space and the virtual space, but also between the production and the consumption of those games produced.

Introduction

The Internet is one of the most significant technological innovations that capitalism has achieved, having a wide range of influences across different scales and scopes of economic realms. Instead of focusing on the accumulation of conventional inputs such as labor and capital, many contemporary macroeconomists along with economic historians have recently emphasized the significance of technological innovation in overall economic growth (Romer, 1990; Grossman and Helpman, 1991; Aghion and Howitt, 1992; Helpman, 1998). Some of these studies use a specific term called "general-purpose technology" (GPT) to describe a drastic "enabling technology" involving "innovational complementarities" (IC) that increases the productivity in a downstream sector (Bresnahan and Trajtenberg, 1995; Helpman, 1998; Malecki, 2002). Distinct from incremental and secondary technological innovations, GPTs such as printing, writing, electricity, factory systems and automobiles are considered revivals of an historical technological tradition instead of a total "discontinuous newness." Malecki (2002), for example, argues that the Internet generally reiterates past technological traditions, especially since the invention of the telegraph, in terms of its strong initial ties with financial institutions, and invisible commodities like financial tallies, a systematically networked economy, and private-owned telecommunications networks.

In this vein, economic geographic studies on the Internet since the early 1990s have contributed considerably to the understanding of recent telecommunications technologies within the context of specific geo-economic scales and the conventional physical flows of capital, labor and goods. Pioneering works in urban and economic geography devoted themselves to the significance of emerging telecommunications and their impacts on the economic, social and spatial dimensions in postindustrial economies (Moss, 1987; Langdale, 1989; Hepworth, 1990; Brunn and Leinbach, 1991). Recent geographic studies are also interested in the multifarious interactions between the spaces of networking flows and real urban places (Graham, 1994; Mitchell, 1995; Graham, 1997; Adams, 1998; Graham and Marvin, 1996; Graham and Marvin, 2001), the utopian and dystopian visions of cyberspace as a public space and related cultural dimensions (Rheingold, 1993; Shields, 1996; Adams, 1997; Kitchin, 1998; Crang M., Crang P. and May, 1999; Crang, 2000; Dodge and Kitchin, 2000), and the geopolitics of global Internet diffusion, connection, and "digital divide" (Brunn and Cottle, 1997; Warf and Grimes, 1997; O'Lear, 1997; Warf, 2001). More recent geo-economic studies focus on diverse constraints and possibilities of the Internet-based e-commerce and its geographic dimensions (Leinbach and Brunn, 2001; Zook, 2000, 2002). Instead of arguing for the end of geography by technological space-time convergence to create a "space of flows" (Castells, 1996), many of the above studies have implied that e-commerce is not bringing about the destruction of economic regions and places, but is providing the impetus to reorganize and differentiate the economic space in which business operates.

Theorizing the Internet as a GPT is a useful framework to elucidate its "complementary" role in commerce and telecommunication sectors, and its "general-purpose" diffusion in social and cultural spheres. At the same time, however, the framework has an overall danger in downplaying the significant "discontinuity" of the emerging Internet economy, an economy that not only appropriates the Internet for complementary telecommunication infrastructure, but also takes the Internet "network" itself as a core, as an alternative economic resource, and a social space of economic activities (i.e., Liebowitz, 2002; McKeown, 2002). Especially is this observation apparent in the realm of the digital contents industry, with its low barrier to market entry and differentials in transaction costs that form the complex geographies of cyberspace (Kenney and Curry, 2001). Within this context, this chapter attempts to lay the groundwork for in-depth discussions on the economic, social and cultural dimensions of the online game business as one of the most successful forms of the contemporary digital contents industry using the Internet. The central queries in this chapter are: "what are the salient characteristics of the online game business as a form of digital economy?", "why has it been one of the most consistently profitable and stable forms of dot.com business?", "what factors are significant in the success and growth of the online game business?", and finally "how is the operation of the online game business associated with game users' social and cultural spheres?" Entangled with other forms of the digital economy, answering these questions requires us to examine scrupulously the cultural economy of contemporary Internet businesses and its societal implications.

This chapter begins by examining some of unique characteristics of the online game business as one of the most exemplary forms of the Internet contents industry. The online game business not only utilizes the digital space of the Internet to make stable profits, but also creates social spatiality through technology-intensive visualization and rhizomatic connections of the game users. It is a frontier form of the digital economy evolving both "through" and "within" the space of the Internet. I suggest that the broadband Internet infrastructure and the construction of the cyber game community constitute two necessary conditions for the economic success of the online game business (and possibly other forms of the Internet business). Especially, drawing on Jean Baudrillard's (1983; 1988; 1998) critical discussion on simulacrum and simulation, I will illuminate the ways in which the simulated hyper-reality of the online game produces certain "spatiality" in the online game, evokes a sense of community among game players, and consequently generates a "third" socioeconomic space in-between (or overarching) the real and the virtual. For an empirical analysis, I specifically investigate the case of the South Korean online game company NCsoft's *Lineage: the bloodpledge*. This game had over 3.2 million registrations and 11 million accumulative registrations in 2002. The latter figure accounts for almost one-fourth of the country's total population. The company generated 44.2 million U.S. dollars of net profit from game players in 2002[1], and has opened operations in Taiwan, Hong Kong, Japan and the United States. The U.S.-based investment bank JP Morgan upgraded the company's shares in 2001, signaling it as the most valuable stock in the South Korean high-tech stock market KOSDAQ (Korea Securities Dealers Automated Quotation System) in 2001[2]. Overall, NCsoft's *Lineage* would be an archetypal online game, featured by massive game players, transnational scope of operation, and stable and high profitability.

The Online Game Business as Digital Economy

The term "online game" is usually distinguished from the network game and the Internet game. The characteristics of online games, such as *Ultima Online* and *Everquest* in the United States can be summarized as an infinity of game participants and exquisite audiovisual technology for digital representation of real space and life. A network game such as the Blizzard's *Starcraft* lacks the former characteristic of an online game while an Internet game such as the MSN's *Gaming Zone* lacks the latter. The differences between the Internet game and the online game are also significant: online games create a simulated "cyber-world" through realistic representations of space, while Internet games are related to simple cyber-games such as billiards, card games, car-racing, checkers, etc.

The online game business, rapidly emerging in a digital economy, has become one of the fascinating Internet contents businesses, including an Internet portal service, e-broadcasting, e-education, e-business solution, and e-security. Because many online game companies maintain their profit models based on "retail game package with online fee" (i.e., *Everquest* and *Ultima Online*) or "free game package with online fee (i.e., *Lineage*)," they have been quite successful in securing continuity and consistency in making profits (Costikyan, 1998; 2000). The online game has actually evolved from the textual structure like MUD (Multiple User Domains) to more elaborately represent graphic networks like MUG (Multiple User Graphics) and currently, MMPOG (Massively Multiple Player Online Game). Usually, MMPOG is played by 50,000 ~ 200,000 multiple Internet users who construct a virtual community in cyberspace through their access to the host computers of the game company (Lee, 2001). It is different from a PC-based network game in which usually 2~20 players can play game at the same time, whereas the online game is played by an infinite number of players in many different places (Lee, 2001). For this reason, most of the online game players consider the cyberspace elements of the game not only as virtual, but also as "real" society. Table 1 shows that the online game industry is generally small, but growing faster than other types of games. Note that arcade and video games still dominate the global game market.

More specifically, there are at least three significant features of the online game business. First, as a form of the contents industry of Internet e-business, the success of the online game heavily depends on users' accessibility to a broadband Internet infrastructure, including xDSLs and cable modems, for it simultaneously inter-connects 50,000 ~ 150,000 game players who rhizomatically communicate large capacities of textual and audiovisual data. Hence, the online game business is one of the most accurate, efficient and inclusive measurements to evaluate the digital economy in association with the Internet and telecommunication infrastructure. Furthermore, the online game technologically depends on a meticulous graphic design, 3-D visualization, and a delicate user-networking structure. It has stimulated a variety of innovations including artificial intelligence techniques, image-processing software and hardware, and super-speed Internet infrastructures.

Table 1. Global market of game businesses

	1998		1999		2000		2001		2002
	Market (billion dollars)	Growth rate (%)	Market (billion dollars)	Growth rate (%)	Market (billion dollars)	Growth rate (%)	Market (billion dollars)	Growth rate (%)	Market (billion dollars)
PC	5.0	14	6.7	34	9.3	39	13.9	49	20.7
Video	39.8	35	43.0	8	49.0	14	55.4	13	62.0
Arcade	60.5	21	75.6	25	98.2	30	129.0	31	170.0
Online	3.3	18	4.5	36	6.5	44	10.2	57	16.0
Total	1,086	25	1,298	19	1,630	26	2,085	28	2,687

Source: http://stat.nic.or.kr (Korean Network Information Center); http://www.gameinfinity.or.kr (Korean Game Promotion Center); http://www.game.or.kr (Korean Entertainment System Industry Association)

Second, as a form of a non-material, information-based business, the online game business does not necessarily require the conventional processes of production, storage, and distribution of material goods, all of which require physical facilities and management systems. Thus, the profit model of the online game business is substantially different from other forms of e-commerce, such as e-shopping, e-auction, and e-bookstore, in which the conventional system of storage and distribution remains one of the most influential factors in their profit models.

Third, an analysis of the online game business is crucial in understanding the contemporary cultural economy in the information age. Playing multiplayer online games not only means it is a game, but it also implies that the game users socialize with other real time players in the game's virtual community. Online game users share similar socio-cultural codes and bonds, and experience a sense of belonging. Therefore, an online game company's role is often not only to create machinic algorithms, rules, and plots for a specific game, but to provide game users with a comfortable cyberspace in which they can enjoy their social associations with one another. In this sense, an analysis of the online game is instructive in investigating the cultural and economic implications of a cyber-community, in which the conventional economic binarism of producer and consumers is often blurred, contested and negotiated.

The Conditions for the Success of the Online Game Business

Broadband Internet Infrastructure

The first significant condition essential for the growth of the online game business is being associated with the development of the broadband Internet infrastructure. The Internet infrastructure is increasingly based on broadband networks that allow hundreds of thousands of Internet users to log on the server at a time and to exchange large-sized date files. While Internet games are played through executing small-sized files and exchanging small data between players, online games usually depend on executing large-sized (10~200 MB) program files and exchanging large data files among real-time players. Furthermore, the online game business requires intensive high-tech innovations for image processing and server management. For this reason, while playing an online game, a large quantity of data flows simultaneously among players, i.e., texts, images, 3D-graphics, sounds, and video clips. Further, not only is broadband a prerequisite for the success of multiplayer online games, but the online game industry itself promotes a greater market demand of broadband.

The U.S. Federal Communications Commission (FCC) defines the term "broadband" as a new generation of high-speed transmission services, which allows users to access the Internet and Internet-related services at significantly higher speeds than dial-up modems (narrowband). The FCC uses the term "advanced telecommunications capability" to describe services and facilities with upstream (customer-to-provider) and downstream (provider-to-customer) transmission speeds exceeding 200 kbps (FCC, 2000). Many professionals use the term "broadband" to describe any of various high speed, always-on Internet connections, including xDSL (x-Digital Subscriber Line), HFC (Hybrid Fiber Coaxial), FTTH/O (Fiber To The Home/Office), PAN (Power Area Network), PLC (Power Line Communication), and B-WILL (Broadband Wireless Local Loop) (Yun et al., 2001). Generally speaking, high-speed broadband refers to a high-capacity, two-way link between an end-user and an access network supplier capable of supporting real-time data rates in megabits per second (Broadband Task Force of Canada, 2002; Adamson, 2003).

Today, successful deployment of broadband Internet connections has become one of the most urgent and significant components in the development of an "information society" for many countries (U.S. Department of Commerce, 2002; Belson and Richtel, 2003). Many contemporary electronic applications require broadband to work "properly." Figure 1 from the Broadband Task Force of Canada (2002) shows the minimum and ideal speeds necessary for some of the more popular applications. The minimum bandwidth for tele-working, video-conferencing, and tele-medicine is above 100 kilobits per second, an almost impossible data-transfer speed for conventional modem users. Furthermore, such applications as movies-on-demand and digital TV require 1,000 kilobits per second for the minimum requirement and 7,000 kilobits per second for getting "suitable operation." Beyond exchanging e-mail, documents and reading e-newspapers, contemporary Internet content providers increasingly deliver a variety of forms of

Figure 1. Bandwidth requirements for selected applications

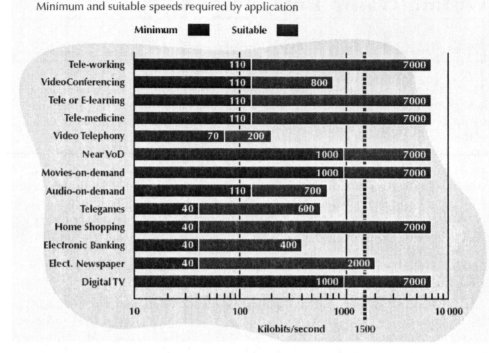

additional services, such as audio-visual data, streaming video clips, real-time Internet broadcasting, and online games (Yun et al., 2002).

According to Hausman's (2001) study of the estimation of cross-price elastics of the Internet infrastructure market, the broadband Internet market is asymmetrically and distinctly separated from the narrowband Internet market. In terms of the characteristics of data flow and traffic, the narrowband Internet connection is not complementary to the broadband Internet market. That is, the narrowband Internet connection is incompatible with data-intensive multiplayer online games.

Sense of Community

One of the most salient characteristics of the online game business is in its relatively long life cycle of more than eight years (Lee, 2001; Themis Group, 2001). *Ultima Online* is currently in its seventh year of live operations. It has more than 200,000 subscribers, and consistently adds more subscribers each year. *EverQuest* reached its second anniversary in May 2001. It had more than 410,000 subscribers as of August 2001 and also appears to be steadily growing. As a result, *EverQuest* and *Ultima Online* respectively generate more than $U.S. 4 million and $U.S. 2.75 million per month (Bartle, 2001).

One basic question remains. What is the factor that consistently makes online game players happy to spend $U.S. 15 ~ 25 each month? According to a report from the Themis Group (2001), past performance shows that there are at least two main phases in the subscriber growth for online game services: the initial "try it out" phase and the second "this is my home, come join my team" phase. Thus it is almost an axiomatic principle among online game providers that players come for the game and stay for the "community" (The Themis Group, 2001). In other words, players may be attracted to a certain genre or style of game and try it out, but ultimately they remain because they make friends and fulfill their need for social interaction within the game's framework. There are also other factors involved, such as the ongoing and persistent ownership of items and in-game property, regular new features and an evolving storyline. But the "key" element is the "social bond" that forms among game players.

In this context, the Themis Group (2001) suggests an interesting lifecycle model of online game players. The stages consist of confusion, excitement, involvement and boredom (see Figure 2). Among them, the third stage (involvement) is the longest subscription period of the player lifecycle and is closely linked with game users' strong involvement with the online game community. If a game player becomes attached to an in-game micro-community, he/she generally becomes involved in the meta-functions of the game, such as an ongoing story plot and sponsoring team events. Players who move into the involvement phase normally continue to subscribe to the game for a period of years. In sum, one of the most important success factors in the multiplayer online game business is constructing the feeling of community and belonging among online game users. In terms of the value chain, while the conventional console and PC-based games have retail-driven forms of the value chain, the multiplayer online game mostly depends on game users' subscription fees. In the online game business, consumer subscriptions generally constitute about 70~80 percent of the total revenues (The Themis Group, 2002). And, in this case, revenues are highly dependent on the extent of the game's community-oriented structuring (in cyberspace) and the game company's promotion of festivals, contests and other meetings for subscribers (in the real world). All are important in evoking a sense

Figure 2. The ideal persistent online game player lifecycle

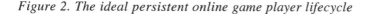
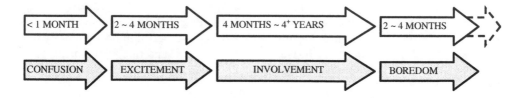

Source: The Themis Group (2001)

of cohesive belonging to a cyber-community among game players. Therefore, it is not an unusual event, for example, in South Korea, for online game users whose animated game characters married in cyberspace to "really" marry in the real world (Macintyre, 2001). Even the following case is quite pervasive throughout the country.

> *Last September Han Sang, a 14-year-old boy in Seoul, stole $35 from his parents to buy sunglasses and other accessories. The petty thievery was bad enough, but what really irked his dad was that none of the stuff he bought was real. They were for the animated character, or avatar, the boy used as a stand-in for himself on the Internet. Han was spending four hours each night hanging out online with his friends and wanted his virtual stand-in to look as cool as possible (Fulford, 2003).*

At least in the online game business, the distinction between "real" and "virtual" is drastically blurred, combined and contested. This process seems to have its own economy. In terms of Jean Baudrillard's (1983; 1988; 1998) notion of "simulation," the figuration of cyberspace as spatial simulacrum undermines the symbolic distance between the real and the imaginary. In the age of a technology-based postmodern culture, the semiotic equivalence between the signifying and the signified gives way to simulation, which is "no longer a question of imitation, nor of reduplication, nor even of parody … rather a question of substituting signs of the real for the real itself" (Baudrillard, 1983). Simulation envelops the whole edifice of representation as itself a "simulacrum," that is, an imaginary construct that has no referent in reality, but is more real than the real (i.e., hyperreal). In the Baudrillardian epistemology, the cyberspace of the Internet as a simulacrum is not a representational space of referents in reality, but it has "real" spatiality with its own geographies almost unconsciously inscribed in such spatial terms as "home" page, e-mail "address" and web "site." The real spatiality of cyberspace is especially salient and significant in the image-enhanced and user-intensive space of the online game. At the same time, we should be careful not to overestimate the relative autonomy of spatiality in the online game, not only because it cannot exist without the network of a broadband-based Internet infrastructure, the game operator, and the massive game uses in reality, but also because it is essentially inseparable from the economic geography of the online game industry. It is in this context that Baudrillard (1988; 1998) considers the notions of simulation, simulacra and hyperreality as the postindustrial (or postmodern) cultural phenomena that have resulted in drastic changes in the consumption sphere. For example, Baudrillard (1998) argues that consumers no longer purchase goods because of real needs, but because of desires that are increasingly defined by artificial images for a commercial purpose, which keep consumers one step removed from the reality of human bodies. In sum, the online game business is located at the frontier of the emerging broadband-based socioeconomic community that creates a "third" economic space in-between "cyberspace" and the "real world."

NCsoft's *Lineage: The Bloodpledge*

The online game business in South Korea has been one of the country's most consistently profitable, sustainable, and successful accomplishments in the midst of other dot.com companies' waxing and waning (IDC, 2001; Kim, 2001; Moltenbrey, 2003). The online game has become in name and reality a national sport, frequently broadcast by television stations and Internet Web sites in South Korea. A considerable number of "professional" online game players visit Seoul from Australia, Canada and the U.S. in order to win large amounts of prize money coming from online game tournaments. Compared to the world game market (see Table 1), the growth of the online game business in South Korea has significantly exceeded PC and video game markets since 2002 (see Figure 3). The arcade game market had been the largest, but the online game market has exceeded other types of game markets since 2002. Most online game companies established in the last four to seven years are small-sized firms predominantly funded from the venture-oriented capital. While employing a relatively small number of employees, these South Korean online game companies have made high net profits and experienced a high

Figure 3. Korean game business market

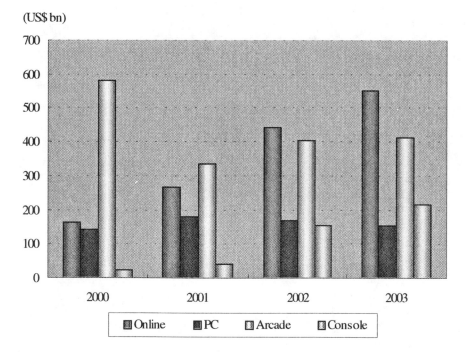

(US$ bn)

Legend: Online, PC, Arcade, Console

Source: NCsoft (2002).

growth rate in their sales. Domestic gamers account for about 80 percent of all registrations, and foreign gamers make up the remaining 20 percent. Also, major South Korean
online game businesses have been expanding their services with success in Taiwan,
Japan, Hong Kong, China and the U.S.

Among the online game companies in South Korea, NCsoft, established in 1997,
accounted for about 40 percent of the domestic online game market in 2002. It is by far
the world's largest online gaming network, with 3.2 million subscribers paying about
$U.S. 25 per month (Fulford, 2003)[3]. This company was considered one of the most
successful venture businesses in South Korea in 1998, and since has expanded into
Taiwan, Hong Kong, Japan and the U.S. The company also aggressively pursued and
acquired the prominent U.S.-based online game companies ArenaNet and Destination
Game. It also established a strategic branch, NC Austin, in Texas in 2001. NCsoft's
Lineage: the bloodpledge has been the principal propellant of the company's rapid
expansion and growth in the global online game market. Figure 4 shows that the average
ratio of operating profit amounted to over 45 percent (77,115 million Korean won, or $U.S.
65 million) of the total revenues (154 million Korean won, or about $U.S. 130 million) in
2002. Most strikingly, out of the total company's 154 million Korean won in revenues,

Figure 4. Revenues, operating profit, and net profit of NCsoft (2000-2003)

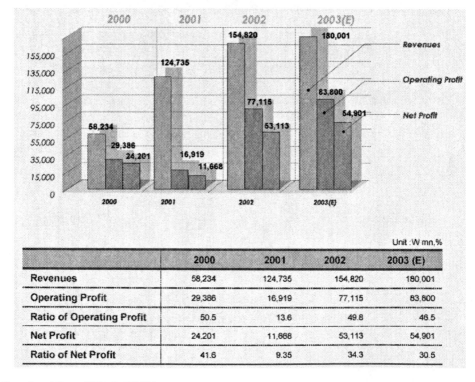

	2000	2001	2002	2003 (E)
Revenues	58,234	124,735	154,820	180,001
Operating Profit	29,386	16,919	77,115	83,800
Ratio of Operating Profit	50.5	13.6	49.8	46.5
Net Profit	24,201	11,668	53,113	54,901
Ratio of Net Profit	41.6	9.35	34.3	30.5

Reprinted from NCsoft (2002).

the cost of goods sold, which includes the Internet operation and other services, is only about 32 billion Korean won (20.8 percent). Hence, the company's total gross profit in 2002 amounted to 154 billion Korean won (79.2 percent), which is nothing short of incredible in terms of conventional Internet businesses.

NCsoft's *Lineage* is a so-called "massively multiplayer online role playing game" (MMORPG) in which more than 120,000 users simultaneously can gain access to the company's game servers and associate with other players. Set in the Middle Ages, *Lineage* is a fantasy game in which each game player chooses to be a knight, wizard, elf, or prince/princess along with other players. *Lineage* requires a high level of co-operation as armies storm castles, platoons need to be organized, and charges planned and executed in cooperation with other players. *Lineage* operates via multiple remote computer servers in which users in different places can constantly meet new counterparts literally around the world who are accessed via the Internet. Most importantly, *Lineage* features over 50 different cyber worlds, and each of them is so large that it takes over six hours for an animated character just to walk from one end to the other. The cyberspace in *Lineage* is not a metaphor but a reality. In this way, according to Taek-Jin Kim, the chief executive officer of NCsoft, "the game has evolved into a new society in the virtual world" (Macintyre, 2001).

Growth of the Internet Sector in South Korea

The necessary condition for the online game business, as noted above, is a broadband infrastructure and Internet environment favorable to dot.com companies. Either fortunately or strategically, NCsoft's *Lineage* was first launched in 1997 when the South Korean government vigorously began following the Asian financial crisis to seek new ways to implement successful economic restructuring projects. These projects include radical rationalization of labor-intensive industries, deregulation of governmental economic policies, decentralization of large conglomerates, and strategic facilitation of high-tech venture businesses (Kim, 2000; Shin, Chang and Belsey, 2002). Although South Korea is still struggling with considerable economic problems such as continuous stagnation and high rates of joblessness, neoliberal governmental policies and institutions in the restructuring process have strongly promoted the country's economic constitution into a more flexible, liberalized and knowledge-based structure (*The Economist*, 1998; Kim, 2000; Bremner and Moon, 2002; Shin, Chang and Belsey, 2002).

Of all these economic transformations and initiatives, one of the most striking successes is South Korea's rapid achievement and its pioneering position as one of the most wired (and wirelessly-wired) countries in the world, all the direct result of its elaborate Internet and telecommunications infrastructure. It thus comes as no surprise to witness the miraculous success of NCsoft's *Lineage* to the South Korean digital economy. According to the Korean Network Information Center (2003), South Korea in 2002 had 25.6 million Internet subscribers, equivalent to 58 percent of the country's total population. Among these subscribers, 10.2 million have broadband Internet connections with 54 percent having xDSLs (x-Digital Subscriber Lines) and another 34 percent high-speed cable modems. Thus, South Korea had the world-highest 20.8 broadband Internet penetration per 100 inhabitants (OECD, 2002)[4]. Furthermore, at least 80 foreign companies have set up research sites in Korea to tap into this gigantic broadband laboratory (Fulford, 2003)[5]. South Korea is one of the most electronically wired countries on the planet, with cheap broadband access available almost everywhere (Lee and Choudrie, 2002; *Internet Magazine*, 2003). In truth, South Korea is now "the powerhouse in broadband and wireless Internet markets" (Rao, 2001), "the bandwidth capital of the world" (Herz, 2002), and "tech's test market: a hotbed for anything new that's digital or online" (Moon and Stone, 2003).

In a broad sense, NCsoft's success should be contextualized within the "national innovation system" (NIS) (Nelson, 1993; Lundvall, 1992; Wijnberg, 1994; Leinbach and Brunn, 2002). National laws, policies and institutions in conjunction play a major role not only in the construction of the broadband Internet infrastructure, but also in promoting domestic capital to invest in small-size and high-tech intensive venture businesses such as NCsoft. In this sense, the South Korean government is considered one of the most interventionist and aggressive in the world in superseding the narrowband market with broadband Internet networks (Rao, 2001; Herz, 2002). Since the mid-1990s, the South Korean government has implemented a series of three master plans for the development of information and telecommunication industries. First, in August 1995, the South Korean government enacted the Framework Act on Informatization Promotion, established the first Master Plan for Informatization Promotion in June, 1996, and established a national organization for planning and implementation of the goals outlined in the Master Plan. The plan presented ten key projects for the realization of an "advanced information society" by the year 2010 (MIC, 2002). Second, in March 1999, the government established "Cyber Korea 21 Project" as the more concretized blueprint for the new information society of the 21st century. The project has become one of the highest priorities among principal structural adjustment programs since the 1997 financial crisis. Through these plans, the government brought South Korea closer to the realization of the information society with the construction of an advanced information infrastructure. More recently, the government launched its third master plan called "E-Korea Vision 2006," which was implemented primarily to cope with four current issues: (1) slow spread of informatization in the public sector, (2) low IT investment in the SMEs (i.e., small-and-medium enterprises), (3) the adverse effects of information and communication technologies such as computer viruses, hacking problems and privacy infringement, and (4) insufficient investment in the R&D sector of advanced information and telecommunication technologies. Especially, in regard to the broadband Internet infrastructure, its policy objective is to have broadband connections of 155 megabytes to five gigabytes available nationally by 2005 (MIC, 2002; 2003). South Korea has also made direct investments of $U.S. 600 million to promote its digital contents industry, and is scheduled to add an additional $U.S. 30 billion into its broadband infrastructure by 2010. These are the results of a combination of government and private investments along with the strong cooperation with the R&D sector such as universities and research institutes (Adamson, 2003; MIC, 2003). As a result, xDSLs and cable modems provide service to 94.7 percent of all Internet connection subscribers in 2003 compared to only 3.3 percent using dial-up modem (see Figure 5).

Figure 5. Internet infrastructure in South Korea

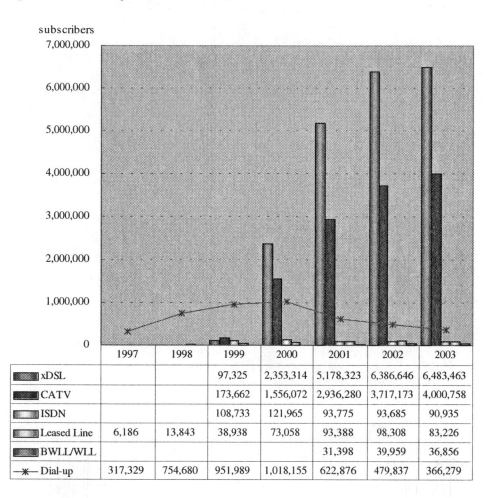

	1997	1998	1999	2000	2001	2002	2003
xDSL			97,325	2,353,314	5,178,323	6,386,646	6,483,463
CATV			173,662	1,556,072	2,936,280	3,717,173	4,000,758
ISDN			108,733	121,965	93,775	93,685	90,935
Leased Line	6,186	13,843	38,938	73,058	93,388	98,308	83,226
BWLL/WLL					31,398	39,959	36,856
—*— Dial-up	317,329	754,680	951,989	1,018,155	622,876	479,837	366,279

An examination of the sales breakdown of NCsoft's *Lineage* (see Figure 6) reveals more about the broadband-based economy of the online game business. While narrowband-based sales are minimal, broadband-based PC-cafes and households account for the most of the company's total sales. From 1998 ~ 2000, PC-cafés in particular were the most important source of NCsoft's revenues[6]. They were mostly privately run facilities that provide super-speed Internet access to those households not equipped with xDSLs and cable modems. In 2002 the number of PC-cafés in South Korea was about 24,000, ubiquitous on almost every street corner in built-up areas and nearby commercial buildings (KNIC, 2003; MIC, 2003). The PC-café is not just a place for Internet access, but also a convenient place for meeting friends and socializing with other online game users. For this reason, despite the rapid growth of the home broadband market, PC-cafés still remain important cultural and social places for Internet users (Lee and Chourdrie, 2002). Finally, as NCsoft began to expand its services for Internet users overseas, the

Figure 6. Sales breakdown of NCsoft's Lineage: The Bloodpledge

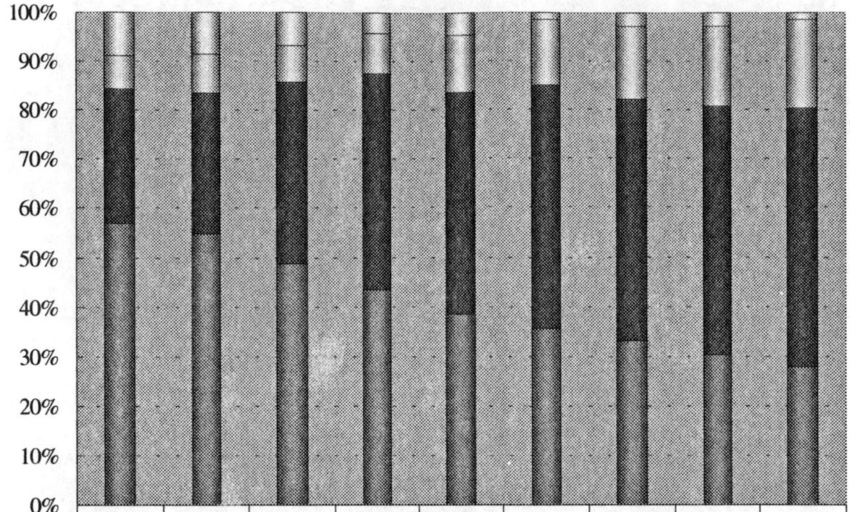

	1Q_01	2Q_01	3Q_01	4Q_01	1Q_02	2Q_02	3Q_02	4Q_02	1Q_03
Narrow-Band	2,209	2,221	2,222	1,682	1,923	568	1,160	1,038	582
Royalty	1,615	2,046	2,608	3,056	4,906	4,833	5,821	6,302	6,746
Personal	6,767	7,405	12,311	17,075	18,602	17,685	19,243	19,195	19,711
PC Café	14,004	14,235	16,409	16,681	15,970	12,845	13,065	11,450	10,447

Source: NCsoft (2003). (Unit: million Korean won)

royalty from foreign countries (especially from Taiwan) increased rapidly, amounting to $U.S. 5.5 million in the first quarter of 2003 (NCsoft, 2003).

Cybercommunity: Social and Cultural Dimensions of the Online Game

A Web-crazed country: Earlier this year, Internet gaming company NCsoft found it had some unwelcome visitors. The Seoul company is the creator of *Lineage*, an online fantasy game in which players do battle in a medieval cyberworld with swords and shields and magical rings that change their identities. Players can swap weapons or buy and sell them using the game's cybermoney. So popular is *Lineage* - and so competitive its fans - that players started buying and selling weapons with real money instead of cyberbucks. (Rings were reportedly going for as much as $300 each.) NCsoft didn't like that practice, and barred two offending players from the game. Soon after, the banned players barged into NCsoft's office and demanded to be allowed back online. The company had to call the police. That's how it is today in South Korea—the Internet seems to have made the whole nation a little crazy (Macintyre, 2001).

What was happening to these two players? What was their desire to purchase rings (or the screen image of the rings composed of digital signals) in the cyberworld for real money? Were game players so crazily intoxicated with the NCsoft's online game that they could not recognize their social positions in-between the cyberspace and the real world? Or is this a coincidence happening in South Korea, where about one-third of the country's 48 million people are logging onto the Internet on a daily basis, one-third are using wireless Internet service on the street, and more than one-half are at home using the Internet through super-speed broadband connection?

In regard to cyberspace as a social space of the Internet, one of the contemporary questions in social sciences has been, "How could the cyberspace of the Internet impact individual users and overall society?" An interesting answer from Poster (1996, 206) is that, "There can be only *one* answer and that is that it is the wrong question." Human beings are usually understood to manipulate the materials for ends that they impose upon the technology from a "pre-constituted" position of subjectivity. But, Poster argues that the problematic aspect of cyberspace would be meaningless without considering the subjectivity of the Internet user, who produces and transforms cyberspace as much as she or he is transformed by cyberspace.

The significance of Poster's argument is strongly embedded in the massively multiplayer online game (MMOG), in which a large number of game players get together, not only because of the game plot's own merit, but because of its external social effects on the game users' socializing with other people, belonging to the game community, and feeling free from the complicated real world. In this vein, online game players are not necessarily users, consumers, or customers. Rather, they are creative producers and consistent maintainers of the contents of the online game. As discussed above, almost all of the online game developers strongly believe that one of the most crucial axioms in the successful online game business is that players come for the game and stay for the "community." The key element of the online game business is to construct "social bonds" among game players in cyberspace.

NCsoft's *Lineage* is noted for its exquisite image-processing graphic technology, through which 3D graphics of animated game characters, land, buildings, and other objects in the game are projected into the two-dimensional digital space on the computer screen. In terms of game players, this spatial representational technology is highly conducive to the production of a "third" spatiality in-between cyberspace and the real world. Here the creation of spatial simulacra accompanies the simultaneous epistemo-logical process of domestication and foreignization of social space. These image-process skills are used for the procession of simulation, which Baudrillard (1983) defines as the image having four successive phases: (1) it is the reflection of a basic reality; (2) it masks and perverts a basic reality; (3) it masks the absence of a basic reality; and (4) it bears no relation to any reality whatsoever, that is, it is its own pure simulacrum. First, *Lineage* contains a variety of simulated images that reflect the basic geographies of reality, including not only large-scaled entities such as mountains, lakes, islands and buildings, but also small-scaled materials such as trees, humans, and even more specific and smaller items. The game's simulation is not based on its high fidelity to basic reality, but rather it appropriates the representational freedom inherent in its digital representation for generating a fantasy and attractive cyber-spatiality in which a medieval knight, monsters, pizza, and candy coexist in a cyberspace beyond the restriction of time and space, or beyond the real and the imaginary. The simulation in *Lineage* both reflects and perverts basic realities. It generates the simultaneity of the unsimultaneous in cyberspace. Therefore, game users commonly share a sense of in-betweenness of the real and the simulated through their audio-visual experience in cyberspace. In this sense, Baudrillard (1988) notes how easily an experience of a series of simulated images can produce a sense of an actual and real experience (see also Nunes, 1995). A *Lineage* player in the U.S. describes her spatial in-betweenness (reality vs. freedom) as follows:

> Recently, I have found something new to share my spare time with, but it wasn't just a "game." It was more like living a "life" in a fantasy world. ... What makes it special is the *realism* such as the reality of actually taking the ferry to the mainland. After leveling up only by killing a lot of orcs and werewolves, I was ready to leave the Talking Island. The first time I left, it gave me a sense of leaving an island like Alcatraz and stepping into a land of freedom and mystique. The land of freedom was a feeling of accomplishment and desire, just like the feeling of the early immigrants to the United States...*Lineage* is more than a game, most importantly, it is the *freedom* that gives this game its specialty. ... It is a real fantasy world and it is this that makes me keep on playing this game, and it is all of us, that makes this unique world a reality in *Lineage* (Player stories from the *Lineage*'s community site, n.d., emphasis added).

The structure of virtual time and space in *Lineage* plays the more significant role in producing a certain sense of "real" community in cyberspace, considerably detached from the real world. In *Lineage*, the actual length of a day is four hours: two hours are daytime and the other two are night. Usually it takes over 22~24 hours, equivalent to almost six days in *Lineage*, for an animated character to walk from one end to the other of each cyberworld in *Lineage*. Because *Lineage* contains 50 simulated cyberworlds, it takes about 1,100~1,200 real-time hours or about 48~50 full real days, equivalent to 288~300 virtual days in *Lineage*, just to travel around the total space in *Lineage*. Thus the time-space compression in cyberspace provides a common spatial and temporal experience among the game players. The cyberspace in *Lineage* is pure simulacrum with its spatiality, for example, when a player states, "A life wouldn't be real if nobody slept or ate, and definitely I had limits on playing this 'life' just like everyone else. I would sleep when the Lineage world was dark and would wake up when dawn arrives" (Player stories from the Lineage's community site, n.d.).

The simulation of the human body in *Lineage* is also important in evoking a sense of community and generating desires for socialization in cyberspace. The game represents not only specific physical characteristics of human body such as hair, muscle, and skin color, but it also visualizes invisible human attributes such as physical ability, resistance to dangers, items for the body, the experience and disposition of hunger, as all these are translated into quantitative values. The physical features of the game character are divided and quantified into six categories that include strength, dexterity, intelligence, wisdom, constitution and charisma. Also, the social disposition of game characters is visually represented. The bodies of game characters are categorized into three colors, each of which representing an ethical value as lawful, neutral or chaotic. These character statistics have a great influence on the progression of the game because they are critical values that define specialized classes (e.g., knight, wizard, prince/princess, and elf) who have different abilities in the game plot. Each player must choose a specific class to belong to and consequently socialize and cooperate with other class-based game players. In other words, while the quantitative simulation of human body enables users to differentiate themselves from other users in *Lineage*, they are structurally and ultimately destined to work together to attain game goals, develop the ability of their game character, and, most of all, to survive the social life in cyberspace. A game character actually requires sleeping, eating and exercise in *Lineage*, just as he or she does in reality.

NCsoft's *Lineage* has another distinctive structure in that game users must construct their own community in order to accomplish specific goals. Figure 7 is a typical screenshot of *Lineage*, in which each animated game character represents an individual game user. The community in *Lineage* is called "bloodpledge" and is composed of about 5~100 game users who can communicate in a private mode and cannot harm one another. They must cooperate in order to defend themselves from other bloodpledges' attacks and to accomplish given goals. In South Korea, there were about 1.2 million cumulative registered communities in mid-2003, of which about 10,000 active game communities have their own homepages on the Web and meet regularly in PC-cafés, pubs and restaurants in the "real" world. Again, the conventional dualism of cyberspace and real world is

Figure 7. NCsoft's Lineage: A leading massively multiplayer on-line role playing game (MMORPG)

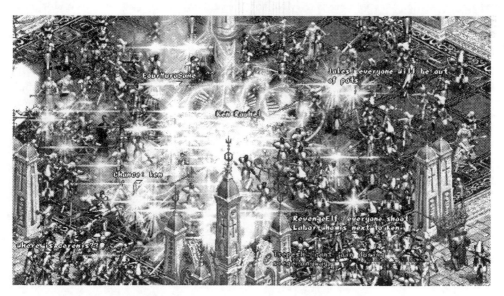

practically blurred and associated. The following game player's story describes *Lineage*'s community-oriented third spatiality:

> I joined a small pledge early on and enjoyed sharing my items with them; we became a family. … My pledge and I would go to the mainland cave, or Dragon Valley, and "work" there. We got a room in the hotel when we were tired and fearlessly went back out to work again. … It was all about teamwork. … Before dusk, many of us would leave for town to enjoy some beers at the bar. However, some of my fellow pledgemates would gamble money on slime races only to lose it all. They would grieve to me how they lost their money, and I would grieve that our king from Kent Castle raised the taxes again. It was a typical life, after gaining some levels we would be back in town talking about our Lineage life, and *most importantly our real lives also*. … Meeting new people from all over the world and gathering together to play this "life" is what makes Lineage so special (Player stories from the *Lineage*'s community site, n.d., emphasis added).

As a part of its marketing strategy, NCsoft periodically holds game tournaments in South Korea and Taiwan with a large amount of prize money for participants and winners. It also sponsors game users' group travel, festivals and other social events. Along with NCsoft's strategy to aggressively promote social bonds among game users, the company also operates multiple servers and frequently updates the game's episodes. In March 2003, NCsoft operated 41 servers in South Korea and 33 servers in Taiwan. And, since *Lineage*'s launching in 1997, NCsoft have released 12 different game plots. Except for the servers used for testing and program-downloading, most of the servers have different episodes, spaces, events and communities so that the company could minimize game users' boredom and maximize their desire to socialize with new people in this "third" space.

However, *Lineage* is not necessarily NCsoft's exclusive, finished and closed world that is produced to exist in the cyberspace. For example, NCsoft invited more than 600 game players and held several public conferences in major six metropolises of South Korea in 2003. Principal topics in the conferences included *Lineage*'s system problems (i.e., networking speed), modification of animated game characters, plotting of the follow-up game episodes, development of *Lineage*'s cyber-communities, etc. Based on these feedback discussions with its customers, *Lineage* is becoming a third socio-economic space that constantly evolves in-between real world and imagined space, and also in-between producer and customer.

Conclusions

Discussions of the Internet as a GPT and a conventional form of technological innovation often conceptualize the new information age as a modified replication of the telegraph era or the telephone age. For example, Button and Taylor (2001) argue that "the new technology has features common to many other network activities, albeit with a few idiosyncrasies of its own, and by and large its role in society can be explained in traditional economic theories, or at least by rather minor variations to that theory." However, aside from the Internet's substantial impacts on conventional transaction costs, financial and labor markets, overall economic productivity and efficiency, etc., the "discontinuous" significance of the digital economy such as the online game business lies in: (1) its heavy dependence on the Internet users' convenient and inexpensive accessibility to the broadband Internet infrastructure, (2) its dispensability with the conventional system of material production, storage and distribution systems, and (3) its principal concern with the creation of social spaces in which game users can comfortably enjoy not only the game itself but also their social association with one another. In this sense, truly, the Internet is arguably "a newly developed *space* with the power to give rise to novel forms of human social interaction in almost any area of human endeavor, commercial or otherwise" (Kenney and Curry, 2001, emphasis added).

In this chapter, I found out that the rapid success and consistent growth of NCsoft's *Lineage* is indebted to two principal factors. The first is the South Korean national innovation systems (NISs) in the Internet broadband infrastructure sector. Especially since the 1997 financial crisis, the South Korean government has implemented massive national projects to construct nation-wide, high-speed, cheap Internet networks in order to boost its knowledge-based and techno-intensive national economy. In this sense, about 24,000 broadband-based Internet-cafés on every street corner in built-up areas played a crucial role in the success of the online game business, not only because they provided convenient and high-quality Internet service along with low price, but also because Internet-cafés were pivotal "off-line" places of the online game users' communities. The second crucial factor is the game company's technology-intensive, elaborate efforts at constructing the cyberspace of *Lineage* as a social space in-between the real and the imaginary. *Lineage* is a simulacrum consisting of not only hyper-real images of basic realities, but also its own spatial and temporal scale. It is a distinct social space in which game users share common time-space compressed experiences and socialize with other game users in order to survive the "society" of *Lineage* in cyberspace. However, at the same time, I suggested that we should not overestimate the relative autonomy of the spatiality embedded in the online game, not only because it is primarily based on the physical network of the broadband-based, Internet infrastructure, but also because it is essentially and directly meets NCsoft's economic purpose. In this sense, in order to reinforce game users' community activities in cyberspace and embed them in the off-line real world, NCsoft has invested a significant amount of money in promoting festivals, game tournaments, public conferences, and other off-line social events for the game user communities.

In this chapter, I have conceptualized such a socio-cultural economy of the Internet business as the economy of a "third space" or "in-between space." Although the digital economy could not be completely separate from convention economic principles, I argue that it has emerging forms of new economic space not only in-between the real space and the virtual space, but also between the production and the consumption of what is produced. And, as we have seen the case of NCsoft *Lineage*, the third space is not just social but also economic space with the game users' "real" consumption of simulacra (e.g., avatar game characters and items in *Lineage*) and its spread effects on other economic sectors in the off-line world. In this sense, the emergence of the digital economy containing certain forms of new economic space would give rise to fertile economic environment in which many businesses especially such as e-business could explore new economic opportunities. This perspective requires us to explore the new "spatiality" of a digital economy. The task does not necessarily connote the economic geography of distance and location, which explores the geographical dimensions of digital economy, such as different production (and distribution) systems, organizational networks, differential transaction costs, and geographical agglomerations. Rather, it behooves us to have a flexible (and possibly multiple) "epistemological" sensibility to understand the complicated entanglement of a digital economy with social and cultural spheres. In this sense, further studies of digital economies, especially in relation to the digital contents industry, such as the online game, should develop analytic frameworks to understand the "third spatial economies" emerging in-between online and off-line. These studies could include the synergetic socioeconomic relations of digital contents in-between providers and customers, the flexible profit models based on this relation, the potential and distinct separateness of the cyber-market generated by the broadband-based Internet infrastructure, the economic implications of the Internet users' active social behaviors, and the specific socio-cultural contexts in which they are embedded.

Acknowledgments

I thank Dr. Kehal for his kind invitation to contribution to this book. I also want to thank the anonymous reviewer, who provided me with a supportive critique and insightful comments to improve this chapter. Most of all, I acknowledge that this chapter would have been impossible without the great support from Dr. Stanley Brunn, who reviewed several drafts and offered several constructive suggestions. Of course, I am completely responsible for all possible errors and limits of this chapter.

Endnotes

[1]   The game's record for the highest number of simultaneous players is 140,000, including 100,000 in Korea and 40,000 in Taiwan. Jung-Hwan Kim, the global relations manager for NCsoft, states that they estimate the cost of their network downtime at $U.S. 400,000 per hour.

[2]   In mid-2003, NCsoft's stock price sold for $132 U.S. a share, which is the highest price for any component in South Korea's digital economic sector.

[3]   NCsoft has the potential to surpass both Microsoft's *Xbox Live* and Sony's *broadband PlayStation networks* in the race to dominate online gaming (Fulford, 2003).

4   Canada is next with about 11 broadband Internet connections per 100 inhabitants. The other runner-up countries are far behind South Korea with fewer than 10 Internet connections per 100 inhabitants (OECD, 2002).

5   Even though Microsoft generates only $200 million in yearly revenue from Korea, it has recently invested $500 million in Korea Telecom, in part to test plans for ubiquitous computing (Fulford, 2003).

6   NCsoft relied on PC-cafés for about 80 percent of its total revenues in 1997 (Lee and Choudrie, 2002).

References

Adams, P. (1997). Cyberspace and virtual places. *Geographical Review*, 87(2), 155-171.

Adams, P. (1998). Network topologies and virtual place. *Annals of the Association of American Geographers*, 88(1), 88-106.

Adamson, W. (2003). How Korea built the broadband that America wanted. *Digital Investor Pty Ltd*. Retrieved June 24, 2003 from the World Wide Web: http://www.digitalinvestor.com.

Aghion, P., and Howitt, P. (1992). A model of growth through creative destruction. *Econometrica*, 60, 323-351.

Bajaj, V. (2002). High-speed connections common in South Korea. *The Seattle Times, October 21*.

Bartle, R. (2001). A wish list for massively multiplayer games. The Themis Group. Retrieved June 24, 2003 from the World Wide Web: http://www.themis-group.com/uploads.

Baudrillard, J. (1983). *Simulations*. New York: Semiotext(e).

Baudrillard, J. (1988). *The Ecstasy of Communication*. New York: Semiotext(e).

Baudrillard, J. (1998). *The Consumer Society: Myths and Structures*. London: Sage.

Belson, K. and Richtel, M. (2003). America's broadband dream is alive in South Korea. *The New York Times, May 5*.

Bremner, B. & Moon. I. (2002). Cool Korea: how it roared back from disaster and became a model for Asia. *Business Week, June 10*.

Bresnahan, T. and Trajtenberg, M. (1995). General purpose technologies: "engines of growth." *Journal of Econometrics*, 65, 83-108.

Brunn, S. and Cottle, C. (1997). Small states and cyberboosterism. *Geographical Review*, 87(2), 240-258.

Brunn, S. and Leinbach, T. (Eds.). (1991). *Collapsing space and time: geographic aspects of communications and information*. London: Harper Collins Academic.

The business case for community management. (2002). The Themis Group. Retrieved June 22, 2003 from the World Wide Web: http://themis-group.com/whitepapers. phtml.

Button, K. and Taylor, S. (2001). Towards an economics of the Internet and e-commerce. In T. Leinbach & S. Brunn (Eds.), *Worlds of e-commerce: economic, geographical and social dimensions*. Chichester: Wiley and Sons.

Castells, M. (1996). *The rise of the network society*. Oxford: Blackwell.

Costikyan, G. (1998). Online gaming's store-shelf chains. Retrieved June 26, 2003 from the World Wide Web: http://www.salon.com/tech/feature/1999/04/21/battlenet/ index.html.

Costikyan, G. (2000). The future of online games. The Themis Group. Retrieved June 26, 2003 from the World Wide Web: http://www.themis-group.com/uploads/ ogrfinal.doc.

Crang, M. (2000). Public space, urban space and electronic space: would the real city please stand up? *Urban Studies, 37*(2), 301-317.

Crang, M., Crang, P. and May, J. (Eds.). (1999). *Virtual geographies: bodies, space and relations*. London: Routledge.

Dodge, M. and Kitchin, R. (2000). *Mapping cyberspace*. London: Routledge.

Fulford, B. (2003, July). Korea's weird wired world: strange things happen when an entire country is hooked on high-speed Internet. *Forbes*. Retrieved July 21, 2003 from the World Wide Web: http://www.forbes.com/forbes/2003/0721/092.html.

Graham, S. (1994). Networking cities: telematics in urban policy – A critical review. *International Journal of Urban and Regional Research, 18*(3), 416-432.

Graham, S. (1997). Cities in the real-time age. *Environment and Planning A, 29*(1), 105-127.

Graham, S. and Marvin, S. (1996). *Telecommunications and the city: electronic spaces, urban places*. London and New York: Routledge.

Graham, S. and Marvin, S. (2001). *Splintering urbanism: networked infrastructures, technological mobilities and the urban condition*. London and New York: Routledge.

Grossman, G.M. and Helpman, E. (1991). *Innovation and growth in the global economy*. Cambridge: MIT Press.

Hausman, J. (2001). Asymmetrical regulation and DSL: the demise of the broadband CLECs. *Proceedings of The Broadband Economy: The Emerging Market Systems in Bandwidth*. New York: Columbia University.

Helpman, E. (1998). Introduction. In E. Helpman (Ed.), *General purpose technologies and economic growth*. Cambridge, MA: MIT Press.

Hepworth, M. (1990). *Geography of the information economy*. New York and London: Guilford Press.

Herz, J.C. (2002). The bandwidth capital of the world. *Wired Magazine, 10*(8). Retrieved May 5, 2003 from the World Wide Web: http://www.wired.com/wired/archive/ 10.08/korea.html.

IDC. (2001, December). *Online gaming-anytime, anywhere: U.S. forecast and analysis, 2000~2005.*

Kenney, M. and Curry, J. (2001). Beyond transaction costs: e-commerce and the power of the Internet database. In T. Leinbach & S. Brunn (Eds.), *Worlds of e-commerce: economic, geographical and social dimensions.* Chichester: Wiley and Sons.

Kim, J.H. (2001). The transition of business model in the evolution of on-line game. *Korea Information Society Development Institute (KISDI) IT focus*, 10. Retrieved May 13, 2003 from the World Wide Web: http://www.kisdi.re.kr.

Kim, T. J. (2001, July). President of on-line game company NCsoft. *Business Week*, July 2, 3739, 32A28.

Kim, Y.G. (2000). The new South: after two years of reform and restructuring, South Korea has pulled through its worst economic crisis. *World and I, 15*(6), 44.

Kitchin, R. (1998). *Cyberspace: the world in the wires.* Chichester: John Wiley.

Korea Information Society Development Institute (KISDI). (2002). *IT Industry outlook of Korea 2002.* Retrieved May 15, 2003 from the World Wide Web: http://www.kisdi.re.kr.

Korean Network Information Center (KNIC). (2003). *2002 Korean statistical Internet yearbook.* Seoul. Retrieved May 15, 2003 from the World Wide Web: http://isis.nic.or.kr.

Langdale, J. (1989). The geography of international business telecommunications: the role of leased networks. *Annals of the Association of American Geographers, 79*(4), 501-522.

Lee, H. and Choudrie, J. (2002). *Investigating broadband deployment in South Korea: broadband mission to South Korea.* London: DTI and Brunel University. Retrieved June 5, 2003 from the World Wide Web: http://www.broadbanduk.org/reports/SKorea_report.pdf.

Lee, H.K. (2001). Present condition of on-line game in South Korea, and its potential problems. *Information and Communication Policy, 13*(5), 20-37.

Leinbach, T. and Brunn, S. (Eds.). (2001). *Worlds of e-commerce: economic, geographical and social dimensions.* New York: Wiley.

Leinbach, T. and Brunn, S. (2002). National Innovation system, firm strategy, and enabling mobile communications: the case of Nokia. *Tijdschrift voor Economische en Sociale Geografie: Journal of Economic and Social Geography, 93*(5), 489-508.

Liebowitz, S. (2002). *Rethinking the network economy: the true forces that drive the digital marketplace.* New York: Amacom.

Lundvall, B.A. (Ed.). (1992). *National systems of innovation: towards a theory of innovation and interactive learning.* London: Pinter.

Macintyre, D. (2001, January). South Korea wires up: overnight, the country has gone overboard for the Internet, kicking off a cultural revolution. *Time, 157*(3).

Malecki, E. (2002). The economic geography of the Internet's infrastructure. *Economic Geography, 78*(4), 399-424.

McKweon, P. (2002). *Information technology and the networked economy*. Orlando, FL: Harcourt College.

Ministry of Information and Communication Republic of Korea. (MIC). (2002). *E-Korea vision 2006: The Third Master Plan for Informatization Promotion*, Seoul. Retrieved June 5, 2003 from the World Wide Web: http://www.mic.go.kr/eng/res/res_pub_db/res_pub_sep_ekv/ekorea_vision.zip.

Ministry of Information and Communication Republic of Korea (MIC). (2003). *Toward a knowledge/information-strong country in the 21ˢᵗ century: Accomplishments and future tasks in the governmental policies for the IT industry in South Korea*. Retrieved June 2, 2003 from the World Wide Web: http://www.mic.go.kr.

Mitchell, W.J. (1995). *City of bits: Space, place, and the Infobahn*. Cambridge, MA: MIT Press.

Moltenbrey, K. (2002). Gaming for the masses: Part 1: Massively multiplayer games are positioned to invade the mainstream market. *Computer Graphics World*, 25(3), 12-17.

Moon, I. and Stone, A. (2003). Special report: emerging tech markets - South Korea: tech's test market. *Business Week, March 4*.

Moss, M. (1987). Telecommunications, world cities, and urban policy. *Urban Studies*, 24, 534-546.

National Broadband Task Force of Canada. (2002). *The new national dream: networking the nation for broadband access*. Report of National Broadband Task Force.

NCsoft. (2003). *IR Report*, Retrieved February 21, 2003 from the World Wide Web: http://www.ncsoft.net/eng.

Nelson, R. (Ed.). (1993). *National Innovation Systems: A Comparative Synthesis*. Oxford: Oxford University Press.

Nunes, M. (1995). Baudrillard in Cyberspace: Internet, virtuality, and postmodernity. *Style*, 29, 314-327.

O'Lear, S. (1997). Electronic communication and environmental policy in Russia. *Geographical Review*, 87(2), 275-290.

OECD. (2002). *Broadband access in OECD countries per 100 inhabitants, September 2002*. Retrieved April 4, 2003 from the World Wide Web: http://www.oecd.org/EN/document/0,,EN-document-13-nodirectorate-no-1-39262-13,00.html.

OECD. (2003). *Share of ICT-producing activities in the non-agriculture business sector*. Retrieved June 19, 2003 from the World Wide Web: http://www.oecd.org/xls/M00035000/M00035780.xls.

Player stories from the *Lineage*'s community site. (n.d.). Retrieved March 10, 2002 from the World Wide Web: http://www.lineage.com/community/particle15.html.

Poster, M. (1996). Cyberdemocracy: Internet and the public sphere, In D. Porter (Ed.), *Internet culture*. New York: Routledge.

Power up! What can the Korean experience of broadband tell us about the future of high speed Internet access in the UK? (2003). *Internet Magazine*. Retrieved June 5, 2003 from the World Wide Web: http://www.internet-magazine.com/features/korea.asp.

Rao, M. (2001). South Korea emerges as powerhouse in broadband and wireless Internet markets. *Technopreneurial.com*. Retrieved June 23, 2003 from the World Wide Web: http://www.technopreneurial.com/articles/madan/national_it_strategies.asp.

Rheingold, H. (1993). *The virtual community: homesteading on the electronic frontier*. Reading, MA: Addison-Wesley.

Romer, P.M. (1990). Endogenous technological change. *Journal of Political Economy*, 98, S71-S102.

Shields, R. (Ed.). (1996). *Cultures of Internet: virtual spaces, real histories, living bodies*. London: Sage.

Shin, J.S., Chang, H.J. and Belsey, K. (2002). *Restructuring 'Korea Inc.': financial crisis, corporate reform, and institutional transition*. London and New York: Routledge.

Subscriber growth in on-line games. (2001) *Consulting services brochure from the Themis Group*. Retrieved June 24, 2003 from the World Wide Web: http://themis-group.com/whitepapers.phtml.

Think small: South Korea plans aid to small and medium-sized firms. (1998). *The Economist*, November 14, 68.

U.S. Department of Commerce. (2002). *A nation online: how Americans are expanding their use of the Internet*. The Economics and Statistics Administration, National Telecommunications and Information Administration, USA.

The U.S. Federal Communications Commission (FCC). (2000). *Deployment of advanced telecommunications capability: Second report*.

Warf, B. (2001). Segueways into cyberspace: multiple geographies of the digital divide. *Environment and Planning B: Planning and Design*, 28(1), 3-19.

Warf, B. and Grimes, J. (1997). Counterhegemoic discourses and the Internet. *Geographical Review*, 87(2), 259-274.

Wijnberg, N.M. (1994). National systems of innovation: selection environments and selection processes. *Technology in Society*, 16, 313-320.

Wired for life: overnight, South Korea has become one of the world's most connected countries - and Koreans are doing just about everything on the Internet. (2000, December). *Time*, 156 (23), B10.

Yun, C.H., Lee, K.H., Kwon, N.H., Oh, J.S. and Yoo, S.S. (2001). The characteristics of super-speed Internet service market, and its future trend. Working Paper of the Korea Information Society Development Institute (KISDI), 01-21.

Yun, K., Lee H. and Lim, S. (2002). The growth of broadband Internet connections in South Korea: contributing factors. *Working paper in Asia/Pacific Research Center*, Stanford University. Retrieved May 16, 2003 from the World Wide Web: http://www.kiet.re.kr/files/econo/20021014-grow.pdf.

Zook, M. (2000). The web of production: the economic geography of commercial Internet content production in the United States. *Environment and Planning A*, *32*(3), 411-426.

Zook, M. (2002). Hubs, nodes and bypassed places: a typology of e-commerce regions in the United States. *Tijdschrift voor Economische en Sociale Geografie: Journal of Economic and Social Geography*, *93*(5), 509-521.

Chapter XVI

Opportunities and Challenges of the New Economy for East Asia

Donghyun Park
Nanyang Technological University, Singapore

Abstract

The IT revolution has sharply reduced the cost of information and increased its availability. This revolution is also said to be creating a New Economy in which the old rules of economics no longer apply. The first part of my paper discusses the economic impact of the New Economy on East Asia. First, we discuss the potential economic benefits of the New Economy for the region. We argue that East Asian countries should focus on applying existing technology to local needs, since doing so promises large tangible returns, especially in terms of improving the efficiency of the manufacturing sector, the main engine of the region's economies. In the long run, the IT revolution will also raise the quality of corporate governance in the region. Second, we point out that while the IT revolution may enable East Asian countries to leapfrog some technological barriers, it does not enable them to leapfrog sound economic policies. Such policies remain as relevant to good economic performance in the New Economy as they did in the Old Economy. Furthermore, the potential of IT to accelerate growth and reduce poverty will be largely unfulfilled in the absence of complementary investments such as a sound infrastructure for transportation and logistics. Third, East Asian countries must fulfill certain pre-conditions to make sure that the New Economy takes hold.

Above all, they must liberalize their telecommunication sectors so as to improve the quantity and quality of telecom services. They should also make the necessary investments in human resource development to maximize their returns from the IT revolution. In short, although the New Economy holds out tremendous economic potential for East Asia, realizing that promise will require a lot of determination and hard work. The second part of this chapter deals with the implications of the IT revolution for regional development. Most of the main points raised in the first part of this chapter apply to the second part and in this sense, the second part is essentially an application of the first part, which addressed the broader issue of economic development, to the narrower issue of regional development. East Asian countries suffer from significant inter-regional economic inequalities and these inequalities often extend into all other spheres of national life. Such inequalities inevitably interfere with well-balanced economic development and impose costs on both the magnet cities and the rest of the country. A more balanced pattern of development is therefore desirable, and IT can make significant contributions toward this objective. In particular, by reducing the concentration of information and knowledge in the main city and disseminating those valuable resources to the rest of the country, IT reduces the inequality of opportunity that lies at the root of the inter-regional economic inequality. However, we must be realistic about what IT can do and cannot do in terms of promoting greater inter-regional equality. IT by itself will not enable poorer regions and cities to catch up with the main cities, and will facilitate regional development only if the fundamental ingredients of regional development are in place. Finally, East Asian economies must fulfill certain pre-conditions, especially greater inter-regional equality in telecom and other IT infrastructure, to fully realize IT's potential benefits for regional development. In the last section of this chapter, we summarize our main points and provide some concluding thoughts. In addition, we discuss the policy implications of our analysis for FDI in Asia, along with implications for potential foreign investors, especially in the telecommunications industry. FDI into IT sectors cannot only be profitable for the investors, but can also promote the host country's economic growth.

Introduction

One of the most fashionable words these days among government officials, academics and the general public alike throughout Asia is the "New Economy," which refers to the economy that is emerging in the midst of the ongoing IT revolution. The IT revolution refers to the sharp reduction in the cost of finding and communicating information that has been made possible by the convergence of information and communication technologies. For this reason, the IT revolution is also known as the ICT revolution. More convenient and more powerful computing equipment, especially personal computers (PCs), in combination with better and more affordable telecommunication services, are jointly driving the IT revolution. Perhaps the most familiar manifestation of this far-reaching revolution is the Internet, which can literally connect us to the rest of the world in the comfort of our homes and offices. The IT revolution is giving rise to a new economic paradigm – the New Economy.

The New Economy is structurally different in many ways from the Old Economy. The latter is based on hardware, whereas software is the defining characteristic of the New Economy. Value added in the New Economy comes from the creation of new knowledge rather than the application of existing knowledge, as in the Old Economy. The current transition from the Old Economy toward the New Economy is therefore a transition from the industrial age of making and consuming products to the information age of creating and absorbing knowledge. While the focus of the Old Economy is on transforming raw materials into goods and services, the focus of the New Economy lies in transforming intellectual capital into new information and knowledge. For example, transforming iron and coal into steel is a classical example of the Old Economy in action, whereas creating new software to process financial data more efficiently fits our mental picture of the New Economy. In short, intellectual capital, instead of the more traditional factors of production such as land, labor and capital, underpin the New Economy.

While there are other forces such as globalization behind the New Economy, its primary driving engine is the IT revolution. This is because the New Economy is based on creating and disseminating knowledge and information, and the IT revolution has significantly reduced the cost of doing so. The ongoing convergence of information technology and communication technology, which lies at the heart of the IT revolution, is accelerating the creation and dissemination of knowledge and information. It is worth noting that knowledge and information are omnipresent but often ignored inputs of production. In the real world, unlike in the world of textbooks, information is costly, so the IT revolution represents a supply-side revolution of falling information costs and hence transactions costs.

Specific examples of firm-level efficiency gains due to IT include lower procurement costs, better supply chain management, and tighter inventory control. According to a 2000 report by Martin Brooks and Zaki Wahhaj at Goldman Sachs, firms' potential savings from purchasing over the Internet range from 2% in the coal industry to 40% in the electronics components industry. They also estimate that doing business online with suppliers can reduce the cost of making a car by as much as 14%. British Telecom claims that procuring good and services online will reduce the direct costs of the goods and services it purchases by 11%. In a comprehensive recent study of the impact of firm-level information technology investments in a wide range of industries in the U.S. between 1995 and 1997, Kudyba and Diwan (2002) find that IT investment has a substantial positive impact on firm productivity and, furthermore, this positive impact increases over time. Although the efficiency gains vary from firm to firm and industry to industry, at least some firms and industries will realize substantial gains. Figure 1 summarizes the impact of the IT revolution at the firm level.

As we can see in Figure 2, at a macro level, the lower information and transactions costs enable the economy to produce more at each price level, resulting in a rightward shift of the supply curve, and a new equilibrium of lower price levels and higher outputs. The positive supply shock entails the best of both worlds – faster economic growth combined with deflationary pressures.

At a micro level, while creativity, innovation and risk-taking have always been essential elements of successful entrepreneurship, there is an even greater premium on those qualities in the New Economy. At the macro level, this means that the most successful

Figure 1. The impact of the IT revolution on firms

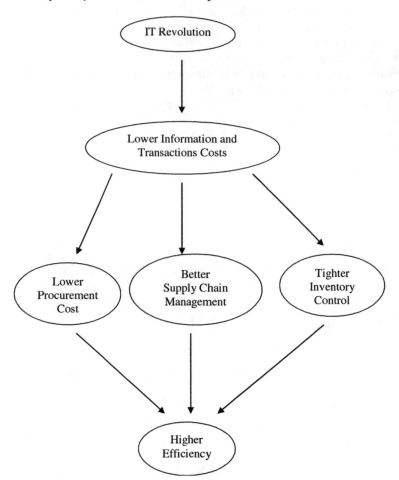

economies will be those that are most effective at creating new information and knowledge by taking full advantage of the IT revolution's information cost savings. Nimble re-allocation of resources associated with flexible and deregulated markets is vital for an economy in view of the fast-paced obsolescence of information and hence technology in the information age. Equally important is human resource development capable of producing workers who can not only absorb existing knowledge but also generate new knowledge.

The transformation of manufacturing products into mass-produced, low-margin commodities is no longer restricted to low-tech products, but is becoming more evident further up the technological ladder as well. This trend, which is a consequence of the globalization of production and economic activity, reinforces the case for a more creative and innovative workforce and economy, especially in higher-income countries that are experiencing a hollowing-out of their manufacturing sector. The IT revolution is provid-

Figure 2. The macro impact of the IT revolution on supply

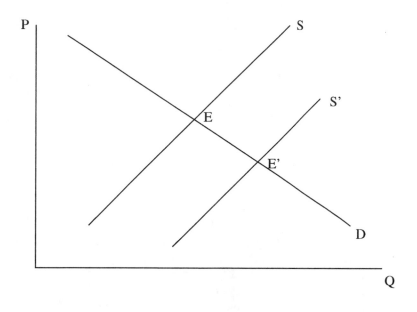

ing further momentum to the shift from manufacturing to services in those countries. Related to this shift in the composition of output is a shift away from mass production and toward customization to suit individual preferences. IT-induced reduction of transactions costs between firms and consumers underlies this trend. At the same time, IT-induced reduction of transactions costs between firms is promoting the contracting out or outsourcing of various services to other firms. To the extent that inter-firm transactions costs dictate the optimal size of the firm, we can expect lower inter-firm transactions costs to result in a smaller optimal size of the firm. This, in turn, implies increasingly higher levels of specialization and thus concentration on core competencies, with beneficial effects for efficiency and productivity.

Economic globalization and the IT revolution are complementary in a very fundamental sense – they both make markets more competitive than ever before. Economic globalization, evident in the sustained growth of international flows of goods and services as well as capital and labor, is breaking down the barriers that protected domestic firms from international competition. By subjecting firms to relentless external competitive pressures, globalization is forcing them to shape up or shut down. By the same token, the IT revolution is making more information about producers and products available to consumers. Armed with more information, consumers are able to choose more selectively from a wider range of producers and products. They are better able to find the best value for their money. The IT revolution thus breaks down consumer ignorance, which protects firms from competitive pressures just as much as tariffs or barriers to entry. Figure 3 summarizes the impact of the IT revolution on consumer choice and welfare.

Figure 3. The impact of the IT revolution on consumers

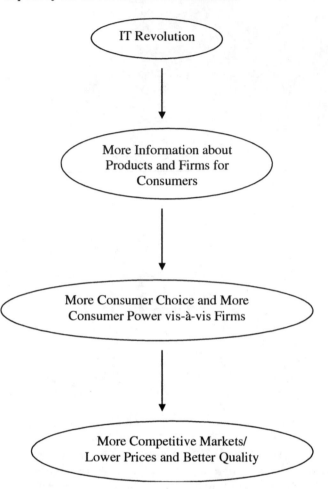

Lower information costs for consumers leaves them with more resources available for consuming goods and services. In other words, some of the time and money consumers spend searching for goods and services can be re-allocated on goods and services themselves. If we think of the cost of gathering information as a tax on consumers, the IT revolution brings about a reduction in this tax. Furthermore, the economy's higher productivity (as a result of the IT revolution) will further increase income and raise demand for goods and services. Therefore, although the primary impact of the IT revolution is on supply, it will also have a positive impact on demand at the macro level, as we can see in Figure 4. This positive demand-side impact will further stimulate economic growth.

E-commerce, which does not require a physical bricks-and-mortar presence, reduces the set-up costs of entering and doing business. In the process, e-commerce reduces the

Figure 4. The macro impact of the IT revolution on supply and demand

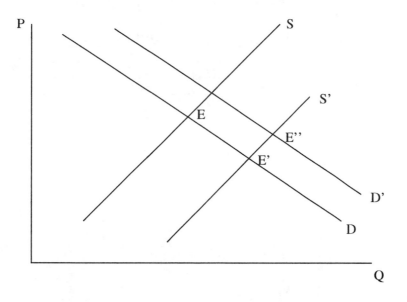

barriers to entering a market and makes markets more competitive. In short, in the New Economy, stronger competitive pressures will force firms to become more efficient and productive over time. Mere survival requires nothing less. We should also note that the division between the New Economy and the Old Economy is not always a clear-cut one. Although the New Economy is associated with industries such telecommunications and telecom equipment, computer hardware and software, biotechnology, and fuel cells and other alternative energy technology, and the Old Economy with low-tech manufacturing, even in the most technologically advanced developed countries such as the U.S., elements of the two co-exist with each other. In addition, many of the efficiency gains associated with the IT revolution, in particular the reduction of information costs, are applicable to the entire spectrum of industries, including those we typically associate with the Old Economy.

In this chapter, I will focus on the economic impact and implications of the New Economy for East Asia in the 21st century. East Asia consists of two sub-regions - Northeast Asia and Southeast Asia. There is a great deal of diversity among the East Asian countries in terms of economic development and income. They range from Japan and the NIEs (i.e., Korea, Taiwan, Hong Kong and Singapore), which are industrialized, high-income economies at one end, to Myanmar and the Indochina countries at the other end, which remain among the world's poorest countries despite recent economic progress. Table 1 shows the population, per capita GDP and per capita GDP in purchasing power parity terms of selected East Asian countries.

Our focus on economics is not to make light of the social, political, and other effects, of which there are bound to be many, some of them profound in their own right, but simply

Table 1. Population and per capita GDP for 2000, selected East Asian economies

Country	Population (millions)	GDP Per Capita, US$	GDP Per Capita, PPP, US$
China	1,262	840	3,920
Japan	127	35,620	27,080
Korea (South)	47	8,910	17,300
Taiwan	22	14,000	N.A.
Hong Kong	7	25,920	25,590
Singapore	4	24,740	24,910
Indonesia	210	570	2,830
Vietnam	79	390	2,000
Philippines	76	1,040	4,220
Thailand	61	2,000	6,320
Malaysia	23	3,380	8,330

Source: World development indicators 2001, EIU for Taiwan

to concentrate on my field of expertise as well as to provide a sharper focus to my reflections on this most important subject. And, as its name suggests, the New Economy is above all an economic phenomenon. Casual observation alone suggests that the rate of technological progress in the information technology (IT) field over the past ten years or so has been absolutely breathtaking. Moore's Law, according to which the processing capacity of silicon chips doubles every 18 months, powerfully sums up the speed of innovation. Although web surfing and e-mailing have now become as much a part of our daily routines as eating and sleeping, they were little more than fascinating novelties until quite recently. Microsoft, Cisco and Sun Microsystems, to name just a few, have come out of nowhere to become among the biggest and most recognized companies in the world. The New Economy is here, and it is here to stay.

But what are the implications of this New Economy for the global economy? The extraordinary macroeconomic performance of the U.S., the undisputed standard bearer of the New Economy with its Silicon Valley, countless dot.coms and venture capitalists, in recent years has led some economists to proclaim the arrival of an economic nirvana in which high growth went hand in hand with low inflation. At the other extreme, New Economy skeptics attribute the remarkable U.S. economy simply to an accidental convergence of growth-promoting cyclical factors such as the IT investment boom and inflation-subduing circumstances such as the strong dollar.

At the heart of this heated debate between the supporters and critics of the New Economy is an empirical issue – the contribution of IT to productivity. That is to say, theoretical arguments aside, by how much has the IT revolution helped workers to actually produce more with a given amount of capital? Whether or not IT enables an economy to achieve faster growth on a sustainable basis without triggering inflation ultimately depends on the magnitude of productivity gains.[1] Although it is too early to make definitive judgments,[2] the preliminary evidence indicates that IT has clearly led to significant productivity gains.

The basic theoretical reason for why IT should promote productivity is intuitively compelling and clear. As anybody who has searched for books on both hard copy library catalogues and online library catalogues knows, IT sharply reduces the cost of information. And, to repeat, the cost of information is as much of a cost of production as the cost of oil or steel. In fact, information is perhaps the most important input of all since all economic transactions require information. To repeat an important example of how IT boosts efficiency by reducing information costs, it delivers lower procurement costs to firms by making it easier for them to find the cheapest suppliers and cut down their transactions costs.[3] Now that we have touched upon some general conceptual issues, we turn our attention first to East Asia.

The Promise of IT

In order to discuss the potential economic benefits of IT for Asia, it is necessary to first look at the region's strengths and weaknesses. In terms of regional strengths, a glance at shops and department stores around the world will reveal that Asia is the manufacturing hub of the world. This is particularly true for Japan and the four newly industrialized countries of Korea, Taiwan, Hong Kong and Singapore. But it is also true, to a lesser extent, for Southeast Asia. A noteworthy development in this connection has been the recent emergence of China as a manufacturing powerhouse, especially for low-tech goods. Table 2 confirms the importance of manufacturing in the region's economies regardless of income level. The only notable exception appears to be Hong Kong.

Table 2. Composition of GDP for selected East Asian economies, 2000

Country	Agriculture (%)	Manufacturing (%)	Services (%)
China	16	35	33
Japan	1	22	66
Korea (South)	5	31	53
Taiwan	2	26	58
Hong Kong	0	6	85
Singapore	0	26	66
Indonesia	17	26	36
Vietnam	24	18	39
Philippines	16	23	53
Thailand	10	32	49
Malaysia	11	33	44

Source: World development indicators 2001, EIU for Taiwan

Note: The numbers do not add up to 100% because they exclude mining, construction, and utilities.

Table 3. Electronics output of selected East Asian countries, 1985 and 1998

Country	Output in Billions of US$, 1985	Output in Billions of US$, 1998
China	5.6	46.9
Japan	89	196
Korea (South)	6.5	39
Taiwan	56	34
Hong Kong	3.7	8.2
Singapore	4.5	38
Indonesia	0.6	5.2
Philippines	1.1	7.3
Thailand	0.6	14.6
Malaysia	1.9	27

Source: Yearbook of World Electronics Data 2000 (Elsevier)

The region has an especially strong comparative advantage in, and is heavily dependent upon, manufacturing and exporting electronics products, the hardware of the IT revolution. This is true even to the extent that the global electronics business cycle has a tangible effect on the economy-wide business cycles of the region's smaller economies. Table 3 shows the output of electronics products in selected East Asian countries for 1985 and 1998. For the region as a whole, electronics production reached around US$120 billion in 1985 and over US$420 billion in 1998. As Table 3 clearly shows, not only is the value of output large, it has grown explosively between these years. It is no exaggeration to say that East Asia is and will continue to be the world's electronics factory.[4] Therefore, in the first instance, the IT revolution has had a direct positive impact on East Asia's output and exports by boosting the global demand for electronics in general and IT-related products in particular.

Global output of electronics reached US$482 billion in 1985 and US$1,088 billion in 1998. In 1985, Japan, the NIEs and other East Asian countries accounted for 18.6%, 4.3% and 2.4%, respectively, of global output. In 1998, the corresponding figures were 18%, 11% and 10%, respectively. The shares of the NIEs and other East Asian countries have risen sharply. The share of East Asia as a whole in global output has grown from 25% to almost 40%. Figure 5 illustrates this upward trend.

Table 4 tells us why East Asia dominates the global exports of electronics. Revealed comparative advantage is a widely used index of a country's comparative advantage in international trade. An index greater than one indicates comparative advantage relative to other countries in the production of a particular good. A higher number suggests a higher degree of comparative advantage. We can see from Table 4 that most East Asian countries enjoy comparative advantage in electronics, which explains their strong positions as electronics exporters in global markets.

Figure 5. The share of global electronics output for Japan, NIEs and other East Asia, 1985 and 1998

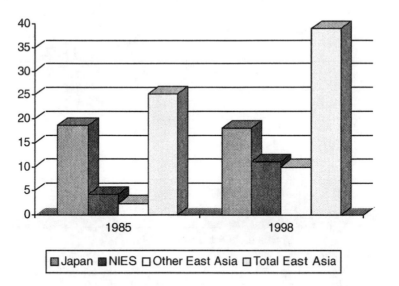

Source: Yearbook of World Electronics Data 2000 (Elsevier)

Table 4. Revealed comparative advantage in Electronics Exports, 1998

Country	Index
China	1.28
Japan	2.53
Korea (South)	1.49
Taiwan	1.52
Hong Kong	0.24
Singapore	1.73
Indonesia	0.54
Philippines	1.24
Thailand	1.34
Malaysia	1.87

Source: Yearbook of World Electronics Data 2000 (Elsevier), WTO (2000)

Figure 6. Share of Global Electronics Consumption, 1997 (%)

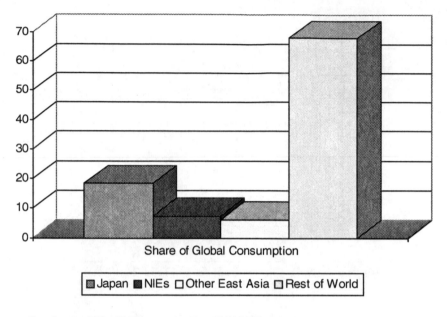

Source: Yearbook of World Electronics Data 2000 (Elsevier)

While electronics exports are a major engine of East Asian growth and the IT revolution has had a strong positive impact on global demand for electronics, East Asia has emerged as a big market for electronics in its own right. That is, while East Asia exports much of its electronics output, the region also consumes a substantial share at home and exports to each other. For example, in 1997, the region accounted for 45% of global output and 32% of global consumption. Figure 6 shows the shares of Japan, NIEs and rest of East Asia in global electronics consumption for 1997.

Despite a widespread tendency to talk up software and services and a corresponding tendency to talk down hardware and manufacturing these days, one should not forget that export-oriented manufacturing was the engine of the Asian miracle and will remain an important engine of regional growth into the foreseeable future. Fortunately for East Asia, the potential benefits of IT for manufacturing are large indeed.[5] While the region does enjoy a comparative advantage in manufacturing, this does not mean there is little room for productivity improvement.

The conventional wisdom in the context of e-commerce or Internet commerce is that although B2C (business to consumer), with its Amazons, e-Bays and Yahoos, grabs all the headlines, B2B (business to business) will generate the lion's share of growth in e-commerce over the next few years. What this means is that whether through lower procurement costs, more efficient supply chain management, or more timely inventory control, East Asian manufacturers stand to gain a productivity windfall if they can capitalize on the IT revolution. Again, the cost of information is a cost of production like any other and its reduction is no different from a reduction in the price of, say, oil. Furthermore, there are good reasons to believe that information costs are quite high in Asia, as best evidenced by a relative lack of corporate transparency, making lower information costs all the more beneficial for the region.[6]

A point worth emphasizing here is that East Asian economies should focus their investment in areas that yield the highest tangible returns, which is the application of existing technology for local needs, especially in the manufacturing sector. There is no need for East Asian economies to compete with each other to create their own Silicon Valleys. At the present, they would do better to focus on localizing and adapting the software and technology developed in Silicon Valley, which enjoys huge advantages in terms of network effects as well as availability of an innovative workforce and venture capital.[7] There are as just as many risks of making "white elephant" investments in the New Economy as in the Old Economy. The main point here is not that East Asia is incapable of its own Silicon Valleys; rather, why waste scarce resources on investments with uncertain payoffs when there are alternative investments with large, certain payoffs?

Returning to the lack of corporate transparency discussed earlier, and combining it with the quality of investments we just talked about, naturally brings us to the issue of corporate governance. With at least some justification, poor corporate governance is widely held to have been a key catalyst in precipitating the Asian crisis.[8] By the same token, improving corporate governance, or the way companies are managed, is central to preventing another crisis and, more generally, improving the performance of East Asian companies.[9] While it is neither feasible nor desirable for the region to have an American-style market for corporate control, there is certainly room for improving the quality of East Asian management, which needs to become less family-based and more market-oriented.

Again, the essence of the IT revolution is to make information, including information about companies, more available and less costly to the man in the street. Lack of corporate transparency, with all its negative implications for corporate governance, ultimately boils down to privileged access to information for the well-connected few and lack of access to information for the not-so-well-connected majority. In an age where information is increasingly available to all, it is only natural to expect the hitherto disadvantaged majority to demand their rights. For example, minority shareholders will no longer sit silently when insiders abuse and manipulate information for their own benefit. In this way, the New Economy will enhance the quality of corporate governance throughout the region in the long run.

Related to the issue of improving corporate governance is the issue of public sector governance.[10] Many governments throughout the region, even in the more advanced economies, lack the confidence and trust of the general public. In some instances, though certainly not all, the introduction of e-services may reduce the scope for undesirable behavior among government officials. Furthermore, by promoting the development of stock markets and bond markets through online trading, the IT revolution can help to weaken the region's over-dependence on banks, which all too often channeled resources toward favored borrowers at the government's behest. Therefore, in the long run, the

New Economy will help to break up the unhealthy aspects of the relationship between the region's governments, corporate sectors and financial systems.

The potential benefit of the IT revolution for improving the quality of the region's financial services points to a more general potential benefit – that of improving the productivity in the service sector as a whole. As we can see in Table 2, services account for a large share of GDP in East Asian economies. The shift away from other sectors toward the service sector is especially evident in the richer regional countries. For example, Hong Kong, which has experienced a massive hollowing out of its manufacturing base to China, now has a tiny manufacturing sector and derives around 85% of its output from services. To illustrate the potential benefits of IT for services, according to Lehman Brothers, a transfer between bank accounts costs $1.27 if done by a bank teller, 27 cents via a cash machine, but only 1 cent over the Internet.

No Panacea

As we have seen in the preceding section, the New Economy does indeed offer enormous economic opportunities for East Asia. Unfortunately, focusing solely on potential benefits, however big they may be, often leads us to unrealistic expectations. And so it is with the New Economy and East Asia. That is, its strongest advocates tout the IT revolution as a solution to everything under the sun – from poverty and malnutrition to war and conflict. Granted, the IT revolution will clearly bring about big benefits for mankind, but we must be realistic about its limitations as well.

In this connection, IT's true believers often bring up India as an example of how a poor country can leapfrog the Industrial Age and move straight into the Post-Industrial Age.[11] India's example is especially relevant for the poorer East Asian countries outside Japan and the NIEs. No doubt India has done well for herself in exporting software and allied services as well as IT-enabled back-office work, and the country has become a global powerhouse in certain niches. So one might be tempted to argue that despite its traditional lack of international competitiveness in manufacturing, India has managed to achieve such competitiveness in services thanks to the New Economy's technological advances and that the country is on its way to becoming the next tiger.

If only the New Economy were that powerful! In the first place, India remains a very poor country by any measure and it is too early to tell whether India's ascent from its Hindu rate of growth will be sustained. Second, although it is untrue that the IT revolution has, as some critics argue, had only minimal impact on India's noticeably better economic performance in recent years, it would be equally implausible to attribute all or most of the improvement to the country's booming IT sector. In other words, IT's impact on the Indian economy extends well beyond the pristine premises of, say, Infosys, but it is simply nowhere big enough to carry the entire economy to a higher level. Third, it may be difficult for poor East Asian countries such as Indonesia, Vietnam or the Philippines to replicate the experience of India, with its millions of English speakers and abundant supply of engineers and other scientific personnel.[12]

Another important area that often generates unrealistic expectations of IT is poverty reduction. One of the most impressive achievements of the East Asian miracle was a remarkable reduction in the proportion of the population living below the poverty line throughout the region. Nevertheless, hundreds of millions of East Asians still live in grinding poverty, especially outside Japan and the NIEs. The Asian crisis has made matters substantially worse, undoing decades of hard-earned progress in countries such as Indonesia and Thailand.

There are several ways in which IT can help East Asia in its fight against poverty, but they all ultimately relate to the essence of the New Economy – the availability of more information at lower cost.[13] The poor, who usually suffer from the poorest access to information (and in fact this is a big source of their poverty), stand to gain the most from the greater supply of information brought about by IT. For example, IT can provide East Asia's small farmers access to valuable timely market information such as the price of inputs and outputs, weather forecasts, and income-maximizing crop mix. IT can also improve the access of the rural poor to education through distance learning and access to health care by training rural health workers. In either case, the end result will be higher productivity and incomes. This matters because agriculture remains a significant part of the national economy in many countries, especially the poorer ones, as Table 2 clearly shows. Furthermore, as Figure 7 indicates, agriculture's share of the workforce is typically bigger than its share of GDP, which means that boosting agricultural productivity matters a lot for reducing poverty.

Figure 7. Agriculture's share of GDP and workforce, selected East Asian countries

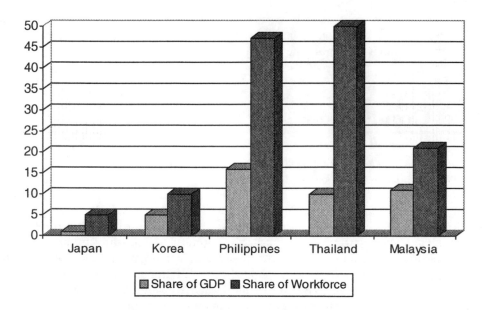

Source: World Development Indicators 2001

However, despite its potential to contribute toward poverty reduction in East Asia, IT by itself cannot do the job. For example, small farmers who gain greater access to information will not be able to make good use of this information if they cannot get their products to markets on time due to poor roads and storage facilities. Or, an artisan who finds new overseas customers through the Internet will find his ability to deliver his products severely constrained by the lack of adequate ports and airports. East Asian economies will not be able to unlock the promise of IT as an anti-poverty tool unless they have good physical infrastructure and other necessary complements.[14]

This brings us to a more fundamental point. All the talk about using IT to leapfrog, bypass and so forth is not merely illusory; it is downright dangerous. Such talk makes us lose sight of the fact that the New Economy does not at all change the fundamental ingredients of economic growth. As we just saw, the New Economy's advent renders good physical infrastructure more, not less, important. And so it is with human infrastructure. East Asia would do well to stick to things that have served it well during the course of its economic miracle – sound macroeconomic policies, openness to foreign technology, an outward-looking, export-oriented development strategy, focus on education, and rapid accumulation of physical capital. The New Economy will not allow countries to leapfrog sound economic policies.[15]

In fact, it is precisely such policies that will maximize the benefits of IT as well as allow IT to take hold in the first place. That is, good policies will not only enable East Asian countries to realize the potential benefits of IT for their economies, it will also accelerate their entry into the digital age. Of course, those policies are desirable for their own sake, but in the New Economy their benefits will go even further. For example, investments in education yield higher returns because IT enables exports of labor-intensive back-office services. At the same time, a strong policy toward the environment will promote domestic and foreign investment in the necessary physical infrastructure for IT, such as an efficient telecom sector. A specific example of a simple but useful IT-enabling policy is to liberalize imports of computer hardware and software, which will sharply bring down their prices and thus accelerate the spread of IT.

Pre-Conditions

Just as there are clear limits to what IT can do, it is also worth remembering that the IT revolution will not arrive throughout East Asia automatically. That is, East Asian economies must work hard to fulfill some basic pre-conditions if they are to enjoy the substantial potential benefits of the New Economy.[16] It is not sensible to discuss the implications of the New Economy for East Asia when it is far from certain whether all the region's economies will experience it in a meaningful way in the first place. Some countries already appear to be doing better than others in terms of creating an appropriate enabling environment for the New Economy. Such an environment requires above all the widespread availability and low cost of the basic hardware of the New Economy – computers and access to telecommunications. As we can see in Table 5, the countries

Table 5. IT diffusion in East Asia, various indicators

Country	1	2	3	4	5
China	7	0.02	74	184	7
Japan	272	11.03	494	214	214
Korea (South)	150	4.22	467	345	378
Taiwan	178	16.71	543	372	206
Hong Kong	310	20.09	584	538	362
Singapore	344	13.45	465	525	244
Indonesia	11	0.11	27	60	4.3
Philippines	16	0.21	32	68	6.7
Thailand	33	0.03	82	116	13.2
Malaysia	78	1.93	205	146	69

Source: World Competitiveness Yearbook 2000, Yearbook of World Electronics Data 2000 (Elsevier), and World Telecommunications Indicators (International Telecommunications Union)

Note: 1 = Computers per 1,000, 2 = Internet hosts per 1,000, 3 = Telephone lines per 1,000, 4 = Secure servers per million, 5 = Internet users per 1,000

of the region vary widely in terms of IT diffusion and hence readiness for the New Economy.

The foundation for the IT revolution and the New Economy is undoubtedly the telecommunications sector. Quite simply, a country that does not have an efficient and well-functioning telecom sector will find itself at the wrong end of the emerging international digital divide.[17] We cannot emphasize enough the central importance of telecom in IT. So much so that ICT, or information and communication technology, is increasingly replacing IT in the jargon to emphasize the convergence of information technology and telecommunication technology in the New Economy. Those of us living in richer countries have a tendency to take affordable and reliable telecom services for granted but, unfortunately, this is not the case in poorer countries.

Therefore, telecom liberalization has to be the point of departure for any East Asian country that wants to join the New Economy. Again, this is especially relevant for the region's poorer countries, where access to telecom services is often limited. Most available evidence indicates that liberalization tends to improve both the quality and quantity of telecom services, as well as encourages more investments.[18] Although bringing in the private sector has not always been successful, liberalization generally does involve a bigger role for the private sector.[19] A sound regulatory framework that promotes competition is required in order to promote efficiency and innovation as opposed to a private monopoly merely replacing a public one. In East Asia, as elsewhere, governments' reluctance to liberalize owes to the fact that public telecom monopolies are a major source of revenues. However, such shortsightedness, costly for the economy as a whole to begin with, will be all the more so in the New Economy.

Figure 8. Gap in IT diffusion between Japan/NIEs and rest of East Asia, 1998

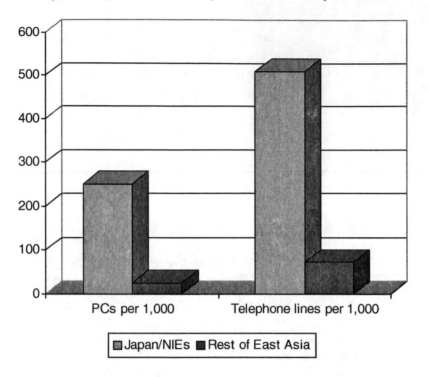

Source: Yearbook of World Electronics Data 2000 (Elsevier) and World Telecommunications Indicators (International Telecommunications Union)

The need for telecom liberalization is particularly urgent in the poorer countries of the region. This is because, as Figure 8 clearly shows, there is a clear digital divide between East Asia's richer economies – Japan and the NIEs – on one hand and the rest of the region on the other. The former are much better equipped to survive and thrive in the New Economy than the latter. Consumers and firms in Japan and the NIEs by and large already have good access to IT hardware such as telecom services and computers unlike in the rest of the region where access is much more limited. Indicators of IT diffusion other than the availability of telephone lines and computers also indicate an unmistakable IT divide between Japan and the NIEs as opposed to the rest of the region. For example, the number of Internet hosts per 1,000 in 1998 reached 13.1 in the former but only 0.39 in the latter. Similarly, the number of secure servers per million in 2001 reached 65 in the former but only 1.4 in the latter.

The digital divide between the richer and poorer countries of the region has clear implications for their readiness to use IT in economic activity. The potential of e-commerce to promote economic efficiency and consumer welfare will go unrealized unless there is the necessary hardware in place. This is true for both B2B e-commerce and B2C e-commerce. For example, buyers who do not have access to the Internet cannot buy

Figure 9. Percentage of online shoppers, 2002

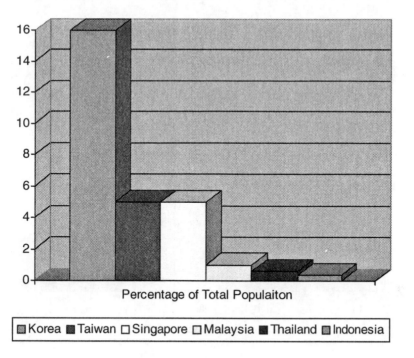

Percentage of Total Populaiton

▨Korea ■Taiwan □Singapore □Malaysia ■Thailand ▨Indonesia

Source: TNS Global E-Commerce Report (2002)

online even when this might be more convenient and less costly. Figure 9 clearly illustrates this gap between the two groups of countries. Notice that the percentage of population that shops online depends not only on the percentage of Internet users who buy online but, more fundamentally, the percentage of the total population that are Internet users. The low percentage of online shoppers in Singapore and Taiwan helps to illustrate another significant point – even in the region's rich countries: e-commerce has a long way to go until maturity. Even in Korea, which has embraced e-commerce with more enthusiasm, B2B e-commerce amounted to less than US$1.5 billion, or less than 2% of total B2B commerce, in 2000. In other words, while the necessary IT physical infrastructure is largely already in place in those countries, companies and consumers have yet to widely use it in their everyday economic activities.

Given such disparity in terms of IT hardware between Japan and NIEs on one hand and the rest of East Asia on the other, it is not surprising that the majority of IT-related success stories are concentrated in the former. For example, in Singapore, the IT industry has become an integral and dynamic part of the local economy. By 2002, total annual revenues from the IT industry had reached about US$18 billion, which represents close to one-fifth of GDP. Figure 10 shows the composition of those revenues. An interesting characteristic of Figure 10 is that in Singapore, more so than in Japan and the other NIEs,

Figure 10. Composition of Singapore's IT revenues, 2002

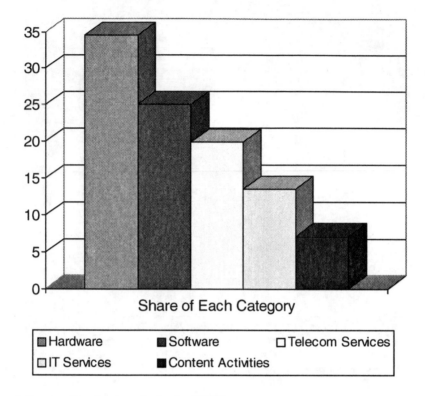

Source: Infocomm Development Authority (2003)

software also plays a big role in the IT industry, so there is a rough balance between hardware and software. Creative Technology, which is a private sector company specializing in the production of sound cards for PCs, is the best-known example of Singaporean success in the software sector. In fact, Creative Technology has become one of the world's leading and most widely recognized brands in sound cards. This success is all the more remarkable in view of the limited role of the private sector in the Singaporean economy and points to a potentially greater role of the private sector in the New Economy. The export market accounted for 53% of total revenues and the domestic market accounted for 47%.

Hardware accounts for the lion's share of the IT industry's output in Japan, Korea and Taiwan while in the case of Hong Kong, the IT industry, along with the rest of the manufacturing sector, has largely shifted production to China. Japan, Korea and Taiwan are all big-time players in the global IT industry. Japanese consumer electronics firms have been and continue to be among the most efficient and most innovative firms in the world, with internationally strong brand name recognition and consumer loyalty. Sony in particular has become a world-class firm synonymous with superior quality and constantly at the technological frontier in terms of introducing new and better products for the consumer to enjoy at home. While Sony has been a global technological leader for a long time in audio-visual hardware based on technologies such as magnetic recording, optical devices, semiconductors and digital signal processing, the company has been strategically and gradually shifting its focus toward establishing a presence in the production of software that plays on its hardware. The acquisition of CBS Records – now Sony Music Entertainment (SME) – and Columbia Pictures – now Sony Pictures Entertainment (SPE) – in the late 1980s marked a giant step in that direction. The success of Sony's PlayStation videogames and digital cameras further illustrates the effectiveness of Sony's strategy of merging hardware and software in the New Economy.

Samsung Electronics of Korea is another company from the high-income part of East Asia that is making waves in the global IT industry. In fact, with its electronics products recognized around the world for their high quality and innovativeness, the company is the flagship of Korea's manufacturing sector and perhaps the country's only truly world-class brand. Samsung Electronics has become a global leader in semiconductor, telecommunication and digital convergence technologies, and the world's largest manufacturer of memory chips, TFT-LCDs, CDMA mobile phones, monitors and VCRs. The company's total sales reached a US$34.5 billion in 2002, and perhaps more tellingly in terms of efficiency, its net income reached US$6 billion for the same year. Samsung has become the world's third largest maker of mobile phones, a product that accounts for a large share of its profits. The company has been able to stay one step ahead of its competitors by spending relentlessly on research and development, investing heavily in new facilities, and keeping a blue-chip client base. For example, in the memory chip business, while its three biggest competitors all recorded losses in 2002, Samsung was able to achieve US$2 billion in profits. The company was able to do this by focusing on specialty products commanding higher profit prices and fatter margins such as graphic chips for game consoles.

Among countries outside Japan and the NIEs, China is best positioned to become a manufacturing hub for IT hardware products and indeed this process is already well under way. The country's computer hardware industry grew dramatically from non-existence in the 1980s to the fourth largest in the world with sales of US$23 billion in 2000. Exports have surged from a mere US$230 million in 1990 to more than US$10 billion in 1998. Local PC makers such as Legend, Great Wall and Founder are dominating the fast-growing Chinese market for PCs through a combination of stronger distribution networks, lower prices and better after-sales service, even though they were expected to be no match for well-established, foreign brands. In fact, the market share of foreign brands has fallen steadily over recent years and is forecast to fall further. The government has actively promoted the development of the computer industry by high tariffs on imports as well as requirements on foreign companies to transfer their technology in exchange for market access. All major Chinese PC makers are involved in technologically beneficial joint ventures with foreign partner firms.

A danger related to greater inter-country inequality inherent in the IT revolution for East Asian economies is that it could exacerbate income inequality within a country. This is especially a concern in countries outside Japan and the NIEs since there is a much closer link between inequality and poverty in those countries. A digital divide, or inequality in terms of access to and use of IT, can only put the less fortunate segments of the society at an even further disadvantage in an age when information and knowledge are becoming ever more important determinants of success and advancement.[20] The essence of the New Economy is more information at lower cost, as we pointed out earlier. So, in principle, IT can serve as a force for greater economic equality. However, in practice, this depends on the extent to which access to IT is available to all. Therefore, once again we come back to our point of departure for the IT revolution – telecom liberalization supported by a sound regulatory framework. The private sector tends to be more flexible and adaptable than the government, yet another big reason why it makes sense to involve the private sector to a greater degree in the telecom sector.

Affordable and reliable telecom services are a start, but only a start in the IT revolution. Human resource development that equips the entire workforce with basic IT usage skills is another indispensable ingredient for an IT revolution.[21] A PC and a telephone line will not do an illiterate person a whole lot of good. Therefore, primary and secondary education that creates a literate and numerate workforce will remain just as important in the New Economy as ever. In addition, primary and secondary schools should introduce computer education as part of their core curriculum. On the supply side, equipping IT workers with the necessary technical skills as well as investing in tertiary education to produce a steady stream of engineers is essential to develop a strong IT sector. Although governments continue to play the leading role in education in East Asia, bringing the private sector into IT human resource development is desirable. In fact, as the proliferation of private IT training institutes across the region shows, this is already happening to some extent. Government regulation of such private sector education should focus on quality control issues.

There is certainly a lot of merit to the widely heard argument that East Asian education systems, with their emphasis on memorization and rote learning, will not serve the region well in the New Economy. Thus the region-wide calls for revamping education systems to allow for more creativity and independent thinking.[22] However, there is also a lot that the region's schools, especially those in Japan and the NIEs, do right, such as emphasis on and their students' excellent performance in science and math. Encouraging greater creativity is fine, but this must not mean wholesale imitation of the curricula of Western countries. Furthermore, we must recognize that the region's education systems, along with the mindset and mentality they have engendered, have been in place for a long time so that the emergence of a mindset and mentality more appropriate for the New Economy will not take place overnight. Also, many talented East Asians still move to Silicon Valley rather than contribute their skills to the region. In this case, the problem is not the education system, but points instead to the lack of a favorable overall environment for IT entrepreneurship.

In particular, Taiwanese have a highly visible presence among the technopreneurs – i.e., technologically proficient entrepreneurs – of Silicon Valley. Thousands of Taiwanese go to U.S. universities each year to study and settle down in the Silicon Valley. In fact, the Taiwanese, along with Indians, have probably been the most influential expatriate community in terms of contributions to the emergence of the Silicon Valley as the epicenter of the global IT industry. Many Taiwanese technopreneurs in Silicon Valley have returned to their home country to play a catalyst role in its transformation into Silicon Valley East or Silicon Island. While there have been several factors behind this transformation, it is difficult to exaggerate Taiwan's close links to America, in particular the role of Taiwanese returnees from Silicon Valley. Just as important as their innovative technical skills have been the spirit of entrepreneurship and risk-taking that they have brought back to their motherland.

Taiwan has a number of globally recognized IT companies, most notably Acer, which ranks among the world's top ten branded PC vendors with sales of US$13 billion in 2002. Taiwan Semiconductor Manufacturing (TSMC) is the world's largest contract chip maker, commonly called a foundry, and its closest rival is another Taiwanese company – United Microelectronics (UMC). The two together accounted for over 60% of the global foundry market in 2002. The prominence of TSM and UMC points to a more general characteristic of the Taiwanese IT hardware industry. Most of the industry consists of component suppliers that supply generic parts, even completely assembled machines, at competitive prices to big foreign brand-name companies that concentrate on marketing and sales. For example, Quanta Computer is the world's biggest designer and manufacturer of notebook PCs, but sells its output to top brands such as Dell and Hewlett-Packard. It was the Taiwanese in the Silicon Valley who first spotted the trend of a division into two tiers – manufacturing and marketing/sales – within the global IT industry and went home to set up many of the component suppliers that form an essential extension of America's IT industry. Again, the role of the returnees from the U.S. has been indispensable to Taiwan's efforts to successfully find a major IT niche for itself.

Central to a favorable overall environment for IT entrepreneurship is the availability of capital for would-be IT entrepreneurs. One of Silicon Valley's biggest advantages over aspiring IT hubs is its large corps of venture capitalists who evaluate the viability of New Economy start-ups and help them grow. Unfortunately for East Asia, the region lacks venture capitalists, and for a good reason.[23] Venture capitalists reflect the depth, width and sophistication of U.S. financial markets. When East Asia's banks and capital markets did a poor job of evaluating risk and monitoring investments even in the Old Economy, and this was one cause of the crisis, it is unrealistic to expect them to do a good job in the much more complex and unstable New Economy. Venture capitalists, just like more independent thinking, cannot be created overnight. However, East Asian countries can make a start by opening up and liberalizing their financial systems so that scarce resources will finally begin flowing to their most productive uses.

Inter-Regional Imbalances

Casual observation suggests there are significant inter-regional economic imbalances within East Asian countries. Capitals and other major urban centers usually account for a disproportionately large share of real output and income. This means that the residents of those areas enjoy higher living standards in comparison with their fellow citizens in other parts of the country.[24] Even in relatively developed and industrialized countries such as Korea, a noticeable economic gap exists among the various regions. Such imbalances are not unique to East Asia and are quite common throughout the world, and they tend to be more pronounced in developing countries.

Concentration of economic power often extends into other areas such as politics, culture, education, medical care, and infrastructure. For example, an oft-cited reason for migration into the major urban centers is the higher quality of education and hence greater opportunities for children in the future. To cite another example, in poorer countries, the lack of adequate basic infrastructure such as power, water supply, transportation and communications practically forces companies to locate in main cities. Geographical concentration of resources in virtually all aspects of national life inevitably interferes with well-balanced economic growth and development.

Of course, we must also realistically acknowledge that the predominant role of Seoul in Korea, Kuala Lumpur in Malaysia, Manila in the Philippines, and so forth are not accidents but rather reflect the evolution and interaction of economical, political, sociological, institutional, and historical forces. Be that as it may, it is equally clear that the geographical concentration of resources entails serious negative consequences, not only for the rest of the country but also for the main cities themselves as well.[25]

For example, the massive flow of labor into the capital and other major urban centers creates congestion, pollution, and excessive strains on infrastructure and basic services. Meanwhile, the rest of the country, especially the rural areas, suffers from brain drain, graying of population, and general decay and loss of dynamism. Paradoxically, while the main cities suffer from the negative consequences of over-population, at the same time some parts of the country suffer from under-population. Narrowing of the inter-regional economic gap is thus a win-win situation that benefits a Jakarta as much as a Kalimantan.

It is worth noting we are not just talking about the urban-rural divide here. The inter-urban divide, in the sense of the contrast between fast-growing main cities versus slow-growing or even declining regional cities, can be equally stark in some cases. The fact that the so many migrants, especially the young and the ambitious, choose to migrate to major cities, despite the unemployment, congestion, pollution, crime, and other problems, attests to the enormous differences in opportunities between the main cities and the rest of the country. Therefore, the key to achieving a well-balanced economic development is to reduce such enormous differences in opportunities.

IT and Imbalances

It is precisely in this area, creating a more level playing field for the various cities and regions of a country, that IT can make a solid contribution.[26] As indicated earlier, the essence of IT is that it reduces the cost of information and thus provides more equal access to information. Physical presence is less important in the New Economy than in the Old Economy due to the high and ever-improving quality of virtual presence. For example, the Internet allows us to constantly stay in touch with other parties and enables us to take care of many businesses that would have required traveling before. Therefore, the physical concentration of institutions and facilities in the main city becomes less of an advantage for the main city and equivalently, less of a disadvantage for the rest of the country, in the New Economy.

Underlying the physical concentration of institutions and facilities is a concentration of information and knowledge. Information and knowledge are immensely valuable resources in any economy, whether Old or New. One of the fundamental sources of the inter-regional inequality of opportunity that is at the root of inter-regional economic inequality has to be the asymmetric inter-regional distribution of information. Fortunately, IT will substantially reduce this information gap and hence promote a more geographically balanced pattern of economic development. We noted earlier that the IT revolution will help to democratize information by spreading information from a privileged elite to masses of ordinary people. By the same token, the IT revolution will devolve information from main cities to other areas.

As noted previously, physical location loses at least some of its relevance in the New Economy. Among other things, the Internet allows for remote or virtual access to a whole new range of employment opportunities.[27] The noticeable increase in the number of stay-at-home workers is changing lifestyles in developed countries, and we have already touched upon how IT has enabled India to become a major leader in back-office services. IT will also bring the central government and bureaucracy closer to those living outside the capital by providing them with improved and more convenient access to administrative services. At the same time, IT will strengthen the local governments in regional cities by enabling them to better serve surrounding rural areas.[28] IT-enabled educational services can reduce inter-regional gaps in the quality of education. One example is online distance education for remote areas. In short, IT holds out a whole lot of potential as a tool for well-balanced development.

Just as we must be realistic about the potential economic benefits of the IT revolution, we must also be realistic about what IT can do and cannot do for regional development. IT will certainly not by itself enable regions and regional cities to leapfrog their way into parity with the main city. To begin with, interactions through the Internet can never completely substitute for face-to-face interactions.[29] A click of the mouse will never feel like a handshake. In this sense, even in the New Economy main cities still enjoy the positive network effects associated with having the vast majority of important people. In many countries, including relatively advanced ones such as Korea, chances are that anybody who is "somebody" will live in the main city. In other words, although IT reduces distances, there is clearly a limit to its ability to do so. To cite just one example, while IT-enabled educational services hold a lot of promise, they can never completely substitute for actual schools and teachers.

We saw earlier that countries have to fulfill certain pre-conditions before they can begin to enjoy the economic benefits of the IT revolution. So it is with regional development. That is, although the benefits of IT for regional development are potentially large, they are neither automatic nor guaranteed. Above all, the realization of those benefits requires the availability of reliable and affordable telecom services throughout the country.[30] In fact, concentration of telecom, IT education and other IT infrastructure in the main city will widen rather than narrow the inter-regional economic gap by creating an inter-regional digital divide.[31] Equally importantly, the basic ingredients of regional development in the Old Economy, such as transportation, education and strong local government, remain as relevant as ever in the New Economy. In other words, IT is a complement rather than a substitute for the fundamental ingredients of regional development.[32]

Concluding Remarks and Implications for FDI

I have limited the discussion to what I believe are the most important issues for the sake of clarity and focus. This means I have omitted some relevant considerations. For example, in addition to telecommunications infrastructure and human resource development, the New Economy requires a well-functioning legal and regulatory environment that covers areas such as contract enforcement and consumer protection. Those issues are especially relevant for Japan and the NIEs since these economies by and large already have the physical and human infrastructure in place. A key issue in the integration of these economies into the New Economy is to encourage consumers and companies to use IT more actively for e-commerce, and a sound legal and regulatory environment will be conducive for making this connection.

Let me briefly repeat the main points of my discussion, in the hope that they may stimulate discussion among East Asia's policymakers and general public on how to best proceed with the New Economy. First, the IT revolution presents many opportunities for East Asian economies in terms of improving efficiency and thus promoting economic growth. Those opportunities are especially inviting in the manufacturing sector, the region's economic mainstay, since the bulk of global growth in e-commerce is expected to come from B2B. Thus the focus of the region's IT investments must be on local applications of existing technology.

Second, while East Asia stands to benefit significantly from the IT revolution, we should be realistic about its limitations as well. In particular, while IT may allow countries to leapfrog some technological barriers, IT will not enable countries to leapfrog sound economic policies. The New Economy may have changed the world, but not by so much as to change the key ingredients of successful economic performance. IT will help East Asian countries achieve sustainable economic growth and development only insofar as they maintain a sound overall policy environment.

Third, sitting back and waiting for the New Economy to arrive is a foolproof recipe for making sure it will never arrive. The New Economy requires basic pre-conditions. Above all, the poorer East Asian countries must liberalize their telecommunications sectors in order to improve the quantity and quality of telecom services. They must also make the necessary investments in human resource development. As for the region's richer countries, where the physical infrastructure is well developed and the quality of human capital is higher, the greater challenge lies in creating socio-economic conditions that are conducive for greater use of IT in economic activities.

Fourth, just as IT holds out a lot of promise for economic growth, it is also a potential catalyst of regional development in East Asian countries. In particular, IT promotes inter-regional equality of opportunity by breaking down the concentration of information and knowledge, and disseminating those valuable resources more evenly throughout the country. However, there are limits to what IT can do in terms of bringing about a more balanced development pattern and, just as importantly, the benefits of IT for regional development will not be realized unless East Asian countries fulfill certain key pre-conditions.

The dawn of the new millenium has thrust upon mankind a technological revolution that is sharply reducing the cost of information. In combination with globalization, the IT revolution is creating a world economy in which competitive pressures are as fierce and relentless as never before. East Asian economies will survive and thrive in this highly competitive New Economy only if they keep doing the things that they have done right, such as saving and investing a lot, while improving the things that they need to improve, such as the quality of corporate governance. If they do so, the New Economy will indeed prove to be a boon for all East Asians.

With respect to FDI, our analysis entails some significant policy implications. Above all, we have seen that affordable and reliable telecommunications services are probably the single most critical enabling pre-condition for the IT revolution and the New Economy. Again, this is especially relevant for the region's poorer economies. What this means is that governments throughout the region should seriously consider opening up their telecom sectors to private sector investors, including big foreign telecom companies with lots of capital and expertise. A big, practical obstacle for the governments of many developing countries in this area is the loss of significant revenues associated with the privatization of state-owned telecom monopolies. However, in light of the critical role of telecommunications in the IT revolution, it would be myopic indeed for governments to place too much weight on those revenue losses. In short, the IT revolution makes the case for telecom liberalization, including opening up to foreign investors, stronger than ever before. Governments of countries that are saddled with backward and under-developed telecom sectors should even consider offering fiscal incentives to attract foreign investors.

At the same time, the IT revolution significantly strengthens the incentive for FDI in the telecom sector. We can expect the demand for telecom services to grow rapidly as the IT revolution, including its commercial applications, takes root in an economy. Precisely because affordable and reliable telecom services are the single most enabling pre-condition for the IT revolution and the New Economy, the telecom industry is likely to offer investors, including foreign ones, higher and more sustainable returns than in the Old Economy. However, the extent to which FDI takes place will depend heavily on the degree of telecom liberalization. Furthermore, telecom liberalization in and of itself will not fully unleash the potential benefits of the IT revolution for economic growth, which, in both the New and Old Economy, requires a sound overall policy environment and helps to determine the returns to domestic and foreign investors, in telecom and beyond.

While FDI in the telecom sector can be a mutually rewarding experience for the host country and well-established foreign telecom companies – the former benefiting from the capital, technology and skills of the latter in improving telecom services, and the latter reaping attractive and sustainable returns on its investments — the IT revolution offers other mutually rewarding investment areas as well. For example, human resource development, which represents another key enabling pre-condition for the IT revolution, is one such area, as are complementary New Economy infrastructures such as logistics and transportation. Computer hardware and software also represent investment areas that can benefit both the host country and the foreign investor, although whether such FDI improves the welfare of the host country depends on the competitiveness of the resulting products vis-à-vis imports.

From the host country's viewpoint, the benefits of FDI into telecom and other IT-relevant sectors are not limited to fostering the New Economy and ultimately faster economic growth. As we have already seen, IT can play a significant role in reducing inter-regional inequality within a country, although there are limits on how much IT in and of itself can do so. To the extent that promoting a more balanced national development is a high-priority objective, governments may offer additional fiscal incentives for foreign investors in less developed regions. Furthermore, FDI into such regions may very well be commercially viable for the investors themselves. For example, stylized facts suggest that there is a strong pent-up demand for telecom services, including satellite-based services, in many backward regions of poor developing countries.

Finally, although the focus of this paper is on East Asia, all of the main lessons are applicable to other parts of the world as well. Our lessons are particularly relevant for developing countries where economic growth and well-balanced development are more urgently needed. In conjunction with sound policies, IT will enable countries to grow faster as well as grow in a more balanced way.

References

Alabau, A. (1997). Telecommunications and the Information Society in European Regions. *Telecommunications Policy, 21*(8), 761-771.

Amirahmadi, H. (1995). Information Technology, the Organization of Production, and Regional Development. *Environment and Planning A, 27*(11), 1745-1775.

Bhatnagar, P. (1999). Telecom Reforms in Developing Countries and the Outlook for Electronic Commerce. *Journal of International Economic Law, 2*(4), 695-712.

Blum, U. and Dudley, L. (1999). The Two Germanies: Information Technology and Economic Divergence, 1949-1989. *Journal of Institutional and Theoretical Economics, 155*(4), 710-737.

Boekema, F., Morgan, K., Bakkers, S. and Rutten, R. (Eds). (2000). *Knowledge, Innovation and Economic Growth: The Theory and Practice of Learning Regions.* Cheltenham: Edward Elgars.

Brennan, E. and Richardson, H. (1989). Asian Megacity Characteristics, Problems, and Policies. *International Regional Science Review, 12*(2), 117-129.

Crocioni, P. (2001). Should Telecoms Liberalization Stop at Call Termination? *Telecommunications Policy, 25*(1-2), 39-58.

Dedrick, J. and Kraemer, K. (1998). *Asia's computer challenge: threat or opportunity for the United States and the world?* New York and Oxford: Oxford University Press.

Dunning, J. (2000). *Regions, Globalization and Knowledge-Based Economy.* New York: Oxford University Press.

The Economist. (2000). Asia Online: The Tiger and the Tech. 5-11 February, 68-70.

Gasper, J. and Glaeser, E. (1998). Information Technology and the Future of Cities. *Journal of Urban Economics, 43*(1), 135-156.

Gera, S., Gu, W. and Lee, F. (1999). Information Technology and Labour Productivity Growth: An Empirical Analysis for Canada and the United States. *Canadian Journal of Economics, 32*(2), 384-407.

Gillespie, A. and Cornford, J. (1996). Telecommunications Infrastructures and Regional Development. In W. Dutton (Ed.), *Information and communication technologies: Visions and realities.* New York: Oxford University Press.

Giuliano, G. (1998). Information Technology, Work Patterns and Intra-Metropolitan Location: A Case Study. *Urban Studies, 35*(7), 1077-1095.

Goldstein, A. and O'Connor, D. (2000). E-Commerce for Development: Prospects and Policy Issues. Technical Paper No. 164. Paris: OECD Development Center.

Goldstein, M. (1998). *The Asian financial crisis: Causes, cures, and systemic implications.* Washington D.C.: Institute for International Economics.

Hanna, N. (1994). Exploiting information technology for development: A case study of India. Discussion Paper No. 246. Washington, D.C.: World Bank.

Harindranath, G. (1995). State Policy and the Development of Information Technology Industries: India and East Asia in Comparative Perspective. *Asia Pacific Business Review, 2*(2), 48-59.

Heeks, R. (1996). *India's Software Industry: State Policy, Liberalization and Industrial Development.* London: Sage Publications.

Heijke, H. and Muyksen, J. (Eds.). (2000). *Education and Training in a Konwledge-Based Economy.* London: Macmillan.

Hicks, D. and Nivin, S. (2000). Beyond Globalization: Localized Returns to IT Infrastructure Investments. *Regional Studies, 34*(2), 115-127.

International Monetary Fund. (1998). *World Economic Outlook May 1998.* Washington D.C.: International Monetary Fund.

International Telecommunications Union. (1999). *Challenges to the Network: Internet for Development.* Geneva: International Telecommunications Union.

Iskander, M. (1999). Corporate Restructuring and Governance in East Asia. *Finance and Development, 36*(1), 42-45.

Izaguirre, A. (1999). Private Participation in Telecommunications – Recent Trends. Private Sector View Point No. 206. Washington, D.C.: World Bank.

James, J. (1999). *Globalization, information technology and development.* London: Macmillan Press.

Jian, T., Sachs, J. and Warner, A. (1996). Trends in Regional Inequality in China. *China Economic Review, 7*(1), 1-21.

Jorgenson, D. and Stiroh, K. (1999). Information Technology and Growth. *American Economic Review, 89*(2), 109-115.

Kanbur, R. and Zhang, X. (1999). Which Regional Inequality? The Evolution of Rural-Urban and Inland-Coastal Inequality in China from 1983 to 1995. *Journal of Comparative Economics, 27*(4), 686-701.

Kim, S. and Hahn, Y. (1998). Venture Capital Industry and Its Role in the United States Economy: Relevance of the United States Model to the Economy of the Republic of Korea. *Asia Pacific Development Journal, 5*(2), 99-116.

Kraemer, K. and Dedrick, J. (1994). Payoffs from Investment in Information Technology.

Krugman, P. (1997, July-August). How Fast Can the U.S. Economy Grow? *Harvard Business Review*, 123-129.

Kudyba, S. and Diwan, R. (2002). The Impact of Information Technology on U.S. Industry. *Japan and the World Economy, 14*(3), 321-333.

Lamberton, D. (1994). The Information Revolution in the Asia-Pacific Region. *Asian Pacific Economic Literature, 8*(2), 31-57.

Lee, B. and Barua, A. (1999). An Integrated Assessment of Productivity and Efficiency Impacts of Information Technology Investments: Old Data, New Analysis and Evidence. *Journal of Productivity Analysis, 12*(1), 21-43.

Lehr, B. and Lichtenberg, F. (1999). Information Technology and Its Impact on Productivity: Firm-Level Evidence from Government and Private Data Sources, 1977-1993. *Canadian Journal of Economics, 32*(2), 335-362.

Malecki, E. and Oinas, P. (Eds.). (1999). *Making connections: Technological learning and regional economic change.* Aldershott, UK: Ashgate.

Mansell, R. and When, U. (1998). *Knowledge Societies: Information Technology for Sustainable Development.* Oxford: Oxford University Press.

Maskell, P. (1998). *Competitiveness, Localized Learning and Regional Development: Specialization and Prosperity in Small Open Economies.* London: Routledge.

NASSCOM. (2000). The Indian IT Industry. Retrieved from the World Wide Web: http://www.nasscom.org.

Norman, A. (1993). *Information society: An economic theory of discovery, invention and innovation.* Norwell, MA: Kluwer Academic.

Organization for Economic Cooperation and Development. (1999). *Asia and the global crisis: The industrial dimension.* Paris: OECD.

Quibria, M. and Tschang, T. (2001). Information and Communications Technology and Poverty: An Asian Perspective. Working Paper No. 12. Tokyo: Asian Development Bank Institute.

Salim, E. (1998). Toward Sustainable Development of the Asian and Pacific Region. *Asia Pacific Development Journal, 5*(1), 1-7.

Schapper, P. (2001). Not Just Narrowing the Divide – Leaping Ahead: Leadership in E-Base Public Administration. Paper presented at the ADBI Capacity Building Workshop on Information and Communication Technology (ICT) for Developing Asia, February 21, 2001, Singapore.

Soete, L. (2000). Technology, Globalization and Employment: Analytical and Policy Challenges. In H. Heijke and J. Muyksen (Eds.), *Education and Training in a Konwledge-Based Economy.* London: Macmillan.

Szczypula, J., Tschang, T. and Vikas, O. (2000). Reforming the Educational Knowledge Base: Course Content and Skills in the Internet Age. In T. Tschang and T. Della Senta (Eds.), *Access to Knowledge: New Information Technologies and the Emergence of the Virtual University*. Oxford: Elsevier Science.

Talero, E. and Gaudette, P. (1995). Harnessing Information for Development – A Proposal for a World Bank Group Strategy. Discussion Paper No. 313. Washington D.C.: World Bank.

Tisdell, C. (1997). The Environment and Sustainable Development in the Asia-Pacific. *Asian Pacific Economic Literature, 11*(1), 39-55.

Wigan, M. (1984). Information Technology and Integrated Regional Development. In P. Nijkamp and P. Rietveld (Eds.), *Information Systems for Integrated Regional Planning*. Amsterdam: North-Holland.

World Bank. (1998a). *East Asia: the Road to Recovery*. Washington D.C.: World Bank.

World Bank. (1998b). *World Development Report 1998/99: Knowledge for Development*. Washington, D.C.: World Bank.

Yorukoglu, M. (1998). The Information Technology Productivity Paradox. *Review of Economic Dynamics, 1*(2), 551-592.

Chapter XVII

Digital Engineering Campus:
Economics, Acceptance, and Impact

Milind J. Mahajan
Mirash Infotech, India

Sunil S. Umrani
Sunind Systems, India

Narendra S. Chaudhari
Nanyang Technological University, Singapore

Abstract

In this chapter, we introduce two existing web-based, e-learning approaches, and examine economic and social aspects of their usage in society. Specifically, we briefly introduce an e-learning initiative in Singapore. Secondly, we give a detailed description of a case study regarding the experiment called "Digital Engineering Campus," which is an NGO initiative to provide supplementary educational facilities for engineering colleges in India. Considering the economic as well as social benefits, using our detailed case-study of Digital Engineering Campus, we argue that developing countries like India have tremendous growth potential in web-based education. Further, the experiences of developed countries with web-based education will prove to be highly beneficial for developing countries like India.

Education and the Web: Economic and Social Aspects

Continued growth of the education sector is very important for improving the standard of living. This sector becomes all the more important for developing countries. Motivated by the International Finance Corporation (IFC) and World Bank (World Bank, 1994, 1996), James Tooley reports factual data about 18 case studies of education projects in 12 countries (Tooley, 2001). A part of Tooley's study also reports the use of Internet for teaching in India (Tooley, 2001).

Professor Roger C. Shank, in his excellent book, "Designing World-class e-Learning," contrasts Internet-based learning with traditional, school-based learning (Shank, 2002). Shank coined the term, "learning-by-doing" for e-learning, and has given seven criteria for assessing the effectiveness of e-learning, specially focusing the freedom of learning. He provides in-depth observations of the e-learning instructional design process, delivery of resources, and accessing the utilization of e-learning resources. He has given concrete illustrations of these points by including the case studies of e-learning initiatives of IBM, GE, Harvard Business School, and Columbia University.

Computing and Web technology has caused widespread economic disruption, limiting growth in productivity (Brown & Duguid, 2000). For example, for the U.S.A., the multi-factor productivity growth rate (labor and capital taken into account) was 2.5% for 1984 to 1973, but it was only 0.7% for 1973 to 1990 (Brown & Duguid, 1996). To explain this phenomenon, the inventor of mouse, Douglas Englebart, states that, "Real social danger today is that the technology is erupting and moving so much faster than it ever has in all of our historical experience … time to start adapting society to this revolution in the technology. There is a lot of potential danger ahead if we do not adapt to it successfully" (Huges, 1986, p.599).

Business writers Downes & Mui (1998) define the "Law of Disruption" as, "social, political and economic systems change incrementally, but technology changes exponentially."

However, Brown & Duguid (2000, p.85) indicate the (future) emergence of new technology to adapt this: "…(e-) technology design has not taken adequate amount of work and its demands … (technology design) has aimed at an idealized image of individuals and information."

Indeed, we see a number of attempts to achieve this goal. Due to influential web-based learning tools, we now witness emerging concepts of distributed intelligence, distributed creation and sharing of knowledge, formation of the social nature of learning ecology, and its social impact.

Singapore gives us a scenario of the fastest growth in the advanced world. In Singapore, the e-learning initiative is largely due to the push of government, and we very briefly comment on this scenario in Singapore, both at tertiary education, as well as primary and secondary schools.

Developing countries like India have tremendous growth potential. In such countries, the government-supported education system is slowly being supplemented by non-governmental organizations (NGOs). To illustrate the interplay of government as well as

NGOs in the evolution of the social fabric, we have chosen to detail a scenario in a developing country like India. We give a scenario concerning India's electronic and educational infrastructure, university system, and attempts for quality assurance in higher education in India. We focus on an engineering education scenario in one of the states, Maharashtra State within India. We include the details about our case study, called "Digital Engineering Campus," a portal designed and maintained by an NGO, Sunind Systems Pvt. Ltd. (SSPL), Pune. More technical details about this experiment are given in Appendix A. We conclude this chapter by giving brief remarks.

E-Learning Initiative at Singapore

To induce its wider impact in Singapore's highly dynamic society, Singapore's government has adopted e-learning initiatives. To increase awareness of e-learning, it organized a month-long campaign during 2000 and 2001. In the past three years, the roots of e-learning have enthusiastically been introduced in educational institutions in Singapore. Nanyang Technological University (NTU) has adopted e-learning initiatives since 1999. The main reason for giving so much importance to this initiative is the wider perception that the traditional models of learning (e.g., classroom model of learning, participation in training programs, conferences, etc.) are too costly, and many times they fail to deliver improved performance.

A uniform web-based platform for delivery of e-learning resources to students was introduced in NTU, Singapore in 2000. The delivery platform is a customized version of Blackboard, and is called "edventure." Within NTU, most of the web-based content is used to supplement and enrich the face-to-face delivery. However, in 2002, many schools in NTU took a major step by deciding to replace the classroom lectures with web-based content.

Lecturers are encouraged to use "edventure" for posting suitable e-content for their courses. It may be noted that security features of "edventure" provide suitable privacy, which can be controlled by the instructor-in-charge for the course. The easiest alternative is to put textual content of PowerPoint presentations on the Web site. A few lecturers have also used voice narration recorded with the PowerPoint slides. Evolution of a complete package with video, voice, slides, and hyperlinks is a recent phenomenon. An independent study relating the effectiveness of such contents has been carried out by Bartsch & Cobern (2003). Teachers, students, as well as administrators have many concerns regarding this initiative: Can the e-lectures be as effective as (or more effective than) the face-to-face lectures? Some studies have been carried out for tackling this problem. However, the discussion about these studies is not within the scope of our discussion here.

Successful integration of Information and Communication Technologies (ICTs) in schools has been studied in last decade (e.g., Sivin-Lachala, 1998). The main focus of the application of ICTs in schools in Singapore is to develop higher-order thinking skills. Ping and Hang (2003) give the study of effectiveness of ICTs within schools in Singapore from the pedagogical and socio-cultural point of view.

India: Electronic & Educational Infrastructure

The Internet is transforming the scenario of imparting education in the developing countries like India at a very fast rate (some related information is available on the Web site: http://www.educationinfoindia.com/onlinedu.htm). Many universities, like Indira Gandhi Open National University, New Delhi (Web site: http://www.ignou.ac.in), Jawaharlal Nehru Technological University, Hyderabad (Web site: http://www.jntu.ac.in/), Punjab Technical University, Jalandhar (Web site: http://www.punjabtechnical university.com/), etc., in India have an "online virtual campus." Even states like Andhra (Web site: http://www.andhraonline.com), and Kerala (Web site: http://www.kerala.gov.in/) have good portals giving a lot of useful information. Many universities in India now have distance education programs and the Internet is now widely used by these universities for facilitating their activities (Web site: http://www.shiksha.com/infobin/corr/corindex.htm).

Indeed, in a two-day conclave of the Confederation of Indian Industry (CII), Gautam Kumra of McKinsey and Company, stated that the cost of education in India is 30 percent of the cost in U.S., and there are several reasons why India can compete globally in the higher education market. He further predicted that it is possible to attract more than 150,000 foreign students to study in Indian Institutions by 2010 (Indo-Asian News Service, 2002). While India has the capability to maintain the quality of education, the investment in maintaining this high quality using Internet resources needs effective co-ordination of web-professionals as well as academic professionals.

At the national level, India has a highly developed satellite program, having launched a wide range of satellites that are used for communications, television broadcasts and remote sensing. In July 2002, the central government of India launched two new satellites (Edusat and Gramsat) to give a boost to education and rural development.

Global Education Market and India

As observed in the Indo-Asian News Service in July of 2002, "Australia was able to increase the number of foreign students studying there from 20,000 in 1990 to 100,000 in 2000 and earned revenue of $800 million." With the economic slow-down, countries like Singapore as well as India and China, are exploring the possibility of tapping the global education market.

India is particularly attractive for foreign students, as it has advantages such as: (i) high fluency of English language amongst its academicia, (ii) low cost of living, and (iii) very high educational standards. In addition to the already existing seven IITs in metros, central government is planning to have five more IITs at relatively smaller places. High educational standards in Indian Institutes of Technologies (IITs) are now spread in relatively smaller places using web-based education. For example, lectures in the K.R. Information Techology School of IIT Mumbai are now available online during the classrooms in institutes located thousands of kilometers away in places like Nagpur,

Indore, Latur, and Pune (Web site: http://www.dep.iitb.ac.in/rc.html). Further, many institutes have been identified as "National Institutes of Technology" (NITs), and they have been given substantial funding for spreading Internet-based education.

Role of Universities in Higher Education in India

Within the field of higher education, India has 259 universities having more than 10,750 colleges affiliated to them, eight million students, and 400,000 teachers. Thus, it has one of the world's largest higher education systems, monitored at the national level by University Grants Commission (UGC), Government of India. With the demonstration of success with experiments like the one in IIT Bombay, their adaptation at wider level has become feasible. Within India, the growth in the field of higher education has resulted in the participation of the private sector in education. The market size of management education alone in India is estimated to be around US$300 million, while the Information Technology (IT) education and training is estimated to be around US$150 million, with an annual growth of 25 percent.

For quality assurance of educational standards, India has the National Association and Accreditation Council (NAAC).

Universities are primarily responsible of maintaining the quality in education. They have direct control over the examination system. Many universities have already established e-learning sites for their students. In our specific experiment of engineeringcampus.com, we are yet to associate it with all universities. However, with a directive from the state government, all the universities will contribute course content to this site.

Engineering Education in Maharashtra State

The infrastructure cost for establishing connectivity facilities are far less important, and the major cost component is in the form of "soft" costs that have to be incurred in the effective usage of Internet facilities. Continuous maintenance as well as updating of information on the web is especially important in fields like education. Many educational institutes in India are realizing this issue in a "hard" way. In the state of Maharashtra, the government is convinced about this problem, and has entrusted this responsibility to professional organizations. We focus on this initiative to support engineering education.

Maharashtra State in India has more than 150 engineering colleges, and has more than 50,000 students studying in them for their engineering degree. Further, the state has more than 110 polytechnic-level institutions, which provide diploma-level engineering education to more than 70,000 students. The state has some of the most prominent universities like University of Poona, Bombay University, who maintain very high standards of engineering education for tens of thousands their students. While the state has well-developed industrial belts like Pune-Bombay, majority of the engineering colleges in the state are located in rural areas, and have significant percentage (more than 50 percent) of students studying in them.

The Government of Maharashtra is concerned about uniformity in the quality of engineering education, especially in remotely located engineering colleges within the state. Techno-savvy solutions like digital course contents, online quizzes, and online evaluation and interactivity with experts using the Internet, have still social resistance in other branches of education. However, in the area of engineering education, this alternative has received a very welcome response widely. While the Government of Maharashtra does not want to commit any financial resources for this activity, it has entrusted the responsibility to Non-Government Organizations (NGOs).

In the remaining part of this chapter, we discuss the socio-economic aspects of one such experiment called "Digital Engineering Campus" (also referred to as engineeringcampus.com). This web-based solution targets a few tens of thousands of engineering students as users. Furthermore, it makes provision for a few hundreds of engineering teachers to interact with these students for imparting a quality education.

In the context of Digital Engineering Campus, in the next section, we also address the following issues:

1. Socio-economic details about the engineering education within the state,

2. Cost-effectiveness of digital solutions,

3. Social acceptance of online as well as off-line materials, especially related to effective questions, and cost-effectiveness of the existing Internet-based system,

4. Future expansions of this system, as well as expected costs involved,

5. Socio-economic impact and challenges in the immediate future.

A Case Study: Digital Engineering Campus

Engineering colleges in Maharashtra state are spread all over the state and most of them are in the rural areas. The students studying in these colleges face the following difficulties:

a. Unavailability of expert staff for teaching,

b. Less number of industries available for summer training, and project work,

c. No career guidance centers,

d. Unavailability of renowned publications, books,

e. Lack of access to expert professors and students of urban engineering colleges.

As the Apex body at the central Government level, All India Council for Technical Education (AICTE) has a responsibility of maintaining the quality of engineering education at the national level. The AICTE act, passed by the parliament, empowers AICTE to provide as well as revoke the accreditation for each college depending upon facilities provided by that college to students.

As the Apex body in state, the Higher and Technical education department of the Government of Maharashtra state is responsible for providing all the necessary facilities to engineering students and overcoming the difficulties stated above. Also it is responsible for improving the quality of education in the state. Though very few colleges in the state are Government run or Government funded, this department has a responsibility for maintaining uniformity in education by controlling the admission process all over the state.

The availability of Internet access in remotely located engineering colleges is still a real problem. Here, AICTE has taken an initiative to provide all Engineering colleges with financial support for establishing Internet facilities in their colleges. Also AICTE has been forcing all colleges to set up a dedicated computer lab only for Internet browsing.

Thus, both state government, as well as AICTE (at national level) is helping technical educational institutes in pursuing Digital E-learning tools to a large extent. Surely these positive steps from government and the participation of NGOs are making an impact on the digital solutions, and e-learning concepts.

As an initiative in this direction, while the Government of Maharashtra does not want to commit any financial resources for this activity, it has supported an NGO, with one of the authors (Mr. Sunil Umrani) as CEO (Sunind Systems Pvt. Ltd.), to pursue these activities. This organization now has a functional "Digital Engineering Campus" (Web site: http://www.engineeringcampus.com/) with hundreds of thousands of engineering students as users, and hundreds of engineering teachers who interact with these students for imparting a quality education.

Socio-Economic Details – Some Observations

Engineering colleges in the state are divided in different categories as follows:

1.   Government colleges – Owned by government,

2.   Semi-Government colleges – Partially funded by government, and,

3.   Private colleges – Privately run colleges (self supporting – financially).

State Government controls the admission process. The main reason for this control is to ensure justice to a large number of candidates desiring the admission to limited seats.

A directive of the Supreme Court of India allows the private colleges to choose their own fee structure (justifying it on the basis of their expenses). Subsequently, Government of Maharashtra gave the freedom to private colleges to decide the amount of fees. However, in September 2003, this led to the situation in which a majority of meritorious students were forced to pay a huge amount of fees for their education, which they could not afford. This effectively denied admission to a large number of such students belonging to the families having average, and lower-income levels. Maharashtra state witnessed huge social unrest disrupting the admission process. While the matter has now been referred to special commissions, and courts, by and large, the existing fee structure in private colleges is as follows:

(a)   Free seats – fee charged is same that of Government college,

(b)   Paid seat – fee charged is pretty high and is approximately eight to 10 times that of free seat. (To control the social unrest, the state legislative assembly is in the process of imposing directives about the fees for these seats.)

Cost-Effectiveness of Digital Solution

There is a scarcity of experienced professors in rural areas. Students in the colleges in rural areas are bound to opt for private coaching classes or search for class notes of renowned professors. They travel to different colleges in urban areas. They spend their valuable time as well as money for this purpose. With a digital solution, they can get the access to these professors at any given time from their computer system.

As a second example, engineering students have to undergo a summer internship program and complete project work in industries in their final academic year. Due to limited industries in many parts of the state, the students of colleges located in the remote and underdeveloped areas have to travel to the industrially progressive belts where industries are in ample numbers. For this they again spend thousands of rupees and valuable time. In spite of spending a lot of money and time, it is not guaranteed that all the students will get projects or summer training. Many of the students fall in traps and buy dummy certificates and ready-made projects from small industries. This not only puts students in monetary losses, but also hampers the quality of graduating engineers.

With Digital Engineering Campus, this situation is overcome by virtually bringing the industries to every student, via the Internet. This site acts as a bridge between the students and the industries. It is a give-and-take policy with a win-win situation, where industries get a centralized database of all the students in the state, and the students get access to the information about the industries. The industries select or search the students' list as per their criteria and inform the colleges through the Internet. Industries also put up their requirements regarding the available projects and training on the web portal. Students can view the list and then interact with the short-listed industries, and personally call upon them or visit them.

Socio-Economic Acceptance of Digital Solution

In 2001, the acceptance of such a new, innovative idea was slow. However, the response is improving very fast. Support of the government in these activities facilitates the expansion of this digital Internet-based, e-learning system. Government recognition plays a very important role in the initial phase, until the time the users of the site are well aware of the usefulness of the contents.

In the study material section, discipline-wise courseware notes designed by subject experts will be provided. Last minute revision is an added advantage. This is to help the students save valuable time, by doing away with referring many books for each and every topic. Subject experts have designed the study material, after extracting information from various books, so as to give the students the best possible course material.

University Question papers of previous years are available to the students. Viva and the Oral Exams section help the students in preparing for the examinations through the Online Oral Exams. In the Forum section, students can place their queries related to their discipline, which are answered by the Subject Experts. This is especially useful for students located in remote areas who can interact with the subject experts at any given time and get their problems tackled on a one-to-one basis. Also, there is the facility to browse the Question Archives and a few more features are included. Students have already reported saving of their precious time and money.

Details and Future Expansion

The facilities provided on the Web site "EngineeringCampus.com" are listed separately (in Appendix A). As a future expansion, a video-conferencing facility will be added to the web portal. This is an innovative module being incorporated into the web-based e-learning program. As the name suggests, the students can not only listen to the lectures (Video Streaming), but also get in touch and interact with (Video Conferencing) eminent lecturers, professors, distinguished persons from within the state or other parts of the country by prior arrangements. Students are informed about the upcoming lectures and seminars by group messages.

Socio-Economic Impact and Challenges in the Immediate Future

Socio-economic impact involves far-reaching positive consequences. It is a gradual and ongoing process where students, especially those from rural areas will benefit immensely. Due to a tie-up with various industries for projects and placements, opportunities for jobs will greatly increase. These trends will motivate the students to excel in academics and at the same time gradually elevate the economic status.

The implementation of this web-based, e-learning portal incorporates distance learning, advanced teaching models, development, visualization, delivery mechanisms of courseware, video-conferencing, use of web browsing and e-mail facilities, facilities which generate employment opportunities, etc.

Acceptance of this innovative e-learning concept as a supplement to the traditional education system is a challenge. Interacting with thousands of students, colleges, universities, faculties, and industries and bringing them all together on a single platform poses an exciting prospect and a challenge. Penetrating rural areas with this latest technology and its implementation is also a formidable task.

Benefits to the Student Community

We briefly give a list of some of the benefits of this initiative to students:

1. Study material, compiled by the highly qualified and experienced faculty, interviews and discussions involving eminent persons and constant contact with these faculties for getting problems and queries solved,

2. Students can send solved answer papers and the experts will evaluate and suggest changes and provide tips, etc.,

3. Students can put forth their views and interact with the elite panel,

4. Students can gain confidence of attending the much-dreaded "Vivas" by going through a question bank of subjective and objective questions with model answers,

5. Placements, summer training, and projects can be selected by interacting with the various industries online, thus saving valuable time,

6. Guidance on the methods of preparation, handy hints and schedules of Post Graduation and other competitive examinations (GATE, TOFFEL / GRE / CAT / CET, etc.) and venues and other relevant details are easily available,

7. Being in touch with the latest developments in the field of science and technology is possible, through publishing of white papers,

8. Placing orders and subsequent door delivery of engineering books (including those which are difficult to procure), as well as CBT kits is done online,

9. Interaction with fellow students of different colleges, for exchange of information like college festivals, picnics, and resale of engineering tools and instruments, hostels, etc., is possible,

10. E-mail and chat facilities are provided,

11. Experts, college authorities and other people from the education department can be contacted easily throughout the year for queries.

More details of digital solutions provided on engineeringcampus.com are given separately in an Appendix A.

Concluding Remarks

Many facets of the web-based model of education have evolved in the last decade, and advanced countries already have tools for implementing many of such important facets. Some of the most important features of web-based education are: (i) learning by doing, (ii) learning through discussion (boards), with the ability to review discussion threads, (iii) quick self-evaluation, and (iv) guided feedback. Companies like Blackboard have already well-established tools for implementing such features. Evaluation of effectiveness of these technologies is frequently carried out in advanced countries. The results of such studies lead to continuous improvements in tools for developing web-based education.

Developing countries like India have tremendous growth potential in web-based education. NGO's have been supplementing such efforts in India. A lot remains to be done about systematic evaluation of the effectiveness of these efforts. However, in general the advantages derived by experiments like "Digital Engineering Campus" are highly useful from socio-economic considerations.

References

Bartsch, R.A. and Cobern, K.M. (2003). Effectiveness of PowerPoint presentations in lectures. *Computers & Education, 41*(1), 77-86.

Brown, J. S. and Duguid, P. (1996). The University in the Digital Age. Times Higher Education Supplement, May 10, 1996 (Multimedia Supplement), iv-vi.

Brown, J. S. and Duguid, P. (2000). *The Social Life of Information.* Boston, MA: Harvard Business School Press.

Digital Engineering Campus Web site. Sunind Systems Pvt Ltd. Retrieved from the World Wide Web: http://www.engineeringcampus.com/.

Downes, L. and Mui, C. (1998). *Unleashing the Killer App: Digital Strategies for Market Dominance.* Boston: Harvard Business School Press.

Huges, R. (1986). *The Fatal Shore: The Epic of Australia's Founding.* New York: Knopf.

Indo-Asian News Service. (2002, July). Retrieved from the World Wide Web at: (i) http://www.symonds.net/pipermail/education-india/2002-July/000009.html; and (ii) http://www.symonds.net/pipermail/education-india/2002-July/000013.html.

Ping, L.C. and Hang, D. (2003). An Activity theory approach to Research of ICT integration in Singapore Schools. *Computers & Education, 41*(1), 49-63.

Shank, R. (2002). *Designing World-class E-Learning: How IBM, GE, Harvard Business School, & Columbia University are Succeeding at e-Learning.* New York: McGraw Hill.

Sivin-Kachala, J. (1998). *Report on the effectiveness of technology in schools: 1990-1997.* Washington, D.C.: Software Publishers Association.

Tooley, J. (2001). *The Global Education Industry: Lessons from private education in Developing Countries.* (Second Edition), London: The Institute of Economic Affairs (IEA). (First Edition, 1999).

World Bank. (1994). *Higher Education: The Lessons of Experience.* Washington, D.C.: World Bank.

World Bank. (1996). *From Plan to Market: World Development Report 1996.* Washington, D.C.: World Bank.

Appendix

Brief Overview of "Digital Engineering Campus"

The students get registered on the Web site and are provided *unique user names and passwords* for logging onto the Web site and making use of the facilities provided. A *joint committee*, comprising of company employees and officials from the education department co-ordinates and monitors the progress and oversees the implementation.

The examples of Digital Engineering Campus (www.engineeringcampus.com) implementation in Maharashtra and Assam states of India are highly encouraging. Maharashtra has nearly 150,000 students pursuing various engineering courses. Here, the project has been successfully implemented at some colleges. Similarly, it is in the process of being implemented in the northeastern state of Assam, which is remotely located and has a hilly terrain. Thus, Digital Engineering Campus is a boon to the engineering students of Assam, who can interact with the best academicians and gain the knowledge in spite of being remotely located. Industries in the country are accessible for summer training, projects and placements.

In Assam, an implementation of a pilot project for the students and faculty of the Government College of Engineering – Guwahati pursuing Bachelor's degree and Post Graduation various disciplines of Engineering has been done. The contents displayed on the web-based, e-learning program are made available to all the students and faculty of the concerned disciplines, separately. Staff and students of the Government College of Engineering – Guwahati are able to access the data pertaining to their disciplines, by use of unique user names and passwords, provided by the company Sunind Systems Pvt. Ltd. (SSPL).

Details of Implementation in Maharashtra State

More than 18 facilities offered to the students are broadly classified under five headings, namely:

1. Academics
2. Industry
3. General
4. User
5. Others

1. The *Academics* section deals with all the academic requirements of the students and provides guidance in the form of study material/question papers/forum to interact with experts/video streaming/video-conferencing, etc. Highly qualified and experienced (10 years+) Experts' panel is responsible for handling the respective disciplines.

2.   *Industry* as the name suggests, provides unlimited opportunities to the students to explore avenues for projects, summer training and jobs. This innovative facility for the first time brings the students and the industry together on a common platform.

3.   Facilities like Online Bookstore, post-graduation (PG) – higher education opportunities, contacts, News from Directorate of Technical Education, etc., are provided in the *General* section.

4.   In the *User* section, information about self (academic/medical/personal), enhancing general knowledge, tests and quiz, being in touch with classmates and other fun-filled activities, etc., are possible.

5.   *Others* section provides information of the college (disciplines/number of seats/staff strength/facilities, etc.) and also helps the parents keep track of their wards' progress in the college.

A brief description of each of the sections is given in the following:

Academics

Study Material: As the name suggests, *discipline wise* courseware notes designed by subject experts, conforming to the university syllabi, is provided in this section. Last minute revision is an added advantage. This is to help the students save valuable time, by doing away with referring to many books for each and every topic. Subject experts have designed the study material, after extracting information from various books/ journals/ papers, etc., so as to give the students the best possible course material. Graphical representations, animations, 3-D models, etc., of theories, mathematical calculations, structural and functional aspects of different systems, are incorporated for better understanding of the subjects. Procedures encouraged by the Dept. of IT – Government of India, like development of courseware, various teaching models, distance learning, etc., have been incorporated here.

Oral Exams: Students face problems during Vivas. This section helps the students in preparing for the oral examinations through the provision of *subjective* and *objective* question bank. Students can assess their knowledge by undertaking practice and online tests, where they can attempt to answer a set of questions. At the end, their performance analysis (based on the topics / number of wrong answers, list of wrong answers) is given. This facility can also help the students for competitive exam preparations.

Question Papers: University Question papers of the previous five years are available to the students. Moreover, Model Answer Sets prepared by the Subject Experts can also be obtained. A question bank is also maintained, which can be used by the students for self-assessment. Solved question papers can be sent to respective subject experts (through us) for assessment and valuable tips can be gained.

Emerging Technology: Students are kept abreast of the global emerging trends and technologies, through this section. White papers on these latest technologies are provided to the students. Details of projects successfully implemented by the ex-students at the industry level are published so as to encourage the thought processes and motivate the students.

Video Streaming & Conferencing: These are two innovative modules being incorporated into the web-based, e-learning program. As the names suggest, the students can not only listen to the lectures (Video Streaming), but also get in touch and interact with (Video Conferencing) eminent lecturers, professors, distinguished persons from within the state / other parts of the country by prior arrangements. Students are informed about the upcoming lectures and seminars by group messages.

Forum: In this section, students place their queries related to their discipline / career, which are answered by the Subject Experts. This is especially useful for students who are shy and feel hesitant to get their problems tackled on a one-to-one basis. Facility to browse the Question Archives for questions that have been asked by fellow students and few more features are also included.

Industry

This facility offers a *common meeting ground* for the student community and the industry. Here, the academic performances and other details of all the students are made available to the industries from all over the country. Industries put up details of their profiles for the benefit of the student community. Industries can easily tap the right students for projects / recruitment, etc., by avoiding tedious campus interviews, placing advertisements, etc.

Projects/summer training: In this section, companies from different disciplines display information related to *projects and summer training* available in their organizations. Students seeking Final Year Projects, Workshops and Summer Training can select the appropriate industries and mail their resumes accordingly. This saves precious time, which can be utilized for academics.

Placement: Various options are provided to the students, so as to help them view the different requirements of the Industries. This facility is also an incentive for the students to fare well and concentrate on academics. Students also do not have to run around in search of placements and their precious time is saved. Industries also save time and money by the omission of screening of candidates and subsequent interviews.

General

Online book store: Here the idea is to make books and Computer-Based Training (CBT) kits available to colleges and students, not only at their doorsteps, but also at discounted rates directly from publishers. Books required by engineering students are listed on our portal and orders can be placed with us – Online. Our company makes sure that the books are door delivered at the desired address. Specific information about each book like Subject, Title, Author, Publisher, Price, Edition, Index, etc., is made available on the web portal. This would help the students and college librarians to select suitable books of desired subjects. Books that are difficult to procure and those, which may not be listed with us, can also be made available.

PG opportunities: Details of universities/colleges/disciplines/number of seats, etc., offering post graduation opportunities are provided here. Brief guidance is provided to students opting for Post Graduation competitive / entrance exams as well.

News from DTE: This section provides information from the Director of Technical Education (DTE) about the List of Universities and Colleges under them, total seats, revisions in DTE guidelines, etc.

Contact: Through this section, students can directly contact University authorities, College Departmental Heads, Directorate of Technical Education (DTE) or any educational officials regarding their queries related to studies or education system.

User

User Portfolio: Here the students maintain their *Personal Diary*, store their *Medical* Profile, record Contacts in the *Address Book*, store their *Academic* Profile and *Company* Profile, etc. The academic profile includes: (i) Details of the total marks sheet for all semesters, (ii) Projects and summer training undertaken, (iii) any other relevant information. The *medical and academic profiles* of all the students are made available to the industry in a specific format.

College Katta: This is a classified section for students trying to avail and provide information about the day-to-day happenings like Hostel accommodations, engineering materials and tools, college activities like cultural programs, seminars, treks and picnics, etc. It is concerned with the day-to-day happenings, where students can share information under five different headings, namely, Travel, Classified, General, Humor and Sports.

Quiz & Contests: This section contains General / I.Q. / Aptitude tests. The quizzes have different levels that will help students to evaluate themselves.

E-mail and Chat: Students can get in touch with their teachers, batch mates through e-mail and chat facilities, when not in regular contact.

Others

Engineering colleges: A platform has been provided for the college to put up relevant information. Students and their parents can procure detailed information about colleges, with the aim of securing admissions to desired B.E. disciplines. The aim of the whole exercise is to present authentic information about the college for the benefit of all users, especially students and industries. Moreover, the college can reach out to students worldwide and indirectly advertise its salient features like disciplines offered, number of seats, hostel and laboratory facilities, staff strength, etc.

Parents: Here the parents / guardians of all students can keep a check on their wards' performance from anywhere. *Academic performance (Report Card), attendance records, performance in extracurricular activities,* etc., can be regularly monitored and remedial action if required can be taken at the earliest. Parents/ guardians are provided unique user names and passwords so as to access their wards' details.

Chapter XVIII

Corporate Strategies in a Digital World:
Supply Chain Management and Customer Relationship Management – Development and Integration - Focus

Purva Kansal
Panjab University, India

Keshni Anand Arora
Indian Administrative Services, India

Abstract

These days, the majority of management literature stresses the concept of "learning organizations", i.e., an organization's capacity to change. However, it is not easy for people to accept this fundamental aspect especially when it comes to the Internet and technologies' growing importance in business operations. They claim it's a temporary trend that will leave little visible change in the way business is conducted. For these businessmen, the philosophy seems to be "keep making better products and offering new services, and the customers will keep buying". They ignore changes occurring in the buying habits of customers and impact of technology. There are some businesses who are happy to follow the leader and adopt tools like supply chain management.

Supply chain management is a recognized discipline to shorten cycle times, reduce inventories, decrease logistics costs and streamline communication process across the business network. On the other hand are the businessmen who understand the learning organization concept and develop a forward orientation. They are prepared to ride the technology wave to new heights and accomplishments by using technology as a defining element in business operations. This chapter suggests a new approach to this new breed of entrepreneurs. In this chapter, we are trying to give supply chain management a customer orientation and to study its results. We highlight the synergistic advantage of linking supply chain management with customer relationship management into a tightly knit network using technology. The main focus is on finding a solution to deal with Internet empowered customers and to learn how to apply technologies demanded in the new digital economy.

Introduction

The corporate strategies drawn by companies in today's digital world have forced them to inculcate technology in all spheres of their operations. Satisfaction in a consumer emanates from the feeling of pleasure or disappointment resulting from comparing the products perceived performance in relation to his/her expectations (Kotler, 1998).

Conceptually, if performance falls short of expectation, the customer is dissatisfied. If it matches his expectations, the customer is satisfied and if it exceeds his expectations the customer is delighted.

As put forth best by Sam Walton, this concept can be simply stated, "There is only one boss, the customer. And he can fire everybody from the chairman on down, simply by spending his money somewhere else" (*Your Customer – Your Boss*, 2003). This has led to the development of customer-oriented markets, i.e., "Buyers Markets." Therefore, successful companies these days are targeting customer delight as a tool for retaining customers and ensuring success. The increasing use of technology in the development and marketing of products has forced companies to turn toward customer retention as an essential ingredient of corporate success.

Moreover, researchers have pointed out that these days retaining customers is a smart strategy. Their work has proven that it is more economical to retain customers than to acquire new ones. The Forum Company estimated as early as 1989 that the cost of winning the new customer is five times as much as that of pleasing an old customer (Sellers, 1989)

On similar lines, Dr. Jason Chen (2002) stated that:

- A 60-100% company profit boost can be achieved by only 5% customer retention efforts

- One dissatisfied customer tells eight to ten people about his experience

- Odds of selling a product to a new customer is 15 % while selling to a existing customer is 50%

- Up to 98% of promotion coupons are thrown away

- Referred customers generally stay, use more products and become profitable customers.

Quantitative analyses like these have motivated companies to understand "customer expectations" and to find tools which would help them achieve customer delight (Gattorna and Walters, 1996) In this paper we discuss two such tools, Customer Relationship Management (CRM) and Supply Chain Management (SCM). The use of technology to integrate these tools has become a focal point in many firms to gain competitive ground.

Many companies have been using these tools profitably however in others the approach has been centered around adopting them individually. In this paper we establish how the singular approach managed to change the expectation set of the customers permanently. However, with the proliferation of these technologies and tools, gaining competitive advantage has become increasingly difficult. Thereby, it is essential for companies to search for new tools to gain a competitive edge in the market.

We explore the feasibility of one such tool, i.e., an interactivity approach between SCM and CRM vis-a-vis India.

India is one of the most rapidly growing economies with a distinct set of customer logics and supply chain. Indian customers have been introduced to the concept of "customer power" only recently with the proliferation of existing and emerging technologies and they are coming to terms with it progressively. This rapid development has made their expectation set very volatile. Meanwhile, there exists a three-tier distribution channel. This leads to sharing of control between manufacturers and channel members. However, this makes the job of offerers, i.e., targeting customer satisfaction, difficult.

In this chapter we explore the option of applying this interactivity tool to the Indian economy.

Customer Relationship Marketing & Supply Chain Management: Tools Used to Satisfy Customers

Customers usually have an intuitive sense of what they want. However, these expectations are continuously influenced by variables like personal needs, past experiences, alternatives available, promises made by manufacturers, etc. (Ziethmal and Bitner, 2003). Companies, in an attempt to win over customers, promise them product and service variables vis-a-vis other products. Thereby, molding the expectations of a customer.

According to the Levitt, "The new competition is not between what companies produce in their factories, but between what they add to their factory output in form of packaging, services, advertising, customer advice, financing, delivery arrangements, warehousing and other things that people value" (Levitt, 1969).

Figure 1. Product variables and CRM and SCM: Relationship

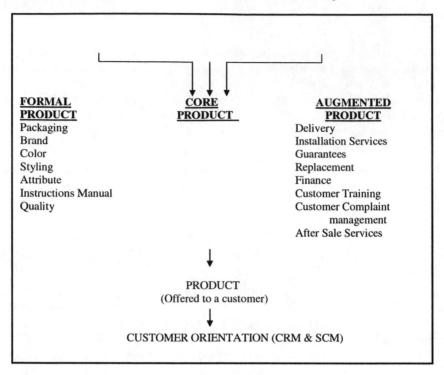

Companies employ varying strategies to differentiate their products, requiring the need for a different set of technologies and business processes.

A product involves its presentation to the consumer as a composite package. It refers to a core product, the formal product, and an augmented product (Figure 1). As pointed out by Levitt, the core product remains the same in an industry, what changes is the formal and augmented product composition.

The formal product variables help customers differentiate a product from that of the competitors. Hence, companies try and customize these attributes. Investment in customization motivates a company to promise customers a certain set of distinct attributes. These promises in turn influence the customer's satisfaction.

The augmented product variables determine the competitive advantage of a company. The level of on-time delivery, customer training, after sales services, guarantee and replacement schemes, influences the customer's satisfaction. Therefore, in order to have competitive advantage in a particular market the manufacturers need to compete not only in terms of what they produce in the factories (core product) but in terms of value-added variables.

The role played by the technological development of the company plays a crucial role at this stage. To date, companies have been adopting their customization strategy by targeting selected variables of augmented and formal product sets. However, the increased levels of competition and technology proliferation have forced companies to look at the product as a whole. Moreover, for a sustained competitive advantage companies need to orient their technologies in their operations and also use them to adapt the variables in a product to a customer perspective. One way of achieving this is through CRM.

CRM - The Concept

CRM refers to the approach adopted by an organization to understand and influence customer behavior through meaningful communication, so as to improve customer acquisition, retention, loyalty and profitability (Deck Stewart, 2003).

CRM is a comprehensive strategy and involves technology and tools used to understand customer needs and behaviors in order to develop stronger relationships with them. It is a process that helps bring together previously dispersed pieces of information about customers and their behaviors, strategies for sales and marketing, their effectiveness and responsiveness and market trends (Raut, 2003).

In a macro sense, the main philosophy behind CRM is to ensure customer delight rather than mere satisfaction by using services as a tool, to provide customers with a service level that exceeds their expectation set. Moreover, having learned from their experiences, customers now demand a product that matches their expectation logics exactly (Ziethmal, n.d.). This involves the integration of data captured by various functions in a company and blending the data to develop a comprehensive knowledge about the needs of the consumer and the product.

The motivation behind companies' efforts to understand their customers is the desire to have a competitive advantage. The more capable a company becomes at understanding its customers and giving them what they want, the more difficult it is for the competitors to entice them away (Switching Costs).

Many corporations have exploited this tool successfully in developed countries. For example Amazon.com, Tipper Tie, Hewlett Packard, Canada Post Corp., Student Advantage, Dell Computers, Microsoft, McDonalds, Pizza Hut, Dominos, etc. These companies are not famous for their advertising campaigns but their service level (Augmented Products). The advancements in present day digital economies have however made some of these technological advances and tools a mere necessity from their earlier status of a highly valued choice.

Case Study: Tipper Tie (2003)

Tipper Tie Inc., owned by Dover Corporation, is a multi-billion-dollar entity publicly traded on the NYSE (DOV). The Tipper Tie Inc. family consists of four companies Tipper Tie, Tipper Tie-Net, Tipper Tie technopack and Tipper Tie Alpina. Their products portfolio includes clippers, aluminum clips, aluminum wire products, electric fence supplies and netting. Tipper Tie was selected as a small-to-midsize enterprise winner of the Spring 2002 Gartner CRM Excellence Awards. Tipper Tie customers (in the food-processing industry) use costly machines for packaging the food items. These packing machines need service, new parts, and plenty of wire and clips. Tipper Tie is a customer-oriented company and their field sales reps and service technicians make personal visits to customers while call center fields their questions, requests and complaints. Believing in the fundamentals of CRM (customer retention) the sales rep used to spend 75% of their time dealing with old complaints and satisfying the old customers (Boeing Center, 2003). This helped the company to increase its customer base and goodwill in the market.

Success stories like these motivate companies to strive for improved customer relations. Therefore, in the past few years, companies increasingly invested huge amounts in CRM infrastructures. The need for such tools has influenced the direction and the development of technological advances needed to satisfy the needs of the companies.

The extensive use of CRM concepts and tools led to a modification of a customers' expectation set.

This led to CRM transiting from its status of a competitive advantage tools to a mere strategy. Therefore companies directed their efforts to look for competitive advantage alternatives which could fill the void left by transition of CRM but do so cost effectively.

Companies having made extensive use of technology to further their cause via CRM then turned to develop further processes and tools to gain competitive ground.

It is against this backdrop that the discipline and philosophy of logistics & supply chain management moved into limelight.

Supply Chain Management – The Concept

In 1954, Paul Converse, pointed out the need for academicians and practitioners to examine the distribution side of marketing (Converse, 1954). Later Peter F. Drucker indicated that physical distribution was akin to the "Dark Continent," i.e., it was an area that was virtually unexplored and hence unknown (Drucker, 1962) He said 50 cents out of every dollar that a consumer spends on goods goes to activities that occur after goods are made, i.e., physical distribution.

Physical distribution is a cluster of activities which creates time, place and form utility through the movement of goods and persons from one place to another.

Over time physical distribution has been expanded to include total materials management and information flows within a channel and is now called logistics (Kapoor and Purva, 2003).

Contributions in these areas from scholars like Heskett (1973) Shapiro (1984) and Sharman (1984) have helped thrust logistics into the spotlight. These days logistics is perceived as a tool for improving efficiency of customer service programs, decreasing total costs and profit leveraging. For example, Michael Dell in his book *Direct from* Dell (Harper Business) Stated, "In 1993, we had $2.9 billion in sales and $220 million in inventory. Four years later, we posted $12.3 billion in sales and had inventory of $233 million. We're now down to less than eight days of inventory [on hand] and we're starting to measure it in hours instead of days" (Allen, 2003). Similarly, logistics deals with reorganizing material handling functions, determining equipment selection and replacement policies, order-picking procedures and stock storage retrieval, etc. Today's digital world has seen a new dimension being added where the product does not have any physical form and can be delivered electronically directly from the Web to the buyer's computer. Use of the Internet and various technologies has also reduced the communication gap between the businesses and consumers.

To synergize these cost reduction benefits, the term logistics has been further expanded to supply chain management. Supply chain management has been defined as the chain linking each element of the manufacturing and supply process from raw material through to the end-user, encompassing several organizational boundaries and treating all organizations within the value chain as a unified virtual business entity (Scott and Westbrook, 1991).

Therefore, anyone or anything that influences a product's time-to-market, price, quality, information exchange, and delivery, among other activities is part of the supply chain.

The supply chain management aims at integrating efforts in terms of target 7R's, i.e., creating the right product, at the right time and right place, in the right quantity and in right condition for the right customer at the right cost (Kapoor and Kansal, 2003). A well-planned SCM system helps an organization achieve

1.   Lower costs
2.   Competitive edge
3.   Reliability of delivery
4.   Order fulfillment accuracy
5.   Flexibility in replenishment
6.   Accuracy of documentation
7.   Continuity of supply
8.   Quality of company sales, technical and service representation.

However, learning from their experiences, the customers expect an offer to cater to augment and formal variables of the product and to have a degree of customization at the same time. This has made the task of exceeding customer expectation very difficult. In present times, to satisfy a customer a company has to be "on its toes" at all times. It is necessary for companies to make CRM and SCM work in synchronization, i.e., target both a formal and augmented levels of the product cost effectively with a degree of customization added to them. It is here that the challenge lies for the companies to utilize the tools and the technologies available to integrate their processes enabling them to enhance their customer satisfaction and retention.

Supply Chain Management and CRM: An Interactivity Relationship

One hard fact of today's cannibalistic market is that only the fittest can survive the competition, i.e., a company which can acquire minimum variance between expected and actual service will exist. However, to flourish actual service needs to exceed expected service. For this approach we need to adopt an integrative approach to CRM and SCM. Let's revert to our Tipper tie example to illustrate this point.

Competition began heating up in late 1990, when overseas competitors entered the United States. The competitors with their alternative packaging methods began enticing Tipper Tie's customers. Executives sought to protect their market share by developing a strategy to respond earlier and more often to their customers.

Company recognizing the fact that it needed to provide easy access to up-to-date customer data to its sales team, technicians and customer call center initiated a linking system. Through this linking system its sales reps in the field and call center were integrated into the same continually updated customer data view.

This helped Tipper Tie to trim the time sales reps had to spend listening to customer complaints leaving them more time for selling. The reps were able to do their homework prior to their sales calls by reading up on technical service problems the customer had logged, machine repairs, parts sales histories and any gripes their call center had entered into the company's centralized system.

This increased efficiency in time and communication lead to decreased cost of generating sales and increased sales revenues from its best customers.

Tipper Tie also implemented Siebel Systems' standalone call center and sales-force CRM modules. Since the system was installed Tipper Tie estimates that each sales rep has had approximately 18 more days per year in face-time selling that they earlier were spending on generating reports or dealing with peripheral issues. The company has also been able to increase its sales territory without increasing its number of sales reps and has trimmed a sales support IT jobs with the automated system in place (Deck Stewart, 2001).

Therefore, SCM and CRM, an interactivity approach would help not only improve customer service but also lead to a decrease in cost. However, this approach would require increased coordination and flexibility not only between various organizational structure elements but also in customer and company relations. This would require efficient communication so that the right information is available to the right person. This information database would allow a company to develop a better understanding of customer buying logics. All of this involves a sizeable shift in the companies' strategies to also employ technology as a tool to enhance the value generated from its operations as against its earlier use to only further enhance the value of its operations.

Multiple variables work in conjunction to shape "customer buying logics" and a consumer uses the standards as reference points to judge actual performance of a company. Any possible bottleneck in understanding can lead to variance which would in turn influence the customer satisfaction and delight level. Gattorna and Walters (1996) describe different types of bottlenecks, which might lead to variance. These are:

- Gap between management perception and customer expectations will influence product quality.

- Gap between management perception and organization system will impact on product delivery.

- Gap between organization system and channel members would determine the actual performance.

- Gap between actual commitment of channel members and promises made by the company would determine the gap between promises made and delivered and thus the goodwill of the company.

As illustrated in Figure 2, CRM helps reduce distance between customer and management, which helps develop an understanding of customer expectations and therefore increase product quality and customer satisfaction. However, for decreasing variance companies require proper cooperation and commitment from employees and other channel members. This would require management of relationships and resources along the whole supply chain. Only then would a company be able to achieve an efficient delivery process.

Therefore, an interactivity or integrated approach between SCM and CRM is essential to achieve increased customer satisfaction. However, practically integration requires phenomenal flexibility, which in turn can arise only from free flow of information. A few decades ago this would not have been possible, but with today's technology SCM and CRM can be integrated to give SCM a customer orientation and CRM a supply process orientation.

In this IT-based approach to integrating SCM and CRM a company employs a wide array of computers, workstations and servers operating with collaboratively developed software. It is a dynamic channel with little friction among the channel participants. Efficient data handling and response to customer choice are more important and therefore to increase flexibility multiple activities are outsourced.

Technology allows customers and suppliers to be seamlessly linked together, throughout the world, exchanging information almost instantly. The velocity of relevant information flow is so fast that, as a result, responding to the inevitable changes in expected vs. actual customer demand will mandate demand-driven manufacturing and supporting processes that provide for faster changes in the actual material flow to match demand. Thereby, helping to reduce the bottlenecks faced by companies (as discussed earlier) in a buyer's market while catering to "customer buying logics."

Figure 2. Customer satisfaction, CRM and SCM: A relationship

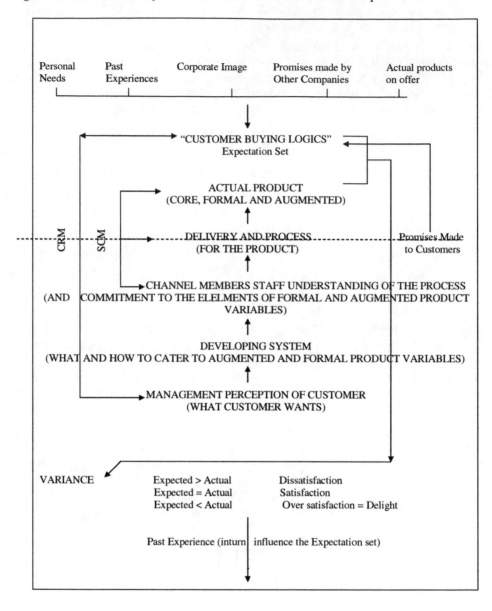

*Adapted from Gattorna & Walters (1996)

Fast access to relevant supply chain information can pay off handsomely in lower costs, less inventory, higher quality decision-making, shorter cycle times and better customer service. One of the biggest cost savings is in the overhead activity associated with lots of paperwork and its inherent redundancies. The non-value added time of manual transaction processing could instead be focused on higher revenue creation activities without proportional increases in expense. Thereby differentiating between companies, which acquire, in the future, or are acquired.

Indian Scenario

Indian businesses, across almost all industries, have a common trait of multiple layers or tiers of distribution between the brand and the consumers. Layers have thrived due to an over-fragmentation of the social class of consumers, tactical location advantage, or purely the liquidity power to hold stock.

There are three primary layers of intermediation:

1.   Consignment & Freight Agents (CFA)

2.   Distributor/Stockist/Wholesaler

3.   Retailer/Dealer

This three-tier distribution channel system increases distance between manufacturer and the customer. Therefore customers in India interact with channel members for product delivery, service, problems, support or to give feedback. Thereby, increasing distance between the manufacturer's perception of customer logics. For example, in the India market segment for luxury cars is defined as people who have a need to be driven rather than drive. Yet all the car accessories controls are with the driver and not in the back with the passenger. This gap, in turn, has a compound effect on bottlenecks outlined by Gattorna.

Therefore, the bargaining power and control of channel members is more in India. Moreover, each layer adds to the price burden of the product.

A company influences the expectation set of the customer by making certain product ad delivery promises. However, lack of commitment, control and coordination from channel members only leads to increase in variance and therefore making the price burden ever more so evident to the customer.

Assume: Mr. Joshi plans to purchase a microwave oven. He has no specifics in his expectation set. He conducts a market survey and collects information about the existing brands. His expectation set is formed by the promises made by these brands. Influenced by the communication, he buys a branded product. He was promised that a representative would come to his house and install and demonstrate the use of the product. After purchasing the product, Mr. Joshi contacts the dealer for a demonstration and he is told that a person has to come from the company's branch office and the dealer gives him the number asking him to contact the company directly. While the company tells him that they, as a policy, entertain the requests for demonstrations only from the dealers. Resultant of this communication is a gap between promises made and delivered. Due to which Mr. Joshi made sure that no one he knew ever brought the same product.

This is a normal experience in India. The problem emanates from the dealers' short-term objective of monetary gains and the customers' lack of knowledge of their own power.

Customers in India have been introduced to the concept of "customer power" only recently (after the liberalization of the Indian economy in the 1990s). They are still learning how to use it and how to demand what they want from the manufacturers. This has in turn made their expectation set very volatile. Therefore, SCM alone will not result in an increase in market share. To satisfy a customer in India the manufacturer has to work at reducing the gap between themselves and the customer and target the Gattorna bottlenecks in totality. Thus it is not just the integration of the SCM and the CRM tools but also the intelligent use of technology to minimize these bottlenecks that is crucial to gaining competitive advantage.

An inspiring success story of this tool is in Public Sector, i.e., the Directorate of Supplies and Disposal, Haryana Government, India. We have chosen a public department to highlight the feasibility of this tool for developing countries. These Government departments work in vertical structure due to which they have limited resources, are plagued by operational inefficiencies, work delays, financial deficits, etc. Despite these limitations, the Directorate of Suppliers and Disposals has been able to save Rs 60 crore per annum in procurement. These savings are to be further complemented by reduction in inventory costs, procurement time, paperwork, human resource, corruption and unnecessary hassles.

Integration of CRM and SCM – The Use of Technological Tools: Case Study

The Directorate of Supplies & Disposals (DS&D), Haryana, is responsible for the purchase of a large variety of items required by the various Government Departments (customers of DS&D). It acts as an intermediary for the Government Departments and the suppliers. This makes the distribution channel two or three-tier (depending on the purchase to be made). The Directorate makes purchases of the order of Rs. 30000 million per annum.

Functions of the Directorate are:

- To act as the purchasing agency for all the State Government Departments.

- To tender advice on matters connected to the purchase and disposal of stores to State Government Departments, Public Sector Undertakings, etc.

- To arrange for disposal of surplus/unserviceable stores.

- To arrange for inspection of stores.

- To arrange for settlement of disputes between the suppliers and indenting departments.

The Present System (Highlighted in Figure 3)

Procurement of goods and services is done by:

- Ad-hoc purchases in which specific quantity and respective department mentions quality.

- Tendering – procurement exceeding Rs. 12,000 (twelve thousand) in value is mandated to follow the tendering process. This is done so as to maintain transparency in the process and also ensure that the Government receives the best value for the money. Tender invitations are published in leading newspapers and all interested supplier or contractors who meet the eligibility criteria are free to submit tenders.

- Rate Contracts – Rate Contracts are used for common user items where demand is repetitive, item values are less, generally required by more than one department and specifications have been standardized. It is an agreement between the respective department and the supplier for the supply of goods at mutually agreed prices & specifications, valid for a specific time period - generally having no quantity limitations.

- Purchase of material against rate contract arranged by Government of India – Director General Supply and Disposals.

- Calling of quotations for proprietary items, which is made by only one company.

- Purchase from approved sources from the State as well as from the Central Government Departments.

Following are the deficiencies of the current system. First, the present system is totally manual and error prone. Second, at present 50 procurement officers manage the process. Thereafter in excess of 10,000 suppliers and on an average 50 indents and two tender inquiries per month containing 40-45 tenders inquiry cases. Therefore, the time lag between placement of a requirement (with the DS&D), purchase, delivery and payment is quite large. Moreover the department for whom the purchase is being made (consumer department), is not allowed to change its specifications once they have been communicated to DS&D. This is a major limitation of the present process. Due to the increased time lag, the environment and expectations sets are prone to changes (expectations set-2). But no provision has been made in the current process for such changes (decreased flexibility).

Lastly, to make the procedure more complex DS&D is a department concerned with only procurement. Therefore it has to make sure that there is no variance among the specifications given by the consumer department (expectation set-1) and the product received. The payment is released only after the consumer department has checked and

Figure 3. Present procurement process at DS&D

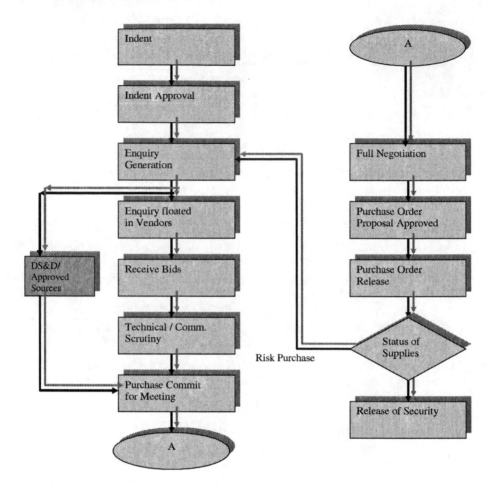

re-checked the product with its expectations set-1. Even after that the supplier has to fill in a ton of paperwork to acquire the payment. This decreases the satisfaction level among the channel members. (decreased cooperation).

To top it all the present system has following deficiencies in terms of specific activity centres:

- Inventory Management
    - Incomplete records of the stock in hand.
    - No proper records as to when the inventory is used.
    - Improper confirmation of supplies received from vendor – there is a risk of

whether the actual supplies have actually been received from the vendor (risk purchase).

- Financial Management

  - Financial planning does not exist and procurement is transactional not strategic.

  - Timely release of funds from finance does not take place at the point of receiving supplies despite formal sanctions. This adversely affects supplier and Department relations.

- Quantifying the Spending

  - Commodity codes don't exist.

  - Supplier codes don't exist.

  - Item numbers are not used for purchases.

  - Spending analysis is a highly manual process and very tedious process.

- Leveraging Contracts

  - Fragmented spending.

  - Inadequate data available in market in order to leverage/control spending.

  - Lack of contract metrics & measurement process.

- Developing Commodity Strategies

  - Lack of established spending baseline.

  - Long cycle time to negotiate contacts (and realize savings) – typically two months from Indent to placement of Supply Order.

  - Limited resources.

  - Limited savings realized to date from sourcing efforts.

  - Unclear user measurements – affects demand management.

  - Buyer skills are transactional and not strategic.

  - The earlier rates and specifications present available on files not easily available.

- Transaction Processing

  - Total processing cost is very significant.

  - Indenting system is manually intensive/redundant.

  - Possibility of errors as system is manual.

  - Excessive cycle time required for purchases.

  - Buyers are busy reviewing and approving Indents instead of managing suppliers.

Figure 4. Functional view of end to end solution

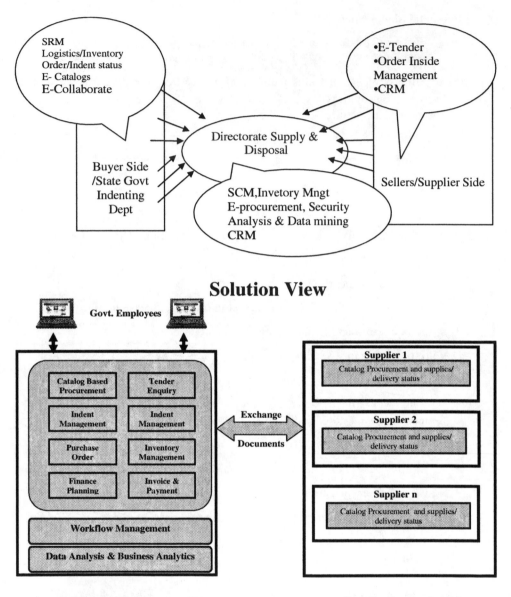

- Too much time reconciling invoices to Purchase Orders.

- Systems are not real-time (mainly manual).

The Proposed System

An integrative approach has been proposed for DS&D. The proposed system will consist of e-procurement and e-supplier enabled solutions. This would help increase flexibility of orders (for consumer departments), reduce procurement time, decrease paper work, and increase communication and coordination. This would help increase satisfaction of all parties concerned.

Buy-Side Procurement – eProcurement Solution for the Government Electronic Procurement (eProcurement) represents the most significant opportunity for the Government to continue to improve operational efficiency. The ability to automate the entire supply chain for goods and services has the potential to deliver enormous cost savings that directly impact the bottom line. In addition, operational efficiency is improved by cycle time reduction, control of purchasing activity is increased, and purchasing professionals can focus on more strategic projects rather than day-to-day transactions.

Sell-Side Procurement – e-Supplier Enablement Solution to have the suppliers integrate with the e-procurement Solution. The success of any procurement system depends on its ability to attract Suppliers.

A functional view of the solution of the proposed system is shown in Figure 4.

The Conceptual Framework of the Solution

- **Views.** The processes as covered in the "**Solutions View**" (Dig 4) shall be automated and a mix of "**Web**" and "**Desktop.**" Interface shall be provided to facilitate the transactions happening at the front office and back office;

- **Portal and Sections.** An Interactive Portal consisting of *separate Sections for the Government Departments, Boards and Corporations, i.e., the buying side and the Sellers/Suppliers on the supplying side shall be created to facilitate separate sections of the supply chain*;

- **Codification.** The present system lacks proper codification for the Departments, Suppliers and the Products/Specifications. Accordingly, the Departments, Suppliers and the Products/Specifications shall be codified in the new system to maintain data integrity and to enable analysis on various parameters;

- **Global Tendering and Participation.** The new system shall enable global tendering and shall invite participation from suppliers from across the globe. This will provide better pricing and quality of the products to the State Government Department.

Government Side

- **Departments' Web Access.** The Departments can Log On to the Web site **using the Web Interface** and know about the status of their Indents placed with the DS&D and the purchase/delivery status of the goods placed in the Indents can be taken online using the Internet. Also, the Departments can update the Tenders and Notices in the concerned section available on the Web site (increase product quality);

- **Indents and Inventory Control Mechanism.** The Departments shall be provided with **authentication-based access rights** to place the indents and update the inventory levels of different indenting items as to how much is available in store and how much has been consumed. This will facilitate not only the Departments in maintaining proper inventory, but shall also facilitate the Government in maintaining a check on the purchases made by different Departments (efficient product delivery system);

- **Budgetary and Financial Planning.** The Government can carry out better budgetary and financial planning as the inventory information along with the indent information shall be available collectively from all the indenting Departments. The budgetary control in terms of the available budget vis-à-vis the purchase price can be monitored on line on a day-to-day basis, which will also result in better financial planning on the part of the Government (decrease cost burden despite multi-tier system);

- **Product Information and Catalogues.** The Departments can access the information about the Catalogue of products offered by different vendors as well as the quotes for these products finalized by the Competent Authorities. Sometimes, the Departments place indents for various products having specifications that are not existing or are outdated. The eCatalogues hosted by different vendors shall help in formulating the right specifications and selecting appropriate products (increase product quality);

- **Testing and Inspections.** The test and inspection reports can also be updated on the dynamic Web site to provide proper access to the user Department. Also, the schedule of tests and inspections to be carried out can be covered on the Portal to provide instantly updated information (increase communication and definition of product quality);

- **Penal Clauses, Risk Purchases and Debarring.** DS&D can impose the penalties as per the terms and conditions of the contract, which can be in-built in the software meant for the e-procurement System. The delay in risk purchases results in loss of revenue/working of the concerned Department. Accordingly, the risk purchase notices, etc., can be expedited by customization depending upon the requirement and can be automated on the basis of delivery period/inspections, etc.;

- **Parameterized Search Facility.** The Government Section shall provide Products Based, Catalog Based, Tender Inquiry Based, Indent Based, Purchase Order Based search facilities in both normal as well as Boolean parameterized mode to the user organizations (increase channel coordination);

- **Workflow and Backend Operations.** DS&D shall have an automated workflow system at the back-end **using the Desktop Interface** to keep track of the indents, purchase orders and invoicing, financial planning, payments and inventory management. The mail messaging and database-driven access control system shall be used to establish the internal Work Flow;

- **Analysis and Data Mining.** Online Analytical Processing (OLAP) Application shall be used for Data Mining and to analyze the purchases done over a period of time on different parameters (increased channel management).

Supplier Side (Better channel management to increase Bargaining power of DS&D)

- **Supplier's Web Access.** The Suppliers shall be able to access the details of the inquiries floated by the DS&D for different products and Departments using the **Web Interface**;

- **Classification of Suppliers.** The suppliers will be classified into two broad categories: Class 'A' and Class 'B' Suppliers. Class 'A' Suppliers includes all those suppliers who had been doing regular successful business with the state government in the past three years and meet defined parameters like annual turnover, Suppliers Financial and Market standing, Suppliers performance and Business in other state governments, etc. All other suppliers will be considered under Class 'B';

- **ECatalogs and Brochures.** The 'A' Class Suppliers shall be given space on the Web site to maintain their Web Catalogs and Brochures; however, other suppliers shall be provided only the limited access to the Tenders and Notices issued by the Department. These Web Catalogs shall contain the detailed information on various products offered by the registered suppliers;

- **Regularly Updated Product Information.** The eCatalogs shall be updated online by the 'A' class vendors to provide updated information to the buyer's side, i.e., the Government;

- **Updating of Status.** The Suppliers that have been given orders by the Department shall be provided access rights to update the status Online about the deliveries, inspections, testing, etc., to facilitate the Indenting Departments. This system will facilitate the Suppliers and shall be called as the Supplier Enablement System.

Analysis of the Results

The interactivity approach will allow Governments to slash printing and mailing budgets by 75%, and that's an immediate savings. By streamlining the work processes associated with purchasing, governments can cut the cost of administering a purchase order by 50%. To add further, the benefits of the e-procurement and the Supplier Enablement solution are:

- *Cost Efficiency*
  - Lower prices via aggregated buying and increased competition
  - Reduction in inventory and supply chain cost via a reduced average PO line item order value
  - Reduced transaction costs
- *Reduced Inventory Costs* – management of inventory and strategic buying would reduce inventory in hand and will result in significant savings for DS&D and other Departments down the value chain.
- *Better Financial Planning and Control* – management of indents and the inventory will result in better financial control and planning. The integrated system of indents and the budget shall help in reducing the cost overruns beyond the budgetary sanctions.
- *Process Efficiency*
  - Lower procurement cycle times
  - Automated transactions (Indent, Ordering, payment)
  - Supplier and procurement process measures and management
  - Increased flexibility and customization options to the customer departments.
- Ensure that goods and services are in accordance with the expectation set (evolved or old) and at best prices.
- *Smart governance* – Make the entire process transparent, this will result in effective customer satisfaction by sharing the channel control with them.

Each of these in turn would help remove the bottlenecks of the old system, while making the expected set equal to actual set in minimum time possible and in a cost effective way. Thus, increase the satisfaction level of the consumer department.

Conclusions

The DS&D department predicts that the benefits of their integration efforts will lead to

- Significant reduction in the DS&D Human Resource requirements.
- Reduction in cycle time from two months to less than a week.
- Reduction in the cost of goods due to better negotiation and volume purchase. It is estimated that the Government will save a minimum of 2% off.

- Inventory and its carrying cost will be reduced to the extent of 10-12% by optimizing the inventory system.

Thereby, providing a strong argument for adopting an integrated approach of SCM and CRM in developing economies. The investment in IT is more than the manufacturers of these countries might be willing to make but in the long-term the benefits would outweigh the initial investment. Moreover, in today's competitive environment where the boundaries are shrinking and spillover effect is leading to increased customer awareness can a manufacturer afford not to cater to customers what they want?

However, the company should not ask themselves if they want to adopt this approach? What they should wonder is if in today's progressively liberalizing developing economies, where cross-border competition is educating customers about their powers, can they afford not to adopt this approach?

References

Chen, J. (2002). Logistics Customer Service. APO Seminar on IT Application for Logistics Management Systems, Representative of China, Department of Business Administration, Ze University, 17th-24th September 2002.

Converse, P.D. (1954). The Other Half of Marketing. *Proceedings of the Twenty-Sixth Boston Conference on Distribution*, Harvard Business School.

Customer-Driven Supply Strategy. (2003). Retrieved May 9, 2003 from the World Wide Web: www.bctim.wustl.edu/articles/pdf/CRM-Success_Stories.pdf.

Deck Stewart. (2001). CRM Made Simple. *CIO Magazine*, September 15, 2001. (Electronic Version). Retrieved May 13, 2003 from the World Wide Web: http://www.cio.com/archive/091501/simple.html.

Deck Stewart. (2001). "What is CRM?" Retrieved May 13, 2003 from the World Wide Web: www.cio.com/research/crm/edit/crmabc.html#what.

Drucker, P.F. (1962, April). The Economy's Dark Continent. *Fortune, 65*(103), 265-270.

Gattorna, J.L. and Walters, D.W. (1996). *Managing the Supply Chain*. London: MacMillan Business.

Gemmy, A. (2003). Module 8: Distribution. Retrieved May 20, 2003 from the World Wide Web: http://ec.mvc.dcccd.edu/IC/module_8.htm.

Heskett, J.L. (1973, March-April). Sweeping Changes in Distribution. *Harvard Business Review, 51*(2), 123-132.

Kapoor, S. and Kansal, P. (2003). *Basics of Distribution Management: A Logistics Approach*. New Delhi: Prentice Hall of India.

Kapoor, S. and Purva, K. (2003). *Marketing logistics: Supply Chain Approach*. New Delhi: Pearson Publication Private.

Kotler, P. (1998). *Marketing Management*. (9th Edition). New Delhi: Prentice Hall of India.

Levitt, T. (1969). *The Marketing Mode*. New York: Tata McGraw Hill.

Raut, P. (2002). Ensuring Customer Delight. Retrieved May 13, 2003 from the World Wide Web: www.crmguru/features/2002a/0124pr.html.

Scott, C. and Westbrook, R. (1991). New Strategic Tools for Supply Chain Management. *International Journal Physical Distribution and Logistical Management, 21*(1), 23-33.

Sellers, P. (1989). Getting Customers to Love you. *Fortune*, March 13, 38-49.

Shapiro, R. D. (1984, May/June). Get Leverage from Logistics. *Harvard Business Review, 62*(3), 119-127.

Sharman, G. (1984, September-October). The Re-discovery of Logistics. *Harvard Business Review, 62*(5), 71-79.

Tipper Tie Inc. (2003). Retrieved May 10, 2003 from the World Wide Web: www.tippertie.com/history.asp.

"Your Customer- Your Boss." (2003). Online Publication of A.T. Kearney (An EDS company) Web site. Retrieved May 15, 2003 from the World Wide Web: http://www.atkearney.com/shared_res/pdf/Your_customer_your_boss_S.pdf.

Ziethmal, V. A. and Bitner, M.J. (2003). *Service Marketing – Integrating Customer Focus Across the Firm*. New Delhi: Tata McGraw Hill Publishing.

About the Editors

Harbhajan S. Kehal is a Senior Lecturer in Economics at the University of Western Sydney, Blacktown Campus, New South Wales, Australia. Previously, he completed his Ph.D. at the University of Western Australia, Perth. The author of chapters in various books, which have been published in Australia and other countries, Dr. Kehal has received international recognition for his achievements in various facets of life. A well-travelled person, he has been a Visiting Fellow and Visiting Professor in many overseas Universities and Research Institutions. His research interests center around digital economy, foreign investment in developing countries, economic relationships of Australia with Japan and other countries. An Academician, Researcher and Philanthropist, his name has appeared in Australasian Who's Who since 1987, Who's Who in the World since 1995, Directory of International Biography since 1996 and many other publications. He is an Eminent Fellow of the American Biographical Institute. He is a member of a vast number of economic societies and is well known in the contemporary economic world for his leadership and active participation in international conferences. His recent conference travels have taken him to Hawaii and Cancun in Mexico, among his trips to Asia and the US.

Varinder P. Singh was born in 1974 in India and earned a Master's in Commerce, specializing in Information Systems from the Faculty of Management, the University of Western Sydney, Australia (2002). Earlier he received his bachelor's and master's degrees in Biochemistry from Panjab University, Chandigarh, India. Being exposed to the field of digital economy during his commitments with this book, in the future he intends to pursue research in the less explored field of health economics emphasizing on the financing and delivery of medical services, with extensive emphasis on federal and state legislation of current policy issues.

About the Authors

Keshni Anand Arora has an M.Phil. from Panjab University, Chandigarh, and an M.B.A. from the University of Western Sydney. She is currently working in Indian Administrative Services (IAS-1983 batch). Her experience portfolio includes supply chain management for Directorate of Supply and Disposal Haryana, Administration of Haryana Industries and strategy formulation for development of rural India. She has presented papers in these areas both at the national and international level.

Parthasarathi Banerjee is a Scientist with NISTADS (National Institute of Science, Technology & Development Studies), New Delhi (India). He has research interests in the areas of economics of technological change, innovation studies, strategy research, ethical and other issues. As visiting faculty, he teaches several papers relating to strategy, ethics and business process. He has nine books and several papers, has organized conferences, advised industrial firms and has undertaken several sponsored research projects. Currently, he is working on knowledge economy and his forthcoming book from Palgrave-Macmillan (London) is Indian Software Strategies, 2004.

Saundarjya Borbora is presently Head of the Department, Department of Humanities and Social Sciences, Indian Institute of Technology Guwahati and is an Associate Professor in Economics. Dr. Borbora completed a Master's in Economics (1983) and then completed a Ph.D. (1993). Dr. Borbora started teaching in 1985. In 1995, Dr. Borbora was selected by the Government of India on deputation under Colombo Plan to work in Bhutan, and served for about three years. In 1998, Dr. Borbora joined IIT Guwahati, has published a number of papers/chapters at national and international levels, and has attended conferences and seminars in India and abroad.

Stanley D. Brunn, Professor of Geography, University of Kentucky, Lexington (USA), has wide interests in human geography. These include electronic human geographies, innovative time-space mapping, visualization, and electronic scholarly communities and communication. He has written chapters and edited books on e-commerce, information and communication, political geography, social geography, ethnicity, world urbanization, the geopolitics of 9-11, and disciplinary history. His co-edited *Geography and Technology* (Kluwer, 2004) contains 25 chapters that examine how advances in various technologies have changed the production and dissemination of geo-information. He has taught at the University of Florida, Michigan State University, and many European and Central Asian universities.

Narendra S. Chaudhari has been with the Division of Information Systems, School of Computer Engineering (SCE), Nanyang Technological University (NTU), Singapore, as an Associate Professor since December 2001. He obtained his Ph.D., M.Tech. (Computer Science), and B.Tech. in Electrical Engineering (with Distinction) from IIT, Bombay (1988, 1983 and 1981, respectively). He has been a Fellow for the Institute of Electronics and Telecom Engineers (IETE), India, since 2000, and member of many professional societies. He has a varied experience in industry and R&D organizations, and had been with Devi Ahilya University since 1988. He has been Professor of Computer Science since June 1990. He has been on various committees of the University and he had been a Dean with the Faculty of Engineering Sciences, Devi Ahilya University, Indore (1995-1997). During this period, the University started the Institute of Engineering and Technology (IET), which currently offers B.E. programs in electronics and comm. engineering, computer engineering, and mechanical engineering. He has more than 80 publications and two books to his credit. He has successfully guided eight Ph.D.'s in Computer Science and Engineering. He had been Chairman with the Computer Society of India (CSI), Indore Chapter (1997-1999). He has been invited by various universities abroad to deliver colloquium lectures/research talks, as well as teaching assignments. The list of countries he has visited includes America, Australia, Germany, and Japan.

Alev M. Efendioglu is a Professor of Management and Information Systems at the School of Business and Management (SOBAM), University of San Francisco (USF) (USA). Having joined USF in 1977, he has served at various times as Chair of SOBAM's many faculty committees (including Peer Review and Academic Standards Committees), as Coordinator of the Management Teaching Area, and as the Coordinator of the USF-EMBA Program for Guangdong Enterprises in China (Hong Kong, Shenzhen, and Guangzhou). He has extensive consulting experience and has authored two books, chapters in two books, and articles in numerous professional publications. These include *Business Horizons*, *Journal of American Academy of Business*, *Journal of Asia-Pacific Business*, and *Journal of Small Business Strategy*. His research "Acceptance and Use of Information Technology among Small Retail and Service Businesses," was awarded "Best Paper in the Small Business/Entrepreneurship Track" at the Western Decision Sciences Institute, 26th Annual Meeting (March 25-29, 1997). He has also earned "Outstanding Research" and "Service" awards from the School of Business and Management, University of San Francisco. He is a member and holds administrative positions in a number of domestic and international professional organizations, including the Academy of Management. He also serves as a member of the board of directors of Ameristock Mutual Fund companies. For more detailed information on Dr. Efendioglu, please visit his Internet home page (http://www.usfca.edu/alev/alev.htm) (developed and maintained on an ongoing basis).

Kai M. Grebe was born in Lich, Germany in 1976. After his school leaving examination and military service, he took up studies in business administration at the University of Bayreuth (German) in 1997. In 1999, he passed his intermediate examinations. His focus as Research Assistant at the Chair of Economic Policy is primarily on Information Management. In 2002, his diploma thesis interrelates specific aspects of electronic commerce to transaction cost economics. At present, he is about to complete his degree and intends to continue research on this subject area as an Assistant Lecturer.

Irene Henriques is an Associate Professor at the Schulich School of Business, York University, Canada. Her research interests span both economics and management and include the economics of R&D, industrial organization, environmental economics and environmental management and sustainability. She has published numerous articles in these areas. In 1997, she was the recipient of the Schulich School of Business Research Award. In 2003, she was won Best Paper Award for the Strategy Division of the Administrative Sciences Association of Canada for "Stakeholder Influences and Sustainability Practices in the Canadian Forest Products Industry." She is currently a member of the advisory board for the Haub Program in Business and Sustainability and is a member of an OECD working group on environmental policy and firm level management.

Purva Kansal is a faculty member at the University Business School, Panjab University, Chandigarh (India). She has an M.B.A. from the International Institute of Management, Himachal Pradesh University, Shimla (1998) and completed her Ph.D. from Panjab University Chandigarh (2002). She is a co-author of *Basics of Distribution Management* (Prentice Hall of India) and *Marketing Logistics* (Pearson Publishers). Her areas of expertise include logistics, SCM, and marketing. She has published articles in the areas of marketing and logistics. She is also actively involved with local industry in their strategy formulation activities.

Yutaka Kurihara is a Professor of International Economics at Aichi University, Japan. He was a Lecturer and Associate Professor at Koryo International College. He majors in international economics, finance, currency integration, market integration, US-Europe-Asia-Japan economic relationship, managerial economics, education, and digital economy. His recent published books are, *Business & Policy Design in the Globalization* (2003), *Intellectual Skills for Freshmen* (2003) and *EU Currency Integration* (2000) (in Japanese). He is a member of the American Economic Association, Business & Economics Society International, European Economic Association, and some academic associations of economics, business and education in Japan.

Milind J. Mahajan has obtained his Bachelor of Engineering (electronics) from Pune University (1988), and a Master of Business Administration (MBA) from the University of Indore (1993). He has more than 15 years of experience in the IT industry and he has been Founder Director of three companies: (i) Sunind Systems Pvt. Ltd. – Pune based company, (ii) Mirash Infotech Pvt. Ltd. – an Indore based company, and, (iii) Milman

Power Technologies Pvt. Ltd. – an Indore based company. He has been involved in the development of educational systems using Java-based web technologies, and is involved in systems analysis and design, as well as monitoring implementation of educational solutions developed by Sunind Systems Pvt. Ltd. His other areas of interest include high power electronic circuit designs, and ERP solutions. He has been on the board of directors of Co-operative Bank at Indore, and has been a member of the Board of Governors, Computer Society of India's Indore chapter.

Simon Mowatt is a Senior Research Lecturer at Auckland University of Technology (New Zealand). He is Visiting Fellow to the Centre for International Business History at the University of Reading (UK), has worked at the Centre for International Business Studies at South Bank University (UK), Loughborough Business School (UK), and has been a Professor Becinario at the Universitat Pompeu Fabra in Barcelona (Spain). He has published in journals such as *Industrial and Corporate Change* and *Industry and Innovation*. Technology, innovation, networks and business history are his main areas of interest and he was awarded the 2002 IBM e-Business Conference Best Paper with Howard Cox.

Chipo Mukonoweshuro is currently conducting doctoral research at Durham Business School, University of Durham, UK, where she gained her M.B.A. (2002). Her research is concerned with the internationalization of Southern African financial service firms. Her professional experience includes employment with PricewaterhouseCoopers in Southern Africa as a Management Consultant, helping key high profile clients to maximize their business performance by integrating strategic change, process improvement and technology enhancement solutions. She has also worked for the Merchant Bank of Southern Africa, participating in various mandates including capital reconstructions and privatization.

Donghyun Park, Associate Professor, has been with Nanyang Technological University in Singapore since June 1995. He has a Ph.D. in Economics from UCLA. His general research interests include international economics, development economics, political economy, applied microeconomics, and East Asian economies. His specific research interests include East Asian financial reform and restructuring, international income distribution and convergence, and the effect of scale economies on firm behavior and international trade. A/P Park has published his work extensively in refereed international journals and presented his research at many international academic conferences. He has taught economics courses at both the graduate and undergraduate levels.

Kyonghwan Park received his M.A. in Geography Education from Seoul National University (2000) and is currently a doctoral candidate in Geography at the University of Kentucky (USA). Drawing on poststructuralist studies of the Internet and cyberspace, he is interested in cultural geographies of contemporary digital economy. He is completing his doctoral work on the development of South Korean transnational economy and its relation to urban spatial changes in the Asia-Pacific region since the 1997 Asian financial crisis.

Thomas Pfahler was born in Treuchtlingen, Germany in 1965. After his schooling he attended the University of Bayreuth (1984-1990) and graduated in Business Administration and Political Economics. His main research interests are in the labor market, transaction cost economics and growth theory. He became an Assistant Lecturer at the Chair of Economic Policy (1990) and was awarded a Ph.D. for a thesis on hysteresis and unemployment policy four years later. In 1999, he qualified as a university lecturer and was then appointed assistant professor. To date he has published several papers, textbooks and a monograph on human capital and efficiency.

Sougata Poddar is on the faculty of Economics at the National University of Singapore. He has received his Ph.D. from CORE (Centre for Operations Research and Econometrics), Belgium. His areas of research interest include industrial organization, imperfect competition and applied game theory. He has held positions as Research Fellow at the Institute of Economics, University of Copenhagen and CORE, Belgium. He has taught at the Indira Gandhi Institute of Development Research (IGIDR), Mumbai. His has written and co-authored articles in the *International Journal of industrial Organization*, *Economic Theory*, *Review of Economic Design*, *Economics Letters* among other publications.

Joanne Roberts is a Lecturer in International Business at Durham Business School, University of Durham, UK. Her research interests include knowledge intensive services, new information and communication technologies and knowledge transfer, and the internationalization of services. She is author of *Multinational Business Service Firms* (Ashgate, 1998), and co-editor of *Knowledge and Innovation in the New Service Economy* (Edward Elgar, 2000) and *Living with Cyberspace: Technology and Society in the 21ˢᵗ Century* (Continuum, 2002). She is also co-editor of the new journal *Critical Perspectives on International Business*, published by Emerald, which will be launched in 2005.

Fjodor Ruzic is Doctor of Information Sciences at the University of Zagreb where he is Lecturer in New Media and Interactive Multimedia Systems. He is currently at the Croatian Government Office for Internet Infrastructure Development as a consultant in information-communications systems, interactive multimedia, and information services. His recent research activities are covering the integration of information content and integration impacts on development of information theory and practice. He has worked in information sciences since 1975, and as an active participant, he is a member of many national and international bodies relating to telecommunications systems integrity, information resources management and multimedia system environment. He was worked on both research and implementation sides of networked databases, educational material, and digital media. He published more than 110 scientific and research papers in various international journals and he is author of four books dealing with graphical user interfaces, multimedia and the Internet.

Perry Sadorsky is currently an Associate Professor in the Schulich School of Business at York University in Toronto (Canada). He has previously taught at the University of California, Riverside, and has been a Visiting International Scholar at the University of California, Davis. He specializes in modeling, simulation and forecasting in economics and finance. His research interests include financial markets and the economy, energy trading and risk management, corporate commitment to the natural environment, and globalization, technology and international trade and finance. He has published extensively in these areas. He is a member of an OECD working group on environmental policy and firm level management.

Gary P. Schneider is an Associate Professor of Accounting and Information Systems at the University of San Diego (USA), where he teaches courses in electronic commerce, database design, supply chain management, and management accounting. Gary has published more than 40 books and 70 research papers on a variety of accounting, information systems, and management topics. His books have been translated into Chinese, French, Italian, and Korean. Gary's research has been funded by the Irvine Foundation and the Office of Naval Research. Gary is a licensed C.P.A. in Ohio. He holds a Ph.D. in Accounting Information Systems from the University of Tennessee, an M.B.A. in Accounting from Xavier University, and a B.A. in Economics from the University of Cincinnati.

Sushil K. Sharma is currently Assistant Professor in the Department of Information Systems and Operations Management, Ball State University, Muncie, Indiana (USA). He received his Ph.D. in Information Systems from the University of Pune. Dr. Sharma has a unique distinction of having been conferred two doctoral degrees. Prior to joining Ball State, Dr. Sharma held the Associate Professor position at the Indian Institute of Management, Lucknow (India), and Visiting Research Associate Professor at the Department of Management Science, University of Waterloo, Canada. Co-author of two textbooks in IT (*Programming in C* and *Understanding Unix*), and four edited books, Dr. Sharma's research contributions have appeared in many peer-reviewed national and international journals, conferences and seminars' proceedings. Dr. Sharma's primary teaching and research interests are in e-commerce, networking environments, network security, ERP systems, database management systems, information systems analysis & design and knowledge management. Dr. Sharma has been a reviewer and a special editor for many renowned journals in information systems area. Apart from teaching and guiding students for various innovative IS related topics, Dr. Sharma has wide experience of consulting in information systems and e-commerce area, network security and has served as a advisor and consultant to several government and private organizations including World Bank funded projects. Dr. Sharma has also conducted a number of Executive Development Programs for corporate world and Government organizations on e-commerce, Networking Environments, and database-related subjects.

Helen Thompson is Manager of the Centre for Electronic Commerce and Communications (CECC) at the University of Ballarat, Australia. Through education, training, research and consultancies, CECC promotes the advancement of electronic commerce, particularly through its practical application. Ms. Thompson has extensive experience in regional development and in managing portal and web-based development projects. In her doctoral research, Ms. Thompson has examined the concept of rejuvenating and sustaining regional and rural communities. She has also explored how community informatics initiatives can be developed in different regional and rural contexts. Ms. Thompson has contributed chapters in several books, published refereed articles and conference papers, and authored a number of reports in her areas of research interest which are primarily related to the role of clustering and of information and communication technologies in a regional and rural development context.

Sunil S. Umrani has obtained his Bachelor of Engineering (electronics) from Pune University (1988). He was actively involved in engineering education at Maharashtra State where he worked in the Vishwakarma Institute of Technology, one of the engineering colleges, as a Lecturer from 1989-1995. At this institute, he has been the recipient of the Best Lecturer Award (1993). From 1995-1997, he worked with a software consultancy firm, ATIC, Pune. Bringing together the unique experience in the field of engineering education as well as web-based solutions, he has been involved with conceptualizing the web-based portal "engineeringcampus.com" since 1998. Currently, he is CEO of Sunind Systems Pvt. Ltd. (India), a Pune-based company having a main focus on web-based engineering education, specially geared for requirements of thousands of engineering students in Maharashtra State in India.

Vincent F. Yip is an International Lecturer and Consultant with wide global experience and contacts. He received his Ph.D. in Materials Science (USC '73) and M.B.A. (USD '76). He was the Chief Scientist and Administrator of the Singapore Science Park (1980-1989) and served as Singapore's Deputy Ambassador to the EC (1989-1991). He consulted in China, the US, Europe, Mexico and Egypt for clients such as World Bank, Asian Development Bank, and UNDP. He was awarded the prestigious French Government Decoration Palmes Academiques in 1989 for important contribution to France's scientific/technology fields. Vincent F. Yip has been a Visiting Professor at Northwestern University's Kellogg Graduate School of Management and Adjunct Professor at Qinghua University and the University of San Francisco. His teaching and research fields include technology policy, cross-cultural management, international talent flow, product management and project management. He is a sought-after international speaker and has written numerous articles for magazines and business journals, and is the author of three books.

Index

A

academic publishing 165
access to government 218
advantages of digital cash 88
advertising revenue model 161
advertising-subscription combination
    model 162
advertising-subscription combined
    revenue model 162
affirmative act 114
Africa One 261
American depository receipts (ADR) 46
AOL-Time-Warner 141
application logic 169
Ararat Online 224
audio recordings 155
Austrian theory 21
authentication 111
automatic teller machines (ATMs) 261

B

bank transfers 63
banking in Africa 254
barter strategies 157
batch deliveries 143

Baudrillard, Jean 288
Bauer 141
biometrics 121
borderless economy 3
bounded rationality 149
branded manufacturers 142
broadband 291
BTX 68
building regional capacity 218
bundles 160
bundling 13
business circuits 22
business functionality 169
business models 99
business processes 62
business transactions 22
buy-side procurement 375
buyer power 142

C

cannibalization 161
capital asset pricing model (CAPM) 44
capital cities 200
case studies 217
Casson 149
certificate of deposit (CD) 87

chilled ready-meals 144
classified advertising 163
classified advertising sites 163
closed loop transaction 86
Coase transactions 27
collaborative relationships 149
communities of interest 218
community-building activities 223
community empowerment 217
community informatics initiatives (CI)
   217
community-level impacts 13
community portals 220
competition authorities 142
competition commission 142
competition in the digital age 137
complimentary assets 148
computer games 155
computer kiosks 240
consignment & freight agents (CFA)
   369
consumer 275
consumer behaviors 278
consumer-driven competition 136, 139
consumer-driven life-span competition
   148
consumer-facing firms 137, 138
consumer protection 107
consumer responsiveness 142
contact cards 118
contactless cards 118
continuous innovation 137
contract journalists 145
convergence 100
corporate strategies 359
cost model 63, 66
cost-of-equity values 39
credence goods 156
credit cards 279
criticism 66
cross-border banking networks 252
cross-border expansion 252
"customer buying logics" 366
customer relationship management
   (CRM) 359, 360
customer selection 89

customization 361
cybercommunity 300
cybercrime 107
cybersecurity 107

D

data entry 242
data warehousing and mining 138
delivery of banking services in Africa
   259
demographic information 161
Dennis and Future Publishing 140
deposit currency 87
desktop publishing systems (DTP) 140
development of e-commerce 273
dhabas 240
differential pricing 157
diffusion rates 72
digital brands 137
digital cash 84, 85, 86
digital cash system 89
digital certificate 113
digital contents 286
digital contents industry 288
digital data highways 64
digital divide 5, 39, 43, 238, 287
digital economy 1, 3, 98, 99, 136,
   201, 252, 288
digital economy environment 98
digital engineering campus 344
digital identity 105
digital processes 63
digital product elements 160
digital products 154, 155
digital revolution 63, 99
digital signature 110, 112, 115, 125
digital signature creation 116
digital signature verification 116
digital solution 351
digital technology 137, 175, 203,
   252, 254, 259
digital world 359
digitally mediated symbol 111
Directorate of Supplies & Disposals
   (DS&D) 370
disadvantages of digital cash 89

document authentication 109
downside risk (DR) 48

E

e-auction 290
e-bookstore 290
e-business 98
e-business legislation 106
e-cash 85
e-commerce 1, 2, 4, 21, 22, 43,
    63, 85, 201, 274, 290
e-commerce activity 277
e-commerce consumption 21
e-commerce development 273, 275
e-commerce in China 273
e-commerce in different environments
    274
e-learning Initiative 346
e-mail service 157
e-marketplaces 100
e-money 85
e-privacy 103
e-shopping 290
e-signature infrastructure 123
e-signature pads 120
e-signature utilization 131
e-supplier enablement solution 375
East Asia 313, 319
economic globalization 242, 317
economic impacts 11
economic restructuring projects 297
economic revolution 99
economies of scale 137
"edge" markets 149
"edventure" 346
electronic authentication 104
electronic databases 202
electronic finance 107
electronic information 203
electronic medium 99
electronic pad system 120
electronic players 6
"electronic purse" 265
electronic signature 98, 99, 104, 110,
    125
electronic signature technology 111

electronic tools 219
electronic transactions and contracts
    107
EMAP 138
embedded social relationships 150
empirical considerations 72
employment ad sites 163
end-consumer 136
eProcurement solution 375
equity 52
equity of service 217
escrow payment services 104
European Union 202
experience good 156

F

file sharing 178
financial capital 40
financial industry digitization 91
financial institution management 90
financial instruments 155
financial management 372
financial market reports 155
financial sector 64
financial services 62, 253
fingerprint 121
fingerprinting 112
food retailing 137
food retailing industry 142
foreign currency 94
foreign direct investment (FDI) 41
foreign indirect investment 41
free seats 351

G

"general-purpose technology" (GPT)
    287
generic systems 149
generic technologies 149
"gentleman's agreement" 147
geographic communities 218
geographical constraints 99
global education market 347
global telecommunications industry 39
globalization 101, 317
globally networked cities 201

Google search engine 200
government policies 218
grocery retailing industries 136
Gyandoot Dotcom 240

H

hardware 315
hash function 116
high crime 90
higher education in India 348
human resource development 334
hyperlinks 200

I

IC card type 86
ICT diffusion 236, 239
ICT economies 200
ICT growth 236
identification 111
idiosyncratic assets 149
idiosyncratic risk (IR) 48
IGOs 202
illegal copying of software 175
image-process skills 301
India 347, 361
Indian IT export scenario 243
information and communication tech-
    nologies (ICTs) 3, 63, 200, 218,
    237, 252, 346
information product 137
information providers 164
information reach 149
information security 107
information society 3, 99
information technology (IT) 23, 40, 85,
    315
information technology (IT) education
    348
information technology online (ITOL)
    220
information-based economy 3
innovation 29
innovation in food retailing 146
innovation networks 145, 148
innovation systems 149
input-output system 30

institutions 64
"integrated information channels" 137
intellectual property 155
intellectual property laws 107
intellectual property rights 164
interbanking transactions 259
interface 64
intermediation 28
internalization 149
international digital divide 236
international finance corporation (IFC)
    345
international monetary fund (IMF) 255
International Telecommunications Union
    (ITU) 42
Internet 201, 273, 286, 287
Internet banking 259
Internet economy 286
Internet usage 43, 276
inventory management 371
IPC 138
IT revolution 313, 314

J

Java card 119

K

knowledge-based economy 3
knowledge-enhanced products 155
knowledge-intensive service (KIS) 148,
    242
knowledge intensive service firms 257

L

labor policy 14
legal boundaries of the firm 149
legislation 98
legislation models 99
licensing approach 157
"life-span" goods 136
life-span products 136, 143, 145
lifecycle model 293
Lineage: The Bloodpledge 286, 288,
    295
local businesses 12

loss of Individuality 9
low technology 137

M

magazine publishing 136, 137
magazine publishing industry 139
management of innovation 137
marginal capitals 213
marginalization 6
marketing channel 157
massively multiplayer online game
     (MMOG) 301
massively multiple player online game
     (MMPOG) 289
master promissory note (MPN) 131
message authentication 114, 122
middleware 170
Mirror Newspaper group 140
mobile phones 64
modes of coordination 67
monopolistic trends 15
multi-national companies (MNCs) 242
multiple user domains (MUD) 289
multiple user graphics (MUG) 289

N

nag boxes 158
narrowband 291
national capitals 201
"national innovation system" (NIS) 298
network arrangements 137
network externality 178, 180
network study 149
network type 86
networked economy 3
networking the nation (NTN) 220
networks 201
new crane 148
new economy 313, 314
"new innovation regimes" 148
new institutional economics 62
New York Stock Exchange (NYSE) 46
niche publishers 141
non-governmental organizations (NGOs)
     202, 345
non-repudiation 122

normative coordination 30

O

old economy 313
online communities 217
online game business 286, 288
online games 165
online services 217, 220
online shopping 138
online technologies 219
open loop transaction 86
OpenCard 119
opportunism 149
organisational changes 11
organizational responses to technologi-
     cal change 137
own-brand contractors 143
own-brand products 143
ownership advantage 257, 258
own-label 143

P

paid seat 351
payment systems 279
personal data protection 107
personal digital assistants (PDA) 64
Personal Identification Numbers (PINs)
     121
"pervasive technologies" 149
phases of a transaction 67
piracy 175, 183
population demographics 276
portfolio investment 41
price-based transactions 28
price discrimination 159
prices 15
pricing issues 154
printing presses 140
privacy 9, 90, 107
production organization 26
productivity growth 40
project-based approach 145
property rights 65
proximity to consumers 148
pseudo-cash 87
public key cryptography 114, 119

public key infrastructure (PKI) 104,
  112, 123
public space 287
publishing firms 145

Q

quantification of transaction costs 66
quantitative modeling 39

R

re-intermediation 21, 25
real economy 94
reason for piracy 178
reason for protection 180
reductions of transaction costs 63
Reed International 140
regional and rural Australia 218
regional development 219
regional portals 217
regional Web portals 217
regulating piracy 175
regulation environment 102
replenishment-based logistics 142
research 273
reservation price 158
revenue model transitions 166
revenue models 154

S

Sainsbury's Magazine, The 148
scale-free delivery 137
scanning technology 138
Schumpeter 148
scoring model 70
search engines 201
secure electronic transactions (SET)
  102
secure sockets layer (SSL) 102
security 102
sell-side procurement 375
"semiperipheral capitals" 213
sequential move 188
"shareware" 158
signature pads 120
signer authentication 109, 114, 122

SIM card 119
simulacrum 288
simulation 288
simultaneity of the unsimultaneous 302
small and medium enterprises (SMEs)
  218
small suppliers 147
smart card/fingerprint reader 122
smart cards 118
SMEs 16
social capital 221
social impacts 5
social isolation 7
social revolution 99
socio-cultural economy 286
"soft" costs 348
software 315
software piracy 175
software protection 181
software technology parks (STP) 247
South Africa 253, 262
South African banking organizations
  255
South African banking sector 258
South African banks 252
South African financial institutions 257
South African multiple option settlement
  (SAMOS) 262
South African reserve bank (SARB) 262
South Korea 286, 295
"space of flows" 287
spam 106
spin-off 144
spin-off title 145
spyware 158
standardization 100
state-wide area network (SWAN) 240
stealthware 158
stock purchases 63
stock theory 93
strategic assets 140
strategic inventory management 142
strategies for success 273
subscription arrangement 158
subscription model 162
subscription revenue model 162

supermarkets 138
supplier relationships 142
supply chain management (SCM) 359,
    360, 364
symmetric key cryptography 120
systematic risk (SR) 48

T

technology, media and telecommunica-
    tions (TMT) 40
telecommunications 297, 329
Tesco 138
time deposit 87
Tipper Tie 363
total risk (TR) 44, 48
tourism 200
traditional industries 137
traditional physical products 155
transaction cost approach 62, 65
transaction cost reductions 157
transaction costs 62, 65
"transaction trust" 277
transactional process 65
transactions 62, 65
transactions cost economics (TCE) 22
transactions costs 317
transactions-cost approach 149
transactions-cost-free market 26
transparent legislation 102
trust 142

U

union power 140
United Nations 202
University of Ballarat (UoB) 221
urban regions 201
URL references 200
USA Funds® 131

V

value at risk (VAR) 45, 48
versioning 159
vertical disintegration 140
vertical integration 140
virtual community 290

virtual private networks (VPN) 102
visible electronic signature protocol 117
voice over Internet protocol (VoIP) 100

W

Wal-Mart 142
watermarking 111
Web advertising 161
Web employment advertising 163
Web pages 200
Web portals 217, 220
Web services 169
websites 202
weightless economy 3
welfare analysis 192
wired world 203
wireless application protocol (WAP)
    100
"wireless in local loop" (WILL) 239
World Bank 345

X

xDSLs 289
XML 128, 169
XML signature 128

Y

Young Australian Rural Network (YARN)
    226

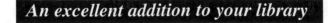